International capitalism and industrial restructuring

TITLES OF RELATED INTEREST

Collapse and survival
R. Ballance and S. Sinclair

Economic analysis and the multinational enterprise
J. Dunning (ed.)

Electronics and industrial policy
S. Jacobsson

The global textile industry
B. Toyne *et al.*

The growth of international business
M. Casson (ed.)

High tech America
A. Markusen, P. Hall and A. Glasmeier

International industry and business
R. Ballance

International production and the multinational enterprise
J. Dunning

Multinationals and world trade
M. Casson (ed.)

New firms
P. Johnson

Politics versus economics in the world steel trade
K. Jones

Production, work, territory
A. Scott and M. Storper (eds)

Regional dynamics
G. Clark, M. Gertler and J. Whiteman

Silicon landscapes
P. Hall and A. Markusen (eds)

State apparatus
G. Clark and M. Dear

Technological change, industrial restructuring and regional development
A. Amin and J. Goddard (eds)

Urban and regional planning
P. Hall

Western sunrise
P. Hall *et al.*

The world mining industry
R. Mikesell & J. Whitney

International capitalism and industrial restructuring

A critical analysis

EDITED BY

Richard Peet

Graduate School of Geography,
Clark University, Worcester, Massachusetts

Boston
ALLEN & UNWIN
London   Sydney   Wellington

Allen & Unwin, Inc.,
8 Winchester Place, Winchester, Mass. 01890, USA
the U.S. company of
Unwin Hyman Ltd
PO Box 18, Park Lane, Hemel Hempstead, Herts HP2 4TE, UK
40 Museum Street, London WC1A 1LU, UK
37/39 Queen Elizabeth Street, London SE1 2QB

Allen & Unwin (Australia) Ltd,
8 Napier Street, North Sydney, NSW 2060, Australia

Allen & Unwin (New Zealand) Ltd in association with the Port Nicholson
Press Ltd, 60 Cambridge Terrace,
Wellington, New Zealand

First published in 1987

Library of Congress Cataloging in Publication Data
International capitalism and industrial restructuring.

Bibliography: p.
Includes index.
1. Industry—History. 2. Industrial organization. 3. Economic
history—1945– . 4. Industry and state. 5. Marxian economics.
6. Capitalism. I. Peet, Richard.
II. Title: Industrial restructuring.
HD2321.158   1987   338.7   86–28870
ISBN 0–04–338132–4 (alk. paper)
ISBN 0–04–338133–2 (pbk. : alk. paper)

British Library Cataloguing in Publication Data
International capitalism and industrial
    restructuring: a critical analysis.
1. Industry 2. Capitalism
I. Peet, Richard
338   HD2328
ISBN 0–04–338132–4
ISBN 0–04–338133–2 Pbk

Set in 10 on 12 point Bembo by Phoenix Photosetting, Chatham
and printed in Great Britain by Billings and Sons Ltd,
London and Worcester

For Enid

Preface

The research which informs this book was begun in 1982 as an academic exercise dealing with a topic of contemporary importance. Personal experiences then changed the nature of my engagement with "industrial restructuring." I returned to the region of my birth after a 20 year absence. I can dimly remember Liverpool, in the north of England, just after the Second World War. The industrial area behind the docks was flattened by German bombing. Several square miles of industrial buildings were reduced to piles of bricks and lumps of twisted iron. Yet, as the crude Orwellian media of the time told us, the "people's spirit had not been broken." What they meant was a good crowd could still be assembled to cheer visiting royalty. What they perhaps guessed was how the anger of the people, nurtured by decades of lining up for a day's work on the docks, seethed beneath the patriotism of the war effort.

The dockland industry was rebuilt and a good part of Liverpool went back to work there – for a while. However by the time of my return "industrial restructuring" had finished what the bombers started. The buildings and warehouses were empty. But the spirit of the people again had not been broken. Despite nightly reminders to the contrary by a media which had become far more sophisticated than Orwell could possibly have foretold, an angry people elected a city council full of Troskyites and left Labourites in open rebellion against a Conservative central government. Class consciousness was on the rise, patriotism laughed at. The harshness of Liverpool's reality broke apart thick layers of false consciousness. 1984 was a year of radical resurgence.

The shape and tone of the book result from the class, regional and intellectual traditions of its author – i.e. working class, North of England and New England, and Marxist structuralism. Other experiences in southern Africa, the Caribbean and the Pacific, and an encounter with dependency theory, have played a role in shaping my concern that the needs of the peasants and workers of the Third World, rather than the profits of the multinational corporations, be met by development.

There is a further aspect of the book which has to be mentioned. For this author, the industrial tradition of the global center was built through the efforts of all workers, "ordinary people" as well as entrepreneurs. The machinery, factories, infrastructure, technology, skills and institutions which make sophisticated production possible come from the labor of generations of workers. They are the gifts of the people of the past to the people of the present. They are not the playthings of corporations. Hence, center industry should not be destroyed, moved, replaced, or "improved" without the consent of its true owners. Nor should industrial development in the periphery be initiated without an expression of the popular will. I do not think either consent has been given, for under capitalism the social patrimony is private property. "Property is theft" said Proudhon. Likewise the movement of productive potential in space is theft. Hence the critical tone of this book.

The book is also a critical reaction to a prevailing mood of false optimism about the future potential for the industrialization of the periphery and the promise of high technology for solving the problems of the center. Optimism is structurally related to a healthy economy under capitalism. Supremely important institutions, like the stock and commodity markets, are directed by the mood of the investor. Presidents, Prime Ministers, cabinet officials, or even widely read commentators dare not make critically accurate assessments for fear of setting off the crises which haunt their dreams. While this may be a way of continuing the existing mode of life for as long as possible, it is not an effective way of handling a society's economic problems.

This book therefore tries to initiate a more critical debate. It is part of a radical academic tradition which sees learning, research and teaching as more than the accumulation and dissemination of ideas. The radical intellectual intercedes in the process being studied. As Marx put it: "The philosophers have only *interpreted* the world, in various ways; the point, however, is to *change* it."

Richard Peet
Clark University

Acknowledgments

The early and middle 1980s were golden years reminiscent of the late 1960s and early 1970s at Clark University where the author works. Some outstanding students passed through my classes and contributed to the formation and maturation of my ideas. Desiree Gran and Dara Kurtbeck helped research parts of the book; too many others to mention endured the first crude versions of my critical remarks on the trajectory of contemporary capitalism. John Silk reviewed the original proposal for the book and critiqued the eventual collection of essays and my own introductions. Paul Sussman arranged a useful discussion of Chapter 2 at Bucknell University. Holly Sklar was instrumental in arranging for Chapter 12 to be reprinted. Lori Wall skillfully redrew several of the maps and diagrams. Margaret Jaquith typed and retyped several chapters with an intelligence and skill which contributed to the production, as well as presentation, of the book's contents. Clark University gave me a faculty development grant at a crucial time. Finally, Enid Arvidson was my loving companion and friend throughout the tense months I worked on the book. Thanks to all for your encouragement and support in a world which particularly does not appreciate its critics.

Contents

1983

List of Tables

List of contributors

Barry Bluestone, Department of Economics, Boston College, 140 Commonwealth Avenue, Chestnut Hill, Massachusetts 02167, USA

Barbara Ehrenreich, *MS. Magazine*, 119 West 40th Street, New York, NY 10018, USA

Andre Gunder Frank, Institute for Socio-Economic Studies of Developing Regions, Jodenbreestraat 23, 1011 NH, Amsterdam, Netherlands

Annette Fuentes, South End Press, 116 St. Botolph Street, Boston, MA 01225, USA

William K. Goldsmith, Department of City and Regional Planning, Cornell University, Ithaca, New York 14853, USA

Bennett Harrison, Department of Urban Studies and Planning, Massachusetts Institute of Technology, Cambridge, Massachusetts 02139, USA

John Junkerman, 10 Summer Street, Somerville, Massachusetts, 02143, USA

Martin Landsberg, Department of Economics, Lewis & Clark College, Portland, Oregon 97219, USA

Doreen Massey, Department of Geography, The Open University, Walton Hall, Milton Keynes MK7 6AA, UK

Rebecca Morales, Graduate School of Architecture and Urban Planning, University of California, Los Angeles, California, 90024, USA

Richard Peet, Graduate School of Geography, Clark University, 950 Main Street, Worcester, Massachusetts 01610, USA

Robert J. S. Ross, Department of Sociology, Clark University, 950 Main Street, Worcester, Massachusetts 01610, USA

A. Sivanandan, Institute of Race Relations, 247 Pentonville Road, London N1 9NG, England

Edward Soja, Graduate School of Architecture and Urban Planning, University of California, Los Angeles, California 90024, USA

Takeo Tsuchiya, Pacific–Asia Resources Centre, P.O. Box 5250, Tokyo International Post Office, Tokyo, Japan

Goetz Wolff, Graduate School of Architecture and Urban Planning, University of California, Los Angeles, California 90024, USA

1   Introduction

RICHARD PEET

In a series of articles entitled "The other Britain: where hard times prevail," a correspondent for the *New York Times* describes how provinces which once generated much of Britain's wealth are now characterized by factory closures, unemployment and social problems. Port Talbot in South Wales had the largest, most modern steel works in Europe, employing 20,000 workers in the 1960s. Now it employs 5,000. In the valleys around the town the unemployment rate is 35 or 40 percent. "The kids in school don't talk any more about what they are going to do when they grow up," says a social worker. A community organizer adds that there has been an increase in the incidence of alcoholism, mental disturbance, and suicide (*New York Times* 1985a: 1, 18).

While Port Talbot represents industrial decline, the Midlands city of Derby has made its economy more efficient by automating. Productivity at Rolls Royce is up by 28 percent in five years. Yet the same period saw 6,000 jobs shaved from Rolls Royce's payroll, while thousands have also disappeared at the city's railway and textile plants. Unemployment rates are estimated to be 25–30 percent in the city center, 15–20 percent in the inner periphery, and 10 percent in the suburbs. "Our worry is that we will never rebuild the industrial base of Derby,' says the (unemployed) deputy leader of the city council (*New York Times* 1985c: 4).

The same issue of the *New York Times* that reports on Port Talbot also calls the steel towns along the Ohio River, in the Middle West of the United States, "a region the recovery never reached." The depression in steel has idled 700,000 steelworkers in the "Rust Belt." One of the main steel producers is bankrupt and attempting to cut wages and benefits by 30 percent. "They want to take us back to the 30s and the good old days of sweat shops," says the negotiator for the United Steelworkers, whose members walked off their jobs in the first strike against a major steel producer since 1959 (*New York Times* 1985b: E4).

Accounts like these, numerous in the recession years of the early 1980s, appear with increasing frequency as the realization grows that manufacturing industry, and the communities that depend on it, have not recovered in the old industrial regions of the advanced capitalist countries. At the same time, there are envious accounts of the Japanese economy and glowing accounts of the miracle economies of certain Third World countries like the Republic of Korea, Taiwan, Hong Kong, Singapore, and Brazil.

The process of economic change referred to in these popular accounts has been variously termed "deindustrialization" (Blackaby 1978, Bluestone & Harrison 1982), "urban and regional transformation" (Goddard & Champion 1983), "industrial restructuring" (Roe 1984), and a variety of other terms implying a world economy in rapid transition (Beenstock 1983). Significant shifts in employment are occurring in the advanced industrial countries of the center (Fothergill & Gudgin 1982, Sawers & Tabb 1984), causing a loss of jobs and unemployment in some regions (Massey & Meegan 1982), yet development in others – high-tech regions of the center and the newly industrializing countries of the periphery (Belassa 1981, Lee 1981). In this book the causes and consequences of the changing location of manufacturing industry in international space are discussed. The term "industrial restructuring" is used to refer to the alternating phases of growth or decline in industrial activity; it emphasizes changes in employment between regions, and links these with change in whole economies. However, we give a somewhat different and certainly more critical interpretation of the term than that expressed in the conventional literature.

The conventional view of industrial restructuring, expressed in a World Bank Technical Paper (Roe 1984), is that shifts in demand, prices, location, technology, and other "exogenous forces" are forcing significant structural adaptation, focused on the industrial sector, in developed and underdeveloped countries. Reallocation of labor and capital are essential to economic efficiency, it is claimed, and "the market does a reasonable job in ensuring that these factor movements take place" (Roe 1984: 1). However, particularly during the recession of the early 1980s, issues of government policy on the restructuring and rationalization of industry have persistently arisen. Market forces, it is admitted, do not always work in a "textbook fashion"; many social, economic and political pains are associated with the restructuring process. Thus government intervention may sometimes be justified, although this should be "market supporting" rather than coercive (Roe 1984: 52).

By contrast, the critical viewpoint expressed in this book sees conventional explanations as disguising, rather than revealing, the causes of industrial change. Explanations of spatial shifts in industry underestimate the problems caused in central countries and overestimate the advantages gained by peripheral countries. Conventional theorists call for government policies which cannot have even the ameliorative effects which their proponents claim. Instead new kinds of explanations are needed which reach beyond "market imperfections" into how capitalist societies are organized and how these structures inevitably generate industrial instability. We need to discuss problems involving long-term unemployment for tens of millions of people as more than the "temporary aberrations" of a market system which "otherwise works well." There is a need for policy solutions which go beyond amelioration to the heart of the matter, even if this means fundamentally changing social structures, substituting planning for the market, and using social rather than private decision making to control industrial change. Industrial restructuring does not only mean adjusting to exogenous change. It can also imply restructuring control over industry, the idea being to make change *endogenous* to a democratically controlled, planned economic system.

There is a critical tradition in Western scholarship, based on Marxism, which discusses issues like industrial restructuring in terms like these. This tradition should not be confused with Soviet Marxism. It has the essential difference that most Western Marxists believe in direct worker control over production, democratic decision making, and freedom of consciousness in the context of responsibility to others. The centers of this thought are working-class institutions, such as certain unions, and the universities, places where a limited freedom prevails, where real alternatives can be pursued, and where analyses can be developed which are deeply critical of the existing society. In Western Europe the Marxist tradition is unbroken since the 19th century. In the United States it is intermittent, at least in the number of adherents. In both it was strengthened by the events of the 1960s, diminished by those of the 1970s, but continues as a powerful generator of insights, ideas, and proposals in the 1980s. In the coming years of crisis Marxism will provide the alternative analysis and vision so necessary to healthy, multifaceted thought.

All the social sciences practiced in Western universities have developed radical, if not Marxist, streams. In this book we draw on material from the rich literature produced by the radical intellectual movement in Britain and the United States. We particularly draw on radical writing in the spatial and environmental tradition centered on the discipline of geography, but including a wide variety of other social sciences. Two types of articles are reproduced. Most of the book is made up of theoretical, analytical articles usually taken from Marxian or radical academic journals. Introductions to some of the key ideas expressed in these articles are provided in the brief introductions to each part of the book. Scattered through the book are articles of a second type; these are more popular, descriptive articles, drawing on the "muck-raking," journalistic stream of radical writing. These are particularly directed at exposing the actual effects of industrial restructuring on individuals, groups, communities, or countries. The idea is that the two types of article should complement each other, provide contrasting types of information and reading matter, and demonstrate the variety of critical styles found on the Left today.

The book is divided into six main parts. In Part I, "Industrial change and economic crisis," the main themes of the book are introduced: "industrial devolution" in the center, "industrial revolution" in parts of the periphery, and the crisis which results from drastic change in the location of manufacturing. In Part II, "Problems of decline in advanced capitalist countries," we take a detailed look at the process of industrial devolution in the advanced capitalist countries, examining the causes of decline in the old regions of the center and its consequences for displaced workers, unions, and the economy in general. Part III, "Contradictions of growth in advanced capitalist countries," contains a critical examination of industrial growth in California, Japan and "high-tech" regions, the aim being to dispel the idea that regional industrial decline is countered by successful industrial growth elsewhere, i.e. that the market reallocates resources successfully. In Part IV, "Disorganic development in peripheral countries," we focus on the "miracle economies" of the Third World in an attempt to discover what kind of development export-oriented industrialization really generates. In Part V, "Industrial policy reexamined," we rejoin the debate of the early 1980s from a new, more critical, radical perspective, focusing on the question of industrial location policy. A brief conclusion to this part draws together the main themes of the book and indicates an alternative (Left) answer to the question "What can be done?" Part VI is a chapter by Frank reformulating many of the issues raised in the book and placing them in the broad context of global transformation.

Each main part contains a brief introductory chapter. I have used these chapters to do more than introduce the reproduced articles which constitute the main contents of the book. By and large these articles explain themselves. However, the introductions are intended to highlight some key ideas and themes in an opinionated, even controversial way. These introductions should stimulate immediate reactions from the reader which may then interact with the equally controversial material presented in the articles reproduced. It goes without saying that the authors of these articles may not exactly agree with the perspective taken in the introductions. But the politics which underlie all the articles presented here are similar enough that an underlying set of assumptions, a common critical stance, and a coherent vision of the future should emerge from the book taken as a whole. The authors of the reproduced articles are extremely critical of the present structures and dynamics of capitalist countries, are deeply concerned about the injuries being afflicted on millions of unionized workers in the center and on further millions of nonunionized workers in the periphery, and think that we should devise a better way of deciding where our most important economic activities are located, how they are organized, what they produce and how they are run. We are people dedicated to a communally owned, democratically run economy, where principles of social need prevail over private profit. We think that the day is rapidly approaching when our ideas will be desperately needed. The events of capitalism in crisis will transform "naive optimism" about the human potential for cooperative action into the pragmatic principles of political economic action.

References

Beenstock, M. 1983. *The world economy in transition*. London: Allen & Unwin.
Belassa, B. 1981. *The newly industrializing countries in the world economy*. New York: Pergamon Press.
Blackaby, F. 1978. *De-industrialisation*. London: Heinemann Educational Books.
Bluestone, B. and B. Harrison 1982. *The de-industrialisation of America*. New York: Basic Books.

Fothergill, S. and G. Gudgin 1982. *Unequal growth: urban and regional employment change in the U.K.* London: Heinemann Educational Books.

Goddard, J. B. and A. G. Champion 1983. *The urban and regional transformation of Britain*. London: Methuen.

Lee, E. 1981. *Export-led industrialisation and development*. Singapore: International Labour Organisation.

Massey, D. and R. Meegan 1982. *The anatomy of job-loss*. London: Methuen.

New York Times 1985a. 'For a Welsh town in decline, London seems a world away.' July 28, 1, 18.
New York Times 1985b. 'A region the recovery never reached' July 28, E4.
New York Times 1985c. 'The home of Rolls-Royce slides into a depression.' July 29, 4.

Roe, A. R. 1984. *Industrial restructuring: issues and experiences in selected developed economics*. World Bank Technical Paper No. 21. Washington, DC: World Bank.

Sawers, L. and W. Tabb 1984. *Sunbelt-Snowbelt: urban development and regional restructuring*. New York: Oxford University Press.

Part I

Industrial change and economic crisis

2 Industrial restructuring and the crisis of international capitalism

RICHARD PEET

Why is manufacturing industry important? Why do changes in manufacturing activity deserve serious attention? Manufacturing industry transforms natural materials into goods which satisfy needs and wants. As distinct from agriculture and mining, manufacturing takes place under humanly created and controllable conditions. As distinct from service activities, manufacturing provides vital material inputs into the continuation of human life. A highly productive, reliable economic activity making the essentials of life is thus available to improve the standard of living, provide employment, and generate economic growth. Manufacturing has played this generative rôle in the economically advanced countries at least since the industrial revolution of the 18th century. As one reviewer puts it: "No major country has yet become rich without having become industrialized. . . . Greater wealth and better living standards under any political system are closely connected with industrialization" (Sutcliffe 1971: 69–70).

As an essential component of the economies of all developed countries, industry employs at least 30 percent of the working population in the advanced capitalist countries. The proportion rises to 35 percent in Japan, 36 percent in the United Kingdom and 44 percent in West Germany (International Labour Office 1984: 45). Workers in manufacturing are more unionized and are paid more than those in other economic sectors; in the United States, for example, manufacturing pays wages which are 11 percent higher than the private sector in general, and 23 percent more than services (United States Bureau of the Census 1984: 427–9). In terms of contribution to employment and earnings, manufacturing thus remains of great importance to economic health. It is a basic activity, a material foundation on which advanced societies are built. What happens to manufacturing is of vital concern to those directly employed and to all who depend on it indirectly for their employment and their consumption.

Change in manufacturing

Dramatic changes have occurred recently in this crucial activity. One of the reasons for manufacturing's success in improving living standards is that it is capable of producing the means of its own improvement – it makes the tools, implements, machines, and computers which enhance the productivity of manufacturing, as well as all other kinds of production. Because it takes place in a controlled environment, manufacturing is particularly amenable to mechanization and automation. This possibility of replacing human physical and (increasingly) mental effort with machines and computers should be welcomed as the source of liberation from labor drudgery, and source of improvement in the standard of living. The workers released from manufacturing could be employed elsewhere, or the savings in necessary labor time could be passed on to everyone in the form of a shorter working week or longer vacations. Here is a place where the finest achievements of the human mind (technology and innovation) could be applied to yield the greatest benefits to human kind.

There is, however, a difference between *technology*, as knowledge providing principles which can be usefully applied, and *techniques*, as the specific ways of applying these principles in making particular products or providing certain services. Thus the liberative potential of the new information–processing technologies, centered on the computer, is actually realized in techniques which already have displaced millions of workers in manufacturing. In the future these techniques will also destroy millions of jobs in the service industries, many of which are involved in simple information processing. Writing in the United Kingdom, Kaplinsky (1984: 148) concludes that "the introduction of new automation technologies, associated as they are with the deepening of economic crisis, is likely to lead to high and sustained levels of unemployment, probably in excess of 12 percent of the labour force. The countervailing tendencies offered by new products, the demand for new skills, the introduction of a shorter week and the resistance to new automation technologies all hold little prospect for substantially altering this perspective". "Liberation from labor drudgery" is thus transformed into the "collapse of work".

How does this reversal happen? One perspective ("technological Darwinism") sees technology developing in response to its own internal logic, with techniques applied in the quest for greater efficiency and only the fittest surviving. Counterposed to this is a second perspective which sees technologies and techniques as social products whose development is conditioned by social relations. According to the second view, the focus of analysis should lie on society rather than the technology it produces. In particular, the competitive conditions of the economic depression which followed the expansionary upswing of

1950–70 have led to the rapid diffusion of new automation technologies, and the resulting loss of jobs has fed back as an additional cause of economic crisis. Competition forces companies to innovate in certain ways which necessarily direct the application of technology towards cost reduction through, for example, the elimination of employment. As crisis deepens the need to compete grows ever stronger and the adoption of labor-saving techniques ever more urgent. In the end the idea of a "choice" of technology becomes virtually meaningless – the social relation of competition assumes the form of an iron hand of determination. Thus a study of alternatives for the British economy in a period of intense international competition finds: "*Remain as we are, reject the new technologies and we face unemployment of up to 5.5 million by the end of the century. Embrace the new automation technologies, accept the challenge and we end up with unemployment of about 5 million*" (Jenkins & Sherman 1979: 113). As Kaplinsky (1984: 180) concludes, given such "options" the investigative problem lies not with technology but with a form of social organization which totally misuses its potential.

A similar argument also applies to the changing geography of manufacturing. Again this has the potential for enormous social good. It may well be that the poluted environments of old industrial regions should be partly disindustrialized. It is certainly the case that underdeveloped regions are in desperate need of manufacturing and the economic growth it can generate. Hence a relative shift of industry to the Third World should be welcomed. But consider also the possibility for social disaster inherent in a changing geography of manufacturing. Regions and even whole nations may lose their manufacturing base. Unemployment, or reemployment in lower-waged service occupations, can so reduce purchasing power that underconsumption pushes the world economy constantly towards depression. In addition, the new regions of the periphery may only receive selected industries, or parts of industries, making them vulnerable to outside control through a new, international–corporate form of imperialism. The new industries may have little relevance to the consumption needs of the local people, yet may pollute their environments, exploit their labor, and change their cultural traditions.

Detrimental consequences such as these flow from an uncontrolled, unplanned movement, one directed not by considerations of social benefit but by the pursuit of private profit. Or, more profoundly, the necessities of competitive survival expressed as profit making may direct the movement of industry even when the socially deleterious consequences are already well known. Thus, for example, it is obvious that the movement of British capital to the Third World is causing massive unemployment at home, destroying people's lives, and causing the permanent loss of valuable skills, plant, equipment, infrastructure, and productive institutions. Yet it is urged on for the survival of "national" corporations in a highly competitive world.

Issues like these demand that we deepen the analysis of manufacturing to include a theory of society, its economy, and the relations which condition decision making. The next section provides a brief introduction to an analysis of this kind.

The economic structure of society

It is impossible for a theory of a particular aspect of society, in this case the geography of manufacturing, to begin and end with the details of the specific case. A more general perspective is needed to order detailed specificities. We need the guidance of a general theory of socioeconomic structure to analyze more effectively spatial change in manufacturing activity and employment. Marx showed a profound ability to reduce complex issues to their most basic elements, from which sophisticated analytical frameworks can be reconstructed. What are these basic social elements?

For Marx, production is the social transformation of nature. Nature is made into useful objects, and the natural environment is transformed by applying social-productive forces: (1) living human labor power; (2) humanly appropriated natural forces, such as soil fertility, waterfalls, fossil fuels, or nuclear energy; and (3) capital equipment, such as tools, instruments, machinery, computers, and infrastructure made by human labor in the past. In the early stages of economic development the productive forces are largely confined to direct human labor. The ability to transform or harness nature is limited, and people find their lives strictly determined by (natural) forces beyond their control. For Marx (1967) the worship of an unknowable, uncontrollable but controlling natural force is the origin of religion. Over time the numbers of human laborers increase, the legacy of implements, machines, and infrastructures grows, and more of nature may be harnessed. This process, involving greater control over human "destiny," and implying a higher standard of material life, is called "economic development." It results in a transformation of the conditions of existence which reaches into all aspects of economic social and cultural life.

But the transformation of life through a transformation in productive ability does not occur everywhere with the same speed, intensity, or character. Environmental determinists, drawing on social Darwinism, argue that natural resources, and inherent human qualities derived originally from nature, determine which areas achieve high levels of productive development (Peet 1985). Marx, by comparison, argues that variations in the level of development come primarily from the different social relations humans enter in the production of their lives. For production to occur there must be a network of different kinds of relations between producers. Relations of distribution determine who gets the products being made – a tribal elder through kin obligations or a resident of Manhattan through market relations. Relations between specialist members of the division of labor determine the allocation of tasks and organize the labor effort as a whole. But for Marx the key social relation lies in the ownership of the productive process. Under what *property relations* is labor performed? For Marx, property is the key to understanding the development of the productive forces and regional disparities in productivity and the standard of living.

With the exception of very early hunting and gathering societies, in which natural territory was considered a communal resource, the productive forces have been owned and controlled by particular individuals or classes of individuals. Nature has long been private property; human laborers have been owned by others as slaves, or have lived under obligation to others as serfs; and the capital equipment made by generations of workers is not the equal legacy of all but private property owned by some. In Marx's analysis ownership and control of these productive resources is the crucial determining social characteristic.

There are two dimensions to the ownership of productive resources. One dimension is the relations between owners, or within the class of owners. Relations within the owning class determine shares of economic, social, and political power. In feudalism these intraclass relations were of a political–military type, with armed conflict as the primary means of defending or acquiring productive resources. In capitalism, economic relations between bourgeois owners of private firms and corporations occur through competition in the market place. Market success determines the size of a corporation and the economic, social, and even political power of its owners.

Competitive market relations between owners are central to understanding capitalist development. Competition in the market focuses on price. Price depends on cost. And cost depends on the amount of productive resources used. Competition forces capitalist producers to use a minimum of resources to reach the highest level of output. Competition also entails the achievement of scale in production to earn lower costs (use less resources), and to control, and if possible monopolize, an area of production. Improvements are bought by investing in advanced methods and buying linked or competing companies. As a competitive system, capitalism is also progressive in that resource savings are built into the economic system. Competition is exactly the source of capitalism's effectiveness as a mode of production.

But what does this mean? Greater productivity occurs not through a consciously reached social agreement to improve the standard of living in the interest of all but through coercion by competitive social relations. Progress in the economy is shaped by competitive relations experienced by each producer as an external, coercive force, whereas historical change takes the form of the development of inherent contradictions and reactions to crises. Thus, although the productive development enabled by competition erodes the power of nature to determine the course of human existence, equally uncontrollable powers, contradiction and competition, have been substituted in its place. The socially uncontrolled nature of the economy is the experiential basis for the retention of religious consciousness in capitalist societies which otherwise comprehend in materialist, scientific terms (Peet 1986).

Competitive relations between owners in the market are one dimension of the social relations of capitalist production. However, if production is understood as the production of existence from nature, then social relations which occur *directly* in the labor process can be understood as the most significant relations of all. In feudalism these relations lay between landowners and serfs. In capitalism they are between shareholders, banks, and corporate management on the one side and waged employees on the other. Relations in the labor process must, in part, be cooperative: without cooperation production would be impossible. Further, the good of the company or corporation is to some degree the good of all: everyone benefits from institutional stability and growth. But Marx's argument is that relations in the labor process are predominantly antagonistic under capitalism. He says that the interests of the two main classes, owners and workers, are fundamentally opposed.

What is the source of this opposition? In Marx's economic theory, "exploitation" does not mean "treating people badly," but rather paying workers less than the value they add to materials during production. At its simplest, this means making a profit from other people's labor by paying less wages than the value being created. Except under certain circumstances, the wages paid for value creation must cover the costs of maintaining and reproducing the value creators. Put more generally, a part of the value added by labor to natural materials has to go to paying the costs of labor's reproduction by supporting the worker and his or her family. However, human labor is capable not only of replacing the value used to ensure reproduction but making a surplus of values. This surplus goes to the owners of productive resources as profit, interest, and rent paid to entrepreneurs, banks, and landowners. This surplus of values is the only reason workers were employed in the first place (Marx 1967).

Hence, on the one side, capitalists must try to maximize the yield of surplus value, because their incomes, and their bankers' incomes, depend on it. On the other side, workers attempt to maximize wages and fringe benefits, for these are the source of improvements in the living conditions of their demanding families. A temporary accord may be struck between capital and labor under which hard work yields high profits *and* high wages. But recall the competitive nature of intracapitalist relations discussed previously. Competition *forces* capitalist producers to extract *hard* work at *minimal* cost despite sentiments about fairness and sharing, or concern for workers' livelihoods. In this context, labor can achieve a greater share of the product only by exerting force on capital – by organizing into unions and, when necessary, going on strike (withholding its value-creating power). Enlightened relations, existing for a time and in certain places, in the end become antagonistic relations. Cooperation is transformed into coercion by competitive necessity.

Why was productivity developed in regions dominated by this particular set of antagonistic social relations? Relations of exploitation between owners and workers channel the surplus into the few hands of owners. *Competition forces them to invest much of this surplus in machines and research to improve productivity*. The ability to produce increases. Struggle between workers and owners diverts some of the surplus to labor. Mass worker consumption provides the markets to absorb the burgeoning output of goods and services. And so the process of productive development develops and continues. Notice again, however, that economic improvement results not from a conscious decision to change the world for the benefit of all but from the continuation of coercion, this time in a social rather than a natural form. This makes the improvements which we have come to take for granted tenuous and unreliable. We cannot be sure about our economic futures because we cannot rely on the competitive, antagonistic relations which determine that future. Thus economic development goes hand in hand with greater social anxiety. Economic development brings with it an increasing insecurity rather than the certainty that life will continue in a predictable, known, and controlled way.

Competition and struggle in global space

With this as background we can now ask: How does change occur in the geography of productive activity? According to the previous argument, revelation should spring from a consideration of the social relations of production: a changing geography of production should result from changing relations between capitalists, and between capital and labor.

In terms of scale, the *relations between capitalist enterprises* are changing rapidly: the struggle for existence leads to the survival of the biggest. Sales by the 200 largest industrial corporations were 18 percent of world gross domestic product in 1960 and 29 percent in 1980 (Cavanagh & Clairmonte 1982: 11). In terms of scope, the never-ending, necessary quest for profits, which made capitalism a world system from the beginning (Wallerstein 1974), has more recently involved internationalization of the whole range of corporate activities: "The World-economy is more integrated by global investment decisions and international sourcing than ever before" (Chase-Dunn 1984: 82). Intraclass relations, between capitalist producers, are thus increasingly characterized by enhanced competition between multinational corporations operating on a global scale. The theme of intercorporate competition is further elaborated in Chapter 4.

Relations between capital and labor have also developed unevenly in time and space. Times of intense capital–labor conflict give way to times of lesser conflict and regions of high conflict lie next to regions of lower conflict. Some regions experience high levels of capital–labor conflict long before others. Arrighi & Silver (1984) argue that the labor movement in the United States showed particular vitality and effectiveness in the interwar years. They attribute the strength of the industrial workers, who spearheaded the union movement, to the growth of labor's workplace bargaining power. Continuous flow production and the assembly line, along with greater concentration, centralization, and integration of capital, increased the vulnerability of capital to workers' direct action at the point of production. Security was bought by capital in the form of high wages and fringe benefits, making US labor expensive, stimulating automation, and fostering the internationalization of capital. Meanwhile greater worker militancy spread to Western Europe in the late 1960s and early 1970s so that capital was confronted by an almost solid array of regions of high levels of conflict in the advanced capitalist countries. The half decade 1968–73 saw an "international strike wave," a period characterized as a "worldwide resurgence of conflict", with further outbreaks occurring until 1977 (Shalev 1983: 434–5, see also Paldam & Pederson 1984). All in all, the period since the 1930s, especially the late 1960s and early 1970s, has seen high levels of capital–labor conflict, increasing unionization, higher real wages, and increasing constraints on entrepreneurial freedom in the old regions of the capitalist center.

Outside these old industrial regions, the level of worker organization, the degree of conflict, and the power of labor to affect the actions of capital are far more limited. Capital–labor conflict, manifested as industrial disputes, varies greatly between world regions and between regions of a given country. Table 2.1 captures some of this variation by presenting wage rates and the level of industrial disputes for the large industrial countries for which reliable statistics are available. Generally speaking, the 1970s and early 1980s saw the advanced industrial countries (AICs) with high wage rates and moderate to high levels of industrial conflict, with the notable exceptions of Germany and Japan, which had remarkably low levels of industrial conflict. The newly industrializing countries (NICs) of Southern Europe had lower wage levels but high levels of conflict. The NICs of Latin America had

Table 2.1 Labor conditions in world manufacturing, 1974–83.

	Average hourly earnings in manufacturing (US$)		Industrial disputes Average annual working days lost per 1,000 nonagricultural workers 1974–83
	1974	1983	
North America			
United States	4.42	8.83	312
Canada	4.46	8.61	836
Latin America			
Venezuela	1.41	3.63 (1981)	45
Mexico	1.10	1.59 (1982)	n.a.
Columbia	0.41	1.00 (1980)	n.a.
Western Europe			
Belgium	3.22	5.29	182 (1974–80)
France	2.17	4.41	167
Germany, Federal Republic	3.45	5.94	26
Ireland	1.94	4.40	798 (1974–82)
Sweden	4.57	6.29	134
United Kingdom	2.61	5.25	470 (1974–82)
Southern Europe			
Italy	1.86	4.95	1088
Spain	2.04	3.63	917 (1974–82)
Turkey	0.60	1.15	1127 (1974–80)
Africa			
Kenya	0.57	0.70	n.a.
Zambia	0.77	1.32 (1980)	317
Zimbabwe	n.a.	2.20 (1982)	66 (1977–83)
South Asia			
Bangladesh	0.23	0.15	460
India	0.18	0.40 (1981)	1696
Pakistan	0.17	0.33 (1980)	47
Sri Lanka	0.19	0.17	383
East and South east Asia			
Hong Kong	0.51	1.26	10
Korea, Republic of	0.38	1.35	2
Malaysia	n.a.	n.a.	26 (1975–9)
Philippines	n.a.	n.a.	53
Singapore	0.52	1.43	2 (1974–82)
Taiwan	0.47	1.67	n.a.
Thailand	n.a.	n.a.	48 (1974–81)
Japan	2.95	6.91	59
Oceania			
Australia	4.95	8.58	577

Sources: Wage rates and disputes from ILO (1984); exchange rates from IMF (1982, 1985).

moderate wages and, based on the case of Venezuela, low conflict levels. However other statistics (e.g., from Peru) suggest that industrial conflict levels would be as high as those of Southern Europe if repression by Latin American governments were not occurring, and qualitative accounts conclude that the "persistence of workers in organizing and fighting to improve their lives remains constant throughout Latin American labor history" (Spalding 1977: xv). Africa had low to moderate wage levels in countries with industrial traditions but very low wage levels elsewhere, although the level of industrial conflict appears to vary tremendously within the continent. South Asia had the lowest wage rates in the world, but the tendency was for high levels of industrial conflict. Finally, the East and Southeast Asian countries were remarkable for low (but increasing) wage rates and industrial peace. Multinational corporations seeking to escape labor opposition and high wages in the center and searching the globe for advantage in a competitive struggle to expand thus find a mosaic of differing relations with labor, which they can put together into various combinations. East and Southeast Asia in particular offer conditions especially suited to labor-intensive manufacturing. (The theme of the geography of class struggle is further elaborated in Chapter 4.)

To summarize, recent changes in the location of manufacturing have occurred under conditions of rapid change in the relations of production. The recent past is characterized by high levels of industrial conflict in the AICs where industry is concentrated. However, a fringe of less developed regions is also available offering various combinations of lower conflict and/or lower wages. The potential exists for considerable advantage to be gained by corporations relocating to, or purchasing from, the various peripheries of the capitalist world system. Opposition from labor in the center is a powerful force propelling capital towards internationalized operations, and lower levels of labor opposition pull capital towards certain parts of the periphery of the world system.

Development of the productive forces

Corporations, however, have to be *able* to make use of this social geography of differential advantage. The development of the productive forces enables natural limitations on corporate freedom of action, such as the limitations of the friction of distance, to be overcome. What has happened recently to capital's technical ability to produce anywhere and traverse space more easily?

In a seminal article on the new international division of labor, Frobel *et al.* (1977) argue that technology and institutions changed dramatically in the 1960s and 1970s. Improvements in transport and communication technologies, like containerization, air cargo, telecommunications, and data processing techniques, reduced the frictional effects of spatial distance. New technologies in the exploration and exploitation of nature, such as satellite photography and deep-sea drilling, made available a wide geographical array of previously inaccessible resources. Changes in technology and design enabled complex production processes, previously carried out by skilled labor, to be decomposed into elementary units performed by unskilled workers. An international capital market, and elements of a transnational superstructure of global institutions and agreements, enabled money to be instantaneously moved and protected anywhere. Such technical and institutional changes liberated capital from its reliance on the organized labor of the industrial heartland.

At the same time there were changes in the human productive forces in the periphery. A huge alternative labor force emerged in mass flight from changing productive conditions in the rural areas of the Third World. This labor force is characterized by extremely low reproduction costs. Workers can be used more hours each day although productivity remains similar to that of the old industrial regions. The enormous size of the workforce means that it can be used and discarded almost at will, for exhausted or injured workers can easily be replaced from the constantly new waves of eager job seekers.

Where did these changes come from? Did production and transport technologies develop in a social vacuum? Did the rural areas of the periphery just suddenly change? Frobel *et al.* (1977: 83) answer as follows:

It was predominantly capital itself which, through its centuries-long expansion and accumulation, produced these conditions in terms of relations of production, forces of production, and superstructure. In one form or other, most of these conditions have been gradually developing for a long time. But as long as the full set was not effectively developed, the reproduction of capital on a world scale only generated the international division of labor in which, essentially, countries producing raw materials exchanged with countries producing capital and consumer goods. . . . Our main thesis is that, roughly speaking in the 1960s, the new set of conditions for capital expansion and accumulation became effectively operative, resulting first of all in industrial relocation of manufacturing. . . . That is, the presently observable worldwide industrial relocation of manufacturing (within the traditional industrial centers and towards the periphery) is the result of a qualitative change of the conditions for capital expansion and accumulation enforcing a new international division of labor.

Change in the spatial division of labor occurred through United States corporations transferring parts of production to Western Europe and

Latin America; European capital moved into southern Europe; and Japanese capital moved into South Korea and Taiwan. At the same time foreign workers were imported into the AICs to reduce labor costs. The geographical framework of multinational production then widened to include a broader periphery, using devices such as free trade zones and extending even into "contract processing" agreements with socialist Eastern Europe. A new global division of industrial labor emerged, characterized by highly sophisticated production in the center and industrial production using familiar technologies in the periphery (Frobel *et al.* 1977).

The changing geography of world manufacturing

As the new set of productive conditions come into effective operation, the rate of world economic growth slowed from its postwar peak. The long-term trend since the late 1960s has involved sharply lower growth rates – indeed "negative growth" in the advanced countries in 1975 and 1982 – and unemployment rates in the AICs have risen to three times the levels of the 1960s (World Bank 1984: 12).

Manufacturing generally grew faster than the world economy during this slower growth period: between 1966 and 1980, world industrial output doubled and trade in manufactured goods tripled. Industries requiring high technology and skills showed the most vigorous expansion, chemicals and machinery accounting for two-thirds of the growth. Yet, like the economy in general, the growth of world industrial output slowed after 1973. In the latter part of the 1970s, manufacturing grew more slowly than gross domestic product in the advanced countries (Leechor *et al.* 1983; OECD 1983).

Change in the geography of manufacturing began in the postwar period of rapid growth, but matured during the period of slower growth (the 1970s and early 1980s). Manufacturing in the AICs continued to grow quite rapidly in the 1960s, with most countries having annual growth rates in manufacturing value added in the 5–8 percent range (Table 2.2). Signs of difficulties first appeared in the oldest industrial country, the United Kingdom, in the form of growth at half this rate (3.3 percent). In the 1970s manufacturing grew only in the 2–3 percent range in the AICs and production actually declined in the United Kingdom. The number of workers in industry, which had been growing until the early 1970s, stabilized in the middle 1970s and then fell in all AICs in the late 1970s and 1980s. The decline in employment was most marked in the oldest industrial countries: Belgium and the United Kingdom lost 28 percent of their manufacturing employment between 1974 and 1983. Even "successful" Germany lost 16 percent of its manufacturing employment.

By contrast, manufacturing grew rapidly in areas of the periphery characterized by lower wage levels: production in Southern Europe and Latin America grew at annual rates of 5–11 percent in the 1960s (except for Argentina) and at rates of 4–8 percent in the 1970s and early 1980s. These growth rates were usually sufficient to support increases in industrial employment: Brazil increased its manufacturing employment by 23 percent between 1976 and 1982, Mexico by 33 percent between 1974 and 1983, Turkey by 32 percent between 1974 and 1982. Spain, with a lower growth of output, declined slightly in manufacturing employment after peaking in the middle 1970s (Table 2.2).

The most rapid growth in manufacturing occurred where low wages and low conflict coincided in East and Southeast Asia. First, however, we must note the growth of Japan, a country characterized by a low level of industrial conflict and yet quite high wage rates. Annual rates of growth in the order of 6–13 percent on an already established base are spectacular indeed. Even so, the potential for automation to destroy manufacturing employment can be seen in a slight decline in the number of industrial workers between 1974 and 1983. Several NICs in the region also had annual growth rates of between 6 and 13 percent a year during the period 1960–82, with two countries, Korea and Taiwan, exceeding even these high growth rates (Table 2.2). As a result manufacturing employment increased 77 percent in Korea between 1974 and 1983, 53 percent in Taiwan, 43 percent in Hong Kong, and 75 percent in Malaysia. In all these countries the rate of growth of female employment was considerably higher than for males.

In the peripheries of South Asia and Africa, the growth of manufacturing was generally slower, although one or two countries, like Bangladesh in South Asia, and Ivory Coast in Africa, were able to achieve high growth rates on very small manufacturing bases for limited periods of time.

From the data in Table 2.2 it appears that the capitalist world's employment in manufacturing has ceased to grow. Between 1974 and 1983 the AICs lost 8 million manufacturing jobs, while the NICs (widely defined to include all peripheral countries listed in Table 2.2) gained 6 million. This is a dramatic change given that employment in manufacturing in the capitalist world was less than 100 million in 1983. We shall refer to the loss of 20 percent of the manufacturing jobs in Western Europe in ten years, and 8 percent of those in North America, as the first phase of an *industrial devolution* which shows every sign of continuing. A major consequence, we argue, is the decreased ability of manufacturing to generate income and demand by providing high-paying jobs. The manufacturing jobs lost in the AICs were paying $4.00–9.00 an hour in 1983, but those gained in the NICs paid $1.50 an hour or less. We conclude that significant deleterious changes are now occurring in the rôle played by manufacturing in generating economic growth.

Table 2.2 Manufacturing in world regions, 1960–83.

Region and country	Value added in manufacturing (billions of 1975 dollars)		Average annual growth rate in manufacturing production		Employment in manufacturing (millions)	
	1970	1982	1960–70	1970–82	1974	1983
North America						
United States	328.2	414.6	5.3	2.4	20.08	18.50
Canada	25.7	32.3	6.8	2.5	1.94	1.86
Latin America						
Brazil	19.2	43.3	n.a.	7.8	6.27 (1976)	7.79 (1982)
Venezuela	3.4	5.7	6.4	4.9	0.29 (1975)	0.41 (1981)
Mexico	14.6	30.2	10.1	6.8	0.40	0.53
Argentina	9.6	9.0	5.6	-0.2	n.a.	n.a.
Columbia	1.6	2.7	5.7	5.2	n.a.	n.a.
Western Europe						
Austria	9.1	13.4	5.2	3.2	0.94	0.85
Belgium	14.4	19.2	6.2	2.3	1.10	0.79 (1984)
France	75.8	106.4	7.8	2.9	5.56	4.78
Germany, Federal Republic	149.1	187.4	5.4	2.0	9.00	7.60
Netherlands	18.7	23.5	6.6	1.9	1.07	0.83
Sweden	16.7	18.0	5.9	0.5	0.67	0.53
United Kingdom	58.7	53.0	3.3	-0.8	7.87	5.64
Southern Europe						
Italy	n.a.	n.a.	n.a.	n.a.	5.19	4.44
Portugal	3.5	6.1 (1981)	8.9	4.5	0.86	0.92 (1982)
Spain	18.3	28.7 (1981)	n.a.	4.1	2.96	2.25
Turkey	3.7	6.9	10.9	5.2	0.78	1.03 (1982)

Africa						
Egypt	1.8	4.8	4.8	9.3	1.35	1.58 (1981)
Kenya	0.2	0.5	n.a.	9.0	0.10	0.15
Ivory Coast	0.4	0.7	11.6	5.4	n.a.	n.a.
Zimbabwe	0.6	0.9	n.a.	-4.1	0.15	0.17
South Asia						
Bangladesh	0.6	1.3	6.6	10.4	0.30 (1975)	0.44 (1981)
India	10.2	16.2	4.7	4.5	5.13	6.19
Pakistan	1.5	3.0	9.4	5.0	0.54	n.a.
Sri Lanka	0.6	0.7	6.3	2.4	0.21	0.18 (1980)
East and South east Asia						
Hong Kong	1.9	3.7	n.a.	n.a.	0.60	0.86
Korea, Republic of	2.4	11.5	17.6	14.5	1.54	2.71
Malaysia	1.0	3.3	n.a.	10.6	0.28	0.48 (1982)
Philippines	2.7	5.5	6.7	6.6	0.51	0.94 (1981)
Singapore	0.8	2.4	13.0	9.3	0.21	0.30
Thailand	1.7	4.8	11.4	9.9	1.69	2.01 (1982)
Taiwan	n.a.	n.a.	15.5	11.5	1.48	2.27
Japan	118.4	252.6	13.6	6.6	12.00	11.75
Oceania						
Australia	20.2	23.6	5.5	1.5	n.a.	n.a.

Sources: Value added and manufacturing production from World Bank (1984: 220–1, 230–1); employment from ILO (1984: 348–57, 1985: 1). Taiwan figures from Republic of China (1984: 4) (employment in manufacturing) and Kuo (1981: 23) (growth rate of manufacturing output, 1961–70 and 1971–78).

The changing pattern of trade

The different regional growth trajectories in manufacturing are also changing the pattern of world trade. The NICs were almost exclusively exporters of primary commodities in 1960. Hong Kong, Korea and Singapore together exported the same value of manufactures as a small European country like Austria. By the 1980s each had manufactured exports equivalent to a medium-sized European country, with the production of sophisticated products (machinery) increasing rapidly in the more advanced NICs and primary exports decreasing rapidly in importance or virtually disappearing in some cases (Table 2.3). Furthermore, although merchandise exports (of all types) from the AICs increased at annual rates in the 3–6 percent range, those of the NICs increased at 8–9 percent a year (Brazil, Mexico, Hong Kong) and 20 percent a year in the case of Korea. This, too, indicates a significant change in the international division of labor in manufacturing.

Notice two other characteristics of the world economy shown in Table 2.3. Certain crucial primary commodities (grain from the United States, oil from Britain) remain extremely important in the exports of the AICs. More significantly, the United States, Japan, and Germany continue to dominate world trade in manufactured goods and, furthermore, the proportion of sophisticated products (machinery and transport equipment) is increasing in the exports of all three countries. Most of these sophisticated exports are exchanged with those of other AICs. However, one-third of the manufactured exports of these three countries go to the underdeveloped countries. Retention of control over the center's production and export of machinery and equipment means that industrialization in the peripheral NICs still entails large and expensive imports of the means of production. Thus in all the NICs, with the exception of Brazil, machinery and transport equipment constitutes a high proportion (23–43 percent) of merchandise imports, fuels being the other main category whose import increases rapidly with industrialization. The implications of this continuing trade structure for the foreign debt situation of the NICs is profound.

External debt and world crisis

Industrialization of the Third World countries has been financed in large part from external sources. The sharp rise in the developing countries' share in world manufacturing and trade, which occurred in the late 1960s and 1970s, was paralleled by a similarly sharp increase in their borrowing on world capital markets (Beenstock 1984: 111, 117–18). As one student of Latin American debt puts it, the growth of underdeveloped country borrowing reflects not unsustainable

Table 2.3 Merchandise exports from selected countries, 1960–82. [a]

| Country | Percentage share of exports | | | | | | | | Value of manufactured exports (in billion US $) | |
| | Primary commodities | | Textiles and clothing | | Machinery and transport equipment | | Other manufactures | | | |
	1960	1982	1960	1982	1960	1982	1960	1982	1965	1982
United States	37	30	3	2	35	44	25	24	17.8	147.8
Japan	21	3	28	4	23	56	28	36	7.7	134.2
Germany, Federal Republic	13	13	4	5	44	47	39	35	15.8	152.8
United Kingdom	16	33	8	4	44	33	32	31	11.3	65.4
Spain	78	29	7	4	2	27	13	40	0.4	14.5
Turkey	97	57	0	20	0	5	3	18	0.01	2.5
Brazil	97	61	0	3	0	17	3	19	0.1	8.0
India	55	40	35	24	1	7	9	29	0.8	4.5
Korea, Republic of	86	8	8	21	0	28	6	43	0.1	19.2[b]
Hong Kong	20	8	45	34	4	19	31	39	1.0	19.3
Thailand	98	71	0	10	0	6	2	13	0.03	2.0
Singapore	74	43	5	4	7	26	14	26	0.3	11.8

Source: World Bank, 1984, 1985.

Notes

[a] In 1962 Taiwan's exports were 54 percent primary commodities, 2 percent machinery and transport equipment, and 44 percent all other manufactures. By 1983 this had changed to 10, 26, and 64 percent. Republic of China (1978, 1984).
[b] 1981.

consumption but increased investment. His examination of the main
Latin American countries during the period 1960–83 shows that
"investment in machinery and equipment induces far more imports
than other expenditures, even in countries with most advanced capital
goods industries (Brazil and Mexico)" (Diaz-Alejandro 1984: 367).

During the 1970s, the NICs began to borrow the capital surpluses
accumulated by the oil-exporting countries, channeled through the
international commercial banks, at high, floating rates of interest
(OECD 1982: 3). Much of this money went to purchasing from abroad
the two main inputs into modern manufacturing – petroleum and
capital goods. As a result, NICs figure prominently in the list of
indebted underdeveloped countries (Table 2.4). Major Third World
exporters of manufactures had foreign debts equal to 38 percent of their
gross national products in 1984 and 109 percent of the value of their
exports (World Bank 1985: 24). This makes them extremely vulnerable
to changes in the world economy. Argentina, Mexico, and Brazil are
particularly vulnerable to such external shocks as rising interest rates,
oil price rises, and downturns in the demand for their exports. As the
1980s proceed the debtor countries have considered various protective
measures. There was a proposal by the President of Peru in 1985 to limit
debt payments to 10 percent of export earnings. (This would create
financial chaos in the international banking world if followed by the
larger debtor Latin countries.) Drastic proposals like this must become

Table 2.4 Underdeveloped countries ranked by debt to foreign banks.

		1983 (in billions US $)
1	Mexico	85.0
2	Brazil	73.7
3	Argentina	24.1
4	Korea	23.4
5	Venezuela	21.2
6	Phillipines	14.7
7	Yugoslavia	14.5
8	Indonesia	13.3
9	Egypt	12.0
10	Chile	11.9
12	Malaysia	10.0
18	Turkey	8.8
23	Israel	5.7
24	Thailand	5.6
25	Greece	5.6

Source: Watson *et al.*
(1984: 89)

This cominal issue ? unexplored

increasingly realistic if world economic growth slows down in the ? second half of the 1980s.

Large external debts are regarded by international agencies like the International Monetary Fund (1984: 63) as "part of the normal growth pattern of developing countries with substantial opportunities for profitable investment that are not met from domestic saving." In this view, providing funds are used for sufficiently productive investments, few problems are envisaged. However, a deeper, structural analysis would suggest that an industrialization financed from abroad through direct and indirect investment, and highly dependent on imported energy and capital goods, is inherently dependent, vulnerable, and unstable. As opposed to the IMF position, Payer (1974: 1) argues: "Capital goods and sophisticated technologies may seem necessary imports to a country that wants to industrialize: but on the other hand they might not be necessary if the country rearranged its priorities or mobilized its own resources more effectively. It is important not to confuse the desire for foreign goods, or even the economic demand for them, with a genuine need." The normal functioning of a dependent economy necessitates a steady inflow of fuels and replacement parts. Yet exports of manufactured consumer goods vary considerably as demand changes with the level of economic growth in the world system, or import policies are adjusted to protect the economies of the market countries.

In the late 1970s the NICs, along with other underdeveloped countries, found themselves faced by two crises simultaneously – a worldwide increase in interest rates, which caused an explosion in debt-service payments, and a decline in the markets for their manufactured exports with the onset of recession in the advanced countries (Bradford 1984: 128). By 1984, debt-service payments (payments of principal and interest) made up 22 percent of the export earnings of all indebted countries, with the largest borrowers having much higher debt service ratios: Brazil would have required 89 percent of the value of its exports of goods and services in 1982 to service its external debt, Argentina 68 percent, and Mexico 57 percent (Larosiere 1985: 163, Wiesner 1985: 24). The problem of paying even the interest on external loans became acute in the early 1980s. Sober analysts made statements that the debt crisis "seriously threatens the stability of the world economic order" (Dale & Mattione 1983: 4), and the international banks stopped lending to Third World countries in 1982 and 1983. Thirty underdeveloped countries with debts of $400 billion were forced into debt restructuring under IMF supervision. Policies were imposed aimed at reducing government spending, reducing the growth of the money supply, and imposing wage restraints, the idea being to curtail imports by slowing the economy. The consequences are higher unemployment and higher prices, and the popular reactions include violent demonstrations and food riots (e.g. Egypt in 1977, the

Dominican Republic in 1984). Hence the debt situation increases the level of conflict, especially in the weaker Third World countries. The IMF, however, functions to deflect criticism away from national governments onto a distant international institution which, in turn, defends itself as merely performing its assigned task; as the director of the IMF sees it, the severity of its terms merely depend on the gravity of a country's overspending (*New York Times* 1984).

Conclusion

As the production of vital material goods in a controlled environment, manufacturing industry comes closest to a situation in which humans make themselves under conditions of their own choosing. The technological and organizational ingenuity enabled by human consciousness can be applied exactly to yield high labor productivity and the possibility of material affluence. In manufacturing, technological discoveries made in theory can be realized in practice: a better idea produces a better machine which enables a better life. It is no accident, therefore, that the transformation in the condition of human life in the 18th and 19th centuries is called the Industrial Revolution. Industry revolutionized itself and the societies in which it developed. What happens to manufacturing is of vital importance to economic development in general. Changes such as extensive mechanization, automation, and computerization may enhance manufacturing's historically beneficial rôle. But they may also "liberate" millions of workers straight onto the unemployment line. Geographic shifts may place more of this growth-yielding activity in underdeveloped areas; but the benefits may be limited by the kind of industry located there, and the people of the advanced regions find international competition undermining their livelihoods.

In an attempt to understand the processes by which potentially beneficial changes can be transformed into actually damaging real events, we examined industry in the context of the social relations of production, the key analytical category of Marxist theory. In capitalism, manufacturing is privately owned and its development privately directed. Yet the class of private owners is related through competition, and capitalists as a whole are antagonistically related with the class of workers. Competition and antagonism increasingly prevent the cooperation necessary for the beneficial realization of manufacturing's productive potential. They become a system of relations with an autonomy and direction of movement of its own. Individual corporate and even national reactions occur under the coercion of massive economic forces which they cannot control. The reaction to one crisis is the fertile ground for the growth of a new one as "solutions" become new problems.

Specifically, the historical development of class antagonism in the old industrial center, and the gaining through struggle of high wages by organized labor, solved the problem of what to do with the myriad products turned out by modern manufacturing. High industrial wages meant mass markets. But this "solution" had flaws. It relied on mass consumption by living labor. Yet the tendency was to replace living labor with machines. And there was the possibility of selling products in the high-waged center which were made by low-waged workers in the periphery. These interrupt the flow of values from production to consumption and back to production again. All these tendencies have hardened into reality under the intensely competitive conditions of the last two decades. A period of economic crisis has resulted which shows little sign of abating despite partial "economic recovery" in the United States. The tendency over the long term is thus towards slower rates of economic growth, particularly in the industrial countries (Table 2.5), and the predictions are for a continuation of these lower growth rates in the foreseeable future (IMF 1985).

We examined in detail one strand of this economic process – the recent shift of manufacturing in world space. In terms of the relations of production, this shift resulted from growth in the size, and expansion in the scope, of the main capitalist productive institutions, along with internationalization of the competitive relations between them. It resulted also from development of the inherent antagonism between capital and labor in regions where capitalist class relations have matured. In terms of the forces of production, we find an increased ability to traverse space and conquer the technical problems of production, together with the emergence of massive cheap labor supplies in Third World cities. Focusing on capital–labor relations in recent years, we find that East and Southeast Asia offered the best combination of wages and labor discipline, with other areas of the periphery, such as southern Europe and Latin America, offering significantly lower wages than the traditional centers of industrial development. These conditions, defined in terms of relations and forces of production, have structured a decline in industrial rates of growth in Western Europe and North America of sufficient magnitude to be termed "industrial devolution," and an increase in industrial growth

Table 2.5 Changes in output by region, 1963–82.

	1963–7	1968–72	1973–7	1978–82
industrial countries	5.0	4.5	3.0	2.0
underdeveloped countries	6.4	6.5	5.8	3.7
world	5.3	4.9	3.7	2.4

Source: IMF (1985, 44).

rates in peripheral regions where a precarious "industrial revolution" is now occurring. This geographical process of differential change has removed industrial production from areas of organized labor opposition and increasingly places it in areas of lower resistance, often in countries where the state represses opposition. Thus capitalism "solves" the problem of heightened class struggle for a share of the product.

However, a number of detrimental consequences flow from this "solution." These interact to form a new crisis period for international capitalism. First, modern capitalist expansion has been based on consumption by the masses of organized high-waged workers of the center. These consumption levels were not easily won: they result from decades of worker struggle based in the manufacturing industries. But now threat of the movement of production in space, and thus the removal of jobs, disciplines organized labor. The pressure to increase wages, and thus consumption levels slackens. More concretely the actual processes of industrial migration and automation have already resulted in a 10 percent decline in manufacturing employment over the last decade in the AICs. Manufacturing employment may have been partly replaced by service employment, especially in the United States where, as a consequence, the unemployment rate stabilized at 7.2 percent in the middle 1980s. (This was enabled by massive public and foreign debts.) But in Western Europe, which lost *6 million* manufacturing jobs between 1974 and 1983, the unemployment rate stuck at 10.5–11.5 percent even during "recovery" with little prospect for significant improvement in the future. This high unemployment rate is a further cause of lack of mass demand in the capitalist world system and thus low growth rates in total production. Escaping from one (labor) problem at one (national) scale capitalism enters a new (underconsumption) crisis at a wider (global) scale.

Second, the industrialization of parts of the Third World occurred in the context of the uneven development characteristic of capitalism's past. Investable surpluses, needed to finance development, have accumulated in the center, necessitating foreign borrowing, whereas the means of production industries remain concentrated in a few advanced countries, necessitating imports of means of production. In addition, a modern industrial technology, and the lifestyle based on it, is energy intensive. Rapid industrialization of the periphery has therefore meant massive imports and external borrowing. While the world economy boomed, the problems of Third World debt were latent. But with the onset of world recession, caused in part by change in the global geography of production, what was latent became painfully real in the debt crisis of late 1982, 1983, and 1984. The crisis was postponed through the intervention of world capitalism's bank – the IMF – and by economic recovery in the United States after 1983. But even this recovery was financed by deficit spending enabled by huge, escalating external debts – in this case by the leading capitalist power, the country which traditionally has provided the bulk of the world's direct investment funds and financed international agencies like the World Bank and the IMF. Can the United States, now one of the world's most indebted countries, afford to subsidize Third World debtors in the next crisis? Probably not. The prospect grows for further crises, centered on the international banks and the international development and financial institutions, involving antagonistic political relations between the debtor underdeveloped and newly industrializing countries and the countries suffering industrial devolution. Economic crisis in the late 20th century will thus occur at the global scale and will focus on the world's most important institutions, the banks which coordinate international capitalism.

References

Arrighi, G. and B. J. Silver 1984. Labor movements and capital migration: the United States and Western Europe in world-historical perspective. In *Labor in the capitalist world economy*, C. Bergquist (ed.), 183–216. Beverly Hills: Sage.

Beenstock, M. 1984. *The world economy in transition*. London: Allen & Unwin.

Bradford, C. I. 1984. The NICs: confronting U.S. 'autonomy'. In *Adjustment crisis in the Third World*, R. E. Feinberg and V. Kalleb (eds). New Brunswick, N.J.: Transaction Books.

Cavanagh, J. and F. Clairmonte 1982. *The transnational economy: Transnational corporations and global markets*. Reprinted by Institute for Policy Studies, Washington, D.C.

Chase-Dunn, C. K. 1984. The world-system since 1950: what has really changed? In *Labor in the capitalist world economy*, C. Bergquist (ed.). Beverly Hills: Sage.

Dale, R. S. and R. P. Mattione 1983. *Managing global debt*. Washington, D.C.: The Brookings Institution.

Diaz-Alejandro, C. F. 1984. Latin American debt: I don't think we are in Kansas anymore. *Brookings Papers on Economic Activity* **2**, 335–89.

Frobel, F., J. Heinrichs and O. Kreye 1977. The tendency towards a new international division of labor, *Review* **1**(1), 73–88.

ILO 1984. *World labour report*, vol. 1. Geneva: ILO.

ILO 1984. *Statistical Yearbook*. Geneva: ILO.

ILO 1985. *Bulletin of Labour Statistics*. Geneva: ILO.

IMF 1984. *World economic outlook*. Washington, D.C.: IMF.

IMF 1985. *Survey*, February 4 and January 21.

IMF 1985. *International Financial Statistics*. Washington: IMF.

Jenkins, C. and B. Sherman 1979. *The collapse of work*. London: Eyre Methuen.

Kaplinsky, R. 1984. *Automation: the technology and society*. Harlow: Longman.
Kuo, S. 1981. *The Taiwan success story*. Boulder: Westview Press.

Larosiere, J. de 1985. Managing director charts course for resolution of debt problems. *IMF Survey* May 27, 162–5.
Leechor, C., H. S. Kohli and S. Hur 1983. *Structural changes in world industry*. Washington, D.C.: World Bank.

Marx, K. 1967. *Capital*, vol. 1. New York: International Publishers.

New York Times, 1984. A turbulent rescue role for the IMF, May 4, D1, D2.

OECD 1982. *External debt of developing countries: 1982 survey*. Paris: OECD.
OECD 1983. *Industry in transition*. Paris: OECD.

Paldam, M. and P. J. Pederson 1984. The large pattern of industrial conflict – a comparative study of 18 countries, 1919–79. *International Journal of Social Economics* **11**(5), 3–28.
Payer, C. 1974. *The debt trap: the International Monetary Fund and the Third World*. New York: Monthly Review Press.
Peet, R. 1985. The social origins of environmental determinism. *Annals of the Association of American Geographers* **75**(3, September), 309–33.
Peet, R. 1986. World capitalism and the destruction of regional cultures. In *A world in crisis*, R. Johnston and P. Taylor (eds.), 150–172. Oxford: Basil Blackwell.

Republic of China 1984. *Statistical Yearbook of the Republic of China, 1984*. Taipei: Republic of China.

Shalev, M. 1983. Strikes and crisis: industrial conflict and unemployment in the Western nations. *Economic and Industrial Democracy* **4**, 417–60.
Spalding, H. A. 1977. *Organized labor in Latin America*. New York: Harper Torch books.
Sutcliffe, R. B. 1971. *Industry and underdevelopment*. Reading, Mass.: Addison-Wesley.

United States Bureau of the Census 1984. *Statistical Abstract of the United States, 1984*. Washington, D.C.: Superintendent of Documents.

Wallerstein, I. 1974. *The modern world system*, vol. 1. New York: Academic Press.
Watson, M., P. Keller and D. Mathieson 1984. *International capital markets: developments and prospects*. Washington, D.C.: IMF.
Wiesner, E. 1985. Domestic and External causes of the Latin American debt crisis. *Finance and Development* **22** (1 March), 24–6.
World Bank 1984. *World development report*. New York: Oxford University Press.
World Bank 1985. *World development report*. New York: Oxford University Press.

Part II

Problems of decline in advanced capitalist countries

3 Introduction

RICHARD PEET

In Part I the topic of recent changes in world industrial regions was introduced. It was argued that there had been significant change, indeed transformation, in the spatial division of labor essentially involving industrial devolution in the center and industrial revolution in parts of the periphery. The underlying reason for this shift involves geographically varying relations between capital and labor, specifically different levels of unionization, strike activity, wage rates, and fringe benefits. The immediate reason for the shift is the internationalization of capital in the context of a greater technical ability to operate globally. The first, variations in the balance of class forces, conditioned the second, the development of multinational production. Furthermore, two contradictions have developed in the new international economy. The removal of high-paying industrial jobs from the AICs has slowed economic growth in the 1970s and 1980s. Retention of control over capital and capital goods by the AICs has meant that industrialization in the periphery involves huge Third World debts. These contradictions intersect as economic crises: slowdowns in the world economy precipitate debt crises in the Third World. An international scale is given to crises, and a new crisis fulcrum forms around the international banks and financial agencies.

We can elucidate this crisis-ridden process by examining the center, the heartland of the world economy in the advanced industrial countries of Western Europe and the northern United States in more detail. The industrial revolution created a core economic region, centered originally on Britain and the Low Countries, but extending in an almost unbroken, single economic space from northern Italy to the Middle West of the United States. This industrial heartland today employs 35 million people in high-paying manufacturing jobs generating the largest mass of disposable income in the world. What happens here determines the development of the entire capitalist world system.

It often seems as though manufacturing activity has a natural history involving youth, maturity, and decline. And it is often said that the world's economic heartland is going through a natural maturation from agriculture, through manufacturing, to services. Thus the decline of manufacturing is merely a natural stage in the evolution to a postindustrial economy. Old industries are displaced outwards in world space to make way for the vibrant new service activities of the high-technology future. Social problems are dismissed as temporary aberrations along an already determined, natural path.

Analogies between society and nature have seduced many a social scientist, particularly in the discipline of geography (Peet 1985). But there are fundamental differences between social and natural processes which make the lessons of evolutionary biology largely irrelevant to human history. There is a difference between the organism's search for life and the human's production of it. Human labor can renew productive resources worn out by use. Old landscapes can be rebuilt to fit new technologies. Indeed the highly productive industrial heartland is exactly the center of accumulation of the capital needed to perform this constant renewal. Under capitalism, however, the reinvestment of capital depends not on the physical age of an industrial region but on its social conditions, especially those relevant to profit making, and in particular the social relation between capital and labor. In the old regions of the center these relations have had time to develop. Trade union membership reaches its highest densities in the home regions of the industrial revolution: 75 percent of the workforce is organized in Belgium, 51 percent in the United Kingdom, 35 percent in the United States Middle West (Walsh 1983: 196, United States Bureau of the Census 1984: 440). Except where industrial relations have been restructured (Germany, for instance), the level of capital–labor antagonism, expressed in strike levels, is high by world standards. Most importantly, worker opposition and union struggle have forced higher wages. A set of social conditions has thus emerged which are inimical to private profit making. As the different national production systems have entered into greater competition, and as multinational corporations have gained greater locational freedom, the different capital–labor relations have exercised their determining influence on the geography of industry.

Let us examine the recent history of the industrial heartland in more geographic detail. Three types of regional experience are characteristic of the recent past: manufacturing employment has sharply declined in the old core of Belgium, the Netherlands, and the United Kingdom; Italy, France, and the Middle Western region of the United States have had more moderate rates of manufacturing job loss; Germany and the Middle Atlantic and southern New England regions of the United States have fared the best (Table 3.1). Unemployment rates in the middle 1980s show a similar tripartite division, being extremely high where manufacturing employment has collapsed and more moderate where the manufacturing base is closer to remaining intact. The only region of the heartland with low unemployment rates, southern New England, has experienced an industrial revival over the last decade. The conclusion can be drawn that manufacturing has not been transcended

Table 3.1 Employment in manufacturing and unemployment in advanced industrial regions.

Country/region	Change in manufacturing employment 1975–82 (%)	Unemployment rate 1984 (%)
Belgium	−23.3	14.0
Netherlands	−15.3	14.0
United Kingdom	−23.2	13.2
Italy	−12.0	10.1
US Middle West	−11.5	9.4
France	−10.5	8.9
Germany	− 7.5	8.1
United States Middle Atlantic	− 7.2	7.6
United States southern New England	+ 7.9	4.8

Sources: ILO 1984, US Bureau of Labor Statistics 1984, OECD 1985.

as a relic of a past stage of life in the economic heartland. Instead retention of the industrial base remains essential to a region's economic health. The future is still made by manufacturing industry, and the postindustrial economy is a long way away.

In the articles reproduced in this part of the book, various aspects of this general process are examined in detail. My article, "The geography of class struggle and the relocation of United States manufacturing industry," reproduced as Chapter 4, develops further some of the ideas expressed in Chapter 2, especially the idea of a causal connection between class relations and industrial location. The United States does not have a politically militant working class. It does have an economically militant workforce, in the sense that labor unions press strongly to increase their members' share of the industrial product. "Class struggle" over wages and benefits has developed more strongly in certain United States regions than others. The old industrial regions have unionization rates and strike frequencies similar to those in Western Europe, and much higher wage rates. In the periphery of the United States by comparison unionization is less prevalent, strikes almost unknown, and wage rates significantly lower. Tied neither to resources (like agriculture) nor markets (like many services), manufacturing has responded to this geographic pattern of class relations by relocating, altering the space economy of the United States by placing employment in low–class–struggle and lower income areas. Chapter 4 concludes that the new geography of employment and income is a signifcant causal factor in the economic recessions of the 1970s and 1980s.

This discussion is cast at the level of massive regions and considered in terms of long-term trends. The selection from Bluestone and Harrison's *The deindustrialization of America*, reproduced as Chapter 5, tells a different kind of story. They document the income losses and impacts on workers' physical and mental health caused by deindustrialization and job loss in the older economic regions of the United States. Detrimental effects ripple outwards from the workers to the immediate community and into the cities and states of affected regions. Disinvestment and job loss damage the "social psyche" creating disorientation and anxiety. Blame for the loss of jobs goes to the unions rather than to corporate decision makers or, more profoundly, the necessities of competition. Hence a popular ideology emerges which precludes a radical politics aimed at the root causes of the problem.

The tendency for industrial "restructuring" to collapse into industrial disintegration is exemplified best by the recent history of the United Kingdom. Significant decline in manufacturing began much earlier and has affected the economy more seriously than elsewhere. A rapid decline in manufacturing employment is now paralleled by a decline in other kinds of employment. The gap widens between the number of people available for work and the employment available. Economic "recovery" in 1984, led by a small increase in service jobs filled by female part-time employees, did not significantly change this disastrous process: manufacturing and other industries continue to decline, 3 million people remain out of work, and the unemployment rate is 13 percent in a social democracy which, until recently, prided itself on its ability to provide work for its people (UK Department of Employment 1985).

Massey's article, reproduced as Chapter 6, sees in this two different historical processes: a long-term decline in basic activities in the oldest industrial regions; and a more recent loss of employment in virtually all industries, but focused on the big cities rather than the small towns. A new map of unemployment is emerging, reminiscent of the 1930s in the continuation of high unemployment in places like Northern Ireland and Central Scotland, but also characterized by high rates of joblessness in regions, like the Midlands, which until recently had low unemployment rates. Lower unemployment rates are encountered in the "British Sunbelt" where employment is generated by control and conception functions, rather than production. Massey interprets these shifts in terms of their social and political effects. These include a changing regional class structure (Massey 1983), economic decline in the heartlands involving a massive loss of union members (Massey & Miles 1984), and weakening in the bastions of support for socialist politics. Britain, rather than the United States, points the way to the future and Massey's article gives some indication of what life will be like. We can see the future and it (literally!) does not work.

References

ILO 1984. *Statistical Yearbook*. Geneva: ILO.

Massey, D. 1983. Industrial restructuring as class restructuring: production decentralization and local uniqueness. *Regional Studies* **17**(2), 73–89.

Massey, D., and N. Miles 1984. Mapping out the unions. *Marxism Today* **28**(5), 19–22.

OECD 1985. *Observer* No. 133, March.

Peet, R. 1985. The social origins of environmental determinism. *Annals, Association of American Geographers* **75** (3, September), 309–33.

United Kingdom, Department of Employment, 1985. *Employment Gazette*. London: HMSO.

United States Bureau of the Census 1984. *Statistical abstract of the United States, 1984*. Washington, D.C.: Superintendent of Documents.

United States Bureau of Labor Statistics 1984. *Employment and Earnings*. Washington, D.C.: United States Government Printing Office.

Walsh, K. 1983. *Strikes in Europe and the United States*. London: Frances Pinter.

4   *The geography of class struggle and the relocation of United States manufacturing industry**

RICHARD PEET

In Marxist theory the relations which organize the material production of life are the economic structure of society. Social relations of production control the development of the productive forces, determining the way nature is transformed into the material basis of continued existence. This structure of determination includes the spatial formation of the productive forces, or the geography of production. Different social relations arrange production space differently. As Buch-Hanson and Nielson (1977: 5) put it: "Each mode of production forms its own territorial structure. . . . Each mode of production thus has its own geography." The geography of production can be comprehended as a particular part of a general theory of modes of production by means of a theory of historical materialism.

Two aspects of the social relations of production are analyzed here. The first, between production units, such as family businesses, or transnational corporations, immediately affects the allocation of the social productive effort, including the distribution of the productive forces in space. Social production, however, is not owned and organized by the entire society; instead, each unit of production is stratified into classes based essentially on ownership, or nonownership, of the productive means, be these natural resources or capital equipment. Struggle between production classes is the second aspect of social relations; the emergence of geographical forms and intensities of class struggle also directs the spatial development of the productive forces. The focus of this chapter is the changing location of United States manufacturing industry as the outcome of the interaction of the two

---

* Edited and updated version of Peet, R. 1983, Relations of production and the relocation of United States manufacturing industry since 1960, *Economic Geography* **59** (2, April), 112–43, reprinted by permission of the editor.

sets of relations of production in the contemporary phase of capitalist development. An approach will be made through social relations of production between capitalists.

Relations between capitalists

Production is collective action directed at changing natural resources into useful products. Advanced production systems involve specialization by production units and exchange relations between them. Capitalism is a mode of production founded on the exchange of commodities and characterized by private ownership of the separate units of production, with competitive relations between members of the class of owners – between capitalists.

COMPETITION

Marx has some interesting things to say about competition and the socio-economic structure made by it. In *Grundrisse* he describes competition as the inner nature of capital experienced by each capitalist as external necessity (Marx 1973: 414). In *Capital* he says that "competition subordinates every individual capitalist to the immanent laws of capitalist production as external and coercive laws" (Marx 1976: 739). Competition imposes the necessity of producing with the greatest efficiency, or with the lowest costs. The most efficient producers capture higher profits, or reduce prices, forcing the less efficient to emulate or be eliminated. To the extent that competition works freely, this aspect of the social relations of capitalist production might be welcomed as a source of productive efficiency. However, competition is not the only way productive resources can be efficiently allocated. And, as Marx points out, with competition efficient allocation is achieved not via a conscious social plan to save scarce natural resources, nor human labor time, but "emerges behind the backs" of the private decision makers. Competition is a social force not controlled by society as a whole. Its central institution, the market, is literally an "invisible hand" which may lead the productive system in directions which allow costs to be saved in the short run but not necessarily in the long run, or advantages to be gained by one (local or national) unit of production at the expense of all others. Savings in resources take the class form of profit for the private owners of production. Organized by competition, the movement of the productive base of capitalist society achieves an autonomous dynamic with production and employment unpredictable and "economic efficiency" sometimes achieved at great social expense.

The overall use of space is also determined by the spontaneous growth and movement of individual capitals which, under the discipline of competition, are forced to locations where natural and social conditions provide the best opportunities for making profit. In the early stages of capitalist development, optimal location was determined by the natural characteristics of places. But with the development of the productive forces this form of locational determination was eroded. Geographic variations in conditions created by social interactions between producers became dominant. Capitalist production became more mobile in space but, paradoxically, as the relation with nature relaxed, not more socially controllable. The process of locational change is still regulated by "external," uncontrollable forces, which exert their influence through cyclical crises: "the spatial division and restructuring of social production occurs through the results of the processes of crises which arise in the accumulation of capital" (Läpple & van Hougstraten 1980: 124).

In brief, under capitalism competition directs the development and location of productive processes. Economic "rationality" is defined in terms of the competitive abilities of individual companies rather than social efficiency directly. Change takes place under coercion rather than through social planning. The structure of space is made by private, profit making decisions, rather than by social agreement.

CONCENTRATION AND CENTRALIZATION OF CAPITAL

Multinational corporations, the dominant institutions of advanced capitalism, emerge as the consequence of tendencies inherent in the nature of capitalist development. Each unit of production must extend its division of labor and employ more workers in the struggle to increase productivity and survive the competitive struggle between companies. Both entail an increase in the minimum amount of capital which the firm must possess. Furthermore, in the modern age higher productivity depends increasingly on the mass of mechanized productive means. Hence the capital needed increases and the size of company necessarily grows larger. The accumulation of capital increases the *concentration* of capital in the hands of individual capitalists. These capitals confront each other as separate entities, and competitive victory results in the *centralization* of capital. Centralization supplements concentrated capital accumulation by enabling individual capitalist firms to again vastly extend the scale and scope of their operations. As Marx says:

> Everywhere the increased scale of industrial establishments is the starting point for a more comprehensive organization of the collective labour of many people, for a broader development of their material forces, i.e., for the progressive transformation of isolated processes of production, carried on by customary methods, into socially contrived and scientifically arranged processes of production. (Marx 1976: 780)

Ind Rev

Centralization of capital achieves revolutions in its organic composition, raising the constant (machine) as against the variable (labor) portion. Automation and mechanization diminish the relative demand for labor. The working population is thereby made superfluous as capital accumulation and centralization progress (Peet 1975). Concentration, centralization and unemployment go hand in hand.

Not always?

Relations of production between capitalists thus increasingly take the form of the centralization of corporate capital, characterized geographically by the regional agglomeration of production on the one hand and the "entanglement of all peoples in the net of the world market, and with this, the growth of the international character of the capitalist régime" on the other (Marx 1976: 929, see also Harvey 1975).

Turning to particular ways in which corporate producers relate, certain kinds of locational advantage are found to play increasingly important parts. Hymer's spatial model of corporate structure provides a useful style for discussing this. Hymer distinguishes between three "horizons" of corporate operations: level I, headquarters concentrated close to markets and control centers, like stock and commodity exchanges, the media, and the government; level II, field offices in large regional cities; level III, day-to-day supervision of productive activities oriented to labor power, markets, and raw materials. Level I of all multinational corporations is increasingly geographically centralized in a few world capital cities; level III spreads across the world's surface because of the multinational corporation's "power to command capital and technology and its ability to rationalize their use on a global scale" (Hymer 1975: 50). Pred, with a similar conception of the spatial structure of "major job-providing organizations," shows that the proportion of jobs controlled by spatially centralized corporations is increasing rapidly.[1] Pred then continues by linking this hierarchical pattern with the differential growth of cities and the question of regional colonialism (Pred 1974). More generally, as a result of the geographic centralization of capital, the degree of central control over decentralized production tends to increase. This occurs through the transfer of corporate head offices towards national metropoli, by the in-migration and rapid growth of the branch plants of multiplant enterprises into dispersed regions of production, and through acquisitions and mergers. Corporate mergers are particularly important in the United States, accounting for a shift in corporate control towards New York, Chicago, and Los Angeles (Dicken 1976, see also Leigh & North 1978, on the similar process in Britain). As shown by Table 4.1, Northeastern and North Central corporations dominate the branching of manufacturing plants in their own areas *and* in the South and West (Birch 1979: 46–7). The location of manufacturing and control over employment thus becomes subject to the competitive necessities experienced by large corporations headquartered in a few world cities. Regional economic development

Or region

Then living decline

Table 4.1 Percentage of net manufacturing job growth in branches controlled by headquarters in regions of the United States, 1969–76.

| Location of headquarters | Controlling branches in | | | |
	Northeast (%)	North Central (%)	South (%)	West (%)
Northeast	53	30	31	29
North Central	34	59	41	39
South	7	4	10	12
West	6	7	13	21
	100	100	100	100

Source: Birch (1979: 46).

or underdevelopment is determined by corporate decisions made by an elite in a few world centers of power.

However, at this crucial point there is a tendency for critical research on corporations to focus only on such questions as the spatial *shape* of control, a geographic analysis which merges easily with a limited liberal critique of the sheer *size* of corporations (Peet 1982). This analysis conveniently ignores the exploitative nature of the labor process in large corporations and small firm alike. Also it assumes that small firms exercising local control are to be automatically preferred over large corporations exercising control from distant central offices. Discussions of corporate acquisitions of smaller companies, for example, always direct criticism at the distant corporate buyer and never the local owners who, despite an intimate knowledge of their employees, and presumably a concern for their fate, still sell their businesses. And finally it assumes that the question of control over production ends at the level of the corporate institution and not the entire structure of interactions between institutions.

How do centralized corporations compete? Enterprises make "surplus profits" from competitive advantages enabled by technical advantage, lower transport costs, and the increased exploitation of labor power.[2] Under present world conditions corporate technologies tend to converge, and the development of transport equalizes locations. Competitive advantage is increasingly linked to the super-exploitation of unemployed females and the workers of the underdeveloped regions and countries of the peripheries. The "logic of profit" leads to the spatial instability of production as capital moves in search of ephemeral competitive loopholes. The policies of the state systematically have to favor the relocation of capital. The most important laws of the organization of space in advanced capitalism result from the *hypermobility* of capital (Damette 1980).

The theme of the hypermobility of corporate capital is picked up by

Bluestone and Harrison (1982). They extended it to the question of the widespread, systematic corporate disinvestment in productive capacity in old industrial regions. In an era of intense worldwide corporate competition, and declining profit rates, capital is forced to move between regions, even countries, in an almost desperate search for new profitable uses or the reduction of costs. This frenzied capital movement leads to a decentralized pattern of production, involving deindustrialization in the abandoned regions of capitalism's origin. Implicit in this analysis is the idea of competition between originally national corporate systems, each with productive bases providing different competitive abilities. Vitally important in the multinational competitive struggle for survival are the results of struggle in the labor process: labor costs and corporate freedom to introduce technology. The regionally and nationally varying opposition from labor conditions intercorporate competition. More generally, class struggle between capital and labor structures the competitive relations between capitalists.

Relations of production between classes

In advanced capitalism corporate decisions made in a few headquarter cities determine the structure of world production. But the centralization of capital does not enable the coercion of competition to be transcended, as a relic of the primitive past. Even the mightiest corporations are forced to conform to directions determined by competition between them. New geographies of production emerge, therefore, not from a process characterized by social planning but under coercion from autonomous relations of production. Under the coercion of competition, corporations may even be forced to make decisions which they already know will, in the long run, end up cutting their own throats. This is the real meaning of "cut-throat competition."

The discussion has so far isolated one relation of production. As with "bourgeois"[3] location theory, it has assumed production is directed solely by relations between production units – in this case capitalist corporations. But for production to take place relations with nature and social relations between capital and labor are also necessary. In the capitalist mode of production natural and social relations are characterized by contradiction, which generates sequences of environmental and social crises, geographically focused on the old centers of capitalist production (Peet 1978, 1979), Such contradictions, established within the very conditions of existence of capitalism, constitute an even deeper basis for the lack of social control over the historical direction and geographical form taken by the production process.

CLASS STRUGGLE AT THE POINT OF PRODUCTION

In Marxist theory, interclass struggle between the owners of capital and its producers is inherent in the capitalist mode of economic life. The very substance of capital, in Marxist theory, *is* value alienated from labor. (Hence capital is "egotistical value.") Forced to sell value-creating labor power to capital, the workers only magnify the power dominating them (Marx 1973: 304–10). Under capitalism the conditions within which production occurs – "the worker works under the control of the capitalist to whom his labour belongs; the capitalist takes good care that the work is done in a proper manner" and "the product is the property of the capitalist and not that of the worker, its immediate producer" (Marx 1976: 292–8) – make daily conflict between capital and labor necessary, and point the way to its multiple forms, struggles over the control of production and over shares of the product. As production relations between owner and worker are increasingly established in the usual way for "commodity owners" (i.e., via the exchange of money), class struggle may also be largely restricted to squabbles over the share of the product rather than the ownership and control of production. This does not, however, resolve the contradiction between classes; it only provides a different channel for the movement of crises.

Until recently, the emphasis in Marxist research has been on interclass relations as the great internal contradiction whose maturation results in the complete destruction of the capitalist mode of production and the substitution of socialism. But worker resistance to capital also causes accommodating change *within* the capitalist mode of production.

Historically, resistance to capitalist factory work first took an individualistic form. The workers came from small-scale and geographically dispersed manufactures or peasant agriculture and learned slowly an urban-industrial "habit of solidarity" suited to the emerging capitalist mode of life. Individualistic resistances of this type mainly occur over the worker's loss of control over life time in the forms of discipline problems, workers arriving late or leaving early, breaking machinery to gain free time, a multitude of different kinds of deception, absenteeism, voluntary quits, etc. Collective resistance developed later, sometimes being organized around the winning back of control over time, but increasingly organized around the workers' share of the product (Friedman 1977).

Worker resistance, particularly of the later collective and organized type, developed unevenly between different groups of workers. Factors determining the strength of organized worker resistance are complex, but large industrial plants with many similar boring tasks, such as automobile factories, seem to favor the building of strong labor organizations. Similarly, workers living in homogeneous communities centered around one particular kind of work, like mining, also tend to have high levels of collective resistance to capital. "In general high resistance appears in relation to the size and homogeneity of workers" situations and the closeness of their contacts. . . . Workers are encouraged to verbalize complaints and to resist oppression if those around them reinforce their feelings, if those around them provide resonance by which these grievances are repeated and magnified" (Friedman 1977: 33). By comparison, heterogeneity of work experience and worker characteristics weaken resistance, while labor segmentation and stratification have similar effects.[4]

For capital the main problem in the labor process is that it buys from the worker only the possibility of exploitation, yet competition necessitates the full realization of this possibility. In Friedman's analysis, the exercise of managerial authority over workers, necessary to get them to work hard, has involved two main strategies: responsible autonomy, which gives privileged workers relative freedom and flexibility; and direct control, under which nonprivileged workers are closely supervised and coercively directed. For years, in the center, managers found cooperation and conciliation to be more effective controls than coercion for core workers (Friedman 1977: 77–9). Other writers stress a wide range of management strategies for controlling workers. Brecher, for example, lists rationalization of production, redivision of labor, changing the technology of production, time study, supervision, hierarchy and job ladders, various forms of payment, hiring and training strategies, corporate welfare schemes, union policies, external institutions of control, ideologies at the workplace, and, significantly for this chapter, workplace relocation (Brecher & the Work Relations Group 1978: 7–15). In summary, the tendency in Marxist research is to discover the "hidden history of the workplace," relating interclass relations to intracapitalist relations, so that "both the nature and intensity of the class struggle as well as competition in the product market are seen to be fundamental determinants of the development of the labor process" (Walker 1981: 46).

In the Marxist understanding, therefore, a fundamental contradiction lies in private ownership and control of the social labor process. Unions are the main device which workers use to pit their collective might against capital. But the social combination of labor does not happen automatically, as though an "essence of contradiction" magically congeals into institutional forms. Labor unions result, instead, from concrete human actions taken within structural constraints, including geographic contexts. In this concrete process certain times and places (conjunctures) are more significant than others. We can begin our account of worker organization by concentrating on one, the organization of labor, and the direction taken by the subsequent development of United States capitalism, in the 1930s and during World War II.

Under the desperate economic conditions of the depression years the classes polarized. The working class fused together bursting into action. Mass action by labor forced recognition by the federal government of organizing and collective bargaining rights (Wagner Act of 1935); an increase in workers belonging to unions, from less than 7 percent in the early 1930s to 24 percent in 1946;[5] and a doubling of wages in manufacturing between 1932 and 1945. This period of transformation in workers' power culminated with 4.6 million people going out on strike in 1946 and 1 percent of the year's working time lost through work stoppages, the closest the United States has come to a national general strike. This forced a reaction by capital, the state, and even the unions. Capital reacted to organized labor via the cooptation and accommodation policies mentioned above; the state limited rights to worker self-organization and collective action (Taft–Hartley Act of 1947); union leaders disciplined their members and eliminated communists; mass worker organizations expelled radical unions (Davis 1980). The relation between capital and labor was successfully maneuvered to center on collective bargaining, a process of accommodation between big business and big labor, aimed at reaching a mutually satisfactory agreement within the existing system (Harbison 1954). In effect, a "social contract" was signed by representatives of the two parties. High wages for workers were exchanged for stable, predictable work for capital. In addition, capitalism effectively turned the workers' concern from the sphere of production to the sphere of consumption. With fragmentation of the work process, which helped destroy the worker's identity as a producer, this led to the abandonment of class struggle as an attempt to transform the capitalist system, inducing instead a union strategy primarily concerned with a "struggle for the beefsteak" (Mallet 1975).

THE GEOGRAPHY OF CLASS STRUGGLE

As the class struggle changed in intensity over time, so also it developed unevenly in space. The strength and effectiveness of workers' resistance to capital depends on the massiveness and centrality of their action.[6] Space arranges workers in different masses (i.e., in factories, communites, etc.). Workers in different geographic settings have different propensities for action, in terms of the development of a collective consciousness and the size and solidarity of organizations. Capitalists likewise are embedded in different settings with different relations between members of the owning class and between capital and the state, both local and federal. As a result, the struggle between capital and labor has a considerable geographic variation, changing in content, intensity, and level of development over space. However, the theme of the geography of class struggle is little developed by academics. It is not even *mentioned* in most conventional social geographies.[7]

Discussions of worker resistance to capital usually emphasize differences in union organization and strike activity between economic activities – manufacturing, mining, and transport are the most active (Friedman 1977, Edwards 1981). Geographic variations in worker resistance to capital have often been assumed to emerge solely from the economic activities present in any space. However, some research has also used an "ecological" viewpoint. This focuses on the territorial processes with structure conflict relations (Stern 1976, Lincoln 1978, Stern & Galle 1978). Most such research contrasts worker organization in urban-industrial centers with that in rural and small-town peripheries within the advanced capitalist societies. Kerr and Siegel (1954) argue that workers living in settings which multiply their contacts have higher propensities to strike than workers living in more diffuse settings. Worker organization is thus easier in large, densely populated cities than in small towns or rural areas (Shorter & Tilly 1974: 283). In urban areas, moreover, strikes spread quickly to large numbers of workers (Gordon 1977: 72), one result being general strikes in which workers take virtual control of entire cities and their economies (Seattle in 1919, San Francisco in 1934). Urban worker demonstrations resound through the corridors of power, whereas those of rural workers echo only through the hills (Shorter & Tilly 1974: 283). Organized workers forming majority populations in urban-industrial concentrations are able to influence state policy, especially at the local level – hence the influence of United States labor in the northern state branches of the Democratic party (Heil 1978). In the large city, moreover, the capitalist class may be divided into factions whose squabbles labor can use to advantage, whereas in the industrial villages and towns of the periphery one capitalist family often holds total power both economically and politically. Finally, big cities are the recipients and makers of diverse ideas, including radical ideas, whereas consciousness in rural small towns is still tyrannized by the powerfully conservative ideologies of religion, nationalism, and local boosterism. Shorter and Tilly thus conclude from a study of the distribution of strikes in France:

> The big city appears a place of militancy and solidarity. It is certain that the sheer intensity of conflict in the big city was higher than in smaller communities. It is certain that the big city, more than the small town, aided the mobilization of workers for strike activity. (Shorter & Tilly 1974: 287).

A study of trade union organization and action in Britain similarly concludes:

> What the city has provided has been quick and easy communication via an elaborate network of informal meeting places and formal organizations. The city too has a large and diverse population and this bestows on the individual a certain social invisibility, an

immunity from the sort of scrutiny and social censorship that is more evident in the small town. The city then, because of its diversity and scale, has provided both a range of organization and a high degree of personal "protection." It is not, therefore, by accident that major campaigns start in cities and ripple outwards with diminishing effect. The more distant and isolated the workplace the less the likelihood of involvement in the big issues. (Lane 1982: 8)

And Gordon argues that the eruption of labor unrest in the late 19th century United States city was stimulated by the dense concentration of workers in central urban neighborhoods; this resulted in the more decentralized city of the 20th century, as manufacturing suburbanized in an attempt to escape organized labor (Gordon 1977). In turn, the dispersal of residence to the suburbs can be seen as an ecological factor changing worker consciousness in the postwar period.

If arguments like these for geographic variations in organized worker resistance to capital have validity, we should find them clearly confirmed by the empirical evidence.[8] In terms of the geographic statistics, differences between urban central and rural peripheral areas are clear. Union membership in the United States declines with the size of the city; it also varies regionally, being lower in the South than the North. One survey found 62 percent of manual workers were union members in northern cities of 100,000 people or more, whereas the figure was 28 percent for similar workers in southern cities of under 2,500 (Kornhauser 1961). One piece of research concludes that northern states, centers of heavily unionized industries, became unionized directly, in terms of the domination of employment by these industries, and indirectly in that when the key industries where organized all industrial sectors tended to become more highly organized (Troy 1957). However, states which remained unorganized by the time of the Taft–Hartley Act (1947) subsequently became more difficult to unionize because they passed anti-union "right-to-work" laws under the Act (Warren & Strauss 1979).[9] The present geographic distribution of union organization was thus more or less set by the timing of an intense reaction by capital to worker militancy in the late 1940s and early 1950s (the McCarthy period). The geography of unions in the 1970s was essentially similar to that in the early 1950s (Troy 1957: 21). Thus workers are unionized in highest proportions in an industrial heartland stretching from New York to St. Louis, with an outlying region of high unionization on the West Coast. The main difference with the 1950s, however, is a decline in worker unionization in southern New England consequent on the decline of the (unionized) mill industries and rise of the (non-unionized) high-technology industries (United States Bureau of Labor Statistics 1979).

Work stoppages show quite directly worker resistance to capital.

Stoppages are highest in organized industries and regions. Work stoppages accounted for 0.03–0.11 percent of working time in lowest-union, most peripheral states and 0.26–0.94 percent in the most organized, heavily industrialized and mining states in the 1970s (United States Bureau of Labor Statistics 1970–80).

Although wage rates depend on productivity, and the degree of competition in an industry, they are also influenced by the organized force exerted by labor on capital: unionism has a significant direct effect on wages and fringe benefits (Lewis 1963, Kahn 1979, Freeman 1981). Hence the geography of earnings in manufacturing parallels unionization, even in such details as relatively low wages in the disciplined New England states. Within this regional pattern there is also a strong correlation between earnings and city size (Fuchs 1967).

Spatial variations in the attitude of the local state towards capital and labor can be measured by the available indexes of "business climate." The most widely used index consists largely of measures of tax levels, union and corporate legislation, the size of government, and other indices measuring the local state's favorability towards business. The 1970s was a period of rapid change in state attitudes as the liberal northern and western states were disciplined by recession and forced into creating the most favorable contexts for private profit making (Goodman 1979). Even so, a 1975 survey indicated that the business climate remained most favorable in peripheral states like Texas, Alabama, Virginia, South Dakota, the Carolinas, and Florida and least favorable in central states like New York, California, Massachusetts, Michigan, Delaware, Connecticut, and Pennsylvania (Weinstein & Firestone 1978: 134–9).[10]

A composite index of the "level of class struggle" can be constructed by ranking all states in terms of the above four measures and summing the rank scores. The map result is shown in Figure 4.1. States with a high level of class struggle are those where the great worker organizing drives of the 1930s and 1940s were most successful and which also retained their industrial structures virtually intact until recently – the "Manufacturing Belt" (excluding New England) and the West Coast. In these states the postwar "social contract" between capital and labor has been in effect. The proportion of plant workers covered by labor–management agreements in large- and medium-sized establishments in 1960–1 was 80 percent in the North Central and Western regions and 77 percent in the Northeast, but only 48 percent in the South; contract coverage also varied with the size of the particular community in which industry was located (Kanninen 1962: 748, 750). Generalizing, we can say that unions and the social contract indeed have a geography. Unions and the contract have been fully in place in the Middle West and the West Coast; they have been partly in effect in regions like New England and the Mid South, contiguous to this high–class-struggle heartland;

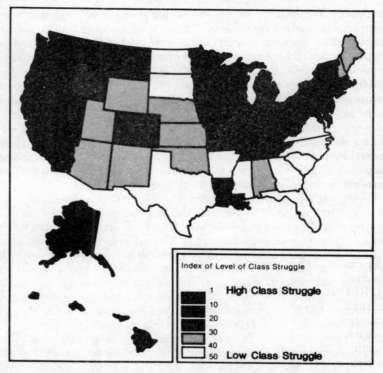

Figure 4.1 The geography of class struggle in the 1970s.

and they have been in effect in peripheral regions only in the urban areas, and there for selected industries.

The "social contract" form taken by class struggle in the postwar years was a primary condition for the type and rate of economic development. Real weekly earnings for industrial workers in the United States increased by an average of 2.2 percent a year between 1947 and 1965, and the proportion of national income going to labor increased from 65 percent in 1947 to 75 percent in 1968 (Backman 1974: 22–3). The mass market provided by the incomes of high-wage, organized labor in particular fueled an economic expansion which pushed the GNP from $212 billion in 1948 to almost $1,000 billion in 1970, a period in which prices only doubled (United States Bureau of the Census 1981: 420, 498).[11] This development was centered in the high–class–struggle (HCS) states; the Middle Atlantic, East North Central, and Pacific states had 52 percent of the national population, but 58 percent of total personal income in 1960 and 56 percent in 1970 (United States Bureau of the Census 1981: 10, 428). In these states there developed an *introverted* exchange between the capital goods sector and the mass consumption goods sector (Amin 1974). This exchange, crucial to modern capitalist development, was discovered through blind struggle between the two great classes. It resulted in a "golden age" for capital and labor which stretched through the years of the 1950s and 1960s. Founded on essentially competitive, antagonistic relations of production, it was, however, inherently insecure. Economic growth faltered in 1958 and 1961 but was kept going by the build-up of the Vietnam War. Then, in the early 1970s, the competitive relations between corporations came into a state of heightened tension, the economy became increasingly unstable, and the relations between capital and labor changed. Instability of the production system in space was one dimension of this more general tendency.

The relocation of United States manufacturing

Would have been useful somewhere in the book!

We cannot trace all the causes of the onset of a period of economic crisis in the late 1960s and the 1970s; these have been outlined elsewhere (URPE 1978, Aglietta 1982, Harvey 1982). Economic crisis in the United States was part of a series of changes in the world economy, involving differential growth and the redistribution of economic activities within a new international division of labor (Frobel *et al.* 1977). As a result, North America's share in world manufacturing value added, which remained stable in the first half of the 1960s, suddenly dropped from 37 percent in 1966 to 27 percent in 1975. Europe's share also dropped, from 30 to 28 percent, but those of Japan and Southeast Asia increased (UNIDO 1979: 37). Explanations for the relative decline of United States manufacturing typically stress increased world competition, with emphasis on the rôle of Japan (Bluestone & Harrison 1982).[12] The profit rate of United States corporations certainly fell as part of this competitive struggle, from an average of 15 percent a year in the 1960s to 10 percent in the 1970s (United States Department of Commerce 1982a: 31). United States corporations reacted via a series of policies which included switching capital in space and relocating productive capacity.[13] However, the exact synthesis of international competition and national economic development in a theoretical framework of the contradictory growth of the world capitalist system remains a matter of controversy. For the moment we shall have to be content with an analysis of certain locational aspects.

FROM FROSTBELT TO SUNBELT
The terms popularly used to rationalize the relocation of United States manufacturing industry as a move from the Frostbelt to the Sunbelt

(implying locational determination by *natural* relations of production) represent an ideological diversion from a more essential truth. Natural resources are used, and space arranged and rearranged, under the control of the *social* relations of production.

Competition between capitals occurs in the social context of different regional–historical relations between capital and labor. Capital–labor struggles at the point of production determine the length of the working day, the intensity of the work, the wages and standard of living of the workers (i.e., the cost of reproducing labor power), and the rate of introduction of new techniques. Labor struggle, strikes, and the high costs of accommodating labor in the old centers of mature capitalism induced pioneering decisions by innovative capitalists to move production to virgin regions.[14] Capitals which moved to regions of low-intensity class struggle were then able to out-compete capitals which remained in regions of high-intensity struggle. These were coerced into drastic adjustments, such as massively replacing living labor by machines and/or disciplining their labor forces, following the pioneers to regions of low-intensity struggle, etc. Differential class struggle was the primary cause of a movement of industrial activity from the Manufacturing Belt to the new industrial regions of a sequence of peripheries especially in the 1950s, 1960s and 1970s. To be exact, changes in the location of United States manufacturing can be explained more effectively by the social geography of intraclass and interclass struggle than by the natural geography of climate and resources.

Employment in manufacturing in the United States was 10 millions in 1939, 18 millions in 1943, almost 21 millions in 1979, and 19.6 millions in 1984 (United States Bureau of Labor Statistics 1980, 1982, 1985). Within this general tendency were cyclical fluctuations. In the period of increasing economic instability since the late 1960s some 2 million manufacturing jobs have continually been gained and (mainly) lost, whereas the interval between economic upturn and downturn has tended to shorten – thus the 'recovery' after 1983 lasted only one year (Figure 4.2). National changes in employment are the synthetic result of sharply divergent rational trajectories. In general, HCS states stagnated in terms of manufacturing employment. East Coast states, like New York, tended to decline constantly in industrial employment from 1953, whereas employment in middle western states, like Ohio, fluctuated around the level reached during the war and immediate post-war period and declined after 1969.[15] Low-class-struggle (LCS) states, by comparison, showed a continual tendency to increase in manufacturing employment with the exception, perhaps, of the 'recovery' from the recession of the early 1980s – there is some evidence that the lowest class-struggle states are now being by-passed in favor of even cheaper labor regions in Mexico and East Asia. On the whole, over the long

Figure 4.2 Employment in manufacturing, 1939 – January 1986 (from U.S. Bureau of Labor statistics, *Handbook of labor statistics* 1980 and *Employment and earnings* 1985, 1986).

term, industrial cycles have had little effect on LCS regional growth patterns. In brief, the increasing instability and loss of United States manufacturing employment in the recent past was largely at the expense of unionized workers of the organized states, while non-unionized regions experienced steady and generally increasing employment.

We can examine the process of geographic change in more detail in Table 4.2 which compares percentage rates of change in manufacturing employment in the United States as a whole with change in the 10 highest, and 10 lowest, class-struggle states. In terms of manufacturing the war effort was mounted with the aid of workers in the older industrial states, which between 1939 and 1943 increased manufacturing employment more rapidly than the national average. With the exception of the 1975–9 upturn, during which California alone added 400,000 manufacturing workers, this was the last time such a more rapid increase was to occur. Since 1943, each national upturn in manufacturing employment has been experienced as a weaker upturn in the HCS states, whereas each downturn occurred more strongly there,

Table 4.2 Percentage change in manufacturing employment in industrial cycles, 1939–84.

Industrial cycle	United States	Ten highest class struggle states*	Ten lowest class struggle states†
1939–43	71.3	78.4	60.0
1943–9	−17.9	−18.5	−12.6
1949–53	21.5	14.8	21.3
1953–61	−6.9	−11.2	13.1
1961–9	23.5	19.6	46.0
1969–71	−7.6	−10.9	−1.7
1971–3	8.2	5.9	11.8
1973–5	−9.0	−10.0	−6.8
1975–9	11.7	12.6	19.8
1979–83	−9.7	−14.6	−1.2
1983–4	5.9	4.5	5.1
1939–84	90.6	58.2	245.5

Statistical source: United States Bureau of Labor Statistics, 1980, 1982, 1985.
Notes
*Michigan, Washington, Pennsylvania, Ohio, Illinois, New York, California, Montana, Minnesota, Oregon.
†Texas, Virginia, North Dakota, Georgia, Arkansas, Mississippi, Florida, South Dakota, South Carolina, North Carolina.

especially the severe declines in employment in 1969–71 and 1979–83. By comparison the LCS states have usually had stronger upturns in manufacturing employment than the national average, whereas downturns have either not occurred or have been much weaker than the national average. Manufacturing growth in the LCS states was particularly strong in the periods 1953–69 and 1975–9. Significantly, it was weak in the recovery of 1983–4.

In terms of the changing geography of manufacturing, the 1960s was a decade of manufacturing employment loss or very small gains in New England, New York, Pennsylvania, and West Virginia; the 1970s and early 1980s showed job loss in the whole region from Connecticut to Illinois (Fig. 4.3). The 1960s was the decade of manufacturing employment gains in the South and parts of the Southwest and the 1970s and early 1980s one of gains in the Southwest, the Mountain States, the Dakotas, Florida, New Hampshire, and Vermont. With the exception of the West Coast, all states gaining significantly in manufacturing employment in these two decades were LCS states, whereas all states losing manufacturing employment in both periods were HCS states.

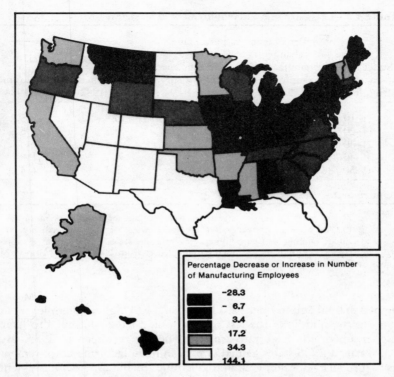

Percentage Decrease or Increase in Number
of Manufacturing Employees

-28.3
- 6.7
3.4
17.2
34.3
144.1

Figure 4.3 Change in manufacturing employment by state, 1970–84.

Further evidence of the relation between class struggle and the location of manufacturing in terms of movements in *total* employment and
unemployment is shown by Table 4.3. There states are grouped into
tens in terms of their index of class struggle. The two highest class
struggle groups (1–10, 11–20) include several West Coast states with
large increases in employment. The general westward spread of
employment is *not* immediately explained by level of class struggle,
which in this case loses its immediate, primary determining effect to
physical environmental, spatial-locational and historical factors, the
rôle of the state (especially defense spending), and to the regional
dimension of ideology and consciousness ("the California image"). This
westward movement requires other dimensions of Marxist explanation, especially those dealing with the rôle of the state and the
geography of consciousness (Peet 1982 on the latter). Overall,
however, the data reveal a definite relation between the level of class
struggle and the changing geography of employment. High-class-
struggle states lost manufacturing employment in the years since 1970,

Table 4.3   Class struggle and employment in 50 states, 1970–84.

States ranked by class-struggle index	Percentage change in manufacturing employment 1970–84	Percentage increase in total employment 1970–84	Unemployment rate July 1982	Unemployment rate 1984
1–10	−10.7	18.5	10.9	8.5
11–20	−7.7	27.0	9.7	7.6
21–30	−0.2	39.2	9.5	6.6
31–40	26.6	56.0	9.1	6.8
41–50	25.0	57.8	8.3	6.4
United States	−0.3	33.0	9.8	7.5

Sources: Rank order of states derived from percentage of employees unionized, working time lost through stoppages, average hourly wage rate in manufacturing, and business climate ranking. 1–10 are highest class struggle states, 41.50 are lowest class struggle states. Employment and unemployment data from United States Bureau of Labor Statistics.

gained in total employment at a lower rate, had higher unemployment rates in the middle of the last recession, and have continued to have higher unemployment rates since economic recovery in 1983. By comparison, LCS states gained rapidly in manufacturing employment as part of an even faster gain in total employment, and unemployment rates were significantly lower than for the HCS states.

The low rate of increase in total employment in the labor heartland indicates the unplanned, economically destructive nature of the change in the geography of manufacturing. Manufacturing accounted for more than a third of employment in all HCS states in 1970. The loss of manufacturing employment in the 1970s and early 1980s which continued through the 1983–5 "economic recovery" in key states like Pennsylvania, Illinois, and New York, occurred in exactly the areas with the lowest ability to re-employ laid-off industrial workers, resulting in state unemployment rates two to five percentage points higher than the national average.

In summary, the change in manufacturing employment during the 1970s and 1980s *is* a move from Frostbelt to Sunbelt so long as "frost" and "sun" refer to the *social conditions for profit making*. Among states which have seen high rates of increase in manufacturing and total employment are North Dakota, Utah, and New Hampshire, hardly sunny, yet all LCS states with low wages, few unions, and (except for New Hampshire) "right to work" laws.[16] More accurately, we have witnessed a reaction by increasingly competitive producers to the uneven spatial development of class struggle, resulting in the migration of all types of employment, but especially manufacturing, from areas of high class struggle to areas where the struggle is less developed.

The Internationalization of United States Manufacturing

The movement of manufacturing to LCS states domestically is only one part of a far wider geographic dispersion of United States manufacturing capital. Direct United States investment in foreign manufacturing started in the early 20th century. The 1940s saw heavy investment in Canada and Latin America; the 1950s in Western Europe; the 1960s and 1970s in Latin America, Western Europe, Japan, the Middle East, and South and East Asia. In the period 1966–77, United States manufacturing assets increased particularly rapidly in Ireland, Austria, Spain, Japan, Brazil, Nigeria, Israel, the OPEC countries of the Middle East, Hong Kong, Malaysia, Singapore (which had the most rapid increase), South Korea, and Taiwan (United States Department of Commerce 1982c: 43). In 1977, some 1,841 United States manufacturing companies had 15,316 foreign affiliates, the result of an accumulated directed foreign investment of $62,019 million, over $40,000 million of which had been made since 1966 (Fig. 4.4)[17] (United States Department of Commerce 1980: 24, 1982a: 20). We shall confine the analysis to the most recent trends in capital movement, What is the attraction of these countries, especially the periphery of Europe and East Asia, for United States manufacturing capital?

The conditions which led to a changing division of labor within the United States are writ larger in world space. The articulation between an expanding capitalist mode of production and the precapitalist modes of the world peripheries is composed, in detail, of processes of conservation and dissolution, with the more powerful capitalist mode "shaping" precapitalist social formations by selectively preserving and changing their constituent elements (Bettleheim 1972). Capitalism destroys selected parts of precapitalist production and social life, releasing rural labor from its attachment to land, forcing desperate migration to urban centers, especially the pathologically ever-growing national capitals (Stuckey & Fay 1981). The accumulation of millions of unemployed or underemployed people in Third World cities, backed by large pools of would-be migrants in rural areas, provides an unending stream of cheap labor for transnational industry, a condition which renders worker unionization extremely difficult.

Indeed, there is so much cheap labor available on the world market that transnational enterprise has been able to pick and choose between alternative regions, requiring additionally that labor be educated and the local state extremely amenable to capital's interests. In many Third World countries, urban labor was organized and politicized prior to industrialization. Indeed labor unions were a major force in the anticolonial

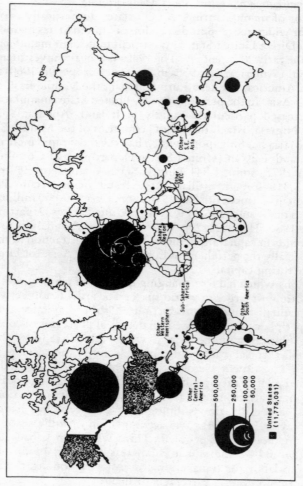

Figure 4.4 World employment in manufacturing by United States corporations (from *Survey of current business*, February 1982: 41).

struggle. The postcolonial state either suppressed labor directly (usually by taking an authoritarian military form) or incorporated the unions into its organizational structure (as parts of *corporatist* political systems). Authoritarian corporatism then completed the requisite conditions for profit-making.[18]

The most relevant locational advantages afforded by countries where these conditions have coincided are as follows. First, the integration of precapitalist labor reproduction systems into the world capitalist system allows the transposition of much of the cost of raising and maintaining labor onto the precapitalist mode.[19] The suppression of labor unions then restricts wages to these low cost levels. As one survey of multinational corporations in the Third world concludes: governments have been vigilant not to allow labor union activities and disputes to create hindrances to the smooth operations of foreign businesses; this reduces union action almost to the vanishing point in multinational corporate subsidiary plants (Kassilow 1978: 153).[20] Wage rates, as a result, even in the newly industrializing countries, are a fraction of United States manufacturing wages. Secondly, the work week is longer[21] and the intensity of work higher, yet labor productivity is comparable with that in the United States. Thirdly, the state intervenes to further enhance these conditions in the free trade zones; there the state provides all necessary services, tightly regulates labor (prohibiting industrial disputes for instance), and often uses its power in local or international capital markets to secure low cost loans (Tsuchiya 1978). What effects have such conditions had on United States corporate investment decisions?

The world manufacturing economy controlled by United States capital consists of manufacturing employment within the country and employment by majority-owned affiliates of United States manufacturing corporations in foreign countries. Table 4.4 presents data on manufacturing employment in the United States for the period 1960 to 1980, broken into employment in 25 high-class-struggle and 25 low-class-struggle states, together with estimates of employment by majority-owned foreign affiliates of United States multinational corporations (0.5 million employees of minority-owned foreign affiliates in 1977 are not included in the table). The data reveal an overall increase in employment by United States manufacturing companies, which contrasts sharply with the stagnation in employment in the HCS states within the country. Although United States manufacturing capital has flowed out for a number of specific purposes, including that of obtaining a superior market position (United States Department of Commerce 1973), the underlying and determining condition of greater profitability in the internationalization of production is the cheapness of foreign labor. United States multinational manufacturing companies paid an average of $8.76 an hour to domestic workers in 1977 and an

Table 4.4 Manufacturing employment in the United States and directly controlled by United States corporations in foreign countries, 1960–80.

| | Manufacturing Employment (millions of employees) | | | | | |
Region	1960	1966	1977	1980	Increase 1960–80	Percentage increase 1960–80
Within United States*	16.9	19.3	19.6	20.3	3.4	20.1
25 HCS states	13.0	14.6	13.7	13.9	0.9	6.9
25 LCS states	3.9	4.7	5.9	6.4	2.5	64.1
Outside United States†	1.6	2.4	3.9	4.3	2.7	168.8
developed countries	1.4	1.9	2.8	3.0	1.6	114.3
underdeveloped countries	0.2	0.5	1.1	1.3	1.1	550.0
total	18.4	21.7	23.5	24.6	6.2	33.7

Sources: United States Bureau of Labor Statistics (1971, 1980, 1982), United States Department of Commerce (1982b).
Notes:
*Includes some employment by foreign corporations in the United States.
†Employment by majority-owned foreign affiliates of United States corporations. Figures for 1960 and 1980 are extrapolated from 1966 and 1977 data.

average of $4.92 in all foreign affiliates, $6.34 in developed countries and $1.74 in underdeveloped countries (United States Department of Commerce 1982a: 48). Normally a rate of return of 13 percent can be expected from foreign investments in manufacturing, 12 percent being the rate in developed countries, but with a profit rate of 16 percent in all underdeveloped countries and 18 percent in underdeveloped countries outside Latin America (United States Department of Commerce 1982c: 17). In part, international investment in manufacturing has kept up the rate of corporate profit by exploiting cheap, nonunionized foreign labor. To some extent this has been forced on United States corporations by competition from producers located in higher profit regions with more docile and cheaper labor supplies.

Faced with high labor costs and restrictions on their activity at a time of increasing competition, United States manufacturers, which until 1960 had predominantly agglomerated in old industrial areas, had four strategic possibilities in terms of alternative regions for investment: (1) the existing areas of industrial agglomeration – the HCS states within the United States; (2) LCS states within the United States; (3) developed foreign countries; and (4) underdeveloped foreign countries. In the early 1960s all four strategies were used. In the late 1960s and the 1970s manufacturing employment was reduced in the HCS states, growth in the LCS states and developed countries continued, but as the 1970s progressed into the 1980s emphasis was increasingly placed on the underdeveloped country locational strategy. The overall tendency was for the increased dispersion of manufacturing investment resulting in a more competitive productive base biased increasingly towards low-wage, higher-profit regions of a number of types. These could then be played off one against the other.

SAVINGS IN WAGE COSTS AND THE ONSET OF ECONOMIC CRISIS

Another way of describing changes in manufacturing location is to estimate the wages saved through each strategy. Within the United States in the 1960–80 period, some 1.7 million manufacturing jobs were lost in the HCS states and gained by the LCS states, due to regional divergence from the national growth rate. The direct yearly saving per job can be estimated from data on average manufacturing wage rates (United States Bureau of Labor Statistics 1980) at about $3,300, making a total annual saving from the locational strategy of emphasizing development in the LCS states of $5,610 million in 1980. In foreign developed and underdeveloped countries, the total number of new jobs opened by United States corporations is multiplied by the difference between multinational corporation wages within and outside the United States for a saving of $22,968 in 1980 (United States Department of Commerce 1982b). The result in terms of savings in wage costs, shown in Table 4.5, is that the underdeveloped country strategy emerges as most significant, accounting for one-half the total wages saved by locating United States-controlled manufacturing jobs in low-wage regions. Table 4.5 also suggests that had the 2.7 million foreign manufacturing jobs started mainly with United States capital been located within the country, and had 1.7 million jobs switched to the LCS states been located instead in HCS states, wage payments to manufacturing workers would have been $28.6 billion higher in 1980 than was the case. The three low-wage locational strategies thus resulted in a 9 percent wage cost saving for United States controlled manufacturing in 1980, making it more competitive. But also 9 percent less income was contributed to the United States economy from manufacturing employment than might otherwise have occurred. Obviously this is a very rough calculation, entailing some gross assumptions, but it is indicative of a general tendency for manufacturing to generate lower worker incomes.

The various low-wage locational strategies made up one aspect of the formation of the economic crises of the 1970s and 1980s. During the 1970s manufacturing employment in the HCS states was highly unstable and tending to decline. Lost manufacturing jobs were replaced (if at all) by jobs in the service sector, which pay about two-thirds as much. Total employment in the 25 HCS states grew considerably less than the national rate between 1970 and 1984, whereas total employment in the 25 LCS states grew far more rapidly (Table 4.3). The movement of

Table 4.5 Wage savings and job relocation: three "strategies" of United States-controlled manufacturing companies.

Within United States	
1.7 million jobs switched to LCS states, 1960–80	
yearly wage savings per job $3,300	
wage saving in 1980	$5,610 million
Outside United States	
Developed countries	
1.6 million jobs opened by United States corporations, 1960–80	
yearly wage saving cf. United States location per job $5,200	
wage saving in 1980	$8,448 million
Underdeveloped countries	
1.1 million jobs opened by United States corporations, 1960–80	
yearly wage saving cf. United States location per job $13,200	
wage saving in 1980	$14,520 million
Total annual wage saving, 1980	$28,578 million
Estimated manufacturing wages paid in United States in 1980	$304,500 million

manufacturing was part of a more general relative movement of all kinds of employment to low-wage states domestically and increasingly to low-wage countries internationally. This shift in place of employment reduced worker incomes and weakened the "central determining relationship" between mass consumption and the capital goods industries at the center of the world capitalist system (Amin 1974). Increasingly, peripheral low-waged workers produced commodities which they themselves could not afford to buy, but central workers also could no longer afford because high-paying, unionized jobs were fast disappearing (Frank 1981). Extraverted production in the periphery increasingly occurred for a world market destroyed by the same extraverted production. Escaping the effects of one set of contradictions, high class struggle, low profits, and high costs in old industrial regions, capital only created another – a lack of demand for industrial products. A realization crisis occurred. Recession set in.

Reification and economic crisis

Contradictions buried in the relations of production create (move through) a sequence of particular economic forms. The determining contradiction lies in the interclass relations of production. Class struggle at the point of production in the United States was ameliorated via a social contract between capital and workers which gave higher wages to organized labor. High wages provided a mass market for consumer goods. Yet high wages also entailed high costs of production for United States manufacturing corporations based in the unionized heartland. International competition coerced these corporations into cost-reducing maneuvers, such as mechanization, and locational shifts to areas where the social contract with labor was not in force. In turn, shifts in employment to the peripheries reduced worker demand for consumption goods and contributed to recession. This process of contradiction–reaction–new contradiction could not be controlled, for its origins lay exactly in the inherently "anarchic" nature of capitalist production.

Under capitalism the reproduction of the material basis of life takes place within social relations mediated by commodities and characterized by competition and struggle, rather than within directly cooperative relations between consciously associated producers. The pursuit of individual gain moves production through time and space rather than the planned satisfaction of human needs. Competition allocates and reallocates the productive effort of the society as a coercive force. Individual firms are forced to follow the dictates of this blind force, regardless of the effects decisions have on the economy, regardless of their contribution to the formation of recessions. The direction taken by economic development has its own dynamic. No agency (including the capitalist state) has either the authority or the knowledge to successfully redirect it. Hence economic "recovery" for the United States manufacturing sector in the middle 1980s was partial and precarious. The prospect is for the permanent decline of manufacturing employment and the implications for the total economy profound: recession is the shape of the future.

Notes

1 Thus 500 companies now control 80 percent of the manufacturing assets in the United States (Erickson 1981: 136).

2 Harvey's conception of competition in space is similarly based on the idea that excess profits accrue to individual producers who sell at the social average, but whose costs are reduced below the social average by relative locational advantage. If producers could relocate at will, such excess profits would be ephemeral; should excess profits be permanent, they would be taken as location rents by land owners. But the frenetic search for competitive advantage which would produce the first is stabilized by inertias imposed by the threat of the devaluation of capital (i.e., loss of socially necessary labor time embodied in material, productive form) which tends to produce the second; hence excess profits can be made for intermediate time periods. There is, however, a permanent tension

between the instability generated by newly forming capital and the stagnation associated with past investment. Breaks with past spatial configur-
ations often entail massive place-specific devaluations; crises unfold
differentially across spatial surfaces, forging organizational structures
more in accord with the law of value and providing the basis for renewed
capital accumulation (Harvey 1982: 388–95).

3   A recent book on conventional location theory describes itself thus: "A
    guide for executives charged with evaluating the placement of a company's
    productive capacity . . . this book seeks to guide and reassure those execu-
    tives burdened with plant location decisions" (Schmenner 1982: vii).

4   The work on labor market segmentation in the United States concludes
    that "the present weakness of the American working class can be traced
    directly to the splintering and subsequent weakness caused by the postwar
    system of labor segmentation" (Gordon *et al.* 1982: 215).

5   In the period 1934–41 one-half to two-thirds of all strikes were concerned
    with issues of union organization.

6   See Brecher's (1972) argument on the significance of *mass* strikes.

7   Harvey, however, discusses the regionalization of class and factional
    struggles (1982: 419–22).

8   The literature on the history of the southern textile industry would tend to
    confirm the difficulty of labor organization in the small and medium towns
    of the Piedmont. There, geographic distance tended to isolate groups of
    workers, the mill owner long retained his position as benevolent patron,
    and antiunion ideologies from the rural past were more effectively retained
    in the worker consciousness (Raynor 1976). Employers were often the
    powerful owners of all the land and buildings in unincorporated mill
    villages, as well as providers of goods and services to their employees
    (Newman 1978). Hence, the failure of the Textile Workers Union in the
    rural South compared with its success in urban New England. However,
    this argument should not be pushed too far. Some industries *were*
    organized in the South (primary metals, petroleum, coal, etc.) and the
    branch plants of northern corporations are often unionized (Bernstein
    1961).

9   On the religious reasons for the passing of a right-to-work law in Utah in
    1955, see Davis (1962).

10 Note that the relative autonomy of the state in the production process is
    reflected in space by a distribution of business climates which vary in detail
    from the geographies of direct production characteristics – unionization,
    work stoppages, and wages.

11 Nonfinancial corporate profits also remained high, averaging 16 percent of
    the corporate gross domestic product in the 1950s and 15 percent in the
    1960s (United States Department of Commerce 1982a: 31).

12 The key competitive advantages usually mentioned are the Japanese rela-
    tions of production between workers and corporations, such as the pattern
    of lifetime employment for workers in large corporations (*nenko*). Such
    relations are the product of a regionally specific history, especially the
    particular articulation between a certain kind of feudal mode of production
    and an already mature capitalist mode. (On the heritage of the Tokugawa
    era see Yashino 1968.)

13   Thus, for example, the Zenith Corporation blamed a "life and death struggle with the Japanese" for the turning to offshore sourcing in Mexico and Taiwan (Hughes 1982: 109).

14   Thus, General Electric reacted to the strikes of 1946 in Massachusetts by decentralizing production into northern New England and the South, and eventually to Singapore (Babson 1973).

15   Ohio alone has some 250,000 manufacturing jobs which are consistently gained and lost in a total state manufacturing employment of some 1.3 millions.

16   There was also a movement from metropolitan to nonmetropolitan areas between 1962 and 1978 (Erickson 1981).

17   United States investment abroad exists when one United States person (United States parent company) has a direct or indirect ownership interest of 10 percent or more in a foreign business enterprise (foreign affiliate) (United States Department of Commerce 1982b).

18   The Republic of Singapore provides a particularly apposite example (Deyo 1981), but all the rapidly industralizing countries of East and Southeast Asia have authoritarian régimes (Sivanandan 1980).

19   The informal sector of the Third World city likewise functions as a mechanism for supporting cheap labor.

20   Singapore has been described as an "Orwellian model of modern and peaceful industrial relations with no labour protest permitted, yet within a neocolonial society where exploitation and poverty are still rampant" (Luther 1979: 298).

21   Korea has 53 hours a week; Singapore, 49 hours a week; Sri Lanka, 10 hours a day; the United States, 40 hours a week (United Nations 1980: 96).

References

Aglietta, M. 1982. World capitalism in the eighties. *New Left Review* **136**, 5–41.

Amin, S. 1974. Accumulation and development: a theoretical model. *Review of African Political Economy* **1**, 9–26.

Babson, S. 1973. The multinational corporation and labor. *Review of Radical Political Economics* **5**(1), 19–33.

Backman, J. 1974. *Labor technology and productivity in the seventies.* New York: New York University Press.

Bernstein, I. 1961. The growth of American unions, 1945–1960. *Labor History* **2**(2), 131–57.

Bettleheim, C. 1972. Theoretical comments. In *Unequal exchange*, A. Emmanuel (ed.). New York: Monthly Review Press.

Birch, D. L. 1979. *The job generation process.* Cambridge: MIT Program on Neighborhood and Regional Change.

Bluestone, B. and B. Harrison 1982. *The deindustrialization of America.* New York: Basic Books.

Brecher, J. 1972. *Strike!* Greenwich, Conn.: Fawcett.

Brecher, J. and the Work Relations Group 1978. Uncovering the hidden history of the American workplace. *The Review of Radical Political Economics* **10**(4), 1–23.

Buch-Hanson, M. and B. Nielson 1977. Marxist geography and the concept of territorial structure. *Antipode* **9**(1), 1–12.

Damette, F. 1980. The regional framework of monopoly exploitation: new problems and trends. *Regions in Crisis*, J. Carney, R. Hudson and J. Lewis (eds). London: Croom Helm.

Davis, J. K. 1962. Mormonism and the closed shop. *Labor History* **3**(2), 169–87.

Davis, M. 1980. The barren marriage of American labor and the Democratic party. *New Left Review* **124**, 43–84.

Deyo, F. C. 1981. *Dependent development and industrial order: an Asian case study*. New York: Praeger.

Dicken, P. 1976. The multiplant business enterprise and geographical space: some issues in the study of external control and regional development. *Regional Studies* **10**, 401–12.

Edwards, P. K. 1981. *Strikes in the United States 1881–1974*. New York: St. Martin's Press.

Erickson, R. A. 1981. Corporations, branch plants, and employment stability in non-metropolitan areas. In *Industrial location and regional systems*, J. Rees, G. Hewings and H. Stafford (eds). Brooklyn: J. F. Bergin.

Frank, A. G. 1981. *Reflections on the world economic crisis*. London: Hutchinson.

Freeman, R. B. 1981. The effects of unionism on fringe benefits. *Industrial and Labor Relations Review* **34**(4), 489–509.

Friedman, A. L. 1974. *Industry and labour: class struggle at work and monopoly capitalism*. London: Macmillan.

Frobel, F., J. Heinrichs and O. Kreye 1977. The tendency towards a new international division of labor. *Review* **1**(1), 73–88.

Fuchs, V. R. 1967. Hourly earnings differentials by region and size of city. *Monthly Labor Review* **90**(1), 32–40.

Goodman, R. 1979. *The last entrepreneurs*. New York: Simon & Schuster.

Gordon, D. M. 1977. Class struggle and the stages of American urban development. In *The rise of the Sunbelt cities*, D. C. Perry and A. J. Watkins (eds). Beverly Hills, Calif.: Sage.

Gordon, D. M., R. Edwards and M. Reich 1982. *Segmented work, divided workers*. Cambridge: University Press.

Harbison, F. H. 1954. Collective bargaining and American capitalism. In *Industrial conflict*, A. Kornhauser, R. Dubin and A. M. Ross (eds). New York: McGraw-Hill.

Harvey, D. 1975. The geography of capitalist accumulation: a reconstruction of the Marxist theory. *Antipode* **7**(2), 9–21.

Harvey, D. 1982. *The limits to capital*. Chicago: University of Chicago Press.

Heil, B. 1978. Sunbelt migration. In *U.S. capitalism in crisis*, Union for Radical Political Economics (ed.). New York: URPE.

Hughes, K. 1982. *Corporate response to declining rates of growth*. Lexington, Mass.: D. C. Heath.

Hymer, S. 1975. The multinational corporation and the law of uneven development. In *International firms and modern imperialism*, H. Radice (ed.). Harmondsworth, England: Penguin.

Kahn, L. M. 1979. Unionism and relative wages: direct and indirect effects. *Industrial and Labor Relations Review* **32**(4), 520–32.

Kanninen, T. 1962. Coverage of union contracts in metropolitan areas. *Monthly Labor Review* **85**(7), 747–50.

Kassilow, E. M. 1978. Regulation and control of multinational corporations: the labor aspects. In *Industrial policies, foreign investment and labour in Asian countries*, Japan Institute of Labour (ed.). Tokyo: Japan Institute of Labour.

Kerr, C. and A. Siegel 1954. The inter-industry propensity to strike. In *Industrial Conflict*, A. Kornhauser, R. Dubin and A. M. Ross (eds). New York: McGraw-Hill.

Kornhauser, R. 1961. Some social determinants and consequences of union membership. *Labor History* **2**(1).

Lane, T. 1982. The unions caught in the ebb tide. *Marxism Today* September, 6–13.

Läpple, D and P. van Hougstraten 1980. Remarks on the spatial structure of capitalist development: the case of the Netherlands. *Regions in crisis*, J. Carney, R. Hudson and J. Lewis (eds). London: Croom Helm.

Leigh, R. and D. North 1978. Regional aspects of acquisition activity in British manufacturing industry. *Regional Studies* **12**(2), 227–46.

Lewis, H. G. 1963. *Unionism and relative wages in the United States: an empirical inquiry*. Chicago: University of Chicago Press.

Lincoln, J. R. 1978. Community structure and industrial conflict: an analysis of strike activity in SMSA's. *American Sociological Review* **43**(2), 199–220.

Luther, H. 1979. The repression of labour protest in Singapore: unique case or future model? *Development and Change* **10**(2), 287–99.

Mallet, S. 1975. *The new working class*. Nottingham: Bertrand Russell Peace Foundation.

Marx, K. 1973. *Grundrisse: foundations of the critique of political economy*. Harmondsworth, England: Penguin.

Marx, K. 1976. *Capital: a critique of political economy*, vol. 1. Harmondsworth, England: Penguin.

Newman, D. 1978. Work and community in a Southern textile town. *Labor History* **19**(2), 204–25.

Peet, R. 1975. Inequality and poverty: a Marxist-geographic theory. *Annals, Association of American Geographers* **65**(4), 564–71.

Peet, R. 1978. Materialism, social formation and socio-spatial relations: an essay in Marxist geography. *Cahiers de Geographie du Quebec* **56**, 147–57.

Peet, R. 1979. Societal contradiction and Marxist geography. *Annals, Association of American Geographers* **69**(1), 164–9.

Peet, R. 1982. International capital, international culture. In *The geography of multinational enterprise*, N. Thrift and M. Taylor (eds). London: Croom Helm.

Pred, A. R. 1974. *Major job-providing organizations and systems of cities*. Resource Paper No. 27, Association of American Geographers, Commission on College Geography, Washington, D.C.

Raynor, B. 1976. Unionism in the Southern textile industry: an overview. In *Essays in Southern labor history*, C. M. Fink and M. Reid (eds). Westport, Conn.: Greenwood Press.

Schmenner, R. W. 1982. *Making business location decisions*. Englewood Cliffs, N.J.: Prentice-Hall.

Shorter, E. and C. Tilly 1974. *Strikes in France 1830–1968*. Cambridge: Cambridge University Press.

Sivanandan, A. 1980. Imperialism in the silicon age. *Monthly Review* **32**(3), 24–41.

Stern, R. N. 1976. Intermetropolitan patterns of strike frequency. *Industrial and Labor Relations Review* **29**(2), 218–35.

Stern, R. N. and O. R. Galle 1978. Industrial conflict and the intermetropolitan structure of production. *Social Science Quarterly* **59**(2), 257–73.

Stuckey, B. and M. A. Fay 1981. Rural subsistence, migration, and urbanization: the production, destruction, and reproduction of cheap labour in the world market economy. *Antipode* **13**(2), 1–14.

Troy, L. 1957. *Distribution of union membership among the states 1939 and 1953*. Occasional Paper 56, Washington, D.C.: National Bureau of Economic Research.

Tsuchiya, T. 1978. Free trade zones in Southeast Asia. *Monthly Review* **29**(9), 29–39.

URPE (Union for Radical Political Economics) 1978. *U.S. capitalism in crisis*. New York: URPE.

UNIDO (United Nations Industrial Development Organization) 1979. *World industry since 1960: progress and prospects*. New York: United Nations.

United Nations, Department of International Economic and Social Affairs 1980. *Statistical Yearbook 1980*. New York: United Nations.

United States Department of Commerce 1980. *Survey of current business*. August.

United States Department of Commerce 1982a. *Survey of current business*. January.

United States Department of Commerce 1982b. Employment and employee compensation of U.S. multinational companies in 1977. In *Survey of current business*, February, 37–60.

United States Department of Commerce 1982c. Growth of U.S. multinational companies, 1966–77. In *Survey of current business*, August, 36–46.

United States Department of Commerce, Bureau of International Commerce 1973. *The multinational corporation*. Washington, D.C.: United States Government Printing Office.

United States, Department of Commerce, Bureau of the Census 1981. *Statistical abstract of the United States 1981*. Washington, D.C.: United States Government Printing Office.

United States Department of Labor, Bureau of Labor Statistics 1971. *Handbook of labor statistics 1971*. Washington, D.C.: United States Government Printing Office.

United States Department of Labor, Bureau of Labor Statistics 1979. *Directory of national unions and employee associations*. Washington, D.C.: United States Government Printing Office.

United States Department of Labor, Bureau of Labor Statistics 1980. *Handbook of labor statistics 1980*. Washington, D.C.: United States Government Printing Office.

United States Department of Labor, Bureau of Labor Statistics, 1970–80. *Analysis of work stoppages*. Washington, D.C.: United States Government Printing Office, annual.

United States Department of Labor, Bureau of Labor Statistics 1982. *Employment and Earnings*, monthly.

United States Department of Labor, Bureau of Labor Statistics 1985. *Employment and Earnings*, monthly.

Walker, J. 1981. Markets, industrial processes and class struggle: the evolution of the labor process in the U.K. engineering industry. *Review of Radical Political Economics* **12**(4), 46–59.

Warren, R. S. and R. P. Strauss 1979. A mixed logit model of the relationship between unionization and right-to-work legislation. *Journal of Political Economy* **87**(3), 648–55.

Weinstein, B. L. and R. E. Firestone 1978. *Regional growth and decline in the United States*. New York: Praeger.

Yoshino, M. Y. 1968. *Japan's managerial system*. Cambridge: MIT Press.

5 The impact of private disinvestment on workers and their communities*

BARRY BLUESTONE and BENNETT HARRISON

Two years after the Lykes Corporation shut down the Campbell Works of the Youngstown Sheet and Tube Company, *Fortune* magazine decided to investigate the subsequent employment experiences of the 4,100 displaced Ohio steelworkers. In an article entitled "Youngstown bounces back," the magazine concluded that after only two years the workers and community were back on their feet (Hayes 1979). How *Fortune* could come to this cheery conclusion must have seemed quite mystifying to those in Youngstown, for even the story's own data appear to contradict it.

Fortune found that 35 percent of those displaced were forced into early retirement – at less than half of their previous salary. Another 15 percent were still looking for work and 10 percent were forced to move. Many of these workers returned after they failed to find adequate jobs elsewhere. Of the remaining 40 percent, some took huge wage cuts. For example, Ric Ayres, a former rigger at the mill, ended up taking a job selling women's shoes for $2.37 an hour. One photograph in the article, showing a young man seated at a piano, was captioned "Crane operator Ozie Williams, thirty-two, has a lot of time to practice his music. He is one of the 600 steelworkers still unemployed."

The "Youngstown bounces back" story turned out to be embarrassingly ill-timed. Only days before the article appeared on the newstands, United States Steel announced the closing of its own massive Youngstown works as well as 13 other plants, prompting outraged workers to occupy the mill. In one day, 13,000 additional workers had lost their jobs. United States Steel chairman David Broderick saw the closings as one more step in the company's strategy to regain its competitive position and boost its profitability. The workers saw the closings in very different terms – the loss of their economic security and

---

* Reprinted from Bluestone, B. & B. Harrison 1982, *The Deindustrialization of America* (New York: Basic Books), by permission of the authors.

the potential destruction of their community. The closings were described by company officials as inevitable, by workers and their supporters as unconscionable.

Assessing the overall impact of plant closings like those in Youngstown is a difficult enough task. Any assessment is always colored by a person's own particular perspective. It matters whether one is the ship's passenger or the iceberg in Carl Sandburg's (1969: 507) "The people, yes."

"Isn't that an iceberg on the horizon, Captain?"
"Yes, Madam."
"What if we get in a collision with it?"
"The iceberg, Madam, will move right along as though nothing had happened."

For United States Steel, consolidating its operations conceivably will lead to increased profits. Its jettisoning of the Youngstown plant along with its other facilities on Ohio and Pennsylvania may allow the corporation to move right along as though nothing had happened in Youngstown. It may even permit new investment elsewhere, creating new employment opportunities for other workers and their families. But for those who comprise the industry's current work force, who own or work in supplier plants, who provide the retail trade and services purchased by steelworkers when they are employed, and who provide the fire and police protection and teach in the schools that steelworkers' children attend, the costs of the closings, like those at Youngstown Sheet and Tube, are real.

The problem, not unlike that encountered in simply adding up the number of plant closings or the number of workers affected by them, is that almost no hard data exist with which to measure these social costs. Gains or losses in corporate profits are easily measured and regularly appear in stockholder reports and on the pages of the *Wall Street Journal*. But the evidence on the social impact of capital mobility tends to be submerged in Gross National Product accounts and disguised by poorly measured and impersonal unemployment figures. The only way to measure these effects – given that we have no set of systematic "social accounts" in the United States – is to appeal to the few surveys run by social scientists and medical researchers to assess the degree of long-term unemployment, income loss, and deterioration in physical and emotional well-being caused by particular plant closings. In only a few cases is there broader-based statistical research on the impact of capital mobility and economic dislocation on workers and their families. Likewise, there is only a smattering of research on the wider community impacts that accompany deindustrialization.

Nevertheless this is what there is to work with; as it turns out, it tells quite a story in itself.

DATA

The loss of jobs

At a minimum, almost any kind of capital mobility produces some short-term, or "frictional," unemployment. A new machine is brought into a plant, an old one is shipped out, and two workers are subsequently let go. If the two readily find comparable jobs, or better ones, the income loss to them and their families, and the productivity loss to society, are inconsequential. At the other extreme, as usually occurs when a plant like the Campbell Works in Youngstown closes down, the displacement can be devastating for some workers. The consequences are especially severe if the shutdown occurs during a recession when the competition for other jobs is fierce, or if it occurs in a small or remote community where no other jobs exist. The serious problems begin with unemployment, but they seldom stop there.

Evidence from a broad array of case studies suggests that long-term unemployment is the result of plant closings for at least one-third of those directly affected. The family income loss that accompanies it is nearly universal and often substantial. In a report prepared for the Federal Trade Commission, C & R Associates (1978) reviewed twelve case studies of factory shutdowns and reported that "in all the studies reviewed the impact on the employees was severe." This is not exactly a new story. In 1961, ten months after Mack Truck abandoned its 2,700-employee assembly plant in Plainfield, New Jersey, 23 percent of its work force were still without jobs, well after unemployment benefits were exhausted (Dorsey 1967). A similar proportion remained unemployed *two years* after the 1956 Packard plant shutdown involving 4,000 workers. Another third of the Packard work force found jobs after the closing but lost these within the first 24 months of the original plant shutdown. Having lost all their seniority, often amounting to ten years or more, these workers were vulnerable to layoffs on their new jobs (Aiken *et al.* 1968).

More recent research corroborates the evidence from these earlier studies. Writing at Cornell University, Professors Robert Aronson & Robert McKersie (1980: 11–12, 36) surveyed workers who lost their jobs in upstate New York when Westinghouse, Brockway Motors, and then GAF shut down operations in their communities between November 1976 and July 1977. The researchers found that nearly 40 percent of the work force experienced unemployment of 40 or more weeks and that one-quarter of the 2,800 affected workers spent a year or more without work. Their vulnerability to unemployment continued even beyond this point. Two years after the closings, 10 percent of the original sample group were still unemployed (Aronson & McKersie 1980: 11–12, 36).

A plant closing during a recession is likely to be even more devastating in terms of reemployment possibilities because of the absence of jobs in other sectors. Thus when Armour and Company closed its Oklahoma City meat-packing plant during the 1960–1 economic downturn and laid off 400 of its work force, 50 percent remained unemployed for at least six months (Young 1963). More recently, the closing of a chemical company branch plant in Fall River, Massachusetts, during the 1975 recession resulted in unemployment that lasted on the average nearly 60 weeks, with some workers idled as long as three years. Thirty-nine percent of the workers in the sample found jobs only after their unemployment compensation had long been exhausted (Barocci 1979: 5). Ironically, despite the obvious economic distress following the closing of Youngstown Sheet and Tube, conditions would have been much worse if employment in the automobile industry had not expanded to partially fill the void in steel. A temporary boom in output at the Lordstown complex of the General Motors Corporation cushioned the immediate blow to the Youngstown community (Buss & Redburn 1980: 7.4).

These particular findings are necessarily based on a handful of plant closings, since only a tiny fraction of all shutdowns have been surveyed by social scientists. Such sobering evidence might therefore be ignored or at least criticized as unrepresentative. However, there is evidence from a nationwide sample of approximately 4,000 men, all over the age of 45, that confirms these findings as anything but atypical (Parnes & King 1977).

Herbert Parnes and Randy King followed this group over a seven-year period from 1966 to 1973. They found that almost one in twenty of this national sample, who had worked for the same employer for at least five years, experienced permanent involuntary separation during the survey period. Even among this experienced group, 20 percent remained unemployed for at least six months before finding another job (Parnes & King 1977). Moreover, the subsequent employment record of those separated from their jobs never regained its previous stability. At the time of the 1973 survey, at least two years after initial separation, 6 percent of the total group of displaced workers were unemployed, as compared with only 1 percent of a control group with the same demographic characteristics, but with no record of permanent job termination. Seventy-six percent of the control group, but only 66 percent of the displaced group, worked all 52 weeks in 1973 (Parnes & King 1977). These results are remarkably consistent with the findings of the individual plant closing studies.

The Parnes and King analysis reveals some surprises. For example, no one appears to be immune to job loss, no matter how well placed. Popular conceptions notwithstanding, displacement respects neither educational attainment nor occupational status. There is virtually no difference in educational background between those displaced and the total population at risk. Similarly, there were no substantial differences among professionals, clerical workers, operatives, and service workers in the chances of being displaced. In the words of these Ohio State researchers: "Apparently the risk of displacement from a job after reasonably long tenure is insensitive to conventional measures of human capital and to the particular occupations in which men are employed" (Parnes & King 1977). When a plant shuts down, or operations are permanently curtailed so that some workers receive layoffs without recall, engineers lose their jobs along with janitors.

This does not imply that all groups are equally vulnerable to dislocation related to capital mobility. In the Cornell study mentioned earlier, women were found to be twice as likely as men to be unemployed for longer than a year (Aronson & McKersie 1980: 39). As secondary earners, it is possible that some married women had the "luxury" of an extended job search, but for most the problem was finding comparable employment. The latter is certainly true for non-white minorities, as Gregory Squires of the United States Civil Rights Commission notes (Squires 1980: 10).

Blacks are especially hard-hit because they are increasingly concentrated within central cities and in those regions of the country where plant closings and economic dislocation have been most pronounced. While blacks constituted 16 percent of all central city residents in 1960 – before the recent spate of primarily northern-based shutdowns – they accounted for 22 percent of the urban population in 1975. Similarly, blacks and other people of color did not share in the suburban housing and business boom of this period. In spite of 15 years of civil rights legislation, they were at best able to increase their share of the suburban population from 4.8 to 5.0 percent by 1978 (US Bureau of the Census 1979). Moreover, as the number of jobs grew more rapidly in the South, whites moved in to take the overwhelming majority of them (Ohio Public Interest Campaign 1981: 7).

To add to the inequity of burden, nonwhite minorities also tend to be concentrated in industries that have borne the brunt of recent closings. This is particularly true in the automobile, steel, and rubber industries. One Washington bureaucrat remarked during the hearings on the Chrysler loan guarantee that it should have been named the Coleman Young bail-out bill and filed under one of the titles of the Civil Rights Act (Young is the black mayor of Detroit). In August 1979 virtually 30 percent of Chrysler's national employment was made up of black, Hispanic, and other minorities, whereas over half of its Detroit work force was nonwhite (Anderson *et al*. 1979: 23). These groups are also at greater risk because they are more dependent than whites on wages and salaries as sources of family income. Eighty percent of minority earnings are derived from wages and salaries, compared to only 75 percent for whites (Hefner 1979: 83).

How capital mobility can have a discriminatory impact, either

intentionally or not, is shown clearly in two examples provided in
Squires's work (Squires 1980: 10). When a laundry located in St. Louis
began to decentralize in 1964, its work force was 75 percent black. By
1975 after it had opened up 13 suburban facilities and reduced its
downtown operations, its black work force was down to 5 percent. In
1976 a Detroit manufacturer relocated production to its facility in a rural
county just over the state line in Ohio. Salaried employees, most of
whom were white, were offered assistance in finding new jobs. Hourly
employees, most of whom were black, received no such aid. As a
result, minorities, who had constituted 40 percent of the work force at
the Detroit facility, comprised barely 2 percent at the Ohio plant.[1]

The nearly immutable code of "last hired, first fired," combined with
entrenched patterns of housing segregation, have left minorities at a real
disadvantage when manufacturing plants close down, retail shops
move out, and economic activity spreads to the suburbs and beyond.
The dream of jobs with high wages and decent fringe benefits that once
lured blacks to the North has turned into a nightmare for those who
now face termination in the once bustling factories of the industrial
Midwest.

Income loss and underemployment

The incidence of job loss and the duration of unemployment are, of
course, only two measures of the personal costs associated with
economic dislocation. Not only do workers lose jobs, but the new jobs
they eventually get do not provide as much income or status.

Again, the Parnes and King national sample confirms what had been
found in the case studies. Almost *three-fifths* of the displaced workers
experienced a decline in occupational status, in contrast to only one-
fifth of the control group. What is most revealing about this result is
that the downward occupational mobility was most acute among professional and managerial workers. In the initial 1966 survey, 27 percent
of the workers eventually displaced, and an identical proportion of the
control group were in these top occupational categories. Seven years
later, the proportion of displaced workers in these categories had fallen
to 18 percent, whereas the proportion among the control group had
actually increased to more than one third (Parnes & King 1977: 88).

In essence, the data indicate that permanently laid-off workers do not
suffer merely a temporary loss. Many appear to make no complete
occupational recovery even after a number of years, and some victims
never recover. One example, provided by Parnes and King, is the
48-year-old accountant who in 1966 had served with his employer for
27 years. His annual earnings were $18,500 at the time of his layoff.
After being unemployed for over a year, he finally found a job as a

salesman. By 1973 he had worked for only 18 weeks at that job, earning $4,000, implying an annual salary of somewhat under $12,000. In another example, in 1966 a 57-year-old metal roller with an eighth grade education and 40 years of service in his job earned $9,000 per year. After his separation from this job, he was unemployed for 13 weeks before finding a job as a gardener at an annual salary of $3,000 (Parnes & King 1977: 90–1).

Thanks to the efforts of researchers at the Public Research Institute of the Center for Naval Analyses in Virginia, there now are some statistical estimates of income loss that apply to entire industries (Holen 1976, Jacobson 1978, 1979). Using social security data, Louis Jacobson and his colleagues have been able to calculate the earnings losses of permanently displaced, prime-age male workers in a number of key industries.[2] To do this, Jacobson calculates the actual earnings of workers in a given industry who remain continuously employed in that sector. This earnings trajectory is then compared with the earnings records of workers who experience permanent layoffs from the same industry.[3] For most cases there is an immediate drop in income subsequent to termination followed by a rise in earnings as those displaced find new employment in other firms. Of course, some job losers are affected quite adversely, with their earnings falling to zero, although others find comparable work almost immediately. The "actual earnings profile" reflects the *average* earnings of the full cohort of displaced workers.

Jacobson's estimates listed in Table 5.1 indicate that in the first two

Table 5.1 Long-term earnings losses of permanently displaced prime-age male workers

Industry	Average annual percentage loss	
	First 2 years	Subsequent 4 years
automobiles	43.4	15.8
steel	46.6	12.6
meat–packing	23.9	18.1
aerospace	23.6	14.8
petroleum refining	12.4	12.5
women's clothes	13.3	2.1
electronic components	8.3	4.1
shoes	11.3	1.5
toys	16.1	− 2.7
TV receivers	0.7	− 7.2
cotton weaving	7.4	−11.4
flat glass	16.3	16.2
men's clothing	21.3	8.7
rubber footwear	32.2	− .9

Source: Jacobson (1978, 1979).

years following involuntary termination, the average annual earnings loss ranges from less than 1 percent for workers formerly employed in the production of TV receivers to more than 46 percent in steel. Even after *six years*, workers in some industries continued to suffer as much as an 18 percent shortfall. Those displaced from the better-paying, unionized industries like meat-packing, flat glass, automobile, aerospace, steel, and petroleum refining experienced the greatest reduction in income. But even in the low-wage sector, including women's apparel, shoes, toys, and rubber footwear, six or more years elapsed before displaced workers caught up with those who had the good fortune to hold on to their jobs.

Presumably, many, if not most, of these workers received unemployment insurance benefits (UIB) when they first lost their jobs. However, during this period, as is true of the present, UIB had a 26-week maximum. Clearly this could only compensate for a small portion of the earnings loss in the first two years and only a minuscule fraction during the full six. Furthermore, workers who found another job immediately following a layoff – even one that paid well below their previous wage – were not eligible for unemployment benefits at all. On the other hand, workers in a small number of industries such as auto manufacturing may have been employed by firms that paid supplemental unemployment benefits (SUB). A few displaced workers might also have qualified for trade readjustment assistance (TRA), but these "better off" workers are by far the exception, not the rule.

This is clearly evident in a recent study of job loss among blue-collar women in the apparel and electrical goods industries conducted by Ellen Rosen (1981). Here it was found that even after including UIB and TRA on top of any reemployment income, 92 percent of the affected workers suffered an annual income loss, with over 20 percent losing more than $3,000. On average, these women ended up losing over one-fifth of their normal yearly income following termination. This figure is nearly identical to the 18 percent cut in median family income found by Aronson & McKersie (1980: 51) in their upstate New York study.

Other research reveals similar degrees of economic loss. When the Mathematica Policy Research Center interviewed approximately 1,500 displaced workers, over 900 of whom received TRA in addition to regular unemployment compensation, it was found that in the first year after layoff, total household income for those in the Mathematica TRA sample dropped by about $1,700 in real terms.[4] Three and a half years after layoff, those who were never recalled by their initial employers still had, on average, lower real weekly earnings than before. Moreover, about 38 percent of the original sample lost their health insurance coverage sometime during the initial unemployment stint.

Workers stand to lose all or part of their pension rights as well. Many

Packard workers were left without a penny after paying into their retirement fund for years. A study commissioned by the Federal Reserve Bank of Boston showed that, during the early 1970s, of all the Massachusetts shoe workers displaced by shutdowns 62 percent lost the pension benefits that they otherwise would have enjoyed had their plants remained in business (McCarthy 1975). Enactment of the Employee Retirement Income Security Act (ERISA) in 1974 curbed many of the earlier abuses of pension rights, but corporate termination of a particular plant or division, or what the United States Department of Labor, Labor-Management Services Administration calls a "partial termination," still can result in some benefits not being paid (United States Department of Labor 1978).

When the Diamond-Reo Corporation went out of business in 1975, 2,300 UAW members, including 500 retirees and 750 vested active employees, were affected. Vested active employees are those who are presently working and have sufficient seniority to qualify for company pensions when they retire. Since the pension plan was seriously under-funded, before ERISA all 750 vested actives would have lost their pension rights and the retirees would have suffered severe cutbacks averaging nearly 80 percent of their monthly pension benefits. Because of ERISA, about four out of five of the retirees suffered only relatively minor cutbacks in their expected pensions. But, for the one in five who chose nonguaranteed early retirement supplements, there were drastic cutbacks. An even more serious loss was borne by the 750 vested employees who had not yet retired (Glasser 1976).

How workers fare after a permanent layoff, if they do not drop out of the labor market altogether, depends on the types of jobs they find when they go to look for new work. Our own research, based on the Social Security Longitudinal Employer-Employee Data file (LEED) – the one used by Jacobson – reveals that postseparation earnings are largely determined by which market segment a displaced worker even-tually enters. By way of example, consider what happened to prime-age workers in the New England aircraft industry when that sector went into a tailspin as a result of slackened procurement for the Vietnam war. Those who ended up in "secondary" jobs did considerably worse than those who remained in the aircraft industry or were able to transfer to other companies in the "primary" segment of the labor market. (The "primary" segment includes most industries in the construction, durable manufacturing, wholesale trade, public utility, and higher-skill service sectors. Generally these are industries that have a more stable employ-ment pattern and normally pay higher than average wages. The "secondary" segment includes most nondurable manufacturing, retail trade, and lower-skill personal service industries, ones usually char-acterized by higher turnover, greater seasonality, and lower average wages.[5])

Aircraft workers who were able to retain their jobs earned 21.1 percent more in 1972 than they did in 1967 (see Table 5.2). Those who left the region following the severe layoffs that began in 1968, to search out aircraft industry jobs elsewhere, did not fare quite as well, averaging only a 16.5 percent earnings gain. Those who left the industry altogether but found work in other parts of the primary labor market had higher earnings in the later year, but their wage gain was only one-third as large as that achieved by those who were able to keep their aircraft jobs.

By contrast, those forced to take menial jobs in restaurants, hospitals, and various other sectors where they could not use their aircraft industry skills lost, on average, 26 percent of their former income levels (even before accounting for inflation). An additional 6 percent of the original sample had no "covered" earnings in 1972, despite the fact that they neither retired nor became disabled. Those in this category either had no wage income at all during the year or worked in jobs not covered by social security, mainly in the federal government. Similar results to those obtained in aircraft were found for the metalworking machinery industry, although those who ended up in secondary jobs were not affected quite so adversely.

To the extent that the relative earnings losses represent real losses in

Table 5.2 What happens to the earnings of workers who leave the aircraft industry (in current dollars).

1972 Industry/region	Number of workers	Percentage in category	1967 Average earnings (US$)	1972 Average earnings (US$)	Percentage change in average earnings
aircraft inside New England	37,700	64.7	9,575	11,595	21.1
aircraft outside New England	600	1.0	9,829	11,455	16.5
other 'primary'[a] industries	11,900	20.4	8,733	9,345	7.0
other 'secondary'[b] industries	2,100	3.6	6,054	4,468	−26.2
not in jobs covered by social security	3,700	6.3	6,175	0	—
disabled, deceased, unknown	2,300	3.9	—	—	—
total	58,300	100.0			

Source: Matthews & Bluestone (1979).
Notes:
[a] "Primary" industries include most durable manufacturing, wholesale trade, public utilities, and some services.
[b] "Secondary" industries include most nondurable manufacturing, retail trade, and lower-skill requirement, higher-turnover personal services.

productivity, Table 5.2 suggests that one-third of the entire New England aircraft labor force experienced a productivity loss ranging from 4.6 percent for those who left the region for aircraft jobs elsewhere to 47.3 percent among those who ended up taking secondary jobs. For those who found no job at all after leaving the industry, the social efficiency loss was, mathematically speaking, infinite.

Leaving the aircraft industry has even worse consequences for women than for their male counterparts. Men who ended up in secondary jobs experienced a 14 percent earnings loss on average, but women lost a whopping 40 percent. Adding to this disparity is the difference in the probability that a woman would end up in the secondary segment. Only one out of fifty men employed in aircraft in 1967 was located in a secondary job in 1972. In sharp contrast, nearly one in eight women experienced such an industrial "demotion." For women, getting into a high productivity, high-wage manufacturing job is a real victory; being forced out involves a real defeat.

Even these numbers present too sanguine a picture of income loss. Unlike other studies, these particular tabulations do not distinguish between voluntarily leaving and involuntary layoffs. Consequently we cannot tell whether the workers who left aircraft or metalworking did so voluntarily, were the subjects of layoff, or experienced a plant closing. Since people who quit often leave because they have found better jobs, the earnings statistics in Table 5.2 almost certainly underestimate the losses of those who left involuntarily.

Loss of family wealth

Families who fall victim to brief periods of lost earnings are frequently able to sustain their standards of living through unemployment insurance and savings. Unfortunately for the victims of plant closings, the consequences are often much more severe, ranging from a total depletion of savings to mortgage foreclosures and reliance on public welfare. Families sometimes lose not only their current incomes but their total accumulated assets as well.

During the Great Depression, the waves of plant closings that spread across the country drove millions of families into poverty. A study completed in 1934 of Connecticut River Valley textile workers showed that two years after the mills closed down, 75 percent of the families affected were living in poverty, compared with 11 percent before the shutdown (Lumpkin 1934: 33). More than one in four families was forced to move in order to find lower rents. Some families lost their houses when they fell behind on mortgages. Thirty-five percent reported no new purchases of clothing, and the consumption of other items was reduced significantly.

This experience did not die out with the end of the Depression. A similar fate is faced by workers and their families who suffer permanent layoff today. When the Plainfield, New Jersey, Mack Truck facility shut down in 1960, workers had to reduce their food and clothing consumption substantially, and they turned to borrowing and install-ment credit for other necessities (Dorsey 1967: 214–17). Aircraft workers in Hartford County, Connecticut – the jet engine capital of the world – responded to the loss of their jobs in the mid-1970s by sharply reducing their expenditures on food, clothing, and medical care, in addition to a long list of "luxury" items such as recreation and house repair. Out of the eighty-one workers interviewed in a study by Rayman & Bluestone (1982), three of these displaced jet engine workers lost their houses to foreclosure. Among participants in the upstate New York study conducted by Aronson & McKersie (1980: 51), 11 per cent reported cutting back on housing expenses, 16 percent reduced their food consumption, 31 percent bought less clothing, and 43 percent spent less on recreation. In what could lead to a mortgaging of their families' health, one in seven reduced their expenditures for medical care. These figures are remarkably close to those found in the Hartford County research.

Such grave consequences are found in other case studies as well. In his study of the Wickwire shutdown (Colorado Fuel and Iron Corpor-ation), Felician Foltman (1968) found that workers were often forced to sell their automobiles and personal possessions in order to qualify for relief payments. Even more recently, the closing of a chemical com-pany in Massachusetts forced families to rely on food stamps and housing assistance after their savings were used up (Barocci 1979: 10). In the wake of permanent layoffs in the mid-1970s at the RCA Moun-taintop semiconductor complex near Wilkes-Barre, Pennsylvania, researchers reported a major increase in young males on state welfare – a condition only permitted by law once someone virtually exhausts all of his savings and cashes in all of his assets (Meyer & Phillips 1978).

Somewhat of an embarassment to the research community is the fact that so little is known about the loss in assets suffered by workers when they lose their jobs. Saving for a rainy day is a normal part of a family's security umbrella, but for many it is never enough to cover the damage caused by the downpour from a plant closing.

Impacts on physical and mental health

The loss of personal assets places families in an extraordinarily vulner-able position; for when savings run out, people lose the ability to respond to short-run crises. The first unanticipated financial burden that comes along – an unexpected health problem, a casualty or fire loss, or even a minor automobile accident – can easily hurl the family over the brink of economic solvency. The trauma associated with this type of loss extends well beyond the bounds of household money matters.

Medical researchers have found that acute economic distress associated with job loss causes a range of physical and mental health problems, the magnitudes of which are only now being assessed. Simply measuring the direct employment and earnings losses of plant closings therefore tends to seriously underestimate the total drain on families caught in the middle of capital shift.

Dr. Harvey Brenner of Johns Hopkins University, along with Sidney Cobb at Brown University and Stanislav Kasl at Yale University, have done careful studies in this area. Kasl and Cobb report high or increased blood pressure (hypertension) and abnormally high cholesterol and blood-sugar levels in blue-collar workers who lost their jobs due to factory closure (Kasl & Cobb 1970, see also Kasl *et al*. 1968, 1975). These factors are associated with the development of heart disease. Other disorders related to the stress of job loss are ulcers, respiratory diseases, and hyperallergic reactions. Higher levels of serum glucose, serum pepsinogen, and serum uric acid found in those experiencing job termination relative to levels in a control group of continuously employed workers suggest unduly high propensities to diabetes and gout (Cobb & Kasl 1977: 179). Compounding these problems is the fact that economically deprived workers are often forced to curtail normal health care and suffer from poorer nutrition and housing.

The Kasl and Cobb findings are by no means unique. Aronson and McKersie write that two-fifths of their sample reported deterioration in their physical and emotional well-being since their termination. Headaches, upset stomachs, and feelings of depression were the most widely-reported health problems (Aronson & McKersie 1980: 57). Aggressive feelings, anxiety, and alcohol abuse were the observed psychological consequences of the Youngstown steel closings. Similar conditions were widely reported among the aircraft workers in the Hartford County study. In most of these cases, the factor of time seems to be essential. Those who need much of it to find another job suffer the most.

Workers generally lose health benefits when they lose their jobs. According to Don Stillman of the United Auto Workers, fewer than 30 percent of the unemployed have any health insurance at all (Stillman 1978: 49). Those who do have to spend 20 to 25 percent of their unemployment benefits merely to continue their former coverage – if continuation is available at all. Premiums for nongroup coverage average twice those for group plans, yet the benefits are lower. There are so many deductibles that nongroup health insurance covers an average of only 31 percent of a family's incurred medical cost.

Brenner's (1976) work gives evidence of yet a much broader and deeper problem. Making use of correlation and regression analysis, he has been investigating the statistical linkages between so-called economic stress indicators and seven indices of pathology. The economic stress indicators include per capita income, the rate of inflation, and the unemployment rate. The indices of pathology are:

- age- and sex-specific mortality rates
- cardiovascular–renal disease mortality rates
- suicide mortality rates
- homicide mortality rates
- mental hospital admission rates
- imprisonment rates
- cirrhosis of the liver mortality rates

Using national data for the period 1940–73, Brenner found that unemployment plays a statistically significant rôle in affecting several forms of "social trauma". In particular, he concludes that a 1 percent increase in the aggregate unemployment rate sustained over a period of six years has been associated with approximately:[6]

- 37,000 total deaths (including 20,000 cardiovascular deaths)
- 920 suicides
- 650 homicides
- 500 deaths from cirrhosis of the liver
- 4,000 state mental hospital admissions
- 3,300 state prison admissions

These results, of course, do not directly address the question of unemployment caused by deindustrialization *per se*. But it is likely that permanent layoffs cause even more "social trauma" than unemployment arising from other causes. For example, in the aftermath of the Federal Mogul Corporation closing of its roller-bearing plant in Detroit, eight of the nearly 2000 affected workers took their own lives (Stillman 1978: 43). This macabre statistic is unfortunately not unusual. In their study of displaced workers, Cobb and Kasl (1977: 134) found a suicide rate "thirty times the expected number".

Of course, suicide is only the most extreme manifestation of the severe emotional strain caused by job loss. Family and social relationships are nearly always strained by protracted unemployment. Richard Wilcock and W. H. Franke, in their now famous work on permanent layoffs and long-term unemployment, suggest that social, medical, and psychological costs may even outweigh direct economic costs in severity. They note:

Perhaps the most serious impact of shutdowns, particularly for many of the long-term unemployed, was a loss of confidence and a feeling of uselessness. . . . The unemployed worker loses his daily association with fellow workers. This loss means not only disappearance of human relationships built up over a period of years, but also the end of a meaningful institutional relationship. When he is severed from his job, he discovers that he has lost, in addition to the income and activity, his institutional base in the economic and social system (Wilcock & Franke 1963: 166, 185).

Loss of a work network removes an important source of human support. As a result, psychosomatic illnesses, anxiety, worry, tension, impaired interpersonal relations, and an increased sense of powerlessness arise. As self-esteem decreases problems of alcoholism, child and spouse abuse, and aggression increase. Unfortunately these tragic consequences are often overlooked when the costs and benefits of capital mobility are evaluated.

Special psychological problems arise when a plant closing occurs in a small community, especially when the establishment was the locality's major employer. Writing about the closing of a plant in southern Appalachia, Walter Strange (1977: 39) notes that the people

lost the central focus which had held the community together – its reason for existence – a focus which was held in common as community property, one which provided not only for economic needs but . . . a structural framework which gave coherence and cohesion to their lives.

These effects typically lessen or disappear following successful reemployment. Yet, "stressful situations" caused by a plant closing can linger long after the final shutdown has occurred. Moreover, feelings of lost self-esteem, grief, depression, and ill health can lessen the chances of finding reemployment; this failure, in turn, can exacerbate the emotional distress, generating a cycle of destruction (C & R Associates 1978: 39). Ultimately a debilitating type of "blaming the victim" syndrome can evolve, causing dislocated workers to feel that the plant closing was their own fault. Strange (1977: 39) argues "that those feelings of self-doubt can create fear of establishing a new employment relationship or complicate the adjustment process to a new job." As the sociologist Alfred Slote (1969: xix) put it, in his seminal work on job termination:

The most awful consequence of long-term unemployment is the development of the attitude, "I couldn't hold a job even if I found one," which transforms a man from unemployed to unemployable.

The "ripple effects" in the community

Although the impact of disinvestment on individual workers and their
families is probably the correct place to begin any inquiry into the social
costs of unregulated deindustrialization, it cannot be the end of such an
inquiry. For when mills or department stores or supermarket chains
shut down, many other things can happen to a community. These can
be extraordinarily costly as they ripple through the economy.

The primary effects are, of course, visited on those closest to the
production unit that ceases operations. The unit's own employees lose
salaries and wages, pensions, and other fringe benefits; supplier firms
lose contracts; and the various levels of government lose corporate
income and commercial property tax revenue. These in turn result in a
series of secondary shocks including decreased retail purchases in the
community, a reduction in earnings at supplier plants, and increased
unemployment in other sectors. Finally, these events produce tertiary
effects in the form of increased demand for public assistance and social
services, reduced personal tax receipts, and eventually layoffs in other
industries, including the public sector. What begins as a behind-closed-
doors company decision to shut down a particular production facility
ends up affecting literally everyone in town, including the butcher, the
baker, and the candlestick maker. By the time all of these "ripple effects"
spread throughout the economy, workers and families far removed
from the original plant closing can be affected, often with dramatic
consequences.

Some of these ripple (or multiplier) effects are felt immediately, but
others take time to work through the economy. Some will dissipate
quickly (especially if the local economy is expanding), whereas others
may become a permanent part of the local economic environment. The
extent of the impact of any particular closing will depend also on
whether the plant or store was a major employer in the area, or an
important purchaser of goods and services produced by other area
businesses. All of these indirect impacts will be multiplied if a number
of closings or cutbacks occur in the area simultaneously.

Systematic research that statistically accounts for all of these crucial
ecological factors is, like the data on plant closings themselves, almost
totally nonexistent. Nevertheless, it is possible to assemble bits and
pieces of evidence that provide at least some sense of what can be
involved at the wider community level when a major employer shuts
down or leaves town. Here the experiences of just a few places –
Newark, New Jersey; Youngstown, Ohio; Detroit, Michigan; Johnstown, Pennsylvania; Cortland County, New York; and Anaconda,
Montana – must suffice. This is not because there are only a few isolated
instances of economic disaster associated with capital mobility, but
because social scientists have not had the foresight or the resources to

produce more than a handful of studies. In fact, literally hundreds of communities have gone through the trials faced by the towns and cities considered here.

J. Wiss & Son, a large cutlery manufacturer, had been in business in Newark, New Jersey, since 1848. When it was acquired by a Texas conglomerate and relocated to North Carolina in 1978, the state AFL-CIO decided to undertake a community-impact assessment, using methods and data suggested by the United States Chamber of Commerce. The direct loss of 760 manufacturing jobs, according to this study, cost the city an additional 468 jobs "in stores, banks, bus service, luncheonettes, taverns, gas stations, and other local businesses." More than $14 million in purchasing power was removed from the local economy, half of which had resided in local bank deposits used for loans to finance mortgages, home improvements, purchases of automobiles, televisions, refrigerators, and other major appliances.

Even charities suffered. No longer available were the annual contributions of $22,000 by the Wiss employees or the $11,000 corporate gift. Among the losers were the community's retarded children who were aided by these funds, the Associated Catholic Charities, the Jewish Community Federation, the Red Cross, the Salvation Army, the Presbyterian Boys Club and Hospital, and the Cerebral Palsy Foundation – all of which were associated with the Essex and West Hudson County United Way.[7]

The planned restructuring of the Bethlehem Steel plant in Johnstown, Pennsylvania, in 1973 would have directly eliminated 4,500 jobs as a result of conversion to electric furnaces from what were justifiably considered archaic coke ovens, blast furnaces, and open hearths. Although the demand for steel increased unexpectedly in 1974 and kept the Johnstown facility booming through the end of 1976, the projected loss of those 4,500 jobs would have induced a $40 million decline in annual payroll from Bethlehem and more than $4 million in canceled orders to area suppliers. Retail sales would have been cut by $20 million. All together, another 3,000 jobs would have been lost as a result of these ripple effects (Metzgar 1980). This estimate turns out to be fully consistent with a United States Chamber of Commerce claim that a community loses, on the average, two service sector jobs every time three manufacturing jobs disappear (*Daily Times* 1980).

Moreover, the steel cutback that eventually did occur in Johnstown in 1979 apparently made the city "an unattractive place to do business, no matter what kind" (Metzgar 1980: 22). In the wake of the downsizing of the firm, other companies pulled up stakes altogether.

In 1980 the Pennsylvania Electric Company (Penclec) announced it would move its administrative headquarters from Johnstown to Reading, dislocating some 120 administrative personnel and eliminating 85 [other] jobs. Then, a local bakery that had been in business for decades in Johnstown closed, throwing 100 people out of work, and a Chevrolet dealership folded after more than sixty years in business, eliminating another 77 jobs (Metzgar 1980: 22).

The employment climate became so bad that the local Bureau of Employment Security estimated that more than 10,000 people had left the area by the end of 1979, most of them under age 40. Even then, the March 1980 official unemployment rate was more than 12 percent.

In Youngstown, the projected community costs were every bit as high. A Policy Management Associates (PMA) study of the Youngstown Sheet and Tube closing concluded that the overall job loss from the 4,100 steel plant layoffs would ultimately reach 12,000 to 13,000 other workers and in turn would cause retail sales to drop by $12–23 million each year (Moberg 1979: 11).

When the company in the classic "company town" closes down, all of these effects are magnified tremendously. The case of Anaconda, Montana, provides a perfect example.[8] Anaconda Copper & Mining Co. had operated a huge copper smelter there for over 75 years when the Los Angeles-based Atlantic Richfield Co. (ARCO) acquired it. Two years later, on September 29, 1980, ARCO announced that it was abandoning the smelter, thus eliminating 80 percent of the entire annual payroll in this community of 12,000 people. Needless to say, the announcement sent a Richter scale shock wave through the town.

The action erased 1,000 jobs in Anaconda and 500 more in neighbouring Great Falls. The fallout was immediate. In two weeks, new unemployment claims added 691 recipients to the rolls and, before long, one in six in the work force was out of work. The food-stamp rolls grew by 190, to 434 families. About 170 workers chose early retirement rather than the $3,500 in severance pay.

But those were just the clackings of the first dominoes to fall here . . . All told, the state estimates, the smelter closing will result in the loss of $42 million in annual payroll in a county with only $51 million in income to begin with. Other dominoes were not long in falling.

First Federal Savings & Loan of Great Falls closed its branch here, eliminating three jobs with a $35,000 annual payroll and a $100,000 operating budget.

Joe Maciag and 70 others lost their jobs at the Butte, Anaconda & Pacific Railway, an ARCO subsidiary that hauled copper for processing.

True Value Hardware cut its two full-time employees to 20 hours each – and reduced their pay from $4 an hour to $3.10, a $98 weekly pay loss.

And Dee, the Chevrolet dealer, kept vacant a $4.50-an-hour apprentice mechanic job after the 20-year-old worker who had held it

decided there was no future here and moved to Cut Bank, Mont.
(Curry, 1981a, 11).

In all these ways, the ARCO smelter closing "echoed through the
city." By December, the Chamber of Commerce found that 36 businesses it surveyed (excluding the railroad) had laid off, on the average,
20 percent of their employees. One-fourth of the businesses said they
anticipated further layoffs, and one-third had canceled expansion plans.
Most reported their business had dropped 10–15 percent, despite both
the severance payments made by ARCO to its recently "pink-slipped"
workers and the various forms of unemployment insurance and public
aid supplied to those directly and indirectly affected.

The secondary victims of the smelter closing often had recourse to
fewer public and private benefits than the smelter workers themselves.
"The businessmen are getting the brunt of it right now," the town's
Chevrolet dealer told a *Los Angeles Times* reporter. "They gave [the
smelter workers] $3,500 in severance pay – I got caught with $500,000
in cars" (Curry 1981a).

The physical and emotional trauma associated with this particular
closing was also striking. Workers sold their $55,000 houses for
$35,000 in order to take jobs elsewhere. Businesses that normally
would have provided a comfortable retirement for their owners went
bankrupt, leaving them with nothing more than social security for their
old age. Visits to the Alcohol Service Center increased by 52 percent,
and there was a 150-percent increase in the number of persons seeking
drug counseling. The patient load at the Mental Health Center jumped
62 percent (Curry 1981b). To add injury to insult, on the day the
smelter closing was announced the local water company raised its rates.
No one in town overlooked the fact that the water company was also
owned by ARCO.

With the immense size of some industries like automobile and steel,
entire regions behave as though they were company towns. The key losses
flowing from the recent automobile layoffs are felt in steel, ferrous castings,
aluminum, synthetic rubber, glass, plastics, textiles, and machine tools.
The United States Department of Labor (DOL) has estimated that for
every 100 jobs in the motor vehicle industry, 105 jobs are wiped out in the
direct supplier network (MacLennan & O'Donnell 1980).

Economists talk about these indirect losses in terms of "employment
multipliers". In this case, the DOL study reveals a multiplier of 2.05,
since an initial loss of 100 jobs leads to an eventual total loss of 205. In
studies of the automobile industry that were performed by the Transportation Systems Center of the United States Department of Transportation, the value of the multiplier was estimated to be even higher –
in the range of 2.4 to 3.0 (MacLennan & O'Donnell 1980).

Our own estimates using the MIT multiregional input–output model

(MRIO) suggest a multiplier in the same range.[9] Beginning with a potential loss of 5,000 jobs in automobile assembly in Michigan, the MRIO permits a measurement of the effect of such a cut on all other industries in the United States on a state-by-state basis. According to this analysis, the original displacement of the assembly workers would eventually affect over 8,000 auto workers in all, as parts suppliers in Michigan and elsewhere eliminate jobs due to reduced orders. Along with Michigan, the midwestern states share the heaviest burden, with Ohio losing over 1,000 auto industry jobs, Indiana another 630, and Illinois and Wisconsin each losing at least 200.[10]

In all, the 8,000 jobs potentially lost nationwide in the automobile industry would ultimately cause a decline in employment among *all industries* of more than 20,600. In other words, more than 12,000 nonauto industry jobs would be affected. For example, iron-ore miners in Minnesota – probably working in that state's northern "iron range" – will lose their jobs because, with fewer domestic cars produced, there is less need for sheet steel and consequently less demand for iron ore. Indeed, because of the staggering complexity and interrelatedness of the economy, nearly *every* industry will be touched sooner or later by the layoffs in the Michigan plants. Somewhere in the production chain – either in the direct manufacture of automobiles or, for that matter, in the weaving of the cloth that goes into the upholstery – workers will suffer short work weeks or temporary layoffs. Some will lose their jobs permanently. The biggest losers in this instance are those who work in closely allied industries such as steel, rubber, metalworking machinery, and metal stampings.

Of course, nonmanufacturing workers are deeply affected as well. Over 1,000 jobs throughout the nation in transportation and warehousing would potentially disappear as a consequence of the original cutback in automobile assembly operations in Michigan. Nearly 1,800 wholesale and retail trade jobs and over 500 jobs in related business services will be affected. Presumably auto dealers, advertisers, truckers, and accountants will feel the pinch when some Detroit assembly lines close down for good. The same is obviously true when a steel or tire factory shuts down or even a major chain of supermarkets or discount department stores. The employment multipliers will differ from industry to industry depending on how well an industry is integrated into the entire production chain. But no instance of a plant, store, or office shutdown is an island unto itself.

Public revenues and social expenditures

The public sector suffers, too. Until recently, Draper Looms was the most important employer in the small town of Hopedale, Massachusetts. In the late 1960s, the 150-year-old mill was acquired by

Rockwell International, which closed down in October 1978, laying off some 3,000 workers. Draper owned 45 percent of Hopedale's land and paid 30 percent of the town's property taxes. When the final shutdown occurred, the town's finances were thrown into disarray, almost to the point of bankruptcy. In testimony before the United States House Committee on Small Business, the town's attorney, Robert Phillips, explained the state of Hopedale's finances in the wake of the closing:

> In summary, in two years, starting with January 1, 1978, and ending on January 1, 1980 – because January 1 is our assessing date – the value of those [Draper] properties dropped from $13.7 million to $8.3 million, which is a loss of $5 million in tax valuation and over $300,000 in tax revenue. That means that $300,000 in tax [burden] has now been shifted over to the residential homeowner and to the small storeowner.
>
> This poses a significant problem in our town finances since practically 70 percent of our local revenues are raised by real estate taxation. That means that, unless we can take this enormous plant and complex and get new businesses in there and keep the thing viable and operative, we are going to suffer a very severe economic loss. The town would almost be eligible for a Chapter 13 bankruptcy reorganisation or something like that. We've got to keep the thing going (United States House of Representatives 1980: 10).

The Massachusetts Executive Office of Economic Affairs has developed a rule of thumb according to which every $10,000 salary-level job lost to the state costs it about $1,336 in foregone state and local taxes.[11] Just in direct property taxes, the closing of the Uniroyal tire plant in Chicopee, Massachusetts, which employed 1,600 people, deprived the city of over half a million dollars in annual revenue. To compensate for this deficit, the city needed to add $5 in taxes per $1,000 assessed valuation to every other property in town (ATSCME Council 93, AFL-CI0 1980).

The same type of losses are suffered by larger towns and cities as well. In the wake of the Youngstown Sheet and Tube closing, Policy Management Associates concluded that, in the first 39 months following the shutdown, the communities around Youngstown would lose up to $8 million in taxes, the county government another $1 million, the state $8 million, and the federal treasury as much as $15 million; for a total tax loss that would approach $32 million. The managers of the Campbell Works themselves projected that the town of Campbell (situated on the edge of Youngstown) would suffer an annual loss of over half a million dollars in personal income taxes and an additional $130,000 in yearly property taxes. They forecast that the school budget deficit would rise by $1 million (Moberg 1979: 12).

The steel firm's managers were not altogether wrong, but they sorely underestimated the financial shock to the community. As a result of the Campbell closing, the townspeople were forced to increase their own property taxes by more than $11 million in one year – from $39.8 to $51 million. More than half the increase came when voters aproved a $5.8 million increase in September 1979. A total of $3.5 million was added to the existing $10.8 million school levy so that the same number of dollars would be produced when valuations dropped. Even then, the Campbell schools had to obtain a $750,000 loan from the state to keep classrooms open, and became the first in Ohio to apply for a second emergency loan from the state to avoid complete bankruptcy.

Moreover, these tax losses can have a hidden cost, to the extent that they impair a municipality's ability to float its bonds. Campbell itself had negotiated the sale of a bond issue just before the shutdown but was unable to complete it when – immediately after Sheet and Tube's demise – the buyer backed out (*Ohio AFL-CIO News and Views* 1980).

The Chrysler Federal Loan Guarantee very likely saved the city of Detroit, the sixth largest city in the country, from immediate bankruptcy. If Chrysler had gone under, 15 percent of Detroit's manufacturing work force would have found themselves on the streets at once. By itself this one automobile company employs over one in twenty of the entire city's labor force. Between the local income tax foregone by those who work in Detroit-based Chrysler plants, and the foregone property tax now paid by the company, a huge chunk of the city's revenue would be lost. Chrysler workers in Detroit pay over $280 million annually in federal income taxes (Anderson *et al.* 1979: 8). Assuming that what Detroit gets in taxes is approximately equal to one-seventh of this amount, based on what was then its 2.5 percent income tax levy, Detroit would immediately have lost $40 million in revenues. Add to this the $34 million that Chrysler pays to the city in its own annual tax payments and the total comes to $75 million. Still, this figure dos not come close to representing the total loss, for it ignores the multiplier effect altogether. As a postscript it should be noted that even though Chrysler was saved (at least for the time being), drastic cutbacks in the company, combined with other automobile industry losses, forced the city to raise the income tax levy to 3.5 percent in July 1981. If the city referendum on the matter had failed, Detroit would have been bankrupt in less than a week's time.

Of course the Chrysler bankruptcy would have had its own ripple effects well beyond the boundaries of the Motor City. So enormous is the national, and international, payroll of Chrysler that a total shutdown would have cut off perhaps half a *billion* dollars in annual federal, state, and local income taxes normally paid by workers in both Chrysler and the businesses linked to it (Transportation Systems Center 1979)[12]. Such is the public cost of widespread deindustrialization.

Disinvestment on a large scale draws on the government treasury in two ways. First, it immediately reduces tax revenues. Then, gradually, it increases the need for additional public expenditures. In some instances, particularly in smaller towns and cities, or when an entire industry lays off a large portion of its work force, both occur simultaneously. Tax receipts fall precisely when the need for public expenditures rise.

Thus, when the Youngstown Sheet and Tube closing was removing $32 million from the public treasury, various relief programs – mainly Trade Readjustment Assistance (TRA) – were costing another $34 to $38 million (Policy and Management Associates, Inc. 1978). By this accounting, the public loss from the shutdown could have reached nearly $70 million in slightly over three years. This amounts to more than $17,000 per displaced worker, very little of which was paid for by Lykes, the conglomerate owners who closed the mill.

A potential loss of the same magnitude, per worker, was calculated by the United States Department of Transportation (DOT) as part of the background material for the Chrysler Loan Guarantee Congressional debate. According to DOT estimates, the average federal cost for one displaced Chrysler worker adds up to $14,100, and the cost to the state government adds another $600 (United States Department of Transportation 1981: 98). Of this total, the average federal tax loss is judged to be $5,000 per worker, extended unemployment compensation $4,400, and TRA $4,700. The state's loss is credited exclusively to foregone state income and sales tax receipts.

These numbers may still underestimate the real net cost to the treasury, for they exclude other public transfers. For example, although the DOT assumes in its 1980 Auto Report that Chrysler workers will receive no food stamps, Medicaid, or welfare assistance, the same report suggests that the cost of these items may reach an average of $3,800 for workers displaced from related supplier plants. These workers are presumed to be lower paid and therefore more likely to qualify for these benefits.

Yet there is ample evidence that these programs *are* used by auto workers and other higher-wage workers and their families when their incomes drop to the point where they are eligible for them. Despite eligibility for TRA and other income supplements, Aronson & McKersie (1980: 85–6) found in the Westinghouse, GAF, and Brockway Motors cases in upstate New York that there was "a large rise in the monthly caseload of food stamps in Cortland County in the three months preceding the shutdown, and the demand remained high for the rest of 1977. . . . The increase in the monthly caseload for food stamps, from 275 in October 1976 to 590 in April 1977, is best viewed as a conjunction of factors, the most important of which was the Brockway termination". The reason food-stamp demand remained high was that many Brockway workers were forced to take jobs that paid substantially below their previous rates and then needed to rely on food stamps to make up part of the difference.

Food-stamp benefits became a major source of income supplementation for the unemployed beginning with the 1975 recession, when the average number of persons participating in the program rose from about 12 million to more than 18 million in two years. By 1979 the average monthly benefit per person was over $30 and total program benefit costs reached $6.5 billion annually (United States Department of Health and Human Services 1980: 79, Table 27).

Even the nation's basic welfare program for the impoverished, Aid to Families with Dependent Children (AFDC), appears to be used when workers lose their jobs. Detailed statistical analysis of the AFDC program has demonstrated a significant link between the level of unemployment in a community and the size of AFDC case loads. Using a "counterfactual" technique that asks what the AFDC case load would be if the unemployment rate were to reach a recession level (8 to 10 percent), researchers at the Social Welfare Research Institute at Boston College (SWRI) found that the number of recipients would be higher by 12 to 29 percent. In Georgia, for example, the case load would have increased from 109,300 to 129,600 – or by 18.6 percent – in fiscal year 1974 under the recession level unemployment scenario. This would have cost the state of Georgia and the federal treasury that shares the AFDC costs almost $35 million in that one year. Similarly in New York City the case load would have been nearly 15.3 percent higher under these depressed conditions. Simulated annual expenditures for AFDC would have risen to over $1 billion in 1974, compared to the actual $880 million paid out (Bluestone & Sumrall 1977: 10–14).

Sensitivity to employment conditions varied between the states, depending on the extent to which AFDC is used as a substitute for unemployment benefits. But in *every* jurisdiction studied, it was a statistically significant factor and usually a more powerful explanator of case-load levels than changes in the benefit level. To the extent that private disinvestment is a significant factor contributing to the elevation of local unemployment levels, AFDC costs are another community impact associated with deindustrialiation.

This is apparently true even when the unemployment is concentrated among relatively high-skilled, well-paid workers. A corresponding SWRI study of the AFDC–UP program – the small public assistance program for *intact* families – showed that the depression that hit the aerospace industry in Seattle, Washington, in the early 1970s led to a boost in case-load and expenditure levels (Sestak 1976: 257). Employment plummeted by 60,000 in a matter of less than two years. Despite the fact that someone can receive AFDC–UP benefits only after exhausting every other income source and practically all family savings, 462 additional applications directly attributed to the layoffs were made to the UP program. Given the average annual AFDC–UP benefit at the time, these applicants cost over $1.2 million in aid. This is a small amount by comparison with unemployment insurance payments, but clearly not trivial for one city. Today, food stamps and Medicaid benefits would have been added to the total for these displaced workers.

It is not easy to calculate the total costs to society of the widespread unemployment caused by deindustrialization, but there are some estimates of the toll that unemployment takes on the federal government and hence on the taxpayer. Research by the United States Bureau of Economic Analysis suggests that in 1980 every percentage point increase in the unemployment rate reduced the nation's Gross National Product by $68 billion and cut federal tax receipts by $20.2 billion. At the same time that tax revenue was sharply lower, federal outlays automatically increased because of the added cost of unemployment benefits and other forms of assistance. Altogether, this cost taxpayers $4.1 billion including $2.4 billion in regular unemployment insurance benefits, nearly $500 million in extra food stamps, and almost $100 million in added AFDC benefits.[13] If the deindustrialization process has been responsible for boosting the average unemployment rate by three percentage points – from somewhere around 6 percent to something closer to 9 percent – then plant closings and other forms of disinvestment may be robbing the nation of $200 billion annually in foregone output, $60 billion in federal tax receipts, and forcing Americans to spend over $12 billion more each year in income assistance. This is obviously no small price to pay, and these figures do *not* include foregone taxes and added expenses for state and local governments.

The revenue and social expenditure costs to local, state, and federal treasuries constitute only the secondary effects of capital flight. In those communities where plant closings take with them a good portion of total local revenues, the entire public sector can suffer. Layoffs among police, fire, school, and sanitation workers are not uncommon in communities hard hit by such closings. This occurred in the Mahoning Valley following the rash of steel shutdowns in that area (Lynd 1981).

It also happened in Detroit as a consequence of the auto crisis. There, hundreds of police officers were furloughed in Sepember 1980 when the city faced imminent bankruptcy (Bulkeley 1981). This was in addition to the more than 700 teachers dismissed by the city after the defeat of a property tax measure in August that was placed on the ballot by the City Council in a desperate move to find revenues to compensate for lost income taxes (Ratliff 1980). These cuts forced the city's school superintendent to reduce the school day at elementary schools by 25 minutes and by nearly an hour at all of the middle schools. Poor schools and inadequate police protection are the key factors behind middle-class flight to the suburbs. The fact that, today, Detroit has fewer city employees than it did 30 years ago cannot portend well for its ability to attract higher-income families (those families who can choose to go where there are quality services and a safe and secure community environment) back to the urban center (Guzzardi 1980).

Community anomie and "antiunion animus"

Thus far, the quantifiable social impacts of business closings have been stressed. But other, and in some respects more profound, impacts are not so easily expressed in numbers, let alone in numbers of dollars.

In terms of a variety of standard indicators, the Brockway closing in upstate New York had a relatively minor impact on the Cortland County community. Nevertheless,

> The situation in Cortland appears to have had very adverse effects on the social cohesiveness of the community. A repeated assertion by members of the community was that: "the psychological effects outweighed the real effects" of the shutdown. Soon after the Brockway termination, a bumper sticker began to circulate that reflected this anomie – "The last person to leave Cortland please shut out the lights." The shutdown was coincident with the departure of the Montgomery Ward store from downtown Cortland, compounding the "depression psychology" prevalent in the community. The gas shortage, retrenchment in the [State University] system affecting Cortland State in 1977, the short work week of many municipal workers – all resulted in a poor job market for Cortland and impeded efforts to help the Brockway dischargees as a group with special needs (Aronson & McKersie 1980: 91).

The state of "anomie" described for Cortland County (evident in community disorientation, anxiety, and isolation) is found almost universally in case studies of plant closings. Those who observed Hopedale, Youngstown, Anaconda, Detroit, Johnstown, Hartford County, and other communities hit by deindustrialization all come to the conclusion that the social "psyche" is damaged by the sudden loss of economic security. The damage, in many cases, has far-ranging consequences beyond the apparent emotional response of anger, frustration, or victimization. Victims lose faith in the "system," leading to a kind of dependency that precludes redevelopment of their communities. Although some struggle heroically to salvage what is left after a major shutdown, there is often the widespread attitude embodied in the statement of one victim: "We put thirty years into building this mill and this community, and it has all come to naught. I can't see that I've the energy to start all over again."

There is a strange silver lining behind all of this – for management. Compelling evidence exists that the layoffs created by plant closings can actually improve the business climate. The swelling of the ranks of the unemployed creates a reserve of malleable workers and even potential strikebreakers. The memory of such drastic dislocation can have what labor relations experts call a "chilling effect" on future labor–management negotiations. Surviving firms in the area gain the advantage of being able to hire the most highly skilled of the dischargees without having to bid them away from their former jobs. This obviously creates the conditions for the previously cited finding that workers experiencing sudden unemployment almost always suffer a significant drop in earnings, at least on their next job.

The strength of the labor relations impact of the three New York state plant closings studied by Aronson and McKersie seems to have especially impressed these researchers. With respect to the GAF closing in Binghamton, they note that "local union leadership felt that the uncertainty regarding GAF's future, and a pool of 1,100 potential strikebreakers in the displacees, severely constrained its ability to strike successfully." (Aronson & McKersie 1980: 69). In the wake of the Cortland shutdown, the researchers reported that they repeatedly encountered an "antiunion animus" related to the widespread belief in the community that it was "the local union's 'exhorbitant' demands and 'intransigent' position in the negotiations" before the shutdown that caused the closing.

> Further, it was rumored that the pall cast over other negotiations by this antiunion sentiment and the fear of job loss had induced other unions bargaining with local firms to settle negotiations quickly. (Aronson & McKersie 1980: 71)

Finally, perhaps the most "socially disconcerting" finding of all was the

> "blacklisting" of Brockway workers. . . . Employers were hesitant to hire persons accustomed to high wages and union benefits, while the community at large felt that the militant stance and strike by the union had caused the closing. In short "they got what they deserved." (Aronson & McKersie 1980: 91)

Conclusion

Whether it is "what they deserve," when deindustrialization occurs, the overwhelming weight of the evidence suggests that workers receive a heavy blow, only a part of which can be systematically quantified. A large majority of those directly affected endure at least temporary income loss, but a significant minority suffer long-term damage to their standards of living and to their physical and emotional well-being. Through the employment and income multiplier effects, a slew of innocent bystanders are victimized as well.

Too simple explan— why can
you get away with it?
Only effects
B. BLUESTONE and B. HARRISON stated +   99
Winners

Deindustrialization affects each community and each individual in a different way. For communities that are experiencing growth in other sectors of their economy, the costs of plant closings are a lot less than for those already mired in a recession. Workers who possess skills that are in great demand are more readily reemployed than those whose skills are made obsolete by disinvestment. Minorities fare worse than whites; in general women fare worse than men. But no one is completely immune. Young workers who are just reaching the point where they have a toehold in the economy can be permanently set back by a plant closing. Middle-aged workers who have reached their peak earning years face giant reductions in income if they are forced out of the jobs where they have experience and still many potential years of productive employment. Older workers face the prospect of being "too old to find new work, but too young to die." Rural boomtowns gone "bust," like Anaconda, Montana, surrounded by mountains and sagebrush, face many of the same problems of older central cities that have lost their industrial base.

Finally, it should be noted that despite the high (personal) costs of disinvestment pictured here, the price paid by workers, their families, and their communities is likely to be much higher in the future. The precedent-shattering reductions in social safety net programs passed by Congress in 1981, including restrictions on extended UIB, the virtual elimination of TRA, the reticence toward any further corporate bailouts, and state government initiatives to cut back on unemployment benefits, all suggest that from now on deindustrialization will entail much more suffering for those who have the misfortune to experience it. WHY?

Notes

1 These figures come from only a handful of specific enterprise case studies. Large surveys indicate the same phenomenon. An Illinois survey involving 2,380 firms that shut down between 1975 and 1978 showed that 20 percent of the affected workers were minorities, compared to a statewide minority work force of just 14.1 percent. See Ohio Public Interest Campaign (1981: 32).

2 The social security data used in these studies are found in the Longitudinal Employer–Employee Data (LEED) file available from the Social Security Administration (SSA). This extraordinary information source contains complete 19-year (1957–75) work histories on 1 percent of all workers covered by social security. This large sample of workers' records is drawn from the quarterly reports submitted to SSA by employers. The work history for each person among the 1.5 million workers on the file includes data on sex, race, and age, and for each year, the state, county, industry, and quarterly earnings for each social security covered job. Each firm is

identified by a unique employer identification code and in most cases each separate unit of a multiunit employer is identified as well. The data therefore permit a comprehensive analysis of job mobility at the county, region, firm, and industry level. The data on quarterly earnings permit an analysis of wage, mobility within a single employer, single industry, or across any of the job mobility patterns described above.

The most important shortcoming of the LEED file is that, in years when a worker is not in covered employment, it is not possible to ascertain directly whether he or she has taken a noncovered public or private sector job, is unemployed, or is out of the labor force. This tends to lead to slight overstatements of earnings loss in studies like those of Jacobson, but the bias is likely to be small.

3   Although the LEED file does not distinguish between normal attrition and displacement for each worker in the sample, Jacobson was able to distinguish between groups with a high probability of being displaced and groups with higher rates of attrition. This was done by dividing workers in each industry on the basis of whether employment in the industry in the worker's Standard Metropolitan Statistical Area (SMSA) was rising or falling in the year of separation. He found, based on an ingenious statistical technique, that the measured loss in earnings for separated workers in SMSAs with falling employment proved to be a "reasonably accurate estimate of the loss due to displacement alone." However, since even the elaborate technique still leaves some voluntary separations in the "displaced group," the earnings loss estimates he generated are *minimum* estimates. Therefore the percentage loss figures in Table 5.1 may seriously *underestimate* real losses of displaced workers and especially plant closing victims. See Jacobson (1978: 3–4).

4   The results of this Mathematica Policy Research Center survey are reported in Gilman (1979).

5   A similar taxonomy of industries is found in Bluestone (1968), *Poverty and Human Resources* 3, no. 2 (April 1979).

6   Brenner has developed estimates of the total foregone income plus direct prison and mental hospital outlays for the years 1970 to 1975 attributable to the 1.4 percent rise in national unemployment since 1970. The cost for these was nearly $7 billion. Adding estimated unemployment and welfare payments of $2.8 billion annually, the Joint Economic Committee staff of the United States Congress calculated a total economic loss of $21 billion from 1970 to 1975 as a result of the increased unemployment.

7   Memorandum from Richard A. Lynch, former executive vice-president, New Jersey State AFL–CIO, n.d.

8   This excellent case study, written by Bill Curry, appeared in the *Los Angeles Times*, January 11, 1981, and continued on February 22, 1981, and April 5, 1981.

9   These estimates are generated using the 1963 multiregional input–output model (MRIO) developed by Dr. Karen R. Polenske of MIT. (See Polenske (1980). Although the data refer to 1963, the relationships between industries still provide a reasonably good approximation to the actual pattern of interaction between industries. The major changes would likely be in the amount of steel and plastics used in the production of

automobiles. Today less steel and more plastic goes into production. There has also been an increase in the amount of electronics used in the modern vehicle. As a result, the estimates presented here may overestimate the number of jobs lost in the steel industry as a result of the Michigan plant shutdown but underestimate the loss in other sectors.

10   These regional impact statistics are probably different today than in 1963. With the greater dispersion of the automobile industry, particularly in the South, the regional distribution depicted is only broadly illustrative of the nature of interregional industry linkages now prevailing. Research that will eventually update the MRIO linkages to 1977 is currently underway at the Social Welfare Research Institute, Boston College, Massachusetts.

11   Arthur Strange, Executive Office of Economic Affairs, Commonwealth of Massachusetts, in an internal memorandum on the "home-based life insurance companies in the state", February 1977.

12   Even smaller, more limited plant closings take an enormous toll on tax revenues. The decision of General Motors to pack up its St. Louis assembly plant and, in effect, move it to Wentzville, Missouri, 35 miles from the city will cost St. Louis $10 million a year in revenue over the next ten years (see MacLennan & O'Donnell 1980). GM currently pays $7.5 million of the city's $23 million merchants' and manufacturers' tax. During the last quarter of 1978 and the first three quarters of 1979, GM employees paid over £2.1 million in earnings taxes. The company paid over $400,000 in other taxes during that same period.

13   These figures are based on de Leeuw *et al.* (1980: Table 5, 29; Table 19, 43).

References

Aiken, M., L. A. Ferman and H. L. Sheppard 1968. *Economic failure, alienation, and extremism.* Ann Arbor: University of Michigan Press.

Anderson, M., G. Byron and J. O'Donnell 1979. *Regional employment and economic effects of a Chrysler shutdown – preliminary data and analysis.* Cambridge, Mass.: United States Department of Transportation.

Aronson, R. L. and R. B. McKersie 1980. *Economic consequences of plant shutdowns in New York State.* Ithaca, N.Y.: New York State School of Industrial and Labor Relations, Cornell University.

ATSCME Council 93, AFL–CIO 1980. Uniroyal closing: a $500,000 tax loss. *Bay State Employees*, ATSCME Council 93, AFL–CIO, Commonwealth of Massachusetts, March 1980, pp. 7–8.

Barocci, T. A. 1979. *Disinvestment in Massachusetts: a case study of personal and economic impacts.* Working Paper no. 1080–79. Sloan School of Management, Massachusetts Institute of Technology.

Bluestone, B. 1968. Low-wage industries and the working poor. *Poverty and Human Resources* **3** (2, April).

Bluestone, B. and J. Sumrall 1977. *An overview of recent state AFDC benefits and caseload dynamics.* Publication no. 25. Boston, Mass.: Social Welfare Research Institute, Boston College.

Brenner, H. 1976. *Estimating the social costs of national economic policy: implications for mental and physical health and clinical aggression*. Report prepared for the Joint Economic Committee, United States Congress. Washington, D.C.: United States Government Printing Office.

Bulkeley, W. M. 1981. Government workers find that job security can suddenly vanish. *Wall Street Journal* July 29, 14.

Buss, T. and F. S. Redburn 1980. *Shutdown: public policy for mass unemployment*. Draft report. Youngstown, Ohio: Center for Urban Studies, Youngstown University.

C & R Associates 1978. *Community costs of plant closings: bibliography and survey of the literature*. Report prepared for the Federal Trade Commission under Contract No. L0362, July.

Cobb, S. and S. Kasl 1977. *Termination: the consequences of job loss*. Public Health Service, Center for Disease Control, National Institute for Occupational Safety and Health, United States Department of Health, Education, and Welfare, Washington, D.C.

Curry, B. 1981a. Smelter closing gives cash registers a hollow ring. *Los Angeles Times* January 11, 11.

Curry, B. 1981b. Town loses its payroll but it finds a will to survive. *Los Angeles Times* April 5, 11.

Daily Times (Erie, Pennsylvania) 1980. Erie shares grant to fight closings. November 13.

de Leeuw, F., *et. al.* 1980. The high-employment budget; new estimates, 1955–80. *Survey of Current Business* **60** (11, November).

Dorsey, J. W. 1967. The mack truck case: a study in unemployment. In *Studies in the economics of income maintenance*, O. Eckstein (ed.). Washington, D.C.: The Brookings Institution.

Foltman, F. 1968. *White and blue collars in a mill shutdown*. Ithaca, NY: Cornell University Press.

Gilman, H. J. 1979. *The economic costs of worker dislocation: an overview*. Paper prepared for the National Commission for Employment Policy, July. Washington, D.C.: National Commission for Employment Policy.

Glasser, M. A. 1976. Diamond-Reo pension plan termination. Inter-office communication to the International Executive Board, United Automobile Workers (UAW), April 9.

Guzzardi, W., Jr. 1980. A determined Detroit struggles to find a new economic life. *Fortune* April 21, 84.

Harrison, B. and E. Hill 1979. The changing structure of jobs in older and younger cities. In *Central city economic development*, B. Chinitz (ed.). Cambridge, Mass.: Abt Books.

Hayes, L. S. 1979. Youngstown bounces back. *Fortune* December 17. 102–106.

Hefner, J. A. 1979. The economics of the black family from four perspectives. In *Class caste controversy*, V. Willie (ed.), 83. Bayside, NY: General Hall. (As reported in Ohio Interest Campaign, n.d.)

Holen, A. 1976. *Losses to workers displaced by plant closure or layoff: a survey of the literature*. Paper of The Public Research Institute of the Center for Naval Analyses, McLain, Virginia.

Jacobson, L. S. 1978. Earnings losses of workers displaced from manufacturing industries. In *The impact of international trade and investment on employment*, W. G. Dewald (ed.). Washington, D.C.: US Government Printing Office.

Jacobson, L. S. 1979. *Earnings loss due to displacement*. Working Paper CRC-385 of The Public Research Institute of the Centre for Naval Analyses, McLain, Virginia.

Kasl, S. and S. Cobb 1970. Blood pressure changes in men undergoing job loss. *Psychometric Medicine* **32** (Jan.–Feb.), 100–22.

Kasl, S., S. Cobb and G. Brooks 1968. Changes in serum uric acid and cholesterol levels in men undergoing job loss. *Journal of the American Medical Association* **206** (November), 1500–1507.

Kasl, S., S. Gore and S. Cobb 1975. The experience of losing a job: reported changes in health, symptoms, and illness behavior. *Psychosomatic Medicine* **37** (2, March–April), 106–22.

Lumpkin, K. D. 1934. Shutdowns in the Connecticut valley. *Smith College Studies in History* **19**. (As reported in C & R Associates 1978: 33.)

Lynd, S. 1981. Reindustrialization: brownfield or greenfield? *Democracy* **1** (3, July), 31.

McCarthy, J. E. 1975. *Trade adjustment assistance: a case study of the shoe industry in Massachusetts*. Boston, Mass.: Federal Reserve Bank of Boston.

MacLennan, C. and J. O'Donnell 1980. *The effects of the automotive transition on employment: a plant and community study*. Draft for the Transportation Systems Center, United States Department of Transportation.

Matthews, A. and B. Bluestone 1979. *Special tabulations of social security LEED file*. Social Welfare Research Institute, Boston College, Massachusetts.

Metzgar, J. 1980. Plant shutdowns and worker response: the case of Johnstown, Pa. *Socialist Review* **10** (5, Sept.–Oct.), 18–19.

Meyer, P. B. and M. A. Phillips 1978. Worker adaptation to internationally induced job loss: final report on a pilot study. Bureau of International Labor Affairs, US Department of Labor, April 27.

Moberg, D. 1979. Shuttered factories – shattered communities. *These Times* June 27, 11.

Ohio AFL-CIO News and Views 1980. Plant closings in Campbell force higher taxes. February 29.

Ohio Public Interest Campaign n.d. *Industrial exodus hits minority workers the hardest* (reprinted in *Shutdown: economic dislocation and equal opportunity*, report prepared by the Illinois Committee to the United States Commission on Civil Rights, June 1981).

Polenske, K. R. 1980. *The U.S. multiregional input–output accounts and model*. Lexington, Mass.: D. C. Heath.

Policy and Management Associates Inc. 1981. *Socioeconomic costs and benefits of the community-worker ownership plan to the Youngstown-Warren SMSA*. (As reported in Moberg 1979: 12.)

Ratliff, R. 1980. Schools – taxes = ? *Detroit Free Press* August 24, G1.

Rayman, P. and B. Bluestone 1982. *The private and social costs of job loss: a metrostudy*. Boston, Mass.: Social Welfare Research Institute, Boston College.

Rosen, E. I. 1981. *Job mobility and job loss: a study of the effects of unemployment and underemployment among blue-collar working women in New England*. Boston, Mass.: Social Welfare Research Institute, Boston College.

Sandburg, C. 1969. The people, yes. *The complete poems of Carl Sandburg*, rev. edn. New York: Harcourt Brace Jovanovich.

Sestak, K. 1976. *AFDC caseload and benefits dynamics – Washington*. Boston, Mass.: Social Welfare Research Institute, Boston College.

Slote, A. 1969. *Termination: the closing of the Baker plant*. Indianapolis, Ind.: Bobbs–Merrill.

Stillman, D. 1978. The devastating impact of plant relocations. *Working Papers* **5** (4, July–August).

Strange, W. 1977. *Job loss: a psychosocial study of worker reactions to a plant closing in a company town in Southern Appalachia*. Washington, DC: National Technical Information Service (NTIS).

Transportation Systems Center, United States Department of Transportation 1979. If Chrysler shuts down. *Challenge* Nov.–Dec., 51–2.

United States Bureau of the Census 1979. *The social and economic status of the black population in the United States: an historical view, 1970–1978*. Current Population Reports (Special Studies P-23, No. 80). Washington, D.C.: United States Government Printing Office.

United States Department of Health and Human Services, Social Security Administration 1980. *Social security bulletin: annual statistical supplement, 1977–1979*. Washington, D.C.: United States Government Printing Office.

United States Department of Labor, Labor-Management Services Administration 1978. *What you should know about the pension and welfare law: a guide to the Employment Retirement Income Security Act of 1974*. Washington, D.C.: United States Government Printing Office.

United States Department of Transportation 1981. *The US automobile industry, 1980: report to the President from the Secretary of Transportation*. Washington, D.C.: United States Government Printing Office.

United States House of Representatives, Committee on Small Business 1980. *Conglomerate mergers – their effects on small business and local communities*. 96th Congress, 2nd Session, Report No. 96–1447, October 2.

Wilcock, R. and W. H. Franke 1963. *Unwanted workers: permanent layoffs and long-term unemployment*. New York: Glencoe Free Press.

Young, E. 1963. The Armour experience: a case study in plant shutdown. In *Adjusting to technological change*, G. Somers, E. Cushman and N. Weinberg (eds). New York: Harper & Row.

6 The shape of things to come*

DOREEN MASSEY

The changing composition of the workforce

The British labor force is not what it was 20 years ago. The immediate disaster of Thatcherism has thrown into high relief major changes in its composition. Employment in manufacturing has collapsed since the 1979 election. Skilled manual jobs are being cut back drastically. There has even been a drop in the total work force. It has felt like devastation, and it has been. But the intensity of the effect of Tory policies should not blind us to the fact that underlying them are longer run processes of change. The working class, and the labor force more generally, are undergoing structural changes in composition.

They are profound changes, profound enough to mean that some of the old ways of thinking and working are no longer adequate or appropriate. The labor movement too, if it is to keep ahead of events, must *Good* restructure itself, recognize the shifts, address new questions.

But it is not only the social composition of the labor force which is changing. Its geography is also being transformed. The urban and regional structure of the Britain of tomorrow (even after, that is, some recovery from Thatcher) will be different from what we have come to know, and to know how to work within. Regional divisions are being broken down. To be sure, the old north–south divide is being reinforced in terms of voting patterns, but it is not the same old north–south divide of the 1930s. Further, the pattern in which most working-class jobs, particularly in manufacturing, were gathered in the towns and cities is crumbling. "Rural areas" are no longer places without major nonagricultural employment.

This changing geography compounds the challenge facing the labor movement. The changing location of industry breaks down established relations between workplaces, and between workplaces and communities. And the new locations are different. The factory or office is situated in

* Reprinted from Massey, D. 1983, The shape of things to come. *Marxism Today* April 18–27, by permission of *Marxism Today*.

a different context, to which previous forms of organization may be inappropriate. Geographic change can, in other words, alter the wider social context of the politics of the workplace at the same time as the social composition of the work force itself is changing. And, indeed, the two processes are related. The geographic reorganization of British capital has been fundamental to all its attempts over the last 20 years or so to become more competitive, hold down wages, restructure itself out of crisis. Geographic restructuring has already been important to capital, and it should be important to labor.

THE NATIONAL LEVEL

At the national level there have been significant changes in balance between different elements of the work force. Figure 6.1 shows one of the divisions which has long been central to labor movement organization – that between manual and nonmanual workers. Manual workers, from having made up over 60 percent of the working population in 1961, are now down to only about 50 percent. This change in the shape of the labor force has been going on throughout the postwar period, manual workers having declined by about 5 percent as a proportion of the total work force in each postwar decade. To some extent what these figures reflect is the loss of jobs in manufacturing. This too is now a well established phenomenon. The number of jobs in manufacturing in 1961 was 8.2 million. Since then it has fallen by a quarter and, from 36 percent in 1961, manufacturing now makes up only 28 percent of jobs in the economy.

These major shifts are mirrored in the changing occupational structure of the workforce (Table 6.1). Within the generally expanding nonmanual groups, it has been the higher-status jobs which have been growing fastest as a proportion of the total workforce. And this growth has been accompanied by shifts in the internal composition of each group. The particularly rapid rise in importance of professionals, for example, has been due especially to public-sector expansion (we are talking here of the last 20 years!) in health and education. Similarly that wide spectrum of occupations referred to in the table as "engineers and technicians" has seen engineering–based professionals, draftspeople,

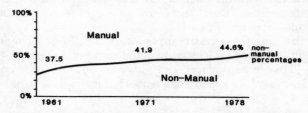

Figure 6.1 The changing balance between manual and nonmanual workers (calculated from the data of Warwick University Manpower Research Group).

and so forth, dwindling in importance, whereas the computer whizzkid and the research scientist increase in both numbers and status. The managers and administrators have expanded in all parts of the economy: public sector and private, manufacturing and services. In contrast, the increase in the number of clerical workers is not so marked; each clerical worker is evidently now supporting more professionals. The declining groups reflect the obverse of these processes. And here, too, there are significant shifts in the internal composition of each category; the generally declining "other operatives" group, for instance, includes a growing army of assembly workers.

PARTICIPATION OF WOMEN

Perhaps best known and most important is the increased participation of women in the paid work force. Figure 6.2 gives some details. The rise in the number of women in the labor force has not in fact been steady (the figure for 1982 is actually below that for 1964). But the increase in the proportion of the work force which is female has been far more consistent. This obviously reflects what is happening to male employment – the recent dramatic collapse of jobs for men resulting in a rise in the importance of women in the work force, even though their own numbers are shrinking too.

But these are all national changes. They are substantial enough as they stand, but they also hide a lot else that has been going on. For these national changes are highly differentiated from one part of the country to another, and very different kinds of class changes and shifts in social composition are underway in different regions. A new geography is in the making.

Table 6.1   Occupational changes 1961–78 (percentage of workforce).

	1961	1971	1978
administrators, managers	6.6	7.8	8.7
professionals	6.6	8.1	9.8
engineers and technicians	3.5	4.2	4.7
clerical workers	14.0	15.0	15.9
craft workers	19.7	17.6	15.9
skilled operatives	3.2	3.1	2.7
other operatives	22.9	20.4	18.5
personal services	8.9	10.5	11.2
other	14.6	13.4	12.5
total	100	100	100

Source: Warwick University Manpower Research Group.

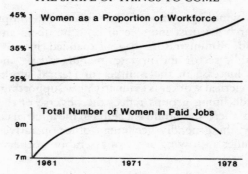

Figure 6.2 Women in the workforce (from ACE data, censuses of population).

Behind this new geography lie a number of interlocking processes. Each of them is related to long-term shifts in the economy as a whole and to the changing place of Britain in the international system. They can, roughly, be divided into two groups: elements of the geography of decline on the one hand and the emergence of new patterns on the other.

The geography of decline

The pattern of employment decline in Britain today is actually the result of *two* different patterns, the one superimposed upon the other. On the one hand there is the long-term decline of a range of "old basic" sectors; on the other hand there is the newer, though by now also well established, loss of employment in manufacturing. These two waves of decline hail originally from different periods, each reflecting the previous dominance of different structures of the British economy. Each, too, has its own particular geography.

THE 1930S REVISITED

First, there is the long-term decline of jobs for men in the old basic industries of the Development Areas – South Wales, Central Scotland, the Northeast of England. The loss of jobs in industries such as coal mining and shipbuilding, which once formed the economic core of these areas, has been going on for much of this century. It was the collapse of these pillars of Empire which lay behind the regional concentrations of unemployment and the appalling poverty in these areas in the 1930s (unemployment rates in the Southeast were relatively low). And it was the sudden and rapid loss of jobs in these industries (particularly shipbuilding) which heralded for British industry the end of the long postwar boom and, with that, the reemergence of the "regional problem." Since then the loss of jobs has varied in pace and been modulated by economic climate and political strategy. The contraction of this central element of the working class, then, is long term, and it has had and continues to have a very definite geographic pattern. It is the decline of employment in these industries which is at the heart of the "traditional" form of the British regional problem.

But that well-known pattern is now being overlaid by another, equally dramatic, pattern of decline.

DEINDUSTRIALIZATION

Deindustrialization – reflected in the loss of jobs in manufacturing – has hit the headlines under Margaret Thatcher. But it, too, is a longer-term phenomenon. The absolute *number* of jobs in manufacturing has been shrinking in the UK for nearly 25 years now – ever since the mid-1960s. And manufacturing's *share* of total employment has been declining for far longer.

Deindustrialization is certainly of a different order under this government. It has accelerated, and it has spread to virtually all manufacturing sectors. Moreover, it is not just employment, it is also output which is now falling. In the late 1960s job loss in manufacturing took place in a context of rapidly rising productivity and technological change (it was the age of the white heat and productivity agreements). Today far more of it is due simply to the closure of capacity. So there is no question but that what is happening now is of a different order. But the decline of jobs in manufacturing is not itself a new phenomenon.

Now, the geography of the decline of manufacturing is very different from that of the decline of the old basic sectors. For one thing, it is more general: it is not confined to two or three regions of the country. But it does have a definite geographic pattern. The first areas to be hit by deindustrialization were the cities. Greater London has seen the most spectacular falls. Every five years from 1961 to 1976, 200,000 manufacturing jobs were lost from the city's economy. By the end of 1983 the number of manufacturing jobs in the former Greater London Council area was only two-fifths of what it had been in 1961.

A large proportion of the overall decline of jobs in urban areas has in fact been due simply to this decline of manufacturing industry. There has been a relative "shift" of employment from bigger cities towards smaller towns and more rural areas. But the term "shift" (the term most frequently used) can give the impression that the whole thing took place through actual geographic movement. It did not. Much of it has been a process of differential growth and decline. A large part of the loss of manufacturing jobs in major urban areas has taken place through straightforward closure, with no new investment elsewhere, or certainly not in the UK.

DECLINE OF THE CITIES

The loss of manufacturing jobs in the cities has not, for the most part, been because they had a high proportion of jobs in industries which were declining fastest nationally. It was not, in other words, a result of the cities' industrial structure, as it was the industrial structure of South Wales and the Northeast which lay behind the collapse of their employment in the 1930s. The cities suffered most because, *within* particular industries, they tended to have the oldest factories and the oldest production techniques. Most of all they had the lowest levels of labor productivity.

There were other reasons, too. In a number of cases we studied in the late 1960s (Massey & Meegan 1979:3), management argued that it was easier to close a plant in a large and complex labor market than in a smaller town: the job losses are absorbed, the unemployment diluted, and less "blame" gets pinned on the individual company. It was also the case that workers in the cities had often won higher wages and, in manufacturing industries, were better organised than those in more out-of-town locations. Whether explicitly motivated or not, the decline of manufacturing industry in the cities has certainly taken with it some of the old bastions of trade union strength.

But it is not *only* the cities which have been hit. As deindustrialization has accelerated, it has spread both to more and more industries and to more and more places. The regions which have been worst affected have been those with the greatest reliance on manufacturing. The economies of the engineering-based regions, in particular the West Midlands and the Northwest, have been shattered. Manufacturing employment in the Northwest has been falling since the early 1960s, gradually picking up speed to lose 20 percent between 1966 and 1976. In the West Midlands manufacturing jobs carried on increasing until the early 1970s. But in the four years from 1978 to 1982 each of those two regions lost over 200,000 jobs, a further 20 percent of the manufacturing work force in each case.

THE CHANGING MAP OF UNEMPLOYMENT

So two contrasting patterns of job loss, stemming initially from very different eras, have in recent years been superimposed upon each other. The result is that the map of unemployment is now very different from the one we have been used to since the 1930s (Fig. 6.3 updated by editor). Some elements have acquired an apparent permanence: the unemployment rate in Northern Ireland is now 21 percent. But the rates in the Northwest and the West Midlands are now equal to that of Scotland. Only the Southeast stands out as significantly better than the national average. And that itself conceals enormous

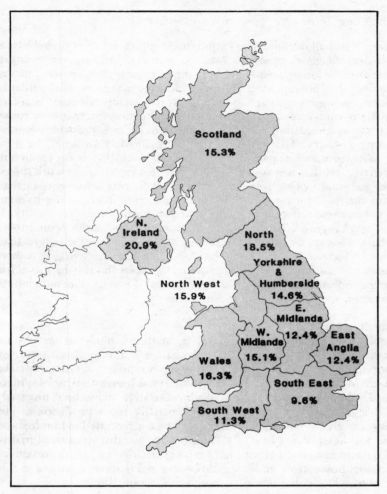

Figure 6.3   The map of unemployment, June 1985 (Department of Employment 1985).

differences. Within each region, the inner cities of the major conurbations have rates of unemployment far above the national average. In London most inner-area boroughs have more in common with inner cities elsewhere than with the outer metropolitan area.

The shape of the new: geographic restructuring

But it is not all decline. The employment which remains is also being restructured geographically. And the sectors which are growing (at least over the longer term) have very different geographic patterns from the ones they are replacing. The way industry makes use of the British space is being reorganized. This process has been particularly marked since the mid-1960s when pressures of increasing international competition and a shifting world order began to enforce a restructuring of British industry. That restructuring has changed a number of times in both its form and its pace in the years since then. But its net result has been to produce a major shift in the social geography of the work force. The geography of each element of that work force is being reorganized. And this is happening at the same time, remember, as the balance between these different elements is also shifting (Table 6.1).

The changing balance of corporate structures in the economy is reflected most obviously in the changing geography of management. This is discussed next. Having established that framework, it is then easier to examine the internal reorganization of the rest of the work force, concentrating here on the categories of production and clerical workers, and scientists and technicians.

THE GEOGRAPHY OF MANAGEMENT

Look first, because it is the simplest, at the changing geography of management. At the heart of this change is the increasing size of individual companies and the growing dominance of the top few hundred firms. As firms have grown there has been a tendency for their head offices and upper echelons of administrative, marketing, financial, and legal staff, etc. to be split off spatially from production, and increasingly the tendency is for them to be concentrated in London and the Southeast of England. As Table 6.1 shows, this stratum of managerial and associated groups has been expanding as a proportion of the national population, and it should be stressed that employment in this kind of white-collar work has been growing in all regions.

But as it has grown it has also become more highly differentiated, both functionally and socially; management hierarchies have lengthened. Hand in hand with this increasing social differentiation has gone increasing geographical differentiation. The lengthening managerial hierarchies, with their associated hierarchies of functions and social status, have been stretched out over space. And the geographic pattern has taken on a very definite form: the higher-level functions, the ultimate control over production and over the relations of economic ownership and possession, and the upper echelons of social strata with which such functions are associated are increasingly concentrated in the bottom right-hand corner of the country. In 1977, some 350 of the top

500 UK companies had their headquarters, and therefore all their top management, in London and the Southeast. In contrast, the lower the level of management, the nearer to actual production it tends to be geographically. With HQs concentrating in the Southeast, the corollary is that other regions are increasingly becoming "branch-plant" economies.

DECENTRALIZATION OF PRODUCTION AND CLERICAL JOBS
In contrast to what has happened to management, and contrary to a long and dearly-held thesis on the Left, the concentration and centralization of capital in ownership terms has *not* led to the geographic concentration of jobs in *production*. Indeed at precisely the same time as the concentration (both spatial and aspatial) of ownership and control has been going on, the location of production itself has become more decentralised, both within individual regions, outwards from cities, and from the Southeast and Midlands of England to the regions of the north and west.

Some of this relative shift has been associated with changes in the technology of production. In a whole range of industries the kind of technological change which has been going on over the past 20 years or so has been associated with a changing demand for labor. Industries such as telecommunications, parts of electrical engineering, and electronics are the most obvious examples. In such industries, both changes in the product (e.g., in telecommunications from electromechanical to semi-electronic switching gear) and changes in the production process towards more highly mechanized techniques or techniques involving major assembly stages have gone along with a shift in the kind of labor employed. The archetypal shift is from male manual workers classified as skilled to female assemblers classified as unskilled or semiskilled.

Such changes in the social composition of the labor force are often accompanied by geographic recomposition. They have "freed" industry from its traditional sources of labor in the old centres of manufacturing skills and have been part and parcel of a significant decentralization to pastures new, and labor forces new. The existing work force has been abandoned and new and different labor employed in areas with no tradition in the industry, or indeed any industry at all. The social recomposition of the labor force, changes in the technology of production, and changes in location are in such cases integral to each other.

THE SERVICE SECTOR
Technical change has been one significant force behind the decentralization of production, but it has not been the only one. There has also been a significant outward movement of manufacturing jobs, particularly jobs traditionally done by women, but where there has been little technological change in production. Here the driving force has been to find cheaper sources of labor. The clothing industry is a good example.

In the 1960s it was caught in a vice. It was under competition from low-cost imports. But its own usual supply of women workers in urban areas (particularly London) was threatened by the expansion of the service sector. Big firms in the industry solved the dilemma by changing location. New sources of labor, more vulnerable and with fewer alternative sources of employment, were sought out. The new source of labor was older, married women; the new locations were smaller towns, trading estates, and sometimes quite isolated locations in the peripheral regions of the country – the rural areas such as the Southwest and old heavy-industry areas such as the coalfields.

Nor has it just been manufacturing which has decentralized. Not many years later the service sector adopted the same strategy, and new geographic patterns of employment were developed there too. Both clerical wages and office rents decline once you get further than about 60 miles from London, and from the 1970s departments of the central state and large private sector firms began decentralizing the more routine elements of clerical work. Clerical workers are an increasingly important part of the labor force (see Table 6.1), and this decentralization is therefore a significant element of its changing geography. Longbenton in the North-east is a classic example: 6,000 clerical workers process you through the DHSS here. Driving licenses are issued by nearly 4,000 similar workers in Swansea. In some areas, such as the Northeast, this has represented an increase in jobs available to women where there had been precious little before. In other cases the service industry arrived to compete with others, in the East Midlands, for example, chasing the shoe industry (with many of the same pressures on it as in clothing) even further north.

SCIENTISTS AND TECHNICIANS

Although these changes have been affecting workers directly involved in production, other things have been going on at the other end of the social spectrum. An increasing proportion of the work force is engaged in research and development and related activities, either in the research establishments of major corporations in a wide variety of industries, or in independent "business services" of various sorts (software consultancies, for example), or in the newly developing hi-tech sectors. To some extent the growth of this element of the work force is bound up with the same technological changes which produced the deskilled and decentralised production jobs. They are the necessary counterpoint to that production labor force in a long process of the separation of conception from execution.

Their geographic distribution, too, is very different. As with managerial hierarchies so with the technical division of labor: the separating out of a whole series of distinct functions, each related to a particular social status, has enabled also their geographic separation. The further you are from production in a functional sense the further you can be distanced geographically. The industrial technologists of a generation and more ago had a far more intimate relationship to the actual process of production than do, except in the prototype stage, the emerging technologists of today. Big companies have taken advantage of that fact, separating out geographically the different parts of the organization into hierarchical geographic structures.

THE BRITISH SUNBELT

The upper echelons of these technocratic strata have increasingly concentrated in a new "region" of the country, which is called the British sunbelt. This belt is the swathe of tamed rurality which stretches between Bristol, Southampton, and round and up to Cambridge (Fig. 6.4) – the outer–outer metropolitan area. In startling contrast to the tedious assembly and clerical jobs which have for years been the main new source of employment outside this belt, and particularly in the old coal and steel areas, these jobs are almost all for graduates, and almost all for men.

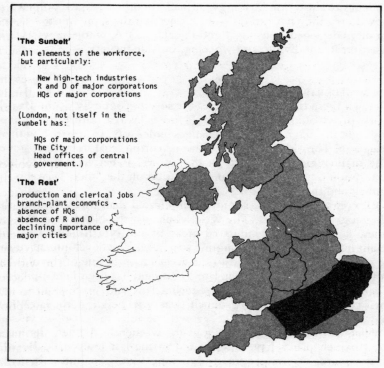

Figure 6.4 The shape of things to come.

But it is not just big companies. It is in this stretch of country that the new, and still small, breed of entrepreneur scientist is gathered. Indeed it is only in this part of the country that "the small-firm sector" lives up to its image of entrepreneurship and dynamism. What are biotechnology and software consultancies here tend in other areas to be sweatshops and scrap-metal dealers.

But why this part of the country? Certainly there are some plausible economic reasons; but there are social reasons too, and it is arguable that they may be at least equally important. The attraction of the area originally was a combination of accessibility to London and nearness to defence establishments. The latter provided both jobs for technicians and contracts for the growing electronics industry. However, since then the place has taken off in another way. The research scientists, the technologists, those working in business services, make up the stratum of the labor force most able to choose where to live, and assume that jobs will follow. And they do. And jobs do follow. The region *itself* now has a status, a cachet, attached to it. The highly interlinked and individualistic nature of the labor market for these groups reinforces the tendency to clustering, making it difficult for other areas to compete. (If they do try they have to do so by projecting the same image – semi-rurality, detached housing, "good" schools.) A whole new style is being created in living, and working, outside the city.

A NEW GEOGRAPHY

Were all these trends to continue, the social geography of the British work force would be transformed. Figure 6.4 is a caricature, but it helps highlight the magnitude of the changes under way. Compare it with 50 years ago. The old regional specialisms (cotton, coal, cars) have gone. The main regional contrast, in this future, is between control and conception on the one hand and execution on the other, between the sunbelt and the rest.

Of course the picture is more complicated than this. Much of the old geography remains. The West Midlands, the Northwest, the big cities, and the heavy industrial areas of the North and West still retain much of their old economic structure. The development of the new geography (as opposed to the accelerated decline of the old) has in fact slowed down over the late 1970s, and has been interrupted by Thatcherism. The expansion of technicians and professionals, and their concentration into the sunbelt, was at its height in the late 1960s and early 1970s. So was the growth of jobs in out-of-town and smaller-town locations. Many jobs for women in the new decentralized branch plants have disappeared in the last few years. But the shift towards a new geography is a long-term one, and is likely to reemerge.

The importance of local diversity

The fact that the social recomposition of the work force also involves geographic reorganization has a number of implications. Most importantly, it means that completely different kinds of social change can be going on in different localities. Not everywhere mirrors the national pattern; in all likelihood very few places do. The classic picture of the dwindling and disintegration of the heart of the traditional labor movement is found most clearly in the old heavy-industry and coalfield areas (for instance South Wales). In these areas, certainly, there is the fragmentation of a previous, relatively coherent economic structure based around a few industries, and a few unions. Here too jobs for women are expanding fast and jobs for men contracting, there is a proliferation of industries and employers, often with little connection to each other, and an expansion of white–collar strata.

But it is not everywhere like this. In some more rural areas the numerical importance and the structural coherence of the working class is actually *increasing* over the medium term as a result of the geographic decentralization of industry. Cornwall is an example. Here, new employment has come into an area where the previous economic and social structure was based around self-employment and small–scale employment in agriculture and tourism. Straightforward wage labor has been a very much less important element here than in other regions. Today that picture is changing. The traditional petty bourgeoisie is declining fast, and though a stratum of managers and professionals is certainly expanding, so too is the working class.

So the directions of social recomposition can be quite different from one area to the next. "National" changes can take highly variegated forms across the country. The decline of the old is not always happening in the same place as the rise of the new. What that means is that different problems are being faced, different battles fought out, in different places.

THE PROCESS OF CHANGE

It is important to remember that recomposition is a *process*. What has to be recognized politically is not just some end state looking very different from what we have been used to, but also a process of social change which may often be difficult and painful. The actual process of change is itself an important determinant of the social and political response. This process of change varies locally. Where an area is coming from can be just as important as where it is going to for understanding the political climate. What are apparently similar numerical changes can have very different implications depending on the regional setting. The impact of rising unemployment, for instance, can vary dramatically depending on the wider social context and on the historical experience of those in the area.

People in the West Midlands are newly coping with not being the
boom centre of the land. To some extent epitomized by the car
workers, it has gone from cocky aggressivity to agreeing to new work
practices. There is a real shock of sudden vulnerability and eroding
status and relative, as well as real, wages. This shock of the new is in
total contrast to the weary and deeply resentful return, yet again, to
high unemployment, the status of disaster area, you feel in South
Wales, the northeast of England or even Merseyside. In London and the
Southeast, the lengthy decline of the East End is apparently more like
that of the older regions, but here the context is so different. From
Docklands you can see the City and if you venture into town you are
faced, still, with well-heeled white-collar workers and the denizens of
the stockbroker belt.

THE GEOGRAPHY OF GENDER RELATIONS

Nor is it just changes in class relations which vary across the country.
There is a geography of gender relations, too. Particularly over the last
20 years, women have been increasingly participating in the waged
labor force in all regions, but the increases have been greatest in the
peripheral regions (Southwest, Wales, Scotland and the Northeast),
both urban and rural, to which jobs have been decentralized. Once
again, the numbers do not tell the whole story. The impact of an
increase in women's participation in paid employment depends on the
prevailing system of gender relations. And this varies a lot between one
part of the country and another.

Possibly the extreme cases are the old heavy industry Development
Areas, especially the coalfields. The "decline" of these regions should be
assessed not just from the point of view that they were heavily working
class areas, and highly unionized, but also from the point of view that
they were extremely *male*. As far as paid employment is concerned, the
opportunities for women have been extremely limited in these regions
throughout the century. This has in part been related to the nature of
employment for men, and the status attached to it. The demands put on
(female) domestic labor by male work down the mine are enormous.
Shiftwork, too, makes it more difficult for both partners to be
employed outside the home. The ideology of a sexual division of labor
between breadwinner and homekeeper has probably been more firmly
entrenched in these areas than anywhere else in the country.

The associated attitudes spread beyond the domestic sphere. In clubs,
in politics, in unions, women have been excluded from all but a very
minor rôle, perhaps especially in postwar years. Attitudes existed
which would be unthinkable in Lancashire, say, or London. The now-
mourned homogeneity of the labor movement in these regions was
based around a rigid sexual division of labor. The shift in the sexual
balance of the paid labor force has sorely disrupted this established set of

practices and relations. So much so, indeed, that the late 1960s and 1970s saw calls, from male trade unionists, academics and politicians alike, for more jobs specifically for men and, in some cases, less jobs for women. A House of Commons memorandum pleaded that the established sexual balance of employment should not be too severely disrupted.

It is interesting to speculate on the degree to which this highly patriarchial past has been one of the conditions for the threat currently posed to it. Certainly, given the previous reliance on female domestic labor, the decline of male employment was an important condition for the formation of the women of these areas into a "reserve of labor." They were, moreover, a particularly attractive one, from industry's point of view. More than almost anywhere else in the country they lacked previous experience of employment in capitalist wage relations. They were real "green labor", and their previous exclusion from public life seemed to make them ideal. To the extent that it was complicit in the rigidity of the sexual division of labor in these regions, and in the exclusion of women from so many social activities, the old traditional heart of the (male) labor movement may well itself have been party to the creation of the new super–cheap labor forces industry was searching out in the 1960s and 1970s. Certainly the geography of gender relations has been an important element in British industry's attempts to re-organize geographically – to restructure itself out of crisis.

LOCAL POLITICS AND NATIONAL POLITICS
In the 1960s and 1970s much of the importance of "local politics" was seen to be in linking the local to the national, the particularities of a local area to the wider underlying mechanisms of a capitalist society. Failure to make that link was often seen as failure of the exercise as a whole. That job is still there; it still needs to be done. But it did perhaps lead to a tendency to see *only* the "wider capitalist system" at work in every local situation. The local particularities were seen as something to be cleared away to reveal what was *really* happening. But part of the importance of local politics is precisely in learning how that "capitalist system" gets worked out in people's lives in the detailed specificity of a vast variety of local situations. "What is really happening" is actually very varied. Unity between those situations is not constructed only by proclaiming that each and every local change is underlain by capitalism; only, in other words, by asserting "the general". It also needs, for a solid foundation, a recognition and understanding of the reality and conditions of diversity, and of the actual processes which link the local particularities.

Geographic diversity matters politically in other ways, too. Above all it can be divisive. It is not just that "national" changes are reflected in a geographically differentiated form, but that geographic diversity can be used as a weapon in a wider politics. The way this happens can vary, has varied, widely. In the 1960s, that combination of technological change and locational change which was mentioned earlier often set workers in one area against those in another, in the context of an individual company. More recently, as that process has slowed down, and high unemployment has spread to more and more places, "interarea competition" has become a weapon in the hands of both individual companies and the state. The Nissan episode, with over 100 local authorities competing against each other, has been the most glaring example of the former.

More generally, areas compete with each other by advertising the nonmilitancy of their labor. Regions are blamed for their own decline. The reputation of militancy of Merseyside workers is the most obvious case. In 1978 there was an attempt to draw up a local social contract; in 1979, just after the election, James Prior, Secretary of State for Employment, visited the area to announce that, if there were no strikes there for two years, some investment might be forthcoming. Only recently, a report on East Kilbride assured would-be investors that the situation was nothing like as bad as they might have thought: an investigation had shown that the workers there were hardly militant at all! Thus the vulnerabilities of particular areas are used in a wider battle between capital and labor.

The politics of recomposition

The joint social and geographic restructuring of the labor force is, then, producing very different conditions for political organisation and representation from those we have come to know and love. It is easy to feel that all is lost. Indeed a quick survey of socialist thoughts upon the subject of the presently emerging geography of the working class would indicate a depressing assessment of its potential as a base for organization.

Certainly we have been witness to the erosion of well established and familiar bases. To the long decline of the industrial unions of the old periphery has now been added the subduing of the strength of the West Midlands. In many areas the accustomed social infrastructure of organization has been torn apart by industrial decline. At the intraregional scale, New Towns are well known for the passivity, in general, of their labor forces. The *process* of geographic recomposition is itself a problem. Much of the strength of the labor movement is constructed around local histories, and their dislocation can produce a sense of placelessness in the strong meaning of that word.

But on its own that negative assessment misses a lot. It is not just decline that is going on; it is recomposition. And there have been such recompositions before. The interwar years saw a massive social and

Simple view of 30's?? (handwritten)

spatial restructuring of employment. It was then that the basic industries plunged into decline; and the new sectors which grew up were completely different. They were at the other end of the country – in the Midlands and Southeast. They demanded different skills, implied a different social structure. The unions which organized in them (TGWU, NUGMW) were different, too. This is *not* to imply that each and every change should be accepted, nor, certainly, that the present form of spatial recomposition is politically inevitable. It is merely to point out that what we have now was once itself new and untried; the organizational frameworks which are now so familiar themselves had once to be built.

Moreover, much of what is now thought of as new has not been absent before; it has simply been ignored. The past which it is commonly thought we are leaving has been inaccurately mythologized. Take this "new" entry of women into manual jobs. Women now represent about 30 percent of all manual workers, which is about the same as in 1911. If anything it has been the intervening years which have been the exception. Again, manufacturing employment has *never* been numerically dominant in the economy. Some of the strongest points of the labor movement have always been outside manufacturing – coal mining is the most obvious example.

So there is a need to readjust our stylized image of the past. Anyway, we should not just be seeking the restoration of the old and well tried. After all, it was not a spectacular success. We cannot recreate the old labor movement of the coalfields, for instance, and it, too, had its share of disadvantages and its own vulnerabilities.

But there *have* been major changes. And they do require a response. Is the outlook, then, as grim as most assessments would have it? Is no response possible?

One counter to the bleakest scenarios of the future is that they are, curiously, very geographically determinist. It is argued, for instance, that the great cities, with their variety of enterprises and industries, and with their anonymity, provided ideal places for union organization, and that is now gone. In one sense it is true. But that union organization had to be constructed, and the form which it took corresponded to, took advantage of, the setting. That was how that particular "geography," the urban form, was used to advantage. But by no means all the old centers of trade union strength had those characteristics. Some of the strongest bases were in small, single-industry settlements – colliery villages for example.

There are now different situations, demanding different strategies and forms of organization. The "new geography" may look pretty unprepossessing at first sight, but there are possibilities. The problems of organizing in multiregional companies are clear, but such companies do open up new potential contact between areas. It is a difficult potential to grasp, but then it was not so simple to build unity on the coalfields either. The growth in numbers, unionization, and militancy of public sector workers offers opportunities at local level for linking employment with community issues, and possibilities at national level for coordinated action entailing a presence in every locality, which no other industry provides.

The problem is that the movement always seems to be on the receiving end of such processes, but never to hold the initiative. The impetus for industrial restructuring has come in an immediate sense from capital. Much of it is a response to, and an attempt to break, established elements of labor movement organization. Certainly this has been true spatially. The decline of the cities has had as one element a relative shift away from better organized workers. At the other end of the process the decentralization of production has certainly seen managements seeking out potentially vulnerable and difficult-to-organize work forces. But the fact that that was part of the rationale does not guarantee success. At each end of the process there is now a fight back. The cities are far from dead politically, however much they might be losing jobs. The fact of decline, together with their changing social structure, has been a basis for some of them to become the seedbeds of a new kind of politics, based around new coalitions and attempting a restructuring more on labor's terms. It is not just the big cities. The examples of Plessey-Bathgate, of Lee Jeans and Lovable, give notice that capital might just have been mistaken in its assumption that the women workers of "the regions" would not get organized.

So the situation is *not* all gloom and doom. There are already attempts to respond, to take back some of the initiative. But for that to be possible in a wider way does demand that we recognize the extent and the depth of the structural changes which are going on. It is certainly not that old bases, either socially or geographically, should be abandoned. However, it is vital to recognize both that they themselves are changing and that new bases must be constructed, both among the expanding elements of the work force and in new parts of the country.

Acknowledgement

I wish to thank Nick Miles for his help in assembling the data for the diagrams in this chapter.

Reference

Massey, D. & R. Meegan 1979. The geography of industrial reorganisation. *Progress in Planning* **10**, 3.

Part III
Contradictions of growth in advanced capitalist countries

7 Introduction

RICHARD PEET

In Part II we dealt with the recent history of industrial devolution in the advanced capitalist countries. Deindustrialization has particularly occurred in industries and regions characterized by organized, economically militant labor forces which restrict corporate profit making by demanding higher wages and opposing technical and organizational changes which they find contrary to labor's interest. Deindustrialization occurs as increasingly mobile corporations relocate production to areas better suited to capital, or as corporations embedded in unfavorable environments are driven out of production by competitors located in areas with more amenable and cheaper labor forces. This impoverishes labor, destroys unions, and enhances the prospect for underconsumption crises. But surely new regions blossom as the old wither away. Does not this new growth balance regional decline? Does not the success of the new regions point the way for the survival of the old? Here, in Part III, recent industrial growth in the advanced countries is critically examined in an attempt to answer these questions.

Japan is the model most frequently presented as the working formula for industrial success. Between 1970 and 1982, when industrial production in the United States and Germany, the other most successful advanced capitalist countries, increased by 26 percent, Japan raised industrial production by 113 percent (World Bank 1985: 187). Whereas the West European industrial countries had unemployment rates averaging 11.5 percent in 1985, and the United States rate was 7.2 percent, Japan's was 2.5 percent (IMF 1985: 24). And when the United States in the middle 1980s was running a record balance of payments deficit, Japan was accumulating a record surplus. Indeed in 1985 Prime Minister Nakasone had actively to encourage Japanese consumers to buy more foreign goods. These evident signs of remarkable achievement have encouraged one of the few growth industries in the West – publishing books on the reasons for Japanese success. Here, however, we briefly examine the social basis of Japan's economic achievement, and take a more critical viewpoint of the methods used to reach the top.

The literature on Japan abounds in myths, many with a (hidden) racial basis. Take, for example, the idea of the docile, slaving Japanese worker, in particular, the tendency not to oppose the wishes of one's

corporate master. The notion that servility is an inborn, natural characteristic can be dispelled by even a cursory look at the history of
Japanese industrial relations. In common with labor in Western Europe
and North America, Japanese workers greeted the immediate postwar
years with an outburst of union activity including widespread strikes
and the taking and running of factories – what is called 'production
control' (Farley 1973, Moore 1983). Japan's Toyota Motor Company,
which has subsequently not lost a day from labor disputes for 30
years, was almost bankrupted at the time by a long, bitter strike (*Far
Eastern Economic Review* 1983: 49). In 1946 there were mass food
demonstrations, prompting a warning from General MacArthur,
Supreme Commander for the Allied Powers, that mass violence under
organized leadership was a menace to the future development of Japan
(Gayn, 1973). United States policy, which had been to encourage the
Japanese labor movement, changed dramatically in the direction of its
confinement as signs of worker radicalism emerged. Indeed General
MacArthur forbade a strike by government employees in 1948. Under
the Dodge Plan, Communists and other radicals were discharged from
their jobs while "democratization leagues" were set up to promote
capitalist values.

Even so the wave of strikes continued until finally being contained by
the middle 1950s through the development of enterprise unionism,
lifetime employment, and other devices designed to integrate the
workers and their unions into the fabric of Japanese enterprise. As one
writer concludes: "The emasculation of trade unions was one of the
preconditions for the extremely rapid increases in productivity and
labor intensity in Japanese industry that began in the late 1950s. In
particular since the late 1960s this emasculation has facilitated the efforts
of the Japan Federation of Employers' Associations to implement and
expand management systems designed to produce the utmost efficiency of labor." He continues that although permanent workers in
large corporations are well paid, the relative share of the product going
to labor in general is lower in Japan than in any other AIC (Tokunga
1983: 319–22). Savings and profits are directed by the state towards
targeted economic activities under a unique system of collaboration
between government and private enterprise – "Japan Incorporated."
Exactly this model invades the dreams of "progressive" capitalist
thinkers in the West.

We can present two kinds of argument in response. The model of
growth, as applied to the West, has an inherent contradiction. On the
one hand, success is attributed to inherent, or deeply seated Eastern
characteristics. On the other, Western capital and labor are told to
emulate immediately the Japanese example. This contradiction stems
from the inadequate (racist) theory of culture which guides this kind of
comparative thinking. But even with a more adequate theory, which

sees culture emerging out of regional historical experience, rather than innate characteristics, the idea that Japanese practices can be transferred to other countries within a decade or two is naive. For example, the particular version of Confucianism which spread to Japan, incorporating a concept of loyalty as devotion to one's lord to the point of self-sacrifice, has been in place for 1,200 years (Morishima 1982). Likewise the extremely rapid transition from feudalism to capitalism which Japan shared with Germany, and which allowed the preservation of feudal values in both, is not typical of the democratic–capitalist historical experience of the United States or the long transition from feudalism in Britain. For these, and many other reasons, it is a mistake to think that the Japanese system can be transplanted to other countries as a quick fix for their economic problems.

We should also critically examine the Japan model itself. Using a case study of Kawasaki, a steel city near Tokyo, the article by Junkerman reproduced in this part of the book (Chapter 8) points out that environmental pollution kills hundreds around the mills, unneeded workers are purged by the thousand, and a wide periphery of underpaid temporary workers and subcontractors is utilized as a buffer zone to absorb the shocks of market fluctuations (see also Galenson & Odaka 1976). Even were it attainable, would we want a system of "extremely intimate relations" between employees and employers when the latter control the destinies of the former? Does this not amount to a new kind of serfdom? Again, if it were attainable, would the Japanese model be sustainable under the prevailing conditions of economic instability in most of the world? Would a "job for life" be realistic in contemporary Britain? We conclude that the Japanese model is the product of Japanese history and allowed by the success attainable by one (unique) country in the world.

We might turn to sunrise industries at home instead of the land of the rising sun. The popular idea is that advances in science constantly generate high technology industries as the abundant employers of the future. However, even when generously defined as activities with higher than average numbers of technology-oriented workers and close to, or higher than, average research and development expenditures, high-technology industry made up only 6.2 percent of total employment in the United States in 1982. By 1995 the present high-tech employment level of 5.7 millions is expected to rise to 7.7–7.9 millions, or 6.5–6.7 percent of total employment (Riche *et al*, 1983). Two million new jobs *cannot* solve national economic problems caused by automation and the massive out migration of employment.

However, it might solve the problems of *selected regions*. An example is New England, where the traditional industries have long been in decline, thus employment in the textile and leather industries in Massachusetts declined from 200,000 in 1948 to 36,000 in 1983. Massachusetts' universities (Harvard, MIT) generated technological break-throughs which then were realized by the state's high-tech manufac-turers in a "second industrial revolution." The computer industry, for example, which is a direct outgrowth of research conducted in Cam-bridge, Massachusetts, has proven vital to the development of "Amer-ica's high-technology region" along Route 128 which surrounds the city of Boston (Browne & Hekman 1981, Kuhn 1982). Presumably as a result of high technology manufacturing Massachusetts' unem-ployment rate was the lowest of any major industrial state in the middle 1980s. If Massachusetts can make it, why not us? ask a thousand economic development agencies from Sunderland to San Diego.

Massachusetts is *the* outstanding example of an old industrial region which has been able to retain part of the high-tech manufacturing generated by its research institutions instead of losing all these pro-duction activities to cheap labor regions. But as shown by Table 7.1 the growth of the two largest high-tech manufacturing industries, elec-tronics and instruments, generated only 42,000 manufacturing jobs in the state in the period 1960 to 1983. By comparison, one of the state's traditional industries (nonelectrical machinery) added 31,000 jobs in the same period. Meanwhile 72,000 jobs were lost in the other big tradi-tional industries (textiles and leather), and total manufacturing employ-ment declined by about the same number. Similarly, a study of the M4 Corridor, Britain's "Sunbelt" between London and Bristol, concludes that the effect on manufacturing employment has been quite limited, not even enough to make up for losses by the traditional industries of the County of Berkshire (Breheny *et al.* 1985). We conclude that high-tech does *not* generate large numbers of jobs in the manufacturing sector and *cannot* be relied on to save the manufacturing base even in the most successful of the restructured old industrial regions.

But what of the *new* industrial regions within the advanced capitalist countries? Saxenian has looked at the Silicon Valley

Table 7.1 Employment in manufacturing in Massachusetts, 1948–83.

Industry	Employment in thousands			
	1948	1960	1970	1983
textile mill products	124.9	48.8	32.8	20.1
leather and leather products	75.1	59.1	34.4	15.9
machinery, except electrical	77.7	69.2	68.7	100.0
electric and electronic equipment	60.4	102.7	93.2	111.3
instruments and related products	21.0	23.8	39.2	56.8
all manufacturing	732.6	698.0	648.2	624.3

Source: United States Bureau of Labor Statistics (1984).

in the San Francisco Bay area of California, an area which boomed due to the growth of 700 electronics-related companies (Saxenian 1985). She argues that, though generating rapid growth, the semiconductor industry also transformed the local class structure and the pattern of urban development in such a way as to cause breakdowns in the housing and transportation systems, along with environmental problems. More significantly, urban problems have increased costs of production in the region, triggering the decentralization of manufacturing out of the area, leaving it as a site for corporate headquarters, high-level research, and prototype production activities (Saxenian 1983). There is little evidence here that high technology generates large amounts of *permanent* manufacturing employment in the immediate vicinity of research institutions.

Soja, Morales, and Wolff in Chapter 9 show that Los Angeles has been outstandingly successful in restructuring its industrial base. High technology industries, particularly aerospace and electronics, are expanding rapidly, due in no small measure to defense and military contracts from the United States government, and now make up more than a quarter of the region's manufacturing employment. Many of these jobs are located in the science-based "outer cities" of the metropolitan area, the kind of place called "technopolis" in Japan. Here the work force is segmented into high and low skills, with the latter vulnerable to replacement or loss of jobs due to industrial relocation. Unionization rates are also significantly lower in places like Orange County, where the union movement collapsed in the 1970s. However, closely associated with the rise of high-tech industries is an accelerating decline in the older (and unionized) industries like rubber and steel. A massive influx of immigrant labor is tied to the rapid expansion of the garment and apparel industries paying minimum or subminimum wages and providing sweat-shop conditions. Los Angeles combines elements of Sunbelt expansion, Detroit-like decline, and free trade zone superexploitation. It symbolizes the process of industrial restructuring, displaying its advantages (industrial growth) but also its disadvantages (cheap labor, decline of unions). Even in Los Angeles, arguably the world's most successful city, industrial growth is contradictory.

References

Breheny, M., P. Cheshire & R. Langridge 1985. The anatomy of job creation? Industrial change in Britain's M4 Corridor. In *Silicon landscapes*, P. Hall and A. Markusen (eds), 118–330. Boston: Allen & Unwin.

Browne, L. and J. S. Hekman 1981. New England's economy in the 1980s, *New England Economic Review*, January and February 5–16.

Far Eastern Economic Review 1983. Not a day lost by dispute in 30 years. December 22, 47.

Farley, M. 1973. Union techniques: production control. In *Postwar Japan*, J. Livingston, J. Moore and F. Oldfather (eds), 143–5. New York: Random House.

Galenson, W. and K. Odaka 1976. The Japanese labor market. In *Asia's new giant*, H. Patrick and H. Rosovsky (eds), 587–671. Washington DC: The Brookings Institution.

Gayn, M. 1973. Food demonstrations and MacArthur's warning. In *Postwar Japan*, J. Livingston, J. Moore and F. Oldfather (eds), 145–9. New York: Random House.

IMF (International Monetary Fund) 1985. *IMF Survey*, January 21.

Kuhn, S. 1982. *Computer manufacturing in New England*. Cambridge: Joint Center for Urban Studies of MIT and Harvard University.

Moore, J. 1983. *Japanese workers and the struggle for power 1945–47*. Madison: University of Wisconsin Press.

Morishima, M. 1982. *Why has Japan succeeded?* Cambridge: Cambridge University Press.

Riche, R. W., D. E. Hecker and J. V. Burgan 1983. High technology today and tomorrow: a small slice of the employment pie. *Monthly Labor Review* **106**(11), 50–8.

Saxenian, A. 1983. The urban contradictions of Silicon Valley: regional growth and the restructuring of the semiconductor industry. *International Journal of Urban and Regional Research* **7**(2), 237–62.

Saxenian, A. 1985. The genesis of Silicon Valley. In *Silicon landscapes*, P. Hall and A. Markusen (eds), 20–4. Boston: Allen & Unwin.

Tokunaga, S. 1983. A Marxist interpretation of Japanese industrial relations, with special reference to large private enterprises. In *Contemporary industrial relations in Japan*, Madison: University of Wisconsin Press.

United States Bureau of Labor Statistics 1984. *Employment, hours and earnings, states and areas, 1939–82* (Bulletin 1370–17) and *1980–83* (Bulletin 1370–18). Washington, D.C.: Superintendent of Documents.

World Bank 1985. *World development report, 1985*. New York: Oxford University Press.

8 Blue-sky management: the Kawasaki story[*]

JOHN JUNKERMAN

They call it "the clean, green steelworks by the sea . . . A new steel mill for the new era." Like most Japanese PR, the tags are a bit too cute and claim too much. But Nippon Kokan's new steelworks, built on the artificial island of Ohgishima in Tokyo Bay, is indeed impressive.

Two mountains were leveled and carted across the bay to form the island, which is connected to the city of Kawasaki by an underwater tunnel. The mill erected there may be the most highly automated, efficient, and pollution-free in the world. Completed in 1979, it cost $5 billion and took a decade to build.

Ore carriers unload raw iron ore and coal at berths on the north side of the island. Automatic conveyors feed the raw material into two massive blast furnaces, operated by technicians at computer terminals in an adjoining building. Self-driven slabs of steel weave their way through pipe and strip mills, emerging into automated cooling yards at the south end of the island, where ships wait to haul the finished steel to Siberian gas fields and North Sea drilling platforms.

American steel executives who visit Ohgishima describe it as a technological dream, something they knew was theoretically possible but is far beyond their means. In contrast to the infernal pit that one associates with steel making, the mill floor in Kawasaki is cool and lonely. Operators sit two stories above in air-conditioned control booths, as glowing, orange planks of steel crash through roller presses, sparks flying. There is scarcely a soul in evidence to read the billboards that exhort, "Put your heart into each slab of steel!"

An air of total rationality and industrial harmony surrounds the Ohgishima works and Nippon Kokan (NKK), the corporation that operates it. An apt symbol, perhaps, are the shimmering carp that swim in ponds of recycled wastewater on the grounds of the mill.

NKK's labor–management relations mirror the tidiness of the mill's operation. The union speaks proudly of close understanding and trust.

* Reprinted with permission from *Working Papers Magazine* (Summer, 1983) 28–36. © Trusteeship Institute Inc.

Charts in the control rooms record the weekly output of quality-control circles, which contribute over 100,000 efficiency suggestions per year. The company basketball team competes in national tournaments, and wins. Vacations are spent at corporate resort hotels. And, of course, NKK employees have lifetime jobs.

It is somewhat startling, then, to emerge from the ordered environment of Ohgishima into the city of Kawasaki. The city to which the steelworks is appended reminds one of nothing as much as a wrecking yard. It is crowded with a chaotic array of small factories and scrap yards, all coated with the rich golden brown of rusting iron dust.

Iron scrap and forged steel are everywhere, heaped in narrow alleys and stacked between rows of weathered frame houses. The ground is soaked with oil and matted with the metal shavings of machine shops.

Kawasaki is one of the oldest industrial cities in Japan. For over 70 years, it has been home base for NKK. The company arrived on the scene when the eastern district of the city was still a salt marsh stretching into the bay. The working-class community of East Kawasaki literally settled in the shadow of Kokan's furnaces.

NKK has been the prime employer for decades, providing as many as 25,000 jobs directly and an equal number through its network of subcontractors. Hundreds of small businesses live off the spillover from Ohgishima. "Throw a stone around here, and you're bound to hit something connected to Kokan," I was told by a high school student who lives in Sakuramoto, a neighborhood just outside the gates to the steel mill. "If it weren't for Kokan, we couldn't live."

But for those on the periphery of the steel giant "living" is not what we have come to expect of the Japanese system. There are no company resorts, no volleyball courts, no color TVs, sometimes not even a promise of work in the morning. It is a world of uncertainty and sacrifice, and without it NKK's gem on the bay would not shine with efficiency.

Nippon Kokan is the second largest steelmaker in Japan, the leader in some fields of speciality steel and seamless pipe but still the "Avis" of the industry. Steel is central to any industrial economy; or as the president of Japan Steel, the No. 1 in the industry, would have it, "Steel is the state." In Japan, it is also the foundation of auto, electronics, and shipbuilding, spheres that the Asian wonder has come to dominate in the past two decades.

Given its place in the economy, and its accessibility – Kawasaki is just 15 minutes by express from Tokyo station – NKK was a natural starting point for a sojourn into the inner workings of the economic miracle. It proved a rich case to study, and, as it happens, of more than academic interest for the United States steel industry. Last July the corporation announced it had begun negotiations to buy a Detroit steel mill from the Ford Motor Company.

The proposed takeover would have been the largest ever by a Japanese corporation, but ten months later the deal fell through. Ford was reportedly unable to gain the concessions from the United Auto Workers that were a precondition to the sale. Battered though it is, Detroit is apparently not yet ready to embrace the Japanese "spirit."

The episode is intriguing. The vaunted harmony between labor and management on the other side of the Pacific has engendered the admiration and envy of American managers. There is little doubt that the Japanese system works, but why does it work in Kawasaki and run aground in Detroit? The question is one of the hallmarks of this decade.

The most common assertion of proponents of the Japanese model is that business, in pursuit of long-term growth and stable markets, has settled into a mode of operation that satisfies both profit goals and human needs. Thus, we are told, workers and managers are part of a "community of shared fate," where common interests override all sources of conflict.

A well-tuned harmony indeed prevails at NKK's mother mill in Kawasaki, but Ohgishima, despite its artificial rationality, has its roots in the shabby neighborhoods back on the mainland. The island and the city are complementary parts of a larger whole, and we cannot understand one without examining the other. The story of NKK is also the history of industrialization of the Kawasaki area. And it is a history of industrial relations that includes personnel relations at the mill, a network of subcontractors who service the company, and the once-militant steelworkers union.

The city of Kawasaki occupies an oblong of land between Tokyo and Yokohama on the Pacific coast. It follows the Tama River from the foothills of Mount Fuji to Tokyo Bay. In feudal times, farms on the fertile river delta supplied rice and vegetables to the neighboring cities, and villagers supplemented their livelihood with part-time fishing. The town also served as a way-station on the famed Tokaido roadway, where inns and brothels provided the nucleus for a thriving, if somewhat seedy, commercial district. The city retains this flavor today: it is famous for its concentration of Turkish baths, Japan's version of massage parlor sleaze.

Cottage industry developed early along the waterfront, and by the mid-19th century the area was a major site of salt and sugar processing and rice-paper manufacture. The leisurely pace of industrialization accelerated abruptly when Japan began its rapid drive to modern statehood in the 1870s. The city's history over the next century provides a capsule version of the nation's industrial development.

The first ironworks was established early in the Meiji period (1868–1912), followed by an electric power plant in 1890 and the first railroad at the turn of the century. The Toshiba electronics company built a factory in 1909, and Nippon Kokan began work on its first steel mill three years later. Farmland quickly gave way to factories, until industrial developers were forced to begin reclaiming the salt marsh to continue their expansion.

By 1925, some 100 factories occupied the East Kawasaki industrial belt; their number swelled by 1940 to 400, centered on steel, machine manufacturing, and electronics. Employees for these companies migrated in a steady stream from the countryside, bringing the city's population to 140,000 in 1933. To meet the growing labor shortage, workers were also shipped in from Japan's colony in Korea during the 1930s and 1940s. They settled in a ghetto called Sakuramoto, just outside the NKK complex, and performed heavy labor at the furnaces.

Thus Kawasaki came to be dominated by industry. The spirit of the times was reflected in the Sakuramoto grade school song. Written in 1934, the song is still in use: a Korean girl, giggling shyly, sang the refrain for me:

> The furnace breathes fire, the anvil rings.
> When we've grown, we'll work for the nation.
> Our town produces, our town moves.
> Our school: Sakuramoto!

World War II flattened Kawasaki, but it soon rose anew, helped along by United States military contracts for Korean War supplies. The government's early reconstruction policy focused on steel, and NKK flourished. The company rebuilt seven blast furnaces and poured steel around the clock.

Subsequent five-year reindustrialization plans nurtured shipbuilding, the auto industry, and electronics, all of which established bases on the Kawasaki shore. The government pursued a conscious policy of industrial concentration, drawing surplus labor from the countryside to factories on the southern coast, where raw materials could be delivered, processed, and exported with a minimum of transportation. Kawasaki was the prototype. The landfill continued to expand, and 1959 saw the opening of the nation's first petrochemical complex.

The city's population tripled between 1950 and 1970, passing one million in 1973. By then, 5,000 establishments were in operation, crammed into the narrow coastal zone. In the relentless drive for industrial growth, little attention was paid to pollution control; one source estimates that the steel industry saved 30 percent on its initial investment by ignoring what it discharged from its smokestacks. Meanwhile, in areas of tight concentration, like Kawasaki, the air turned gray with ash and metal dust blown from the blast furnaces: poisonous fumes from the chemical refineries made it death to breathe.

By the mid-1960s, East Kawasaki was no longer suitable for human habitation. Those who could afford to move retreated to the foothills and neighboring suburbs, leaving an underclass of Koreans, day laborers, the elderly poor, and newly arrived migrants to populate the industrial zone. These marginal citizens became the first victims of "Kawasaki asthma," a debilitating emphysema caused by the fouled air.

Despite the seriousness of the environmental problem, opposition was slow to develop. Not only was there a popular consensus in support of growth, but the corporations made the most of their rôle as suppliers of jobs and affluence. "Nipon Kokan was god," an unshaven man in his fifties told me one day. He was sitting on a stool outside his scrap metal yard, drinking sake at midday. "Nobody would speak against them. I came here in 1962 from the south. My cousin said I should come." He paused. "Sure, it was filthy, but I was glad to have work."

It was only in the early 1970s, when the number of victims rose dramatically and antipollution movements emerged across Japan, that countermeasures began to be taken. By 1975, over 2,500 Kawasaki asthma victims had been officially certified and 128 had died. Vociferous demonstrations were mounted outside the gates of NKK and a score of other major polluters, and the Kawasaki tragedy became a national disgrace.

In response, a ban was placed on further industrial construction in the city, and the factories were ordered to clean up. The most dramatic measure was taken by NKK: the construction of the "clean, green" Ohgishima steelworks. About $1 billion was invested at the new works in pollution control, ranging from state-of-the-art desulfurization facilities to tire baths to wash dust from trucks leaving the island.

An apparent change in attitude also took place. NKK now shows an admirable civic-mindedness toward the surrounding community. A monthly newspaper, the *Common Circle*, is published for the citizens of the Sakuramoto area. The corporation's giant swimming pool is open to neighborhood kids during the sultry summers. The track field hosts a boisterous community meet every spring.

Blue skies have returned to Kawasaki, and NKK's image has rebounded. Unfortunately, the suffocation and death continues. The number of certified pollution victims reached 4,500 in 1982, and fatalities stood at 575 last June. A new death is recorded every five days, primarily among those with little resistance – the elderly and children. The air has been cleansed of sulfur and ash, but it still contains poisonous nitrogen oxide, much of it from the furnaces on Ohgishima. The gas is invisible, but deadly.

The transformation of steel production at NKK's Kawasaki works could not have been accomplished without parallel efforts on the mill floor. This reform effort began shortly after the war and took hold only gradually, but it was firmly in place by the time NKK shifted production to the ultramodern Ohgishima complex. The process included a number of characteristic features. Union leadership was consulted prior to the beginning of construction on the new mill, and agreement was reached on ground rules for the transition. NKK committed itself to heavy retraining of workers on the new system, and the union won assurances that no one would be forcibly laid off.

As a result, the move to the island was accomplished with a minimum of friction. "The workers were highly motivated to make the new plant work," reported NKK's labor relations director. "Many worked long overtime to master the system, learned English in their own time, and studied computer manuals."

The transition was not, however, painless: NKK shed 10,000 employees when it brought in the computers. The union's rôle, according to general secretary Hachiro Yamagishi, "was to persuade the membership to accept the pain of rationalization to ensure the future base of the company and their employment."

Some 4,000 of the younger displaced workers moved halfway across Japan to a newly opened NKK mill (the largest in the world) near Hiroshima. The remainder, mostly older workers, took the "golden handshake" and left. Some found work with NKK's subcontractors. Others ended up taking tolls on the nearby superhighway.

This admirable cooperative spirit, an apparent manifestation of Japanese harmony, is actually the product of a conscious, long-term management strategy to defuse volatile and strife-ridden relationships on the mill floor. In the first 20 years after World War II, NKK experienced annual wage strikes, frequent wildcats over manning levels and safety measures, and bitterly adversarial confrontations over management efforts to rationalize production. The move from conflict to cooperation was brought about by a strategy called, ironically, "blue-sky management." The components of the strategy were adapted from the American steel industry and skillfully utilized to buttress managerial authority.

The search for an effective approach to managing began in the chaos of the early postwar period. It was a time of confusion and malaise for mill supervisors, recalled NKK education director Kenji Okuda, one of the architects of the new system. Freed from the prewar constraints of Japanese fascism, the labor movement had grown explosively and exercised its new voice to challenge management at every turn. The Occupation-inspired democratization had stripped management of its absolute authority and granted workers unprecedented rights to organize, bargain, and strike.

In 1950, NKK underwent its first "Americanization." The Labor Ministry introduced the company to TWI (Training Within Industry), a management program developed in American munitions factories during the war. "It provided a substitute for the total control managers enjoyed before 1945," Okuda recalled. TWI gave the corporation a model of employee education and job design that was heavily seasoned with the psychological principles of the human relations school of organizational behavior. It was to provide the foundation for NKK's "people-oriented" philosophy of management.

To implement the new system, however, NKK had to tangle with the traditional organization of the mill floor. Since the early history of the steel industry in Japan, supervision of the work force had been the responsibility of the *oyakata* (roughly equivalent to a job-boss). The *oyakata* recruited his own work team, served as gang leader, and also functioned as a master craftsman who provided apprenticeship to the steelworker. The first loyalty of many workers was to their *oyakata*, which placed them outside the grasp of the company. In the early postwar period, many *oyakata* also became leaders in the union.

The path around this bottleneck was discovered by a study group that NKK dispatched to the United States in 1955. They returned with two key souvenirs: the foreman system and a job progression ladder. Both were adopted, with key modifications that increased their effectiveness as mechanisms of control and motivation.

Beginning the following year, the foreman gradually replaced the *oyakata* over the period of a decade. He absorbed the latter's rôle as team leader, but now he was seen as the first rank of "line management" (the staff–line corporate model, common in the United States, was also adopted in Japan at this time). He is responsible for both the supervision of labor and the technical aspects of production. The foreman also evaluates workers for wage increases, though, in sharp contrast to American practice, he remains a member of the union. He is thus the critical link in the chain of authority, the border straddler between management and worker, in place of the barrier the *oyakata* represented.

The training rôle once filled by the *oyakata* was taken over by NKK's education department. The company was expanding, hiring each spring a flood of high school graduates with good technical backgrounds. At the same time, automation had reduced the skill requirements of the job, so the company could provide the necessary training in less than a year.

The changes eliminated the need for an apprenticeship, but they also undermined the rationale behind the traditional age-based wage system. Young workers grew increasingly discontented with the gap between their wages and the pay of older workers, since their technical training gave them a level of competence approaching that of their elders. In response, the traditional pay system was modified to reflect education and skill levels.

At the same time, NKK instituted a job progression ladder that specified the requirements for promotion from general laborer through team leader to foreman, and, theoretically, on to white-collar management. It was the open door to opportunity that the company called "blue-sky management." At least on the surface, it represented a substantial departure from the rigid status distinctions of the past.

"It brought a revolution in consciousness," observed Satoshi Yamakawa, a mill worker who was hired in 1956 at age 15. "The promotion system was proof that the company recognized skill and that you could become a manager if you worked hard enough." Naturally, very few high school graduates pass the white-collar examination; it takes about 30 years to get that far. "You end up polishing the barriers so long you can see your face reflected." Yamakawa commented. "But without this belief in the possibility of advance, the labor–management system would not work."

NKK introduced one significant modification into the job ladder it borrowed from American industry. Each job grade was subdivided into as many as ninety subgrades; advance through the subgrades is awarded by an annual performance evaluation. Each worker ends up with a different base pay, in contrast to the "equal pay for equal work" principle of American industry. This setup provides a strong incentive for workers to comply with the authority of management; dissidents soon find their annual pay lagging thousands of dollars behind their peers.

Makoto Kumazawa, a critical academic, argues in a recent analysis of NKK that the corporation's structural reforms succeeded in fragmenting the shop-floor organization into a collection of atomized workers, who now compete against one another for wages and promotions. The elimination of the *oyakata*, the deskilling of the mill work, and the new wage structure undermined the independent power base from which the union had challenged management. By 1963, Kumazawa reports, workers identified directly with the enterprise and there was a dramatic drop in support for the union.

During this same period, Nippon Kokan introduced quality control (QC) circles into the Kawasaki mill. "The circles," mill worker Yamakawa observed, "deal with matters that used to be the union's concern, such as dangerous conditions in the mill. But the circle is led by a manager. The activities of the QC circle and the weakness of the union are actually the same thing," he suggested.

"For some people, QC provides an opportunity for self-realization," Yamakawa continued. Fostering this sense of personal growth through work is perhaps the primary goal of the circles. With the average education of mill workers rising in recent years, the company is concerned that employees will become bored and frustrated with their increasingly routine and automated jobs.

The NKK hopes for QC as a creative outlet are reflected in the company's QC credo, which reads in part: "Take pride in turning a new page of history with your hands. Make something worthy of your life in the shop. . . . You are not merely a gear in a big organization, but a hero."

Despite the weariness of the metaphor, NKK officials insist that the company operates as a family. It is a tightly structured family, and its relationships are spelled out in a labor agreement that runs to 375 pages and weighs a pound. It reads like a code of civil procedure, specifying lines of promotion, spheres of authority, and the rights and responsibilities attached to each rank within the company.

But if NKK operates as a hierarchically structured state, the boundary between citizen and alien is clearly drawn. At the Kawasaki works, for example, there are about 8,500 NKK employees (*seishain*; roughly, "official employees"). Working side by side with them are over 5,000 second-class subcontract workers. They are employees of about 40 companies, ranging in size from a 900-employee warehousing firm down to a 40-employee slag processing company.

The use of subcontract employment is widespread in Japanese industry and has a long history. Its importance in steel has grown in recent years to the extent that nearly half of the workers at most major steelworks are outside employees. The largest subcontractors are designated "associated enterprises" and are fully integrated into the operations of the primary employer. As one descends the hierarchy of subcontractors, wages, job security, working conditions, and status fall. At the bottom of the ladder, older workers toil at menial and dangerous tasks for about half the pay of top-class employees.

The stratified labor market performs a number of functions. Perhaps most important, it provides a vehicle for adjusting employment during downturns in the business cycle: since jobs are guaranteed for "official employees," it is the outside contract workers who are cut when demand slackens. Secondly, by separating off dead-end, unrewarding jobs from the main work force, the system isolates dissent, often among unorganized workers. A third function of the hierarchy is to foster competititon between the various ranks and to reinforce the elite consciousness of the workers on the top of the heap.

Subcontract employment in the steel industry is an outgrowth of the traditional use of temporary workers to perform many of the more disagreeable tasks in the mills. In the 1930s, Japan Steel reportedly had 70 percent of its employees on temporary status. In time, as the mills grew, small companies began to develop whose specific purpose was procuring temporary workers. These companies proliferated, often competing against similar small firms to win business from the primary employer.

Early in the postwar period, however, these temporary workers were granted the right to organize and they began to press demands on their primary employers. To limit these claims, companies began to draw a formal distinction between "official employees" and subcontract workers. The temporary employees thus became subcontract employees who were not guaranteed job rights or access to the job progression structure. The subcontract system was formalized further when changes in labor laws made it illegal for a company to engage exclusively in the procuring of labor; the subcontractors were required to own the equipment their employees operated. The response of the steel majors was to transform the maze of subcontractors into a smaller number of "associated enterprises," often with capital investment by the primary employer.

Despite its formalization, the subcontracting network remains labyrinthine. "We have a hard time grasping the conditions of subcontractors," conceded one NKK union staffer. "There are so many, and there are so many layers." Many subcontractors employ subcontractors of their own. There are as many as four tiers of employment in some cases.

At Kokan's main subcontractors, wages average 70 to 80 percent of the primary company levels, even taking into account the fact that subcontract workers put in an average of 10 percent more hours of overtime. The union staffer estimated that 250,000 of Japan's half million steelworkers are subcontract employees; of these, only some 50,000 have been organized.

The largest impediment to organizing the lower-ranked workers is the leverage exercised by the parent company. "If the subcontract workers organize and win higher wages," a union organizer told me, "they face the threat of being cut off by Kokan. It has happened often enough that they resist joining the union."

But the steelworkers union itself has a contradictory posture toward the subcontractors. Since its members are overwhelmingly from the elite companies, the union has a vested interest in maintaining the privileged status of the majors.

"We operate under a triple handicap," one unionized subcontract worker told me. "We have to contend with the management of the parent company, the management of the subcontractor, and finally the union from the parent company." The parent union screens wage demands from the subcontract union before they are submitted to negotiations; demands that would disrupt the hierarchy are not allowed.

The subcontract system, with its inequalities of status, power, and compensation, that undergirds the operations of Nippon Kokan and the other steel majors is replicated outside the large companies. For example, the Japan Casting Company, a NKK subsidiary, has about 1,100 employees. Ten percent of them work for thirteen subcontractors employed by the firm. Japan Casting also has a subsidiary, Keihin Machines, with about 70 employees; a dozen of these workers are employed by a couple of subcontract firms.

Ironically, it is at the level of the sub-subsidiary that a family atmosphere is actually in evidence. Personal relationships function according to principles of mutual obligation and trust. The boss may still hand out paychecks on Saturday afternoon and thank each worker for the week's effort. At Keihin Machines, workers often continue working, at reduced pay, for years after formal retirement: the oldest worker is 71. Some craft pride is maintained by these workers, whose jobs are often highly specialized. Other workers at this level told me they preferred to work for the small companies, despite low wages, because they enjoyed less pressure and greater freedom on the job.

At some of the small companies, however, working conditions are atrocious. The workers responsible for marking NKK's seamless pipe, I was told, breathe dangerous lacquer fumes all day long. Those who clean the blast furnaces when they are down for maintenance breathe dust-laden air that coats the lungs. These firms, at the very bottom of the system, employ people who have nowhere else to turn.

It is commonly argued that the dual structure of Japanese employment is a carryover from early industrial times that is likely to disappear with continuing modernization. Under conditions of labor shortage that obtained in the high growth period, the wage gap between large and small firms narrowed considerably, a development that was thought to signal the end of the duality. But the gap has widened again since the mid-1970s, especially in the last few years. There are still a vast number of small and tiny enterprises: in Kawasaki in 1980, 90 percent of the establishments employed fewer than 30 workers. Nationwide, 35 percent of all workers are in such small enterprises; another 30 percent work for firms with fewer than 500 employees.

Dual labor markets exist in most industrialized countries, but the Japanese system is probably unique in the coherence and rigidity of its stratification. Once tracked into a smaller company, it is virtually impossible to gain entry into an elite firm. Nor can one move from one elite firm to another; in most cases a change of employer requires one drop down in the hierarchy.

Several of the people I interviewed drew an analogy between the gradations of status in Japanese corporations and the official ranking system for citizens of feudal Japan. The feudal shoguns enforced a system of four ranks, called *shi-nō-kō-s'hō*, referring to the samurai–farmer–artisan–merchant order of status in the society. The fact that Japan was a late industrializer and that its feudal past is more recent than in any other industrialized country undoubtedly did provide fertile ground for the emergence of hierarchical authority relationships in the twentieth century. Indeed, NKK education director Okuda traces the current system to the Confucian premise that "management leaders are moral people."

Others argue that in Japan's short modern history, industrial workers did not crystallize into a class that was conscious of interests distinct from the employer class. The Japanese economy instead sped through the stages of development experienced in the West and quickly entered the post industrial world of fuzzy class lines. Workers came into industry from the countryside with their sights set on upward mobility, and there has been sufficient opportunity to keep these hopes alive, the theory goes. As a result, there is little support for efforts to remedy the inequities of the dual labor market. An NKK unionist, acknowledging that even in industrial Kawasaki there is little sense of a working-class culture, sighed and commented, "The dual structure of the economy has entered people's consciousness."

"The theory of economic orderliness" is perhaps the clearest summation of the character of the Japanese system. The phrase is, tellingly, not the concoction of management but of the Japanese steelworkers union, and it gives an indication of how far the union has come in embracing the status quo. Economic orderliness is used to describe the union's approach to wage bargaining, but the term can be applied with equal aptness to the structure of authority within the enterprise and the hierarchy of subcontracting that surrounds it. It contains an implicit acknowledgment of the stratification of status and power among the various classes of worker.

The steelworkers union was not always so willing to endorse the established order. Between the end of World War II and 1960, the union and much of the labor movement was directed by an explicitly class-conscious leadership. This period was characterized by intense conflict and the process that molded the labor movement into a cooperative ally of management was crucial to the consolidation of the Japanese system.

Because Japanese unions are organized on an enterprise rather than industry-wide basis, there has always been a tension between enterprise-specific interests and the broader collective interests of the labor movement. In an attempt to overcome the limitations of the enterprise union, the early leftist leadership tended to emphasize political issues: opposition to the business-dominated government, challenges to Japan's ties with American foreign policy, demands for social welfare and full employment. There was always, however, a significant right wing in the movement that is committed to bread-and-butter trade unionism.

In the early years, the Left held the balance of power. And the Left developed the innovative Shunto ("spring struggle"), an annual wave of strikes that was intended to address political and economic issues simultaneously. Shunto involves coordinated, national strikes in support of a platform of political issues and a target wage demand. A prosperous industry is usually chosen to set the national wage pattern, and the steel industry became a key battleground soon after the Shunto strategy was first attempted in 1955.

The left wing of the union, centered at NKK, held a loose grip on power during most of the 1950s and led strikes nearly every year, often in support of unions under attack in other parts of the country in addition to its own demands. Then in 1957, when steel demand fell sharply, the manufacturers joined together and refused to offer any wage increase at all. "It was unprecedented in Japanese labor relations," recalled Masaharu Konda, who directed NKK's labor division at the time. The union responded with a series of eleven 48-hour strikes, "but we turned them back," Konda relates.

The following year, the union bided its time, building up a strike fund for the coming battle. In 1959, NKK adopted a novel strategy, presenting a first and final offer – a considerable wage increase, which they declared was what they could afford to pay, and no more. It took a 49-day strike to convince the union they were serious, but when the strike was over, the offer had not changed. A pattern had been set: "one answer bargaining," they call it, and it is practiced today. The union has never since mounted a unified strike; there has not been a strike at NKK since 1963.

The year after the strike, the right wing took control of the steel-workers union. They were led by Yoshiji Miyata, originally from Yawata Steel in southern Japan and still one of the most prominent right-wing labor leaders in the country. Tactics began to change immediately. Wage bargaining, in particular, became a process of consultation, in which the corporations would explain their financial situation to the union, allow the union to make a case, then come up with a single offer. Trust and understanding were said to attend the process, but in any case there was no strike threat.

At NKK as well, the leftist leadership was deposed. From the perspective of the current "trade unionist" leader, the right's victory was a repudiation of the struggle tactics of the left. "The membership began to wonder if the sacrifices of the strikes were worth it. The philosophy began to develop in the union that we should think of the union's interests, not the class interests," said general secretary Hachiro Yamagishi.

Meanwhile, the national leadership of the labor movement suffered a serious political setback in 1960 when the United States–Japan Security Treaty was extended. With the economy booming, politics took a back seat. During the extended period of rapid growth, the labor movement turned its attention toward catching up with the living standards of the West, and strikes became ritualized.

By 1965, the steelworkers' wage settlement had become permanently established as the pattern by which all other bargaining was conducted. The process soon took the shape of an informal national incomes policy, which awards wage increases on the basis of increases in productivity with allowances for inflation. There is little suspense in the negotiations: their outcome can be predicted weeks in advance.

Since the oil crisis of 1973 brought an end to the rapid growth era, the union has developed its "theory of economic orderliness" to guide its bargaining. The theory points out that steel is the basis for Japan's central industries, including auto, electronics, and shipbuilding. If labor costs push up the price of steel, all industries will suffer and Japanese exports will lose their competitive edge. Thus, moderation is in order, especially during a time of economic crisis.

This is a philosophy management would be glad to call its own. And it is not ashamed to say so. In March 1981, Yoshishiro Inayama (former chairman of Japan Steel, now head of the Federation of Economic Organizations, Japan's paramount business organization) spoke at a union banquet at a posh hotel in Tokyo. "Steel labor and management are absolutely unified," he told the gathering of dignitaries from business, government, and labor. "This has been the foundation for Japanese prosperity."

He continued even more effusively. "Steel's one-answer bargaining is great, because it prevents inflation. It makes me feel like I am a member of the union."

Discounting a bit for hyperbole, this is still a pretty remarkable statement by the leading spokesperson for the business world. Inayama completed his paean to the union by declaring, "People could come from all over the world to copy it, but we wouldn't be able to teach labor–management relations like those in the steel industry."

Is this the implication of NKK's unsuccessful takeover bid in Detroit, that "adversarial" Americans are constitutionally incapable of Japanese-style cooperation? I don't think so. We have seen how Japanese steel-makers created their brand of industrial harmony through a conscious program that included protracted battles with labor, the strategic leverage provided by the dual economy, and the introduction of personnel policies borrowed from American industry. It took the better part of 20 years for the new relationships to mature. Similar raw materials are available to Japanese employers in the United States; despite the setback in Detroit, we should not be surprised to encounter "blue-sky management" on our shores in the years to come.

9 Industrial restructuring: an analysis of social and spatial change in Los Angeles*

EDWARD SOJA, REBECCA MORALES, and GOETZ WOLFF

[handwritten annotations: TYPICAL OF BOOK / we know what's happening kind sometimes / meaty]

> I should be very much pleased if you could find me something good (meaty) on economic conditions in *California*. . . . California is very important for me because nowhere else has the upheaval most shamelessly caused by capitalist centralization taken place with such speed.
>
> Letter from Karl Marx to Friedrich Sorge, 1880

The area circumscribed by a 60 mile radius from downtown Los Angeles encompassing the built-up area of five counties (Los Angeles, Orange, San Bernardino, Riverside, and Ventura) is one of the largest industrial metropolises in the world. Moreover, since the late 1960s, it has experienced a concentration of industrial production, employment growth, and international corporate finance that may be unparalleled in any advanced industrial country. Between 1970 and 1980, when the entire United States had a net addition of less than a million manufacturing jobs, the Los Angeles region added 225,800 (while New York lost 329,800). In the same decade, total population grew by 1,300,000, the number of nonagricultural wage and salary workers increased by 1,315,000, and an extraordinary office-building boom marked the emergence of Los Angeles as a global city of corporate headquarters, financial management, and international trade (Security Pacific National Bank 1981a).

Sustaining this rapid centralization of industrial activity, financial control, and corporate wealth has been a series of structural changes which have significantly modified the social and economic geography of the region. A comprehensive process of *urban restructuring* has been

* Edited version of Soja, E., R. Morales & G. Wolff 1983, Restructuring: an analysis of social and spatial change in Los Angeles. *Economic Geography*, **59**(2), 195–230, reprinted by permission of the authors and editor.

[handwritten annotation: Is tristre might armed other.]

taking place since the late 1960s, affecting the organization of the labor process and the composition of the work force, the location of industry and the sectoral distribution of employment, the organization of the working class and the patterns of class conflict. These changes have juxtaposed substantial aggregate economic growth and expanding concentrations of affluence against extensive job layoffs and plant closures, deepening poverty and unemployment, the reemergence of industrial sweatshops reminiscent of the 19th century, the intensification of ethnic and racial segregation, and increasing rates of urban violence and homelessness.[1]

In many ways, the Los Angeles region appears paradoxically to combine the contrasting dynamics of both "Sunbelt" and "Frostbelt" cities, adding to this mix many of the features of intensified industrialization characteristic of Third World export processing zones. This has created a peculiar composite metropolis that resembles an articulated assemblage of many different patterns of change affecting major cities in the United States and elsewhere in the world – a Houston, a Detroit, a Lower Manhattan, and a Singapore amalgamated in one urban region.

Making sense, both theoretically and politically, of this distinctive combination of expansionary growth and urban social and spatial restructuring requires an interpretive perspective which can set the particular local experience into a broader context. What initially may appear as paradoxical or unique within the Los Angeles region can be more appropriately understood as a particular concatenation of several different patterns of social and spatial restructuring identifiable within the larger economic system. To demonstrate this relationship, we present a detailed empirical examination of the effects of urban restructuring in Los Angeles since the late 1960s.

Restructuring in the Los Angeles urban region

Los Angeles never experienced the intensive geographic centralization of production that characterized the 19th century *Industrial Capitalist City* and shaped the early expansion of most large American cities east of the Rockies. Although founded in 1781, the city of Los Angeles remained a small peripheral outpost until a century later, when the urbanization process had become more decentralized, extensive residential suburbanization had begun, and clusters of separately incorporated municipalities started to rim the central metropolitan city. The rapid population growth between 1880 and 1920, when Los Angeles County expanded from 35,000 to nearly a million inhabitants, was thus primarily shaped by the social and spatial relations of the *Monopoly Capitalist City*.

Government, financial and commercial activities were concentrated in the downtown core and a sizeable industrial zone developed just to the south, toward the port of San Pedro (annexed in 1909) and adjacent Long Beach (to this day the second largest city in the multicounty region). The prevailing pattern of residential and industrial location, however, was already polynucleated and decentralized, with relatively low overall densities. Even with the aggressive annexation policies which increased the size of the city of Los Angeles from 85 to 362 square miles in the decade 1910–20, the incorporated areas of the county grew more rapidly in population than the city itself. From 1920 to the present, the city of Los Angeles was never again to experience an intercensus population growth rate greater than the suburban areas of the county (Hoch 1981).

From 1920 to 1940, covering the years of the Great Depression, Los Angeles County added nearly 2 million inhabitants, roughly evenly divided between city and suburbs. Petroleum refining and the aircraft industry were solidly established, and during the depression four major auto manufacturers opened assembly plants, attracting rubber tire and other auto-related industries to the area. Los Angeles remained, however, an economic center of relatively small firms, engaged in food processing, garment manufacturing, furniture production, tourism, and movie making. Despite a history of vigorous workers' struggles, Los Angeles also remained a preeminent center of effective labor control, an area where the open shop was virtually a law in the 50 years following the 1890s depression.[2]

The impact of the Great Depression, although somewhat cushioned and delayed in Los Angeles given its particular employment mix, was accentuated by the influx of large numbers of homeless and unemployed seeking jobs and housing. This accumulating and manipulable labor pool, sustained through the depression by New Deal programs and California state welfare policies, smoothed the way for massive war-based expansion of the economy. Manufacturing boomed from the beginning of World War II, moving far ahead of the previously larger service and trade sectors in employment by the early 1960s. During the Korean War period, 1950–3, total employment increased by 415,000 jobs, 95,000 in the aircraft industry (by then reoriented from an emphasis on aircraft frames to a more diversified aerospace–electronics-guided missile manufacturing). By the early 1960s, the city of Los Angeles contained 2.5 million people, matching almost exactly the total population of the surrounding incorporated areas. Los Angeles County's population reached over 6 million, more than doubling its size in 1940.

The Los Angeles region was the exemplary American "growth pole" of state-managed capitalism, with its economy keyed directly to defense expenditures, government housing assistance and mortgage programs, and the propulsive industrial growth sectors of the national economy. A low-density sprawl of residences and workplaces was meshed with a network of freeways, and another round of decentralization brought new industrial and residential expansion to Orange and other surrounding counties. One of the largest urban industrial zones in the world stretched over 20 miles from downtown to the port, cutting through rigidly segregated areas of black and poor white workers, tens of thousands of whom had migrated there during the war. The downtown core, never as dense or as developed as in major eastern cities, was reduced further as a regional focus with the accelerated growth of peripheral shopping centers and massive suburban expansion. Flexing their muscles again, powerful corporate interests crushed what had promised to be one of the largest public housing programs in the country under the banner of "fighting socialism" (Palloix 1978), shifting the focus of public expenditure toward major renewal programs aimed at reviving the central city business district and upgrading the extensive areas of deteriorated housing surrounding it.

As the quintessential center of statemanaged capitalist urbanization, Los Angeles also epitomized the crises borne by it from the mid-1960s to the global recession of 1973–5. The Watts riots in 1965 and the less widely known Chicano demonstrations in the following years[3] challenged the foundations and ideological legitimacy of the post–World War II economic order and marked a period of widespread urban rebellion in the United States and western Europe. Recession in 1969 and 1970 ended a decade in which many different trends were either reversed or rapidly accelerated. The proportion of the Los Angeles County work force employed in manufacturing peaked at 32 percent and began to decline precipitously with the concurrent surge of employment in services, wholesale and retail trade, finance, and government. The aerospace sector intensified its shift away from airframe construction to electronics and ordnance, contributing to a dramatic increase in industrialization in Orange County. The relative economic stagnation in Los Angeles County was reflected in enormous increases in welfare expenditures. Total welfare payments more than doubled between 1964 and 1969 and Aid to Families with Dependent Children nearly trebled.[4] After the end of the 1973–5 global recession, there was a brief period of recovery and rapid economic expansion in Los Angeles and elsewhere, but only after a significant social and spatial restructuring had begun.

Since 1979, another round of deepening crisis has accelerated the restructuring process. Recognizing three subphrases (roughly from the 1960s to the early 1970s, 1972–9, and from 1979 to the present), it is possible to identify a series of empirical trends in the restructuring of the Los Angeles region, trends which can be linked back to the historical and theoretical arguments introduced earlier.

THE CHANGING SECTORAL STRUCTURE OF PRODUCTION AND EMPLOYMENT

Postwar employment growth in the Los Angeles five-county region has been rapid and relatively steady. Around half a million new jobs were added in the 1950s, over 800,000 in the 1960s, and more than 1.3 million between 1970 and 1980, pushing the regional total to over 5 million today. Other large urban areas – Atlanta, Miami, Dallas, and Houston – grew at a somewhat faster rate from 1970 to 1980, but even Houston's net addition of 685,900 non-agricultural wage and salary workers was barely half the Los Angeles total.

Accompanying this aggregate job growth has been a significant change in the sectoral and spatial distributions of employment manifested clearly in the late 1960s and continuing to the present, a restructuring of employment patterns which is largely masked by persistent expansion in job numbers. Some of the changes which have occurred, such as the declining share of manufacturing in total employment and the concurrent expansion of the service, trade, finance, insurance and real estate sectors, reflect broad national trends. So too does the relative decline in government employment (especially federal), a dramatic contrast to the preceding decades. Other changes, although not unique, are more specific to the Los Angeles region, at least in their particular combination.

To describe the broad patterns of sectoral growth and change, considering both national trends and localized divergences, a series of shift–share analyses were conducted for the Los Angeles region on employment changes across all sectors and within manufacturing for three time periods, 1962–7, 1967–72, 1972–7, based on available Census of Manufacturing data (Morales *et al*. 1982). Particular attention is given here to estimated regional share indices, which represent the residual number of jobs "gained" or "lost" after considering aggregate national growth rates and national sectoral growth patterns.[5] Regional share values are presented in Figure 9.1 for seven sectors (excluding government) in the region as a whole and for Los Angeles, Orange, and San Bernardino, Riverside, counties.[6] Also shown are sectoral growth patterns (including government) for the 1960s and 1970s.

Major changes between the two decades include the increasing percentage growth of manufacturing and construction and the decelerating growth of most other sectors, with the decline most pronounced for government. The accompanying regional share values for the whole period 1962–77 bring out the relative growth of regional manufacturing even more prominently, with most of the +92,033 value accounted for by a +75,865 for the period 1972–7. Also evident is the marked contrast between Los Angeles County sectoral growth patterns and those in surrounding counties, especially Orange, which show positive increases in virtually every category, topped by manufacturing and trade. What these regional share values show is an internally

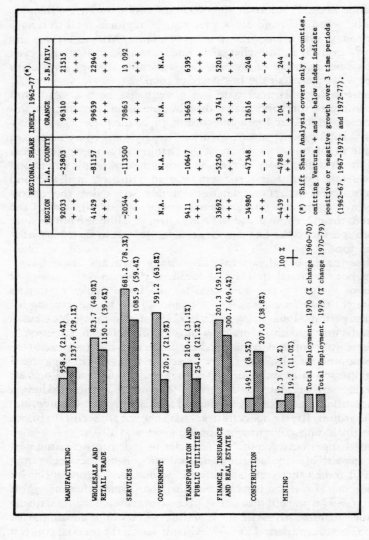

Figure 9.1 Changes in sectoral employment, 1960–79 (California Employment Development Department).

differentiated and increasingly decentralized urban area which is growing much faster than the rest of the country in trade, finance, insurance,
and real estate, and especially manufacturing, and slower in services and
construction.

Although its margin has been decreasing considerably, manufacturing remains the leading employment sector in the region. Moreover,
relative to the rest of the United States, manufacturing has been
expanding significantly, reinforcing Los Angeles' postwar position as a
leading industrial growth pole in a slowly and selectively deindustria-
lizing advanced capitalist world. According to Bureau of Labor Statistics estimates, of the less than 1 million net increase in manufacturing
jobs for the entire country in 1970–80, the Los Angeles region
accounted for 225,000, more than the next two leading urban areas (San
Francisco and Houston) combined (Security Pacific National Bank
1981b). In contrast, New York, Chicago, Philadelphia, and Detroit
together lost a total of 651,000 jobs. Within manufacturing, this job
growth has been concentrated primarily in durable goods production
(68 percent), led by the machinery, electrical machinery, primary and
fabricated metals, and transportation equipment subsectors (SIC codes
33–37 accounted for 45 percent of total manufacturing employment
growth). By far the leading subsector in nondurable goods manufacturing was apparel, which grew nearly 60 percent between 1970 and
1980, representing 12 percent of manufacturing employment growth
and the net addition of over 32,000 jobs.

Probing more deeply into these changing employment patterns,
especially with regard to manufacturing and to the geographical distribution of changes across the five counties, brings out the strikingly
composite character of the region and its structural reorganization. Since
the 1960s, Los Angeles has shifted from being a highly specialized
industrial center focused on aircraft production to a more diversified
and decentralized industrial–financial metropolis. This shift has been
the product of a combination and complex linking together of several
different patterns of restructuring which exist individually in other
major regions but appear as an integrated ensemble in Los Angeles to a
degree that is perhaps unmatched anywhere else in the United States.
On the one hand, the region has been experiencing a characteristically
"Sunbelt" expansion of high-technology industry and associated
services, centered around electronics and aerospace, at a rate which
compares with developments in Houston or northern California's Silicon Valley. At the same time, however, there has been an almost
Detroit-like decline of traditional, highly unionized, heavy industry, a
deindustrialization centered in the huge industrial zone stretching from
the downtown south to the twin ports of San Pedro and Long Beach.
This combination of stereotypically Sunbelt and Frostbelt dynamics
has produced many of the features of a recycled labor force, successfully

disciplined to sustain a new round of industrial expansion based upon more manipulable pools of highly skilled and unskilled workers. In this sense, a better comparison might be made to the current industrial "revival" of the Boston region (Harrison 1981).

Added to this combination (and very much an integral part of it) has been the growth of "peripheralized" manufacturing and service sectors which resemble the superexploitative industrialization of a Hong Kong or Singapore, based on a tightly controllable supply of cheap, typically immigrant and/or female labor. Many of the same conditions which characterize the numerous export processing zones that have multiplied throughout the Third World have developed within the Los Angeles region, well before the idea of "enterprise zones" was suggested by the Reagan administration.

Finally, Los Angeles has also emerged as a control and managerial center for international capital, the "New York of the Pacific Rim," a global capitalist city of major proportions. This has brought about a dramatic transformation of downtown Los Angeles and the corridor, running along Wilshire Boulevard 20 miles to the Pacific, into a major focus for transnational capital headquarters, financial, accounting, and insurance firms, and a full range of supportive business, entertainment, hotel, and restaurant services. Once true to its popular description as "a hundred suburbs in search of a city," Los Angeles now has a downtown which is becoming commensurate with its size and global economic influence.

Through this combination of changes, Los Angeles has concentrated many different aspects of the contemporary restructuring process in one region. As the following examination of each of these aspects will attempt to show, the result of this distinctive mix has been the emergence of a particularly successful example, from the point of view of capital as a whole, of the social and spatial reorganization of capital and labor in response to economic crisis and social unrest.

THE EXPANSION OF "HIGH-TECH" INDUSTRY AND SERVICES

Table 9.1 presents employment growth statistics between 1972 and 1979 in the Aerospace and Electronics (A/E) cluster of seven industrial sectors, the core manufacturing segment of the Los Angeles region, and the largest such employment concentration in the United States, perhaps in the world. During this period, the A/E cluster grew by 50 percent adding over 110,000 jobs and raising its percentage of total manufacturing employment from 23 to 26 percent. Leading this growth were the electronics sectors, especially electronic components and accessories (SIC 367), whereas aircraft and parts (SIC 372), still the largest single manufacturing sector at the three-digit SIC level, declined slightly.

This cluster not only covers aerospace and electronics but also

Hi Tech Reg^n ?

combines civilian and military-related production, all of which have become increasingly difficult to separate. Indeed, what ties the seven industries together most directly is a shared dependence upon technology arising out of Department of Defense and NASA research and development activities and a heavy reliance on military and defense contracts. The Los Angeles region has been a leading recipient of prime defense contracts ever since the war, averaging around 10 percent of the total in recent years. Employment directly attributable to military spending in the A/E sector was at least 70,000 in 1978, probably even higher, and there is no doubt that the recent increases in defense spending are further swelling these figures substantially, albeit somewhat more slowly than expected (*Los Angeles Business Journal* 1982).

The rapid expansion of this cluster of high-technology industries represents an augmentation of employment equivalent to the addition of a Silicon Valley to the Los Angeles regional economy[7] and is greater than the entire increase of manufacturing employment in Houston over the same time period, 1970–80. Moreover, it has been closely associated with significant changes in the geographic distribution of industry and in the organization of the labor process, changes which relate closely to the rise of neo-Fordism (Palloix, 1976).

Geographically, what might be called the "new Houston" of the Los Angeles region is centered in Orange County and in the area around Los Angeles International Airport (LAX), with a smaller subcenter emerging in the West San Fernando Valley (Fig. 9.2).[8] Employment growth in these areas has been part of the development of what some have called "outer cities," a contemporary manifestation of the urban decentralization begun in the 19th century.[9] Rather than being satellites of heavy industry and blue-collar workers or suburbanized office and retail nodes, these new outer cities are large conglomerations of technologically advanced industry and services, huge new shopping and leisure-oriented complexes, and high-income and expensively housed technicians, managers, and professionals, sprawling science-based New Towns described by one developer as having a "work-oriented, highly scientific, no-nonsense atmosphere" (*Los Angeles Times* 1982c).

The "atmosphere" so described referred specifically to the LAX region, which contains a resident population of about 550,000 but an estimated daytime population of over 750,000 and more adjacent hotel and office space than any other urban airport, a product primarily of the past 15 years. Also clustered around the airport focus are such aerospace and electronics corporations as Hughes Aircraft (the largest military electronics producer in the country, which in its several locations employs more people throughout the region than any other single manufacturing employer), Hughes Helicopter Division and offices of the parent Summa Corporation, Northrop Aviation, North American

Table 9.1 Employment change in the aerospace and electronics industries.

SIC code	Sector		Total employment 1972	Total employment 1979	Percentage United States employment in sector 1972	1979
372	aircraft and parts	Region	108,501	100,956	21.8	19.2
		LA County	103,076 (95.0)	90,153 (89.3)		
		Orange	3,581 (3.3)	7,369 (7.3)		
		SB/R/V	1,844 (1.7)	3,434 (3.4)		
376	guided missiles and space vehicles	Region	not a separate SIC category	56,805	—	44.4
		LA County		47,297 (83.3)		
		Orange		7,500 (13.2)		
		SB/R/V		2,008 (3.5)		
357	office and computing machines	Region	20,146	30,967	9.2	9.1
		LA County	15,815 (78.5)	14,431 (46.6)		
		Orange	3,969 (19.7)	15,886 (51.3)		
		SB/R/V	362 (1.8)	650 (3.5)		
365	radio and TV equipment	Region	8,016	8,695	6.6	9.3
		LA County	8,016 (100)	7,514 (86.4)		
		Orange	—	1,181 (13.6)		
		SB/R/V	—	—		
366	communications equipment	Region	50,179	64,158	11.7	12.1
		LA County	27,699 (55.2)	36,698 (57.2)		
		Orange	22,480 (44.8)	25,984 (40.5)		
		SB/R/V	—	1,476 (2.3)		

SIC	Industry	Area				
367	electronic components and accessories	Region	28,043		53,384		8.6	11.4
		LA County	19,715 (70.3)	29,308 (54.9)		
		Orange	4,879 (17.4)	17,510 (32.8)		
		SB/R/V	3,449 (12.3)	6,566 (12.3)		
382	measuring and controlling devices	Region	7,224	17,485	7.9	8.1
		LA County	7,224 (100)	12,807 (73.2)		
		Orange	—	4,266 (24.4)		
		SB/R/V	—	412 (2.4)		
	TOTAL	Region	222,109	332,450		
		LA County	181,545 (81.7)	238,208 (71.6)		
		Orange	34,909 (15.7)	79,696 (24.0)		
		SB/R/V	5,655 (2.6)	14,546 (4.4)		
	total as percentage of regional manufacturing employment		23	26		

Source: United States Department of Commerce, 1972, 1979.

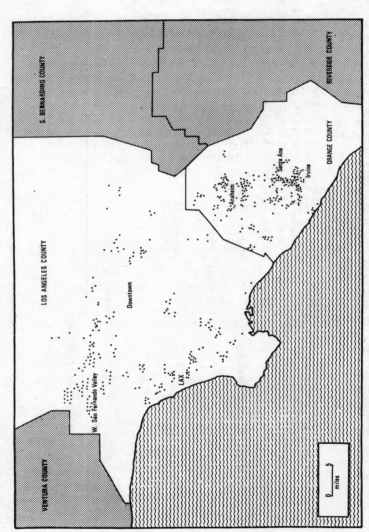

Figure 9.2 Location of electronics component plants, 1981.

Rockwell, TRW (specializing in guided missiles and space vehicles), Xerox, The Aerospace Corporation, and Control Data, as well as major banks, insurance companies, and business service organizations. Such communities as Marina Del Rey, Redondo Beach, and El Segundo have received thousands of new residents since 1970, primarily those employed in the occupations which have experienced the largest percentage increases in the country: computer systems analysts, designers and other professional and technical workers, managers and administrators, computer equipment operators, banktellers, etc. (Leon 1982). The LAX region also contains some of the largest areas of undeveloped urban land in the country, currently being proposed as the sites for massive new housing and office projects, the most ambitious under the aegis of the Summa Corporation.

Of even greater magnitude has been the growth of Orange County, especially in the sprawling development master-planned by the Irvine Company around Irvine New Town, Tustin, and Newport Beach. Although aircraft production has remained highly concentrated in Los Angeles County, the electronics industry has become more decentralized. About 33,500 new electronics jobs were added to Orange County during the 1970s, mainly around the booming Irvine complex, the densest cluster of the over 500 electronics firms currently operating. Total manufacturing employment in the county is now estimated to be 255,000 (Houston had 251,000 in 1980), of which nearly 60 percent are in various high-technology sectors (*California Business* 1982b). Further indication of this wave of expansion in the 1970s can be seen by comparing the employment growth rates of Los Angeles and Orange counties in certain key service activities: business services (69.2 versus 232.5 percent); banking, credit and securities (26.3–161.4); insurance (10.2–124.3); real estate (39.2–133.0); health (48.4–123.9); legal (80.0–186.3). From all available evidence, this trend has continued, if not accelerated, since 1979, with 30,000 jobs added in Orange during the recession year April 1981 to April 1982.

The decentralized expansion of the high-technology industries into these science-based outer cities has had important repercussions on the labor process. It has contributed to increasing labor control by further dispersing and segregating certain segments of the workforce[10] and by polarizing workers into a "felicitous balance" of very high skilled, capital-intensive operations (e.g., engineering and circuit design) and low-skilled, labor-intensive processes (e.g., the cutting of wafers and packing of circuits). The latter can take maximum advantage of available, cheap, unskilled, nonunionized labor supplies (or alternatively be exported overseas, an always effective bargaining threat). Workers in the middle are thereby reduced in numbers and influence (draftsmen being bypassed by engineers, machine operators and traditional office workers mechanized or computerized out of jobs), and knowledge of the whole production process by the individual worker is further fragmented.

Associated with these changes has been a marked reduction in unionization and the attendant improvement in what is called the "business climate." Following national trends, the percentage of California workers in unions declined from 30.9 percent in 1971 to 23.5 percent in 1979, figures which are very close to those for Los Angeles County. The change in Orange County, however, was even more pronounced, dropping nearly ten percentage points over the same period to 13.8 percent. In Orange County manufacturing, there was an almost total collapse, with the unionized work force moving from 26.4 to 10.5 percent, representing an *absolute decline* of over one-quarter of the union membership existing in 1971.[11]

SELECTIVE DEINDUSTRIALIZATION: PLANT CLOSURES, LAYOFFS, AND CAPITAL MOBILITY

Closely associated with the rise of high-tech industries has been an accelerating decline in older, established manufacturing activities, especially over the past four years. During this period, Los Angeles automobile production, once second only to Detroit, virtually disappeared, as did the entire rubber tire industry (Goodrich in 1975, followed more recently by Firestone, Goodyear, and Uniroyal) and a major portion of the auto-related glass, steel, and steel products sector. Counting a few major "indefinite" layoffs, over 70,000 workers have lost their jobs due to plant closure since 1978, almost 75 percent of the jobs in the auto, tire, steel, and civilian aircraft sectors.[12] Most (about 75 percent) of this job loss was concentrated in the old manufacturing belt running from downtown Los Angeles to the ports of San Pedro and Long Beach, and secondarily in a band stretching east of downtown into San Bernardino County (to the industrial area called the "Inland Empire"). Even Orange County, however, has not been totally immune, although the firms closed have been relatively small (Fig. 9.3).

Industry has been decentralizing from its traditional core in Los Angeles County for decades, and some plant closures and business failures are to be expected in any urban economy. However, the quickening pace and the particular sectoral and locational focus of recent closings demands a more conjunctural interpretation. It is no coincidence that actual and threatened plant closures have been concentrated in areas and industries which are the most highly unionized, pay relatively high blue-collar wages, and have employed large numbers of minorities. The corporations involved also represent the core of United States domestic capital: General Motors, Ford, Firestone, Goodyear, Lockheed, McDonnell Douglas, General Electric, Kaiser, United States Steel, and Bethlehem Steel – all major leaders and beneficiaries of

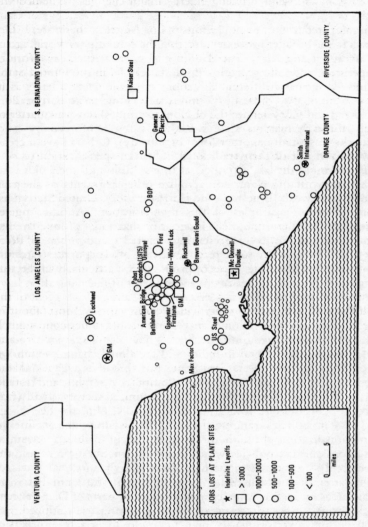

Figure 9.3 Plant closings and major layoffs, 1978–82.

the postwar boom. Boom and successful working-class initiatives fostered a national decentralization and rapidly rising real wages and benefits in these core, primary sector industries. Crisis and recession, however, has subsequently engendered major changes in the postwar order.

An interpretation of plant closings in Los Angeles, therefore, brings us back to the broader processes affecting the contemporary restructuring of capital and labor. Faced with excess capacity, heavy foreign competition, and falling profits, domestic capital in the United States has moved in many different directions over the past 15 years in its effort to rationalize older heavy industries. Some large corporations (Lockheed and Chrysler are the obvious examples) have survived primarily through massive state subsidies, often reinforced by labor givebacks (essentially another form of subsidy). Others have increasingly moved out of their traditional industrial specialization to conglomerate more diverse activities, at times "milking" their older and often still profitable plants to capitalize other segments of the conglomerate network (Bluestone and Harrison 1982). United States Steel is one of many examples of this diversification. Another related strategy has been a pronounced internationalization – of investments, production, and profits – representing a partial abandonment of domestic labor. There is also some recent evidence of a corporate strategy of reconsolidation into older areas of production, particularly in the auto industry, to take advantage of advanced forms of mechanization (e.g., the use of robots) (Anderson 1982).

All these strategies have several key features in common. They are aimed clearly at a restoration of increasing profits under conditions of crisis and general economic decline. They also have involved an accelerated pace of capital mobility and locational change, extending not only throughout the United States but abroad as well. And they have been accompanied by vigorous attempts to discipline and restructure the labor force, especially the most unionized sectors. This whole process of corporate restructuring and labor discipline has been facilitated by state policies, ranging from a tariff system which encourages internationalization through direct government bailouts, antiunion legislation, and tax policies which indirectly encourage relocation to "greenfield" sites versus modernization of older plants.

This attempted restructuring of both capital and labor has made certain areas in the Los Angeles region resemble parts of Detroit or the South Bronx, at least in terms of selective deindustrialization, population decline, extraordinarily high unemployment rates, increasing crime, and general urban decay.[13] A more appropriate comparison, however, may be with Boston and other parts of New England, where a deep and prolonged process of labor disciplining, plant closures, and capital flight has created the basis for a renewed expansion based on high-technology industries and services and a polarized labor force increasingly segmented along the lines discussed earlier with respect to the technical division of labor in the electronics industry.[14] This has allowed the Boston region to be added to the list of booming national electronics centers (along with Silicon Valley, Houston, and Orange County) and to have maintained relatively low levels of unemployment due to an expansion of low-paying service jobs.

The deindustrialization and recycling of labor in Los Angeles has been described as a "K-marting" of the population. When the President of the United Electrical Workers Local was asked what jobs her 1,000 members – the majority of whom were skilled women earning $10 to $12 an hour – would be able to find after General Electric closed down its flatiron plant in Ontario (San Bernardino County), she replied, "Clerks at the local K-Mart store." In recent years, however, even retail trade has felt the impact of deepening recession, with increasing store closures and bankruptcies.[15] Concurrently, the "public face" of plant closings must also be recognized. Although state and local governments accounted for over 10 percent of regional job growth in the period 1972–8, a fiscal crisis, exacerbated by the Proposition 13 "tax revolt" in 1978, led to a severe contraction in the expansion of government employment. Indeed, state and local government employment declined by 3 percent between 1978 and 1981 and was accompanied by a concomitant reduction in public services.[16]

Whereas the public sector had previously absorbed large portions of the growing labor force, that buffer against expanding unemployment is now gone. The leading areas of job growth in Los Angeles County today, according to California Employment Development Department projections, are very revealing. The following figures present estimated average annual job opportunities and 1982 average wages: secretaries and typists (17,637, $4.70–$8.20), bookkeepers (4,820, $9.40), assemblers (3,928, $5.50), cooks (3,630, $5.70–$7.10), cashiers (3,539, $5.50), sewers and stitchers (3,493, $4.50), janitors (3,469, $5.00–$6.80), registered nurses (3,440, $10.10–$11.60), waiters and waitresses (3,394, $3.35+), and real estate agents (3,254, n.a.). Except for janitors and real estate agents, these are all occupations primarily held by women. Given current conditions, however, male competition is likely to increase significantly over the coming years.

"PERIPHERALIZATION" AND THE RÔLE OF UNDOCUMENTED LABOR
Tied directly into the restructuring process has been an enormous influx of immigrants into Los Angeles, primarily from countries along the Pacific Rim. The magnitude and diversity of the immigration since the 1960s can be compared only with the wave of European migrants to New York City in the late 19th and early 20th centuries. If one includes the increasing black population (now approaching 1 million), the county of

Los Angeles has become a Third World metropolis. Thirty years ago, Los Angeles County was over 85 percent "Anglo." Today, Hispanics (or Latinos), blacks, and Asians together comprise over 50 percent of the population, with the Latino segment expected to surpass "Anglos" (non-Hispanic whites) as the largest single group some time in the present decade. Although proportionately smaller, the Asian population, especially Philippinos, Chinese, Thai, Vietnamese, and Koreans, has also been expanding at a very high rate in recent years. Koreans, for example, grew from less than 9,000 in 1970 to perhaps as many as 180,000 in 1982.

Greatly underestimated in the ethnic map of Los Angeles (Fig. 9.4) derivable from the 1980 census (Western Economic Research Company 1982a) is the large "undocumented" or "illegal" immigrant population, numbering somewhere between 400,000 and 1.1 million.[17] Mexicans are by far the largest portion of this group, but there are representatives from almost every country in the world. Together with the majority of the new "legal" immigrants over the past decade, the "undocumented" population has provided Los Angeles economy with perhaps the largest pool of cheap, manipulable and easily dischargeable labor of any advanced capitalist city. Although transforming the cultural geography of Los Angeles, it has also radically altered the local labor market by introducing a peripheral work force and working conditions that approximate those existing in the huge export processing zones of East Asia or in the Mexican *maquiladoras*.[18]

Accompanying this peripheralization and mass immigration has been a process of intensified segregation based on ethnicity and income (Kushner 1981). Using a simple "index of dissimilarity," a recent study showed a marked increase in what was called "ghettoization" for the Latino population, with percentages of Hispanics reaching over 95 percent in some parts of the *barrio* of East Los Angeles (*Los Angeles Times* 1981b). Black ghettoization declined slightly, but the black population of Los Angeles County was by 1970 one of the most geographically segregated in the country. Comparisons with New York City (Manhattan), Chicago, Birmingham, and other large cities marked Los Angeles to be, across all groups combined, the most highly ghettoized. An examination of census tract income data also shows an increasing concentration in the lowest income tracts since the 1960s, particularly in the ring of communities surrounding downtown, south-central, East Los Angeles, and the Pacoima–San Fernando area in the San Feranando Valley – precisely those areas which stand out in Figure 9.4 as more than 50 percent Hispanic or black.

Closely tied to the peripheralization process and the resulting pool of cheap manipulable labor has been the rapid expansion of the garment and apparel industry, noted earlier as being one of the leading manufacturing growth sectors in the regional economy. Almost 20 percent of

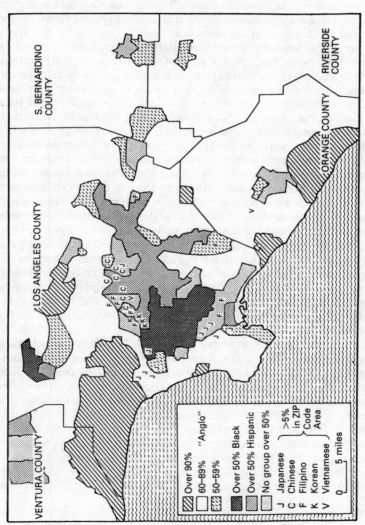

Figure 9.4 Distribution of major ethnic groups, 1980.

the net increase of manufacturing jobs in Los Angeles County between 1970 and 1979 was in SIC 23, apparel. Most of this was concentrated in women's, misses', and juniors' outerwear which, because of its need to be flexibly adaptive to rapidly changing fashions, has tended to be more labor intensive, less technically innovative, and more organized in small shops than the more standardized men's garment sector (still heavily concentrated in New York City). The apparel industry in Los Angeles, for this and other reasons, is very volatile, with many openings and closings occurring each year. Although California Employment Development Department figures show a decrease in employment for the apparel sector in 1980 in Los Angeles County, the County Health Department noted that 2,746 garment factories were founded and licensed in the same year.

Estimates of current employment in the garment industry range up to 125,000, with perhaps 80 percent consisting of undocumented workers and more than 80 percent being women. Only 20 percent of the industry is unionized and in a recent investigation by the County Health Department, nearly 80 percent of the shops surveyed fell below legal health and safety standards (Wolm 1981). Similarly, labor standards enforcement officials found in 1979 that over 80 percent of Los Angeles County garment firms were in violation of minimum wage and/or overtime provisions. Garment factories which bring to mind the unsanitary working environments, long working hours, meager wages, and other exploitative labor practices of the sweatshops of the 19th century have multiplied rapidly throughout the Los Angeles region. They exemplify vividly the localized effects of the recomposition of the regional labor market due to massive immigration.

It must be recognized, however, that immigrant labor forms a key part of the entire rationalization and restructuring process in Los Angeles, affecting virtually all sectors of the regional economy. In the last decade, undocumented workers have become particularly important in three employment areas (Morales 1983). The first consists of small highly competitive firms that depend on low-skilled, often transient labor that can be paid extremely low wages. This would include not only the garment industry but also other light manufacturing activities, hotel, office, and restaurant services, and even many firms in electronics. In Los Angeles, many companies too small or, for other reasons, unable to go abroad have expanded locally due to the advantageous approximation of Third World labor market conditions. They are the primary violators of labor standards, health, and safety laws, the revivers of sweatshop conditions, and the subcontractors most likely to turn to homework (the taking of assembly work home by workers to do on a piece rate basis, be it sewing articles of clothing or cleaning circuit boards for electronic components). Much of the expansion in office space, restaurants, and hotels has been facilitated by the specialized labor market conditions provided by undocumented workers.

A second group of employers, overlapping somewhat with the first, pay at least the minimum wage and are able to operate within the legal boundaries of what constitutes adequate employment. Given that the minimum wage produces an annual salary for a family of four (with only one worker) that is below the federally determined poverty level, many United States residents cannot afford to take these jobs. The immigrant workers who do take up employment in these firms – which include food processing, glass, plastics, and metal fabricating – are almost *forced* to be transient, for they too cannot live permanently in the United States with their families at such low wages. The outcome of Project Jobs, the factory sweep by the Immigration and Naturalization Service and Border Patrol during the last week of April 1982 in nine United States cities, including Los Angeles, sustains this interpretation. A follow-up study in Los Angeles showed that within three months 80 percent of the undocumented workers were back on the allegedly well-paying jobs expected to be eagerly taken up by the native unemployed (*Los Angeles Times* 1982b).

The third major group of employers of undocumented workers in Los Angeles are firms in those core, primary sector industries that are undergoing major structural changes. One study of auto-industry firms which employ undocumented workers found that the companies usually pay well and may even be unionized, but the employers seemed to value having easily controllable workers who can be released when necessary (Morales 1983). For these firms, the employment of undocumented workers represented a temporary strategy, maintaining production until a longer-term market solution could be established, such as moving to Mexico or elsewhere overseas, changing the product line, or automating. Most of these firms were subcontractors or subsidiary branches forced to bear the market uncertainties passed on to them by the main assemblies or headquarters.

To this pattern must be added the expansion of the Los Angeles economy across the Mexican border. Not only has the periphery been brought into Los Angeles, but many Los Angeles-based firms have reached into the most proximate periphery to construct plants in the nearby United States–Mexico borderlands. Of the over 200 United States firms listed in a recent congressional hearing as having factories in the Mexican border towns of Tijuana, Tecate, and Ensenada, approximately 50 percent were headquartered in Los Angeles (United States Congress 1976). They include not only such giant corporations as Hughes Aircraft, Northrop, and Rockwell but dozens of small firms involved in apparel, food processing, furniture, auto parts, and electronics. The boundaries of the Los Angeles regional labor market thus need to be stretched to include this special outlier which occupies an important position in the urban restructuring process.

INTERNATIONALIZATION AND THE CONCENTRATION OF INDUSTRIAL AND
FINANCIAL CONTROL

Over the past 15 years, Los Angeles has drawn ahead of San Francisco
and consolidated its position as the financial hub of the western United
States and the primary gateway to the Pacific Basin. Moreover, it has
emerged to rival New York City as a management and control center
for global capital, a development that is tightly intertwined with the
combination of trends previously discussed. The internationalization of
the labor force has been accompanied by both an expanding global
reach of firms and institutions based in Los Angeles and a large-scale
penetration of the regional economy by foreign capital. The result of
this two-way movement has been a growing concentration of finance,
banking, corporate management, control, and decision-making functions that has significantly transformed the urban landscape (Fig. 9.5).

By 1980, the Los Angeles region was second only to the 21-county
Greater New York area in total deposits and savings in financial institutions. The gap remained large ($294 to $104 billion) but had narrowed
in the 1970s, and Los Angeles leads by a substantial margin in the
holdings of savings and loan associations and credit unions (Security
Pacific National Bank 1981b). The largest California banks are still
about evenly divided between Los Angeles and San Francisco, but 11 of
the 12 largest United States banks headquartered outside California
have their sole California office in Los Angeles (*Bartlett's* 1979). The
Los Angeles region has been increasing its share of Fortune 500 headquarters and contains over 60 percent of California's largest industrial
firms.[19]

Complementing this domestic concentration is the increasingly
international character of banking and finance in Los Angeles. Crocker
and Union Banks are owned by British firms; the Bank of California is
owned by the Bank of Tokyo; and the former Manufacturers Bank is
now Mitsui Manufacturers. Recent newspaper headlines are indicative
of this trend: "Singapore group to buy American City Bank," "Danish
bank signs preliminary pact to buy Long Beach Bank," "First L.A. bank
okays takeover by Italian firm." Of the 78 foreign agents of international banks in California, 57 are based in Los Angeles, the largest
number being Asian, especially Japanese (*Bartlett's* 1979). Four of the
"Big 8" international accounting firms are located in downtown Los
Angeles, occupying nearly 400,000 square feet of office space, and a
fifth is in the Mid-Wilshire area. All are British owned.[20]

Accompanying this expansion has been a major office building
boom. The low-density sprawl of the Los Angeles region and the
unusually low level of development of the downtown area resulted in
many prime locations being undervalued when compared to the office
markets of other major world cities. This latent potential for expansion,
however, has only recently begun to be fully realized, primarily in

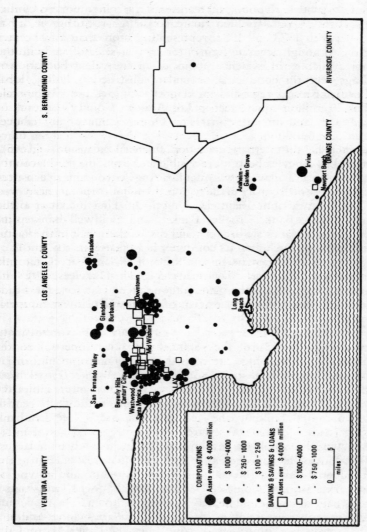

Figure 9.5 Corporate and banking headquarters of the Los Angeles region.

conjunction with a major influx of foreign capital, the expansion of military and defense-based industries,[21] and the availability of cheap labor to service high-rise office buildings and related food provision and hotel activities, all important features of the contemporary restructuring process. Over 30 million square feet of high-rise office space was added between 1972 and 1982, representing more than a 50 percent increase. Although accurate figures for smaller-scale office buildings are not available, all evidence points to an equivalent boom. New buildings recently completed or under construction (with 45,000 square feet or more, regardless of height) as of October 1982 contain another 20 million square feet in Los Angeles County (*Los Angeles Times* 1982d), and similar estimates for Orange County run well over an additional 6 million.

Nowhere has the internationalization, financial expansion, and office boom in Los Angeles been more visible and pronounced than in the downtown area. Today, downtown Los Angeles contains over a third of the high-rise office space in the region, 13 major corporate headquarters (including Atlantic Richfield, Union Oil, First Interstate Bank, Security Pacific Bank, Crocker Bank,[22] and Coldwell Banker, the nation's largest real estate broker), and the southern half of the Pacific Stock Exchange (including its computer headquarters). An unusually high turnover of landownership (a third of all land parcels recently surveyed by the *Los Angeles Times* had changed hands at least once since 1976) and continuing land bargains (although rental rates are among the highest in the country, the price of land remains well below comparable sites in Chicago, Manhattan, San Francisco, or Denver) have drawn in large domestic and foreign capital at a rapid pace. It is currently estimated that at least 21 of the 75 most valuable properties on the downtown's western edge are owned by foreign companies or by partnerships with foreign-based companies (*Los Angeles Times* 1982a). Japanese capital (in the Crocker Bank Plaza, the Bonaventure Hotel, the New Otani Hotel) and Canadian firms have been the most active, with Canadian capital building the new Manufacturer's Life Insurance building (with over 400,000 square feet of office space) and the proposed new California Plaza development (to include when completed 3,200,000 square feet of office space, 220,000 square feet of retail space, 750 residential units, a 100,000 square foot museum, and a five-acre urban park). British, Chinese, German, Dutch, Swiss, and Iranian interests have also invested heavily in the downtown. The remaining high value properties are owned by bank subsidiaries (about a fifth of the total), insurance companies, oil companies, the Times–Mirror Corporation, and other industries and local businesses.

Downtown Los Angeles is the anchor of a control-headquarters complex which stretches westward to the Pacific in Santa Monica and contains such major nodes as Beverly Hills, Century City, and

Westwood. In this almost unbroken ribbon of office development are another 49 major corporate headquarters and an additional one-third of the region's 100 million square feet of high-rise offices (Western Economic Research Company 1982b). The rapidly growing western half of this ribbon has specialized in professionals and service-oriented tenants, with 25 percent of recent office leases made to attorneys alone and much of the remainder to business service firms, engineers, architects, and accountants (Coldwell Banker 1981). Recent completions and current construction are expected to add 5.5 million square feet of new office space to the whole Wilshire Corridor, matching the equivalent new additions to the downtown area.

Branching off from this corridor is the LAX region, a center for aerospace and related high-technology industry, services, and military activities. This booming outer city contains 7.5 million square feet of high-rise office space (an increase of 150 percent in the past decade) and many additional major projects under construction which are expected to add another 5.4 million square feet of high- and low-rise office space in 1982–4. This new space, added to the growth of the Wilshire Corridor and downtown, comes to a total of nearly 17 million square feet currently being brought on the market.

The Orange County outer city matches the LAX area in high-rise office space and high-technology orientation, but it has become an even larger concentration of medium-sized research, development, and management firms and "middle-market" banking (to the point of claiming the title of Wall Street West). The primary office clusters are in Santa Ana, Orange, and along the MacArthur Boulevard Corridor, stretching from just south of the Latino *barrio* of Santa Ana to the luxury resorts of Newport Beach. Thousands of small and many large firms are located in these areas, which also contain or connect with the University of California, Irvine, John Wayne International Airport, several of the largest regional shopping complexes in California, and major branches of the financial and banking firms headquartered in the city of Los Angeles. The total inventory of office space in Orange County reached almost 25 million square feet in mid-1982, up from 17.6 in December 1980 (*California Business* 1982b).

Smaller nuceli of corporate headquarters and office buildings are found in the San Fernando Valley (which between 1977 and 1980 absorbed more new office space than any other area in Los Angeles County and is currently adding 2.4 million square feet in new construction), the San Gabriel Valley (Burbank, Glendale, and Pasadena), the port–industrial complex of San Pedro–Long Beach (the third busiest in the United States after New York and New Orleans), and in such locations as the City of Industry and the City of Commerce. The latter sites are peculiar cities, with very small residential populations. They were incorporated primarily as industrial parks during the postwar boom and remain relatively free from the tax burdens associated with providing local social services (Hoch 1981). Both Industry and Commerce have moved over the past ten years from heavy manufacturing to warehousing and distribution and now to research and development activities and corporate management.[23]

Not surprisingly, the office boom and internationalization process have spawned a major increase in highly specialized industries that service the growing concentration of control and management functions. Employment in the finance, insurance, and real estate sector grew by 47 percent between 1972 and 1979 (versus 32 percent nationally) and even higher rates of growth were experienced in various business services (SIC 73), especially in management consulting and public relations. Particularly revealing is the new service category of *temporary help*, for which the Los Angeles region has one of the highest concentrations in the country.

All of these developments have contributed to making the Los Angeles region an epicenter for global capital, an *internationally* defined growth pole which combines substantial industrial production, rapidly expanding financial management and control functions, and a social and spatial environment unusually conducive to international investment.[24] Under these conditions, overseas capital has continued to flow into Los Angeles even during the current deep recessionary period, not only into real estate, office development, banking, and industrial production but also into a wide range of supportive services: hotels and restaurants, luxury shops and boutiques, country clubs and recreational facilities, entertainment, and the media. Twenty years ago, this international presence was virtually nonexistent.

Conclusion

The pace and scope of urban restructuring in the Los Angeles region since the 1960s has been truly extraordinary. More than any other major urban area, Los Angeles has combined and linked together many different structural shifts and readjustments arising in response to the still deepening crisis of contemporary capitalism. Out of this amalgamation of trends has emerged a restructured social and spatial environment organized for more effective labor control and for the restoration of rising profits, at least for certain key fractions of capital. Selective deindustrialization and reindustrialization have been occurring simultaneously, polarizing the labor force and resegmenting the labor and housing markets. A growing cluster of technologically skilled and specialized occupations, claimed to contain the largest concentration of scientists, mathematicians, and engineers in the world, has been complemented by the even more rapid expansion of a massive reservoir of low-skill, poorly organized, low-wage workers, fed from above by a recycling of labor out of declining heavy industry and pressured from below by a growing pool of Third World immigrants and part-time workers. Homework and sweatshop conditions, labor code violations and job accident rates, the complete abandonment of job search, and the amassing of an expanded "underclass" have all increased concurrently.

Sprawling, low density Los Angeles has always been a centrifugal, fragmented metropolis with a pervasively privatized urban environment having a reputation for more unlisted phone numbers, more fenced or walled-in residences, and more conspicuously consumption-oriented households than any other American city. Its rapid population growth before 1960 was built most heavily upon a stream of migrants from small-town America eager to fulfill personal dreams and to escape the tightness of small-town social life. An accomodative urban spatiality absorbed the newcomers into a compartmentalized mosaic of municipalities and household clusters, connected by the automobile into spreadout networks rather than propinquitous communities. In much of Los Angeles, the casual pedestrian was an oddity – or a walking threat to the civic order.

In so many ways, Los Angeles epitomized the *State Capitalist Metropolis*. Not surprisingly, it was also directly and immediately affected by the crises which emerged in state-managed capitalism at the peak of its postwar economic expansion. The already socially fragmented and geographically segregated labor force, however, combined with a still tractable land market filled with speculative bargains (not the least of which was the underdeveloped downtown) to provide a particularly attractive and manipulative context for the transformation of the quintessential *State Capitalist City* into an internationalized focus for global capital, an emerging *Global Capitalist City*. A heavy stream of foreign investment along with a concentration of banking, finance, and corporate management (itself increasingly involved in global economic ventures) fuelled an office-building boom and reshaped the urban landscape, whole selective deindustrialization and massive immigration peripheralized and disciplined the labor force and segmented it even more finely than before. Long dominated by real estate and development interests and without a strong tradition of local community solidarity, the congeries of local governments tended to be willing and encouraging partners in this expansion, even when fiscal stress increased.

The growth of global capital is keyed to local control over labor and the accentuation of capital mobility, enabling investment to move anywhere higher profits can be assured. The "settling" of global capital in the Los Angeles region (however temporary it may be) is an implicit recognition of its accommodative ecology. It is not surprising then that there has been relatively little direct reaction and mass resistance to urban restructuring. The struggles which have developed have, for the most part, tended to be relatively weak and disconnected. Indeed, the ineffectiveness of collective struggles against deindustrialization and plant closures, union breaking, heightened capital mobility and economic dislocation, increasing unemployment, declining real wages, increasing ethnic segregation, fiscally decimated local communities, reduced public services, and unresponsive local governments has been an integral component of the urban restructuring process.

Will the urban region which has combined the many facets of contemporary restructuring most completely become the locus for a particularly pronounced political response to continuing crisis and further restructuring efforts? Or will Los Angeles continue in the vanguard of a reconstituted capitalism, successfully able to recover from the current crisis and, with the assistance of new exogenous "shocks" to the global economy, to establish the basis for renewed economic expansion? These are not academic but political questions.

Notes

1 A recent article in the *Los Angeles Times* (1982e) on the "new homeless" in the United States estimated the number of homeless in Los Angeles County to be 30,000, 40 percent of whom are considered mentally ill. Homelessness in Los Angeles and throughout the United States is thought to be greater today than in any other time since the Great Depression.

2 Perry & Perry (1963: vii) claim that "with the possible exception of San Francisco in the 1920s, it is doubtful if the labor movement has ever faced anti-union employer groups so powerful and well organized as those in Los Angeles."

3 These ranged from the high-school boycotts in 1966 to the Chicano Moratorium antiwar demonstration in August 1970. The latter involved 30,000 people and was thought to have been the largest hispanic political demonstration in recent United States history.

4 *Fact sheets,* published by the Los Angeles County Department of Public School Services in 1979, noted a 1964–9 rise of total welfare payments from $20.3 to $43.7 million and of AFDC payment from $7.4 to $22.2 million. Although not as severe as in New York City, urban fiscal problems and related austerity programs (including financial bailouts, cuts in public services, and reductions in public employment) have characterized the city and county of Los Angeles since the early 1970s.

5 Shift-share analysis breaks down the actual employment change in a sector into three components: national growth (the number of jobs that would have been added assuming the sector grew at the aggregate national growth rate across all sectors); industrial mix (the number of jobs that would have been added or lost assuming that the sector changed at the same rate it did at the national level); and regional share (the derived change

in employment after national trends are accounted for). For example, the actual increase of 219,288 in regional manufacturing employment from 1962 to 1977 is apportioned into +393,853 (reflecting a national growth rate of 48 percent for all sectors together), −265,598 (showing the negative growth of manufacturing nationally), and +92,033 (an indication of the degree to which the region departed from national norms).

6 Ventura County was excluded due to problems of suppressed data in the Census of Manufacturing. It is included, however, in all other regional statistics.

7 Total employment for the same seven sectors in Santa Clara County, California (which contains Silicon Valley) was 146,658 in 1979. Its employment is ahead of the Los Angeles region only in office and computing machines, is slightly less for electronic components, and much less in the other sectors.

8 The data for Figure 9.2 were collected by David Angel (Department of Geography, UCLA). All maps were drawn by Marco Cenzatti (Department of Geography, UCLA).

9 Other examples of these outer cities include Silicon Valley in Santa Clara County, the Texas "Metroplex" between Dallas and Fort Worth, Nassau and Suffolk Counties on Long Island, Florida's "Gold Coast" between Fort Lauderdale and Palm Beach, and the string of communities along Routes 128 and 495 around Boston.

10 1980 census data on occupations were not available at the time the article on which this chapter is based was written, but existing evidence strongly suggests increasing occupational segregation in the Los Angeles region. See, for example, the series on Orange County in the Los Angeles Times, beginning July 4, 1982. For a more general analysis of the residential sorting out of the "high-tech" labor force in space, see Storper & Walker (1983).

11 Also interesting are figures for average days idle per employee per year (a measure of work stoppages). For 1971–80, the United States average was 0.44; Los Angeles County scored slightly higher at 0.48; and Orange County's average was 0.23, with 1975–80 figures dropping to an average of 0.08. Data sources for unionization were calculated from the California Department of Industrial Relations (1974–80) reports on union membership and California Employment Development (1982–83) data. Work stoppage data were calculated by dividing the number of man-days lost in the ten-year period (as reported by the United States Bureau of Labor Statistics 1973–82) by the size of the work force (based on United States Bureau of Labor Statistics 1974–81).

12 Measuring plant closings is extremely difficult because of the absence of any centralized reporting agency. Even the Employment Department data (California Employment Development Department 1982, Los Angeles Business Journal 1983), the primary source for the estimates used, are considered to be incomplete. Figure 9.3 was based upon firm-specific data collected by the Plant Closure Research Project, a group affiliated with the state-wide Coalition Against Plant Shutdowns.

13 Parts of south–central Los Angeles, including Watts, are economically worse off than they were at the time of the Watts riots in 1965. During the

1970s, the area experienced the greatest deterioration of any community in the city of Los Angeles: population fell by 40,000; the labor force was reduced by 20,000; and by 1977 the unemployment rate hit 11.1 percent. Median family income in the city areas around Watts fell to $5,887 in 1977, over $8,000 below the citywide median and $2,500 below the city median for Blacks (*Los Angeles Times* 1980).

14 Harrison (1981) summarizes the findings of the New England Economy Project, a major collection of studies which chart the regional restructuring of New England since World War II.

15 Plant closings have not gone forward without struggle. Leading the effort against economic displacement has been the Los Angeles Coalition Against Plant Shutdowns (LACAPS). As plant closures have confronted various communities, LACAPS has provided organizational and technical assistance (as in the United Electrical Workers fight against the shutdown of the General Electric flat-iron plant) and applied pressure on state and local government agencies to help create or increase the level of special services and programs for displaced workers. The coalition was also instrumental in introducing and pushing for state legislation requiring advance notice of plant closings and compensation to displaced workers and affected local communities. Significantly, a national campaign which seeks to link plant closings, runaway shops, and union busting has recently targeted Litton Industries, the Beverly Hills-based multinational conglomerate, as a leading representative of the corporate assault against the working class. In the past year, the national campaign has resulted in several major demonstrations in Los Angeles, bringing together independent unions, the AFL-CIO, community, and church groups. Reports of these events have appeared in the *Wall Street Journal* (1982) and *Business Week* (1982).

16 Cutbacks in health services, for example, have involved the closing down of health centers, the introduction of new fees for services, direct job layoffs, and more extensive "contracting out." The latter, affecting other public services as well, privatizes public employment and union-organized jobs such as dietary workers, laundry, and client financial services, jobs which are overwhelmingly held by black and brown minorities.

17 For more details on the politically sensitive debates estimates of the size of the undocumented population in Los Angeles, see Wolinsky (1982) and Cornelius *et al.* (1982).

18 *Maquiladoras* are assembly plants in Mexican export processing zones. They have increased rapidly in numbers since the initiation of the Border Industrialization Program in 1965.

19 The number of Fortune 500 firms in Los Angeles increased from 14 to 21 between 1957 and 1982. Information on headquarters of California's largest industrial and financial firms was derived from *California Business* (1982a) and the *Los Angeles Times* "Roster" of leading California firms (May 18, 1982).

20 The accounting firms are: Price Waterhouse; Peat, Marwick, Mitchell; Coopers Lybrand; Deloitte Haskins and Sells; and in the mid-Wilshire area, Touche Ross.

21 It has been estimated that 25–30 percent of the total new office space in the Los Angeles region is being absorbed by defense-related industries (*Los Angeles Times,* April 5, 1981.)

22 Crocker Bank, now British owned, has a dual headquarters, having added a Los Angeles center to its original headquarters in San Francisco.

23 Los Angeles County (Los Angeles–Long Beach SMSA) has the largest square footage of industrial floor space of any SMSA in the county, estimated by Coldwell Banker (1981) to be 526 million in 1980 (versus 516 for New York and 512 for Chicago). In Commerce, Industry, and the LAX area, much of this space is currently being recycled into office construction.

24 The formation of "World Cities" is explored in more general terms by Friedmann & Wolff (1982).

References

Anderson, M. 1982. Shake-out in Detroit: new technology, new problems. *Technology Review*, 57–65.

Bartlett's Guide to Commercial Banking and Corporate Finance 1979. Santa Monica: Bartlett.

Bluestone, B. and B. Harrison 1982. *The deindustrialization of America*. New York: Basic Books.

Business Week December 27, 1982.

California Business 1982a. California's top 500 corporations. May, 96–118.

California Business 1982b. A California Business Magazine Economic report: Orange County, 1982. Special Selections. September, 1–30.

California Department of Industrial Relations 1974–80. *Union labor in California* Bi-annual reports, 1973–1979. Sacramento: Department of Industrial Relations.

California Employment Development Department 1982/1983. *Annual Planning Information*: Los Angeles Long Beach SMSA, 1982–1983 and Anaheim Santa Ana Garden Grove SMSA, 1982–1983. Los Angeles: Southern California Employment Data and Research.

Coldwell Banker 1981. *Los Angeles County, 1981: the commercial real estate market*. Los Angeles: Market Research Department Coldwell Banker.

Cornelius, W., L. Chavez and J. Castro 1982. *Mexican immigrants and southern California: a summary of current knowledge*. Working Papers in US Mexican Studies, 36. San Diego: University of California.

Friedmann, J. and G. Wolff 1982. World city formation: an agenda for research and action. *International Journal of Urban and Regional Research* **6**, 309–44.

Harrison, B. 1981. *Rationalization, restructuring, and industrial reorganization in older regions: the economic transformation of New England since World War II*. Cambridge, Mass.: Harvard–MIT Joint Center for Urban Studies.

Hoch, C. 1981. *City limits: municipal boundary formation and class segregation in Los Angeles suburbs*. Unpublished Ph.D. Dissertation, School of Architecture and Urban Planning, UCLA, Los Angeles.

Kushner, J. 1981. *Apartheid in America*. Frederick, Md.: Associated Faculty Press.

Leon, C. 1982. Occupational winners and losers: who were they during 1972–80. *Monthly Labor Review*, Department of Labor, Bureau of Labor Statistics, June.

Los Angeles Business Journal 1982. "Local aero space hiring boom is some time off experts say," September 27.

Morales, R. 1983. *Undocumented workers in manufacturing*: Boston University, Institute for Employment Policy, Massachusetts.

Morales, R., T. Azores, R. Purkey, and S. Ulgen 1982. *The use of shift-share analysis in studying the Los Angeles economy, 1962–77*. Graduate School of Architecture and Urban Planning Publications. Report 58, UCLA, Los Angeles.

Palloix, C. 1976. The labour process: from Fordism to neo-Fordism. In *The labour process and class strategies*. Conference of Socialist Economics (ed.). London Stage 1.

Perry, B. and R. S. Perry 1963. *A history of the Los Angeles labor movement, 1911–1941*. Berkeley and Los Angeles: University of California Press.

Security Pacific National Bank 1981a. *The sixty mile circle: the economy of the Greater Los Angeles area*. Los Angeles: Security Pacific National Bank.

Security Pacific National Bank 1981b. *Statistical supplement to the 60-mile circle*. Los Angeles: Security Pacific National Bank.

Storper, M. and R. Walker 1983. The spatial division of labor: labor and the location of industries. In *Sunbelt–Snowbelt: the political economy of urban development and regional restructuring*, W. Tabb and L. Sawers (eds) New York: Oxford University Press.

United States Bureau of Labor Statistics 1973–82. *Analysis of work stoppages*. Annual Reports, Bulletins 1777. 1813, 1877, 1902, 1940, 1996, 2066, 2092, 2120. Washington, D.C.: Government Printing Office.

United States Bureau of Labor Statistics 1974–81. Establishment Data, state and area employment. *Employment and Earnings*, May 1974, 122; September 1977, 116; May 1980, 128; May 1981 126.

United States Bureau of Labor Statistics 1980. *Employment and earnings*, Table A–23.

United States Congress, House Committee on Ways and Means, Subcommittee on Trade 1976. *Special duty treatment or repeal of articles assembled or fabricated abroad*. Hearings, 94th Congress, 2nd Session, March 24 and 25. 126–33.

United States Department of Commerce, 1972. *Country Business Patterns*. Washington, D.C.: United States Government Printing Office.

United States Department of Commerce, 1979. *Country Business Patterns*. Washington, D.C.: United States Government Printing Office.

Wall Street Journal December 7, 1982. Western Economic Research Company 1982a. 1980. *All races and ethnic data by ZIP codes in California, Los Angeles 5 County Area*. Sherman Oaks: Western Economic Research Company.

Western Economic Research Company 1982b *Hi-rise office buildings in the Los Angeles Orange County region*. Sherman Oaks: Western Economic Research Company.

Wolm, M. L. 1981. Sweatshop: undercover in the garment industry, *Los Angeles Herald Examiner*, sixteen-part series beginning January 14.

Wolinsky, L. C. 1982. Latinos assail illegal alien study, *Los Angeles Times*, April 9, Section II. 1,4.

Part IV
Disorganic development in peripheral countries

10 *Introduction*

RICHARD PEET

The regions of industrial growth in the advanced industrial countries were explored in Part III. It was argued that growth, particularly in high-technology regions, has been precarious and contradictory, even generating urban and environmental problems which choke off the manufacturing component. Here, in Part IV, the analysis is extended to the new industrial countries of the Third World. As in previous parts of the book, we take a critical stance, focusing on the effects recent industrialization has had on economies and people. The kind of industrialization experienced in Taiwan and South Korea may be the best a Third World country can hope for within the existing internal and external constraints. It can also be not good enough, in terms of its contribution to the welfare of the people of the Third World.

The idea that peripheral countries should emulate those of the center by developing through industrialization is hardly new. However, as long as manufacturing remained relatively unimportant in terms of contribution to the national economies of the Third World this path to development was regarded as theoretically desirable, but practically impossible. Starting in 1969 growth rates in manufacturing employment in certain underdeveloped countries rose dramatically, and the share of Third World countries in world manufacturing output, which had remained steady at about 8.0 percent during the 1960s, increased to 11.0 percent in 1980 (UNIDO 1979: 33, 224). It suddenly became almost realistic to call for an even greater relative shift of industry to the Third World as part of a new international economic order. Indeed the second general conference of the United Nations Industrial Development Organization (UNIDO) meeting in Lima in 1975 optimistically set a target of 25 percent as the share of the underdeveloped countries in world manufacturing output by the year 2000 (UNIDO 1975). It soon was apparent, however, that significant industrial growth was limited to a few Third World countries. A report by the Organization for Economic Co-operation and Development (OECD 1979) referred to Brazil, Hong Kong, the Republic of Korea, Mexico, Singapore and Taiwan (plus Greece, Portugal, Spain, and Yugoslavia in the First World) as the newly industrializing countries (NICs); and UNIDO (1979: 42) pointed out that ten Third World countries contributed 73 percent of the growth in manufacturing value added between 1966 and

1975. The burning question became what distinguished this small group of countries from the rest?

In an analysis typical of this genre, Belassa (1981) argued that, though important, "objective factors" like a country's size, resources, location, education, and social conditions should not be exaggerated. Instead he proposed a "stages of development" model emphasizing choice of industrial policy. Industrial development begins in response to demand by, and investment from, the primary sector, with protection from tariffs and quotas. The first, or "easy" stage of import substitution entails the local manufacture of previously imported nondurable consumer goods and the inputs into these. At first these industries, conducted at a small scale and requiring unskilled labor, provide rapid growth. But with the completion of import substitution growth is confined to increases in local consumption. Maintaining high rates of growth entails either second-stage import substitution or exporting. Second-stage import substitution, involving the replacement of imports of intermediate goods (petrochemicals, steel), producer durables (machinery) and consumer durables (automobiles etc.) by domestic production, was undertaken in the post-World War II period by the Latin American countries, some South Asian countries, and the Eastern European countries. Problems such as the small size of the market in industries characterized by considerable economies of scale led to heavy protection; in fact in several underdeveloped countries the cost of protection amounted to 6 or 7 percent of the GNP. Economic growth was distorted in environments protected from outside competition, exports suffered, and the countries following this strategy lagged behind. These deficiencies led to policy reforms, generally consisting of reductions in important protection and subsidization of exports. Outward-oriented policies were adopted by Japan in the middle 1950s, Korea, Singapore, and Taiwan in the early 1960s and the Latin American countries in the middle and late 1960s. Korea, Singapore, and Taiwan implemented "free trade régimes" in which exporters could choose to use local or imported inputs in their manufacturing. Increases in manufactured exports in the early 1960s were most rapid in these countries, and in the late 1960s and early 1970s various incentives for exporting led to further growth in manufacturing employment, reduction of unemployment and higher incomes. Countries in Latin America (e.g., Brazil) that reformed their system of incentives also experienced (somewhat lower) increases in exports and employment. Countries which remained with inward-looking strategies (India, Chile, Uruguay) remained at the bottom of the industrial growth league. For Belassa (1981: 16–17) the evidence is conclusive: "Countries applying outward-oriented development strategies had a superior performance in terms of exports, economic growth, and employment whereas countries which continued inward orientation encountered increasing economic difficulties." Choice of economic policy was the differentiating factor, and export-led industrialization is the promise of the future for the underdeveloped world (see also Ballance *et al*. 1982, Krueger 1983).

This argument is debatable on two grounds: could it work; and should it be emulated? First, could export orientation be promulgated as a general stage of development? Belassa (1981: 22–3) argues that East Asian countries with high educational levels could replace Japan in exporting skill-intensive products, the Latin American countries could expand their capital-intensive production, whereas countries at lower stages of industrial development could export products requiring unskilled labor, yielding a widening circle of industrial development which eventually would include all. The plausibility of this suggestion essentially depends on the availability of markets for the (huge) volume of goods which would be made. Who buys the exported manufactures? Three-fifths go directly to the AICs (World Bank 1980: Table 3.3); indirectly the proportion is probably higher. Export-led industrialization therefore depends on the continued ability and willingness of the AICs to absorb manufactured imports. Belassa (1981: 22) thought that gross domestic product in the AICs would grow by 3.9 percent and manufactured imports by 12.5 percent a year between 1978 and 1990. The World Bank (1985: 139–40), however, projects AIC growth at 2.7–3.5 percent a year between 1985 and 1990 and exports from major exporters of manufactures in the Third World to grow at rates of 5.5–10.5 percent a year, substantially lower than Belassa's estimate. The reality may be even lower growth rates than these. In addition, *ad hoc* protectionism (against specific products) is growing in the AICs. Although the NIC's exports make up a small proportion of the consumption of manufactures in the AICs (Kirkpatrick & Nixson 1983: 36–7, 66), the proportion is high for certain commodities (textiles, clothing, electronics) produced in specific regions of the AICs. As conditions deteriorate in Northern Ireland, Wallonia, or the Ohio Valley, sectional political pressure for increased protection grows. For the moment, the United States is absorbing an increasing proportion of manufactured exports (see Table 10.1).

Taiwan, in 1983, sent 45 percent of all its exports to this one market; less than 10 percent went to Europe (Republic of China 1984: 333). In the middle of 1985 a slump in high-tech sales in the United States caused layoffs in the "Four Tigers" of Southeast Asia (*Business Week* 1985: 4). Furthermore, 85 percent of the exports from Latin America to industrial countries in the early 1980s went to the United States, and even advanced countries such as West Germany and Japan relied on rapidly increasing exports to the United States to stimulate their economies after the recession of 1979–83 (*New York Times* 1985: F3). But the annual rate of economic growth in the United States dropped to 2.3

Table 10.1 OECD imports from five East Asian NICs, 1979–84 (billion dollars).

	1979	1980	1981	1982	1983	1984
Singapore	5.1	7.0	6.6	6.6	6.9	8.3
Korea	10.8	11.1	12.5	12.7	14.6	18.1
Taiwan	11.9	13.8	15.2	15.6	18.4	23.7
Hong Kong	10.2	12.3	12.6	12.2	13.3	15.5
Malaysia	8.3	9.2	7.7	7.2	7.7	10.1
total	46.2	53.4	54.6	54.2	60.8	76.0
of which imported by United States (%)	17.6	20.4	23.0	24.1	29.7	39.8

Source: OECD (1985: 22).

percent in 1985, and tensions from huge balance of payments deficits and the continued selective erosion of the manufacturing base in the United States (240,000 manufacturing jobs were lost in 1985) must eventually force a change in state policy away from free trade towards protectionism regardless of the theoretical beliefs of the President. In other words, export-led industrialization assumes a rising world economy; the reality is an international economy increasingly shaped like a doughnut – it has a hole developing in the middle.

Second, a number of arguments can be made on the grounds of *should* the existing model of export-oriented industrialization be promulgated? Here we turn to the articles reproduced in this section. In Chapter 11 Sivanandan argues that the world assembly-line technique practiced by the global corporations produces disorganic development in the Third World – a form of "development" that makes no sense in terms of local cultural and political institutions. Focusing on women, who make up the largest part of the work force in the "export platforms" of the NICs, Fuentes and Ehrenreich (Chapter 12) document the long hours, terrible working conditions, low pay, and sexual harassment that accompany multinational corporate employment in the Third World. They too point to the disorganic nature of factory employment, as "older working women" (in their late 20s!) are rejected by their own societies. A study by Grossman (1978–9) similarly concludes that female employment in the semiconductor industry in Korea is temporary. Separated from their families and communities, former workers often end up as prostitutes (see also Nash & Fernández-Kelly 1983). Landsberg (Chapter 13) takes a further critical look at the kind of industrialization occurring in countries like Korea and Taiwan. He argues that export-led industrialization, particularly the system of international subcontracting, blocks the development of an internally articulated, self-expanding economy. Instead he calls the result "dependent industrialization" (see also Cardoso & Faletto 1979). It should be noted that this last conclusion has been challenged, even within the Left, for example by Barone (1983) who counterargues that Korea has completed a successful transition to industrial capitalism.

The articles reproduced here lend more than a note of cautious skepticism to the chorus of acclaim for "Korean miracle" economies. Export-oriented industrialization may well have been a temporary phenomenon, characteristic of a brief period when demand for imports in the AICs was growing rapidly despite the onset of decline in their industrial base. With slower growth at the center, this route to industrialization in the periphery will be cut off. And this may be a good thing given the effects export-oriented manufacturing has on the workers and cultures of Third World countries.

References

Ballance, R. H., J. Ansari and H. W. Singer 1982. *The international economy and industrial development*. Totowa, N.J.: Allanheld, Osmun and Co.

Barone, C. A. 1983. Dependency, Marxist theory, and salvaging the idea of capitalism in South Korea. *Review of Radical Political Economics* **15**(1), 41–67.

Belassa, B. 1981. *The newly industrializing countries in the world economy*. New York: Pergamon Press.

Business Week 1985. September 16.

Cardoso, F. H. and E. Faletto 1979. *Dependency and development in Latin America* (trans. M. M. Urquidi). Berkeley: University of California Press.

Grossman, R. 1978–9. Women's place in the integrated circuit. Joint issue of *Pacific Research* **9**, 5–6, and *Southeast Asia Chronicle* **66**.

Kirkpatrick, C. H. and F. I. Nixson (eds) 1983. *The industrialization of less developed countries*. Manchester: Manchester University Press.

Krueger, A. O. 1983. *Trade and employment in developing countries*. Chicago: University of Chicago Press.

Nash, J. and M. P. Fernandez-Kelly 1983. *Women, men and the international division of labor*. Albany: State University of New York Press.

New York Times 1985. Only the World Bank has the means. August 25.

OECD (Organization for Economic Co-operation and Development) 1985. *Observer* **134**, 22.

OECD 1979. *The impact of the newly industrializing countries on production and trade in manufactures*. Paris: OECD.

Republic of China 1984. *Statistical yearbook of the Republic of China*. Taipei: Republic of China.

UNIDO (United Nations Industrial Development Organization) 1975. *Lima declaration and plan of action*. New York: United Nations.

UNIDO 1979. *World industry since 1960: progress and prospects.* New York: United Nations.

World Bank 1980. *World development report, 1980.* Washington, D.C.: World Bank.

World Bank 1985. *World development report.* New York: Oxford University Press.

11 Imperialism and disorganic development in the silicon age *

A. SIVANANDAN

One epoch does not lead tidily into another. Each epoch carries with it a burden of the past – an idea perhaps, a set of values, even bits and pieces of an outmoded economic and political system. And the longer and more durable the previous epoch the more halting is the emergence of the new.

The classic center–periphery relationship as represented by British colonialism, and the interimperialist rivalries of that period, had come to an end with World War II. A new colonialism was emerging with its center of gravity in the United States of America; a new economic order was being fashioned at Bretton Woods. Capital, labor, and trade were to be unshackled of their past inhibitions. The world opened up to accumulation on a scale more massive than ever before. The instruments of that expansion – the General Agreement on Tariffs and Trade, the International Monetary Fund and the World Bank – were ready to go into operation.[1] Even so, it took the capitalist nations of Western Europe, Japan, and the United States some twenty-five years to rid themselves of the old notions of national boundaries and "lift the siege against multinational enterprises so that they might be permitted to get on with the unfinished business of developing the world economy" (Rockefeller). The Trilateral Commission was its acknowledgement.

Britain, hung up in its colonial past, was to lag further behind. It continued, long after the war, to seek fresh profit from an old relationship, most notably through the continued exploitation of colonial labor, but this time at the center. So that when the rest of Europe, particularly Germany, was reconstructing its industries and infrastructure with a judicious mix of capital and labor (importing labor as and when required), Britain, with easy access to cheap black labor and easy profit from racial exploitation, resorted to labor-intensive production. And it was in the nature of that colonial relationship that the immigrants should have come as settlers and not as laborers on contract.

* Reprinted from Sivanandan, A. 1979, Imperialism and disorganic development in the silicon age, *Race and Class* 21 (2, Autumn), 111–26, by permission of The Institute of Race Relations.

The history of British immigration legislation, including the present calls for repatriation, is the history of Britain's attempt to reverse the colonial trend and to catch up with Europe and the new world order (Sivanandan 1976, 1978).

That order, having gone through a number of overlapping phases since the war, now begins to emerge with distinctive features. These, on the one hand, reflect changes in the international division of labor and of production, involving the movement of capital to labor (from center to periphery) which in turn involves the movement of labor between the differing peripheries. On the other hand, they foreshadow a new industrial revolution, based on microelectronics, and a new imperialism, accelerating the "disorganic" development of the periphery. It is these new developments in capitalist imperialism that I want to consider, moving between center and periphery, and between peripheries, as the investigation takes me, bearing in mind that these are merely notes for further study.

The early postwar phase of this development need not detain us here, except to note that the industrialization undertaken by the newly independent countries of Asia and Africa (Latin America had begun to industrialize between the wars) put them further in hock to foreign capital, impoverished their agriculture and gave rise to a new bourgeoisie and a bureaucratic elite (*Ampo* 1977). The name of the game was import substitution, its end the favorable balance of trade, its economic expression state capitalism, its political *raison d'être* bourgeois nationalism. Not fortuitously, this period coincided with the export of labor to the center.

Capital and labor migration

By the 1960s, however, the tendency of labor to move to capital was beginning to be reversed. The postwar reconstruction of Europe was over, manufacturing industries showed declining profit margins, and capital was looking outside for expansion. The increasing subordination of Third World economies to multinational corporations made accessible a cheap and plentiful supply of labor in the periphery, in Asia in particular. Advances in technology – in transport, communications, information and data processing, and organization – rendered geographic distances irrelevant and made possible the movement of plant to labor, while ensuring centralized control of production. More importantly, technological development had further fragmented the labor process, so that the most unskilled worker could now perform the most complex operations.

For its part, the periphery, having failed to take off into independent and self-sustained growth through import substitutions,[2] turned to embrace export-oriented industrialization – the manufacture of textiles, transistors, leather goods, household appliances and numerous consumer items. But capital had first to be assured that it could avail itself of tax incentives, repatriate its profits, obtain low-priced factory sites and, not least, be provided with a labor force that was as docile and undemanding as it was cheap and plentiful. Authoritarian régimes, often set up by American intervention, provided those assurances, and free trade zones provided their viability.[3]

The pattern of imperialist exploitation was changing, and with it the international division of production and of labor. The center no longer supplied the manufactured goods and the periphery the raw materials. Instead the former provided the plant and the know-how and the latter supplied primary products and manufactures. Or, as the Japanese Ministry of Trade in its "Long Term Vision of Industrial Structure" expressed it, Japan would retain "high-technology and knowledge-intensive industries" which yielded "high added value" whereas industries 'such as textiles which involve a low degree of processing and generate low added value [would] be moved to developing countries where labor costs are low."

Or, as Samir Amin wrote in *Imperialism and unequal development*, "The centre of gravity of the exploitation of labor by capital (and in the first place, by monopoly capital which dominates the system as a whole) had been displaced from the center of the system to the periphery."

The parameters of that new economic order are best expressed in the purpose and philosophy of the Trilateral Commission. Founded in 1973, under the sponsorship of David Rockefeller of the Chase Manhattan Bank, the Commission brought together representatives of the world's most powerful banks, corporations, communications conglomerates, and international organizations plus top politicians and a few "free" trade unions and trade union federations (from North America, Europe, and Japan) to reconcile the contradictions of transnational capital, while at the same time checking "the efforts of national governments to seize for their own countries a disproportionate share of the benefits generated by foreign direct investment" (Frieden 1977). As Richard Falk (1975) puts it: "The vistas of the Trilateral Commission can be understood as the ideological perspective representation, the transnational outlook of the multinational corporation [which] seeks to subordinate territorial politics to nonterritorial economic goals."

And for the purposes of that subordination, it was necessary to distinguish between the differing peripheries: the oil-producing countries, the "newly-industrializing" countries, and the underdeveloped countries proper (which the Commission terms the "Fourth World").

The implications of this new imperial ordinance for labor migration – not, as before, between center and periphery but between the peripheries themselves – are profound, and the consequences for these countries devastating. The oil-rich Gulf states, for instance, have sucked in whole sections of the working population, skilled and semi-skilled, of South Asia, leaving vast holes in the labor structure of these countries. Moratuwa, a coastal town in Sri Lanka, once boasted some of the finest carpenters in the world. Today there are none: they are all in Kuwait or in Muscat or Abu Dhabi. There are no welders, masons, electricians, plumbers, mechanics – they are all gone. The doctors, teachers, and engineers have been long gone: some left in the first wave of postwar migration to Britain, Canada, the United States, Australia and others in the second to Nigeria, Zambia, Ghana. Today Sri Lanka, which had the first free health service in the Third World and some of the finest physicians and surgeons, imports its doctors from the Philippines. What that must do to the Filipino people is another matter, but all that we are left with in Sri Lanka is a plentiful supply of unemployed labor, which is now being herded into the colony within the neocolony, the Free Trade Zone.

Or take the case of Pakistan, which shows a similar pattern of emigration, except that being a Muslim country the pull of the Gulf is even stronger. Besides, the export of manpower, as a foreign exchange earner, is official policy, a Bureau of Emigration having been set up in 1969 to facilitate employment overseas. Consequently Pakistan "is being progressively converted into a factory producing skilled manpower for its rich neighbours" (Ahmed 1976).

But the export of skilled workers is not the only drain on Pakistan's resources. Apart from its traditional export of primary products, its physical proximity to the oil-rich countries has meant also the smuggling out of fresh vegetables, the sale of fish in mid-seas and the export, often illegal, of beef and goat meat. (The Gulf states raise no cattle.) "The adverse effects of this trade," laments Feroz Ahmed, "can be judged from the fact that Pakistan has one of the lowest per capita daily consumptions of animal protein in the world: less than 10 grammes" (Ahmed 1976).

The Middle East countries in turn have only invested in those enterprises which are geared to their own needs (textiles, cement, fertilizer, livestock) and rendered Pakistan's economy subservient to their interests. To make this "development of underdevelopment" palatable they harked back to a common culture, Iranian cultural centers sprouted in every major town in Pakistan, outdoing the Americans; and the teaching of Arabic and Persian was fostered by official policy. A Pakistani paper said "We the Pakistanis and our brethren living in Iran are the two Asiatic branches of the Aryan Tree who originally lived in a common country, spoke the same language, followed the same religion, worshipped the same gods and observed the same rites. . . . Culturally we were and are a single people" (Dawn 1973, cited in Ahmed 1976).

But if Pakistan has been relegated in the pecking order of imperialism "to the status of a slave substratum upon which the imperialist master and their privileged clients play out their game of plunder and oppression" (*Dawn* 1973), the privileged clients themselves exhibit a distorted "development." Take Kuwait for instance. In the pre-oil era Kuwait's economy was based on fishing, pearling, pasturing, trade, and a little agriculture. Today all these activities, with the exception of fishing, have virtually ceased; and fishing has been taken over by a company run by the ruling family. The oil industry, though providing the government with 99 percent of its income, affords employment only to a few thousand. Almost three-fourths of the native work force is in the service sector, with little or nothing to do. (A United Nations survey estimated that the Kuwait civil servant works 17 minutes a day – *Monthly Review* 1978.) But more than 70 percent of the total work force and over half the total population consists of non-Kuwait immigrant labor. And they are subjected to harsh conditions of work, low wages, no trade union rights, wretched housing, and arbitrary deportation. Kuwait is, in effect, two societies, but even within the first "the ruling elite lives in a swamp of consumer commodities and luxuries, while those at the bottom of the Kuwaiti social pyramid are being uprooted from their traditional productive activities and thrown on the market of unproductiveness" (*Monthly Review* 1978).

The pattern of labor migration in Southeast Asia is a variation on the same imperial theme, and its consequences are no less devastating. The first countries to industrialize in this region were Taiwan in the 1950s and, in the 1960s, South Korea, Singapore, and Hong Kong. Taiwan and South Korea were basically offshore operations of the United States and Japan; and, by virtue of their strategic importance to America they were able to develop heavy industry (shipbuilding, steel, vehicles) and chemicals in addition to the usual manufacture of textiles, shoes, electrical goods, etc. By the middle of the 1970s these two countries had gone over from being producers of primary products to producers of manufactured goods. Singapore's industrialization includes ship repair (Singapore is the fourth largest port in the world) and the construction industry. Hong Kong, the closest thing to a "free economy," is shaped by the world market.

What all these countries could offer multinational capital, apart from a "favorable climate of investment" (repatriation of profit, tax holidays, etc.), was authoritarian régimes (Hong Kong is a colony) with a tough line on dissidence in the work force and a basic infrastructure of power and communications. What they did not have was a great pool of unemployed workers. That was provided by the neighbouring countries.

Hong Kong uses all the migrant labor available in the region, including workers from mainland China, and is currently negotiating with the Philippines government for the import of Filipino labor. South Korea's shortage of labor, by the very nature of its development, has been in the area of skilled workers. (Not illogically South Korea has been priced out of its own skilled workers, some 70,000 of them, by the developing oil-rich countries of the Middle East). But it is Singapore which is the major employer of contract labor – from Malaysia mostly (40 percent of the industrial work force) but also from Indonesia, the Philippines, and Thailand – and that under the most horrendous conditions. For apart from the usual strictures on gastarbeiters that we are familiar with in Europe, such as no right of settlement, no right to change jobs without permission, and deportation if jobless, Singapore also forbids these workers to marry, except after five years, on the showing of a "clean record", and then with the permission of the government – and that on signing a bond that both partners will agree to be sterilized after the second child is born. Lee Kuan Yew, with a nod to Hitler, justifies the policy on the ground that "a multiple replacement rate right at the bottom" leads to "a gradual lowering of the general quality of the population" (Selangor Graduates Society 1978). Their working conditions too are insanitary and dangerous and makeshift shacks on worksites (like the bidonvilles) provide their only housing.

And yet the plight of the indigenous workers of these countries is not much better. The economic miracle is not for them. Their lives contrast glaringly with the luxury apartments, automobiles, and swinging discos of the rich. To buy a coffee and sandwich on a thoroughfare of Singapore costs a day's wages. In South Korea 12- and 13-year-old girls work 18 hours a day, 7 days a week, for £12 a month; and Hong Kong is notorious for its exploitation of child labor (Easy 1977).

How long the repressive régimes of these countries can hold down their work force on behalf of international capital is a moot point; but multinationals do not wait to find out. They do not stay in one place. They gather their surplus while they may and move on to new pastures their miracles to perform.

The candidates for the new expropriation were Indonesia, Thailand, Malaysia, and the Philippines, whose economies were primarily based on agriculture and on extractive industries such as mining and timber. Like the first group of countries they too could boast of authoritarian régimes – ordained by the White House, fashioned by the Pentagon, and installed by the CIA – which could pave the way for international capital. Additionally, they were able to provide the cheap indigenous labor which the other group had lacked – and the free trade zones to go with it. What they did not have, though, was a developed infrastructure.

Multinationals had already moved into these countries by the 1970s and some industrialization was already under way. What accelerated that movement, however, was the tilt to cheap labor, as against a developed infrastructure, brought about by revolutionary changes in the production process.

To that revolution, variously described as the new industrial revolution, the third industrial revolution, and the postindustrial age, I must now turn, not so much to look at labor migration as labor polarization between the periphery and the center and within the center itself, and its social and political implications in both.

Capital and labor in the silicon age

What has caused the new industrial revolution and brought about a qualitative leap in the level of the productive forces is the silicon chip or, more accurately, the computer-on-a-chip, known as a microprocessor. (You have already seen them at work in your digital watch and your pocket calculator.)

The ancestry of the microprocessor need not concern us here, except to note that it derives from the electronic transistor invented by American scientists in 1947, which in turn led to the semi-conductor industry in 1952–3 and to the integrated circuit industry in 1963. Integrated circuits meant that various electronic elements such as transistors, resistors, diodes, etc. could all be combined on a tiny chip of semiconductor silicon, "which in the form of sand is the world's most common element next to oxygen" (Stewart & Markoff 1979). But if industrially the new technology has been in existence for 16 years, it is only in the last 5 that it has really taken off. The periodization of its development is important because it is not unconnected with the postwar changes in the international division of production and of labor and the corresponding movements and operations of the multinational corporations.

The microprocessor is to the new industrial revolution what steam and electricity were to the old, except that where steam and electric power replaced human muscle microelectronics replaces the brain. That, quite simply, is the measure of its achievement. Consequently, there is virtually no field in manufacturing, the utilities, the service industries, or commerce that is not affected by the new technology. Microprocessors are already in use in the control of power stations, textile mills, telephone-switching systems, office heating, and typesetting, as well as in repetitive and mechanical tasks such as spraying, welding, etc. in the car industry. Fiat, for instance, has a television commercial which boasts that its cars are "designed by computers, silenced by lasers and hand-built by robots" – to the strains of Figaro's aria (from Rossini). Volkswagen designs and sells its own robots for spot welding and handling body panels between presses. Robots, besides, can be reprogrammed for different tasks more easily than personnel can be retrained. And because microprocessors can be reprogrammed, automated assembly techniques could be introduced into areas hitherto immune to automation, such as batch production (which incidentally constitutes 70 percent of the production in British manufacturing). From this has grown the idea of linking together a group of machines to form an unmanned manufacturing system, which could produce anything from diesel engines to machine tools and even aeroengines. "Once the design of the unmanned factory has been standardized, entire factories could be produced on a production line based on a standard design" (ASTMS 1978). The Japanese are close to achieving the "universal factory."

A few examples from other areas of life will give you some idea of the pervasiveness of microelectronics. In the retail trade, for instance, the electronic cash register, in addition to performing its normal chores, monitors the stock level by keeping tabs on what has been sold at all the terminals and relays that information to computers in the warehouse which then automatically move the necessary stocks to the shop. A further lineup between computerized checkouts at stores and computerized bank accounts will soon do away with cash transactions, directly debiting the customer's account and crediting the store's. Other refinements such as keeping a check on the speed and efficiency of employees have also grown out of such computerization – in Denmark, for instance (but it has been resisted by the workers).

There are chips in everything you buy – cookers, washing machines, toasters, vacuum cleaners, clocks, toys, sewing machines, motor vehicles – replacing standard parts and facilitating repair: you take out one chip and put in another. One silicon chip in an electronic sewing machine for example replaces 350 standard parts.

But it is in the service sector, particularly in the matter of producing, handling, storing, and transmitting information, that silicon technology has had its greatest impact. Up to now automation has not seriously affected office work which, while accounting for 75 percent of the costs in this sector (and about half the operating costs of corporations), is also the least productive, thereby depressing the overall rate of productivity. One of the chief reasons for this is that office work is divided into several tasks (typing, filing, processing, retrieving, transmitting, and so forth) which are really interconnected. The new technology not only automates these tasks but integrates them. For example, the word processor, consisting of a keyboard, a visual display unit, a storage memory unit, and a print-out, enables one typist to do the work of four while at the same time reducing the skill she needs. Different visual display units (VDUs) can then be linked to the company's mainframe computer, to other computers within the country (via computer network systems), and even to those in other countries through satellite communication. All this makes possible the electronic mail and the electronic funds transfer (EFT) which would dispense with cash completely.

What this linkup between the office, the computer, and telecommunications means is the "convergence" of previously separate industries. "Convergence" is defined by the Butler Cox Foundation as "the process by which these three industries are coming to depend on a single technology. They are becoming, to all intents and purposes, three branches of a single industry" (Butler 1978, quoted in ASTMS 1978). But "convergence" to you and me spells the convergence of corporations, horizontal (and vertical) integration, monopoly. A "convergence" of Bell Telephones and IBM computers would take over the world's communication facilities. (Whether the antitrust laws in America have already been bent to enable such a development I do not know, but it is only a matter of time.)

Underscoring the attributes and applications of the microprocessor is the speed of its advance and the continuing reduction in its costs. Sir Ieuan Maddock, Secretary of the British Association for the Advancement of Science, estimates that "in terms of the gates it can contain, the performance of a single chip has increased ten thousand fold in a period of 15 years." And of its falling cost, he says, "The price of each unit of performance has reduced one hundred thousand-fold since the early 1960s" (Maddock 1978).

"These are not just marginal effects," continues Sir Ieuan, "to be absorbed in a few percent change in the economic indicators – they are deep and widespread and collectively signal a fundamental and irreversible change in the way the industrialized societies will live. Changes of such magnitude and speed have never been experienced before" (Maddock 1978).

The scope of these changes has been dealt with in the growing literature on the subject (see, for instance, ASTMS 1978, Hines 1978, Harman 1979, Barron & Curnow 1979, Jenkins & Sherman 1979, TUC 1979). But they have mostly been concerned with the prospects of increasing and permanent unemployment, particularly in the service industries and in the field of unskilled manual employment, in both of which blacks and women predominate.[4] A study by Siemens estimates that 40 percent of all office work in Germany is suitable for automation – which, viewed from the other side, means a 40 percent layoff of office workers in the next ten years. The Nora report warns that French banking and insurance industries, which are particularly labor intensive, will lose 30 percent of their work force by 1990. Unemployment in Britain is expected to rise by about 3 million in that time (Cambridge Economic Policy Group 1978). Other writers have pointed to a polarization in the work force itself, as between a small technological elite on the one hand and a large number of unskilled, unemployable workers, counting among their number those whose craft has become outmoded. Or, as the chairman of the British Oil Corporation, Lord Kearton, puts it, "We have an elite now of a very special kind at the top on which most of mankind depends for its future development and the rest of us are more or less taken along in the direct stream of these elite personnel".

All the remedies that the British Trades Union Congress has been able to suggest are "new technology agreements" between government and union, "continuing payments to redundant workers related to their past earnings" and "opportunities for linking technological change with a reduction in the working week, working year, and working life time" (TUC 1979). The Association of Scientific, Technical, and Managerial Staffs (ASTMS), whose members are more immediately affected by automation, elevates these remedies into a philosophy which encompasses a changed attitude towards work that would "promote a better balance between working life and personal life", "recurrent education throughout adult life" and a new system of income distribution which in effect will "pay people not to work" (ASTMS 1978).

But, in the performance, these are precisely the palliatives that enlightened capitalism (i.e., multinational capitalism as opposed to the archaic private enterprise capitalism of Margaret Thatcher and her mercantile minions) offers the working class in the silicon age. Translated into the system's terms, "new technology agreements" mean a continuing social contract between the unions and the government wherein the workers abjure their only power, collective bargaining (and thereby take the politics out of the struggle) and a new culture which divorces work from income (under the guise of lifelong education, part-time work, early retirement, etc.) and provides the *raison d'être* for unemployment. Already the protagonists of the establishment have declared that the Protestant work ethic is outdated (what has work got to do with income?), that leisure should become a major occupation (university departments are already investigating its "potential"), that schooling is not for now but for ever.

I am not arguing here against technology or a life of creative leisure. Anything that improves the lot of man is to be welcomed. But in capitalist society such improvement redounds to the few at cost to the many. That cost has been heavy for the working class in the center and heavier for the masses in the periphery. What the new industrial revolution predicates is the further degradation of work where, as Braverman (1974) so brilliantly predicted, thought itself is eliminated from the labor process, the centralized ownership of the means of production, a culture of reified leisure to mediate discontent and a political system incorporating the state, the multinationals, the trade unions, the bureaucracy and the media, backed by the forces of "law and order" with microelectronic surveillance at their command. For in as much as liberal democracy was the political expression of the old industrial revolution, the corporate state is the necessary expression of the new. The qualitative leap in the productive forces, ensnared in capitalist economics, demands such an expression. Or, to put it differently, the contradiction between the heightened centralization in the ownership of the means of production – made possible not only by the technological nature of that increase – and the social nature of production (however attenuated) can no longer be mediated by liberal democracy but by corporativism, with an accompanying corporate culture, and state surveillance to go with it.

But nowhere in all the chip literature is there a suggestion of any of this. Nor is there in British writings on the subject,[5] with the exception of the CIS report (CIS 1979), any hint of a suggestion that the new industrial revolution, like the old, has taken off on the backs of the workers in the peripheries or that it is they who will provide the "living dole" for the unemployed of the West. For the chip, produced in the pleasant environs of Silicon Valley in California, has its circuitry assembled in the toxic factories of Asia. Or, as a Conservative Political Centre publication puts it: "While the manufacture of the chips requires expensive equipment in a dust-free, air-conditioned environment little capital is necessary to assemble them profitably into saleable devices. And it is the assembly that creates both the wealth and the jobs" (Virgo 1979).

Initially the industry went to Mexico, but Asia was soon considered cheaper (besides, "Santa Clara was only a telex away"). Even within Asia the moves were to cheaper and cheaper areas: from Hong Kong, Taiwan, South Korea, and Singapore in the 1960s to Malaysia in 1972. Thailand in 1973, the Philippines and Indonesia in 1974, and soon to Sri Lanka. "The manager of a plant in Malaysia explained how profitable these moves had been: 'One worker working one hour produces enough to pay the wages of 10 workers working one shift plus all the costs of materials and transport'" (cited in Grossman 1979).

But the moves the industry makes are not just from country to country but from one batch of workers to another within the country itself. For, the nature of the work – the bonding under a microscope of tiny hair-thin wires to circuit boards on wafers of silicon chip half the size of a fingernail – shortens working life. "After 3 or 4 years of peering through a microscope," reports Rachael Grossman, "a worker's vision begins to blur so that she can no longer meet the production quota" (Grossman 1979). But if the microscope does not get her ("Grandma, where are your glasses?" is how electronic workers over 25 are greeted in Hong Kong), the bonding chemicals do.[6] And why "her"? Because they are invariably women. As a Malaysian brochure has it: "The manual dexterity of the oriental female is famous the world over. Her hands are small and she works fast with extreme care. Who, therefore, could be better qualified by nature and inheritance to contribute to the efficiency of a bench assembly production line than the oriental girl?" (cited in Grossman 1979).

To make such intense exploitation palatable, however, the multinationals offer the women a global culture – beauty contests, fashion shows, cosmetic displays, and disco dancing – which in turn enhances the market for consumer goods and Western beauty products. Tourism reinforces the culture and reinforces prostitution (with packaged sex tours for Japanese businessmen), drug selling, child labor. For the woman thrown out of work on the assembly line at an early age, the wage earner for the whole extended family, prostitution is often the only form of livelihood left (Neumann 1979).

A global culture then, to go with a global economy. It is serviced by a global office the size of a walkie-talkie held in your hand (Large 1979). The global assembly line is run by global corporations that move from one pool of labor to another, discarding them when done. There is high technology in the center, low technology in the peripheries, a polarization of the work force within the centre itself (as between the highly skilled and unskilled or deskilled), and as between the center and the peripheries, with qualitatively different rates of exploitation that allow the one to feed off the other. Finally, a corporate state is maintained by surveillance for the developed countries, authoritarian régimes and gun law for the developing. That is the size of the new world order.

Disorganic development

All this is not without its contradictions. Where those contradictions are sharpest, however, are where they exist in the raw – in the peripheries.[7] For what capitalist development has meant to the masses of these countries is increased poverty, the corruption of their cultures, repressive régimes – and all at once. All the GNP they amass for their country through their incessant labor leaves them poorer than before. They produce things of no real use to them, yet cannot buy what they produce, neither use nor exchange value, neither the old system nor the new.

How they produce has no relation to how they used to produce. They have not grown into the one from the other. They have not emerged into capitalist production but been flung into it – into technologies and labor processes that reify them and into social relations that violate their customs and their codes. They work in the factories in town to support their families and their extended families in the village – to contribute to the building of the village temple, to help get a teacher for the school, to sink a well. But the way of their working socializes them into individualism, nuclear families, consumer priorities, artefacts of capitalist culture. They are caught between two modes, two sets, of social relations, characterized by exchange value in the one and use value in the other. The contradiction disorients them and removes them from the center of their being.

Neither the workers nor the peasants have escaped the capitalist mode. All it has done is to wrench them from their social relations and their relationship with the land. Within a single lifetime they have had to exchange sons for tractors and tractors for petrochemicals. These things too have taken them from themselves in space and in time.

What happens to all this production from the land and from the factories? Where does all the GNP go, except to faceless foreign exploiters in another country and a handful of rich in their own? Who are the agents but their own rulers?

In sum, what capitalist development has meant to the masses of these countries is production without purpose, except to stay alive; massive immizeration accompanied by a wholesale attack on the values, relationships, gods, that made such immizeration bearable; rulers who rule not for their own people but for someone else. This is a development that makes no sense, has no bearing on their lives, is disorganic.

This can be stated at another level. The economic development that capital has superimposed on the peripheries has been unaccompanied by capitalist culture or capitalist democracy. Whereas in the center the different aspects of capitalism (economic, cultural, political) have evolved gradually, organically, out of the center's own history, in the periphery the capitalist mode of production has been grafted on to the existing cultural and political order. Peripheral capitalism is not an organized body of connected, interdependent parts sharing a common life; it is not an organism. What these countries exhibit, therefore, is not just "distorted" or "disarticulated" development (Samir Amin), but disorganic development: an economic system (itself "extraverted") at odds with the cultural and political institutions of the people it exploits. The economic system, that is, is not mediated by culture or legitimated by politics, as in the center. The base and the superstructure do not complement and reinforce each other (but that is not to say that they are in perfect harmony at the center). They are in fundamental conflict. Exploitation is naked, crude, unmediated, although softened by artefacts of capitalist culture and capitalist homilies on human rights. That contradiction is not only general to the social formation but, because of capitalist penetration, runs right through the various modes of production comprising the social formation. At some point, therefore, the political system has to be extrapolated from the superstructure and made to serve as a cohesive, and coercive, force to maintain the economic order of things. The contradiction between superstructure and base now resolves into one between the political régime and the people, with culture as the expression of their resistance. It is cultural resistance which, in Cabral's (1973) magnificent phrase, takes on "new forms (political, economic, armed) in order fully to contest foreign domination."

However, culture in the periphery is not equally developed in all sectors of society. It differs as between the different modes of production but, again as Cabral says, it does have "a mass character". Similarly at the economic level the different exploitations in the different modes confuse the formal lines of class struggle but the common denominators of political oppression make for a mass movement.

Hence the revolutions in these countries are not necessarily class or socialist revolutions. They do not begin as such anyway. They are not even nationalist revolutions as we know them. They are mass movements with national and revolutionary components that are sometimes religious, sometimes secular, often both, but always against the repressive political state and its imperial backers.

Notes

1   GATT was set up to regulate trade between nations, the IMF to help nations adjust to free trade by providing balance-of-payments financial assistance, the World Bank to facilitate the movement of capital to war-torn Europe and aid to developing countries.

2   Even in the period of import substitution, more succinctly described by the Japanese as "export-substitution investment," the multinational corporations were able to move in "behind tariff barriers to produce locally what they had hitherto imported" (*Ampo* 1977).

3   The first free trade zone was established at Shannon airport in Ireland in 1958 and was followed by Taiwan in 1965. In 1967 the United Nations Industrial Development Organization (UNIDO) was set up to promote industrialization in developing countries and soon embarked on the internationalization of free trade zones into a global system. South Korea established a free trade zone in 1970, the Philippines in 1972, and Malaysia in the same year. By 1974, Egypt, Gambia, Ivory Coast, Kenya, Senegal, Sri Lanka, Jamaica, Liberia, Syria, Trinidad and Tobago, and Sudan were asking UNIDO to draw up plans for free trade zones (*Ampo* 1977). Sri Lanka set up its free trade zone in 1978, soon after a right wing government had taken power, albeit through the ballot box.

4   Of course there are those (guess who) who suggest that automation will not only release people from dirty, boring jobs and into more interesting work, but even enhance job prospects.

5   American writers, however, have done better in this regard. See in particular Stewart & Markoff (1979) and Grossman (1979).

6   Workers who must dip components in acids and rub them with solvents frequently experience serious burns, dizziness, nausea, sometimes even losing their fingers in accidents. "It will be 10 or 15 years before the possible carcinogenic effects begin to show up in the women who work with them now" (Grossman 1979).

7   For the purposes of the general analysis presented here. I make no distinction between periphery and developing periphery.

References

Ahmed, F. 1976. Pakistan: the new dependence. *Race and Class* **XVIII** (1, Summer).

Ampo 1977. Free trade zones and industrialisation of Asia. Special issue 8(4), 9(1–2).

ASTMS (Association of Scientific Technical and Managerial Staffs) 1978. *Technological change and collective bargaining*. London: ASTMS.

Barron, I. & R. Curnow 1979. *The future with microelectronics*. London: Frances Pinter.

Braverman, H. 1974. *Labor and monopoly capital*. New York: Monthly Review Press.

Butler, D. N. *The convergence of technologies* (abstract). Report Series no. 5, Butler Cox Foundation.

Cabral, A. 1973. *Return to the source*. New York: Monthly Review Press.

Cambridge Economic Policy Group 1978. *Economic Policy Review* March.

Counter Information Services 1979. *The new technology*. Anti-report no. 23, Counter Information Services, London.

Easey, W. 1977. Notes on child labour in Hong Kong. *Race and Class* **XVIII** (4, Spring).

Falk, R. 1975, A new paradigm for international legal studies. *The Yale Law Journal* **84** (5 April).

Frieden, J. 1977, The trilateral commission: economics and politics in the 1970s. *Monthly Review* **29** (7, December).

Grossman, R. 1979. Women's place in the integrated circuit. *Southeast Asia Chronicle* 66, January–February.

Harman, C. 1979. *Is a machine after your job*? London: Socialist Workers Party.

Hines, C. 1978. *The chips are down*. London: Earth Resources Research.

Jenkins, C. & B. Sherman 1979. *The collapse of work*. London: Eyre Methuen.

Large, P. 1979. The day after tomorrow. *The Guardian* February 17.

Lin Neumann, A. 1979. "Hospitality girls" in the Philippines. *Southeast Asia Chronicle* 66, January–February.

Maddock, I. 1978. Beyond the Protestant ethic. *New Scientist* November 23.

Monthly Review 1978. Oil for underdevelopment and discrimination: the case of Kuwait. **30** (6 November).

Selangor Graduates Society 1978. *Plight of the Malaysian workers in Singapore*. Kuala Lumpur: Selangor Graduates Society.

Sivanandan, A. 1976. Race, class and the state: the black experience in Britain. *Race and Class*, Pamphlet no. 1.

Sivanandan, A. 1978. From immigration control to induced repatriation. *Race and Class*, Pamphlet no. 5.

Stewart, J. & J. Markoff 1979. The microprocessor revolution. Pacific News Service, "Global Factory" (Part II of VI).

TUC (Trades Union Congress) 1979. *Employment and technology*. London: TUC.

Virgo, P. 1979. *Cashing in on the chips*. London: Conservative Political Center.

12 *Women in the global factory*[*]

ANNETTE FUENTES and BARBARA EHRENREICH

In the 1800s, farm girls in England and the northeastern United States filled the textile mills of the first Industrial Revolution. Today, from Penang to Ciudad Juarez, young Third World women have become the new "factory girls," providing a vast pool of cheap labor for globe-trotting corporations. Behind the labels "Made in Taiwan" and "Assembled in Haiti" may be one of the most strategic blocs of womanpower of the 1980s. In the past 15 years, multinational corporations, such as Sears Roebuck and General Electric, have come to rely on women around the world to keep labor costs down and profits up. Women are the unseen assemblers of consumer goods such as toys and designer jeans, as well as the hardware of today's "Microprocessor Revolution."

Low wages are the main reason companies move to the Third World. A female assembly-line worker in the United States is likely to earn between $3.10 and $5 an hour. In many Third World countries a woman doing the same work will earn $3 to $5 a *day*. Corporate executives, with their eyes glued to the bottom line, wonder why they should pay someone in Massachusetts on an hourly basis what someone in the Philipines will earn in a day. And, for that matter, why pay a male worker anywhere to do what a female worker can be hired to do for 40 to 60 percent less?

United States corporations call their international production facilities "offshore sourcing." To unions these are "runaway shops" that take jobs away from American workers. Economists, meanwhile, talk about a "new international division of labor," in which low-skilled, labor-intensive jobs are shifted to the "newly industrializing" Third World countries. Control over management and technology, however, remains at company headquarters in First World countries like the United States and Japan. In 1967, George Ball, senior managing director of Lehman Brothers Kuhn Loeb (an international investment company) and a former undersecretary of state, described the phenomenon this way:

[*] Excerpted from Fuentes A. & B. Ehrenreich 1983, *Women in the global factory* (Boston, Mass.: South End Press), and reprinted by permission of Institute for New Communications.

Today a large and rapidly expanding roster of companies is engaged in taking the raw materials produced in one group of countries, transforming these into manufactured goods with the labor and plant facilities of another group, and selling the products in still a third group. And, with the benefit of instant communications, quick transport, computers and modern managerial techniques, they are redeploying resources and altering patterns of production and distribution month to month in response to changes in price and availability of labor and materials. (Ball 1967: 26)

The pace of multinational production has accelerated rapidly since the mid-1960s. The electronics industry provides a good example of the new international division of labor: circuits are printed on silicon wafers and tested in California; then the wafers are shipped to Asia for the labor-intensive process in which they are cut into tiny chips and bonded to circuit boards; final assembly into products such as calculators, video games, or military equipment usually takes place in the United States. Yet many American consumers do not realize that the goods they buy may have made a global journey and represent the labor of people in several countries, or that the "foreign" products that worry United States workers may have been made in factories owned, at least in part, by United States corporations.

Women on the global assembly line

We need female workers; older than 17, younger than 30; single and without children; minimum education primary school, maximum education one year of preparatory school [high school]; available for all shifts.

                    Advertisement from a Mexican newspaper

A nimble veteran seamstress, Miss Altagracia, eventually began to earn as much as $5.75 a dày . . . "I was exceeding my piecework quota by a lot." . . . But then, Altagracia said, her plant supervisor, a Cuban emigré, called her into his office. "He said I was doing a fine job, but that I and some other of the women were making too much money, and he was being forced to lower what we earned for each piece we sewed." On the best days, she now can clear barely $3, she said. "I was earning less, so I started working six and seven days a week. But I was tired and I could not work as fast as before." Within a few months she was too ill to work at all.

                    Story of 23-year-old Basilia Altagracia,
                    a seamstress in the Dominican Republic's
                    La Romana free trade zone

                             Flannery 1978: 4

There are over 1 million people employed in industrial free trade zones in the Third World. Millions more work outside the zones in multinational-controlled plants and domestically owned subcontracting factories. Eighty to ninety percent of the light-assembly workers are women. This is a remarkable switch from earlier patterns of foreign-controlled industrialization. Until recently, economic development involved heavy industries such as mining and construction and usually meant more jobs for men and, compared to traditional agricultural society, a diminished economic status for women. But multinationals consider light-assembly work, whether the product is Barbie dolls or computer components, to be women's work.

Women everywhere are paid lower wages than men. Since multinationals go overseas to reduce labor costs, women are the natural choice for assembly jobs. Wage-earning opportunities for women are limited and women are considered only supplementary income earners for their families. Management uses this secondary status to pay women less than men and justify layoffs during slow periods, claiming that women do not need to work and will probably quit to get married anyway.

Women are the preferred work force for other reasons. Multinationals want a work force that is docile, easily manipulated, and willing to do boring repetitive assembly work. Women, they claim, are the perfect employees, with their "natural patience" and "manual dexterity." As the personnel manager of an assembly plant in Taiwan says, "young male workers are too restless and impatient to be doing monotonous work with no career value. If displeased they sabotage the machines and even threaten the foreman. But girls, at most they cry a little" (Cantwell et al. 1978: 14).

Multinationals prefer single women with no children and no plans to have any. Pregnancy tests are routinely given to potential employees to avoid the issue of maternity benefits. In India, a woman textile worker reports that "they do take unmarried women but they prefer women who have had an operation," referring to her government's sterilization program (Chhachi 1981: 7). In the Philippines Bataan Export Processing Zone the Mattel toy company offers prizes to workers who undergo sterilization.[1]

Third World women have not always been a ready workforce. Until two decades ago, young women were vital to the rural economy in many countries. They worked in the home, in agriculture, or in local cottage industries. But many Third World governments adopted development plans favoring large-scale industry and agribusiness as advocated by such agencies as the World Bank and the International Monetary Fund. Traditional farming systems and communities are now crumbling as many families lose their land and local enterprises collapse. As a result of the breakdown of the rural economy, many families now send their daughters to the cities or the free trade zones in an attempt to assure some income.

The majority of the new female work force is young, between 16 and 25 years old. As one management consultant explains, "When seniority rises, wages rise"; so the companies prefer to train a fresh group of teenagers rather than give experienced women higher pay. Different industries have different age and skill standards. The youngest workers, usually under 23 years old, are found in electronics and textile factories where keen eyesight and dexterity are essential. A second, older group of women work in industries like food processing where nimble fingers and perfect vision are not required. Conditions in these factories are particularly bad. Multinationals can get away with more because the women generally cannot find jobs elsewhere.

Not all companies want young women, although this is the exception rather than the rule. In Singapore, some companies had problems with young women workers who went "shopping for jobs from factory to factory." Management consultants suggested "housewives-only" assembly lines. Older and too responsible for "transient glamour jobs," housewives would make better candidates, they reasoned. One consultant recommended that "a brigade of housewives could run the factory from 8 a.m. to 1 p.m. and leave. Then a second brigade would come in [and] take over till 6 p.m. This way housewives need only work half a day. They will be able to earn and spend time with their families. The factories will get a full and longer day's work. Deadlines will be met." (*New Straits Times* 1978).

Corporate apologists are quick to insist that Third World women are absolutely thrilled with their newfound employment opportunities. "You should watch these kids going to work," said Bill Mitchell, an American who solicits United States business for the Burmudez Industrial Park in Cuidad Juarez. "You don't have any sullenness here. They smile." A top-level management consultant who advises United States companies on where to relocate their factories said, "The girls genuinely enjoy themselves. They're away from their families. They have spending money. They can buy motor bikes, whatever. Of course, it is a regulated experience, too – with dormitories to live in – so it's a healthful experience." Richard Meier, a professor of environmental design, believes that "earning power should do more for the women of these countries than any amount of organization, demonstration and protest. . . . The benefits and freedom to be gained by these women from their employment in these new industries are almost always preferred to the near slavery associated with the production of classical goods, such as batik" (Meier 1977: 32).

Liberation or virtual slavery? What is the real experience of Third World women? A study of Brazilian women working in a textile factory drew (Saffioto 1981) positive conclusions: work "represents the

widening of horizons, a means of confronting life, a source of individ-
ualization. The majority of women . . . drew a significant part of their
identity from being wage-workers." By earning money and working
outside the home, factory women may find a certain independence
from their families. Meeting and working with other women lays the
foundation for a collective spirit and, perhaps, collective action.

But at the same time, the factory system relies upon and reinforces
the power of men in the traditional patriarchal family to control
women. Cynthia Enloe, a sociologist who organized an international
conference of women textile workers in 1982, says that in the Third
World,

> the emphasis on family is absolutely crucial to management strategy.
> Both old-time firms and multinationals use the family to reproduce
> and control workers. Even recruitment is a family process. Women
> don't just go out independently to find jobs: it's a matter of fathers,
> brothers and husbands making women available after getting
> reassurances from the companies. Discipline becomes a family mat-
> ter since, in most cases, women turn their paychecks over to their
> parents. Factory life is, in general, constrained and defined by the
> family life cycle.

One thing is certain: when multinational corporate-style development meets traditional patriarchal culture, women's lives are bound to
change.

East Asia: the "Oriental Girls"

> The manual dexterity of the Oriental female is famous the world
> over. Her hands are small, and she works fast with extreme care. . . .
> Who, therefore, could be better qualified by nature and inheritance,
> to contribute to the efficiency of a bench-assembly production line
> than the Oriental girl?

Malaysian government investment brochure

> I've sold five years of my youth to the company. I need a rest from
> this brain-numbing work for two or three weeks. But there is no way
> I can leave without quitting or taking a big loss. There are so many
> regulations you feel you are tied up with ropes till you can't budge an
> inch. And I've given them five years of my life!

Taiwanese factory worker
Arrigo 1980: 34

Half a million East Asian women are estimated to be working in export
processing zones. Women are heavily employed in export manufacture

outside the zones as well. In South Korea women between 16 and 25 years of age comprise one-third of the industrial labor force (UNIDO 1980: 12). A great percentage of these "factory girls" come from rural areas, drawn to the burgeoning urban centers by reports from friends or older sisters who have landed an assembly job. When there is not a large enough pool of would-be factory workers in the cities, companies go out recruiting in the countryside, often enlisting the help of village authorities and the fathers and brothers of factory-age women. In Taiwan, large companies work with junior high school principals who offer up busloads of recent graduates to labor-hungry plants (UNIDO 1980: 27). For the majority of women, it is their first job experience. They may even be the first wage-earners in their families.

Although some women live close enough to factories to remain with their families and commute by bus, most workers are forced to find accommodation near the plant. Housing is scarce and expensive for their meager wages. In Malaysia, researcher Rachel Grossman of the Institute for Labor Education and Research found women employees of a United States company living four to eight in a room in boarding houses, or squeezed into tiny extensions built onto squatter huts near the factories. Access to clean water is often nonexistent or severely limited. Where companies do provide dormitories for their employees, they are not of the "healthful" collegiate variety described in corporate propaganda. Dormitory rooms are small and crowded, with beds shared by as many as three shifts of workers: as one worker gets up to go to the factory, another returning from work takes her place in bed. As many as 20 women may be crammed into a tiny space. In Thailand, staff members of the American Friends Service Committee (AFSC) found filthy dormitories with workers forced to improvise a place to sleep among splintered floorboards, rusting sheets of metal, and scraps of dirty cloth.

The great majority of the women earn subsistence-level incomes, whether they work for a multinational corporation or a locally owned factory. Although corporate executives insist that their wages are ample in view of lower standards of living, the minimum wage in most East Asian countries comes nowhere near to covering basic living costs. In the Philippines, starting wages in United States-owned electronics plants are between $34 and $46 a month; the basic cost of living is $37 a month for one person. In Indonesia, the starting wages are about $7 less per month than the basic cost of living (Grossman 1979: 10). And that basic cost of living means bare subsistence: a diet of rice, some dried fish and water, lodging in a small room occupied by four or more people.

Contrary to corporate belief, most women do not use their wages to buy motor bikes and personal luxury items. A much-advertised Coke is a "luxury" that might cost half a day's wage. Meager as their wages are, however, most women are important wage earners for their families. A

1970 study of young women factory workers in Hong Kong showed that 88 percent were turning more than half their earnings over to their parents. In Malaysia, women electronics workers contribute 25 to 60 percent of their wages to their families (Lim 1980: 28). There is a growing pressure on women of both farm and lower-income urban backgrounds to postpone marriage and find work to help out their families.

Health hazards

Subsistence wages are only part of the picture. Most women work under conditions that can break their health or shatter their nerves within a few years, often before they have worked long enough to earn more than a subsistence wage.

Consider first the electronics industry, which is generally thought to be the safest and cleanest of the export industries. Inside the low, modern factory buildings, rows of young women, neatly dressed in company uniforms or T-shirts, work quietly at their stations. There is air conditioning, not for the women's comfort, but to protect the delicate semi-conductor parts they work with. High-volume popular music is piped in to prevent talking. Electronics is near the top of the list, prepared by the United States National Institute on Occupational Safety and Health (NIOSH), of high-health-risk industries. Open containers of dangerous carcinogenic acids and solvents, giving off toxic fumes, are commonplace in electronics factories. In a Hong Kong clinic survey of workers who use chemicals, 48 percent had constant headaches, 39 percent were often drowsy, and 36 percent had frequent sore throats (*Global Electronics Information Newsletter* 1982).

Anthropologist Linda Gail Arrigo was in Taiwan when 12 women died from inhaling toxic fumes at a Philco–Ford plant. "One 18-year-old woman was stricken after only three weeks on the job," she said. "The company claimed she had a mysterious hereditary disease. After the news of those cases got out, the company gave her parents $2,500 – less than half of her medical bills for a slow, painful death."

At one stage of the assembly process, workers have to dip the circuits into open vats of acid. According to AFSC staffpersons Irene Johnson and Carol Bragg, who toured a National Semiconductor plant in Penang, Malaysia, women who do the dipping wear rubber gloves and boots. But these sometimes leak and burns are common. It is not uncommon for whole fingers to be lost in the process.

Electronic companies require perfect vision in new employees, but most women need glasses after a few years on the job. During the bonding process women peer through microscopes for seven to nine hours a day attaching hairlike gold wires to silicon chips. One study in

South Korea found that most electronics assembly workers developed eye problems after only one year of employment: 88 percent had chronic conjunctivitis; 47 percent became nearsighted; 19 percent developed astigmatism (Lim 1980: 25). The companies treat these health complaints with indifference. "These girls are used to working with the scopes. We've found no eye problems. But it sure makes me dizzy to look through those things," said a plant manager at Hewlett-Packard's Malaysia operation (Grossman 1979: 12).

Unlike electronics factories, conditions in the garment and textile industry are visibly unhealthy, rivaling those of any 19th-century sweatshop. The firms, generally local subcontractors to large United States (and European) chains such as J. C. Penney and Sears, show little concern for the health of their employees. Some of the worst conditions have been documented in South Korea where the garment and textile industry helped spark that country's so-called "economic miracle." Workers are packed into poorly lit rooms, where summer temperatures rise above 100 degrees Fahrenheit. Textile dust and lint, which can cause brown-lung disease, fill the air. The dampness that is so useful in preserving thread, causes rheumatism and arthritis among the workers.

In her diary (originally published in a magazine which has since been banned by the South Korean government) Min Chong Suk, a sewing-machine operator, wrote of working from 7 a.m. to 11:30 p.m. in a garment factory:

> When [the apprentices] shake the waste threads from the clothes, the whole room fills with dust and it is hard to breathe. Since we've been working in such dusty air, there have been increasing numbers of people getting tuberculosis, bronchitis, and eye disease . . . it makes us so sad when we have pale, unhealthy, wrinkled faces like dried-up spinach . . . It seems to me that no one knows our blood dissolves into the threads and seams, with sighs and sorrows.

Stress and high anxiety permeate the women's work lives, contributing to health problems. Most factories operate several shifts, requiring workers to rotate day and night shifts every week or two. These irregular schedules wreak havoc with sleep patterns and foster nervous ailments and stomach disorders. Lunch breaks may be barely long enough for a woman to stand in line at the canteen. Visits to the bathroom are treated as a privilege; in some cases workers must raise their hands for permission to use the toilet. Waits up to a half hour are common. When production deadlines draw near or there are rush orders, women may be forced to work overtime for as much as 48 hours at a stretch. Management often provides pep pills and amphetamine injections to keep the women awake and working; some of the women have become addicts (*ISIS International Bulletin* 1978–9: 12).

Sexual harassment is another hazard of factory work, especially for women who are out late at night working the graveyard shift. In the Bataan Export Processing Zone in the Philippines, sexual harassment is a common practice among male supervisors. "We call our company 'motel,'" says a worker at Mattel, "because we are often told to lay down or be laid off. It is hard to know what to do when that happens because we can't afford to lose our jobs."[1]

Naturally, women's entry into the work force has dramatic effects in countries where their lives have always been centered around the family and home production. On the one hand, factory work does offer women some autonomy, earning power and freedom from parental control. In Malaysia, says Rachel Grossman, "they come for the money, of course, but also for the freedom. They talk of freedom to go out late at night, to have a boyfriend, to wear blue jeans, high-heeled shoes and makeup . . . They revel in their escape from the watchful eyes of fathers and brothers" (Grossman 1979: 13).

On the other hand, factory workers often pay a high price for that newly won freedom, limited though it may be. Because of their relative independence, westernized dress and changed lifestyles, women may be rejected by their families and find it hard to reassimilate when they can no longer find employment on the assembly line. "Factory girls," especially those living away from their families in company dormitories or urban housing are thought to be "loose" sexually. The issue of women workers' morality is a burning one in many East Asian countries, debated by women's groups, politicians and community leaders.

Women who work in factories are often scorned by men as unsuitable marriage partners. Although pressure to marry is great, women have a harder time finding a mate after spending their prime marriageable years in the factory. By age 27 or 28, an unmarried woman is something of a misfit and if she has worked in a factory the stigma is even greater. Competition among the workers for eligible husbands is intense. Social isolation, says Linda Gail Arrigo, is a growing problem among these young women. Caught between traditional rôles and their new status as workers, the "Oriental girls" are at home nowhere.

South of the border, down Mexico way

> Have your cake and eat it too . . . Live in the U.S. Pay your [Mexican] employees $6.64 a day.
>
>   Advertisement in an El Paso business publication

For tourists, Mexico is the land of cheap vacations, spicy food and *sombreros*. For United States business, Mexico is the land of cheap labor. Southwestern agribusiness has long been dependent on that labor in the form of *mojados* (wetbacks) who slip across the border for work.

From 1942 to 1964 the Bracero Program regulated the flow of *braceros* (contracted migrant workers) into the United States. When the program was stopped, 200,000 farm workers were suddenly jobless. Unemployment reached 50 percent among the manual laborers in border cities like Mexicali and Ciudad Juarez. The Mexican government, anxious for a solution to the crisis, reacted enthusiastically when the Mexican secretary of industry and commerce was invited to visit new United States assembly plants in Hong Kong and Taiwan. United States industrialists proposed the creation of a free trade zone on the United States/Mexican border that would both fulfill United States manufacturers' need for cheap labor and create jobs for Mexico's unemployed (Woog 1980: 50). Mexican officials assumed (wrongly, it turned out) that transfer of technology and skills would be part of the bargain. Thus was born the Border Industrialization Program (BIP) in 1965 with the *maquiladora* system of twin plants, one on either side of the border. Labor-intensive processes were to be located in Mexico. Precut garments, electronic components, and artificial flowers, among other things, would be sent from United States-based plants to the *maquiladora* for sewing, welding, gluing, and assembly and shipped back to the United States for distribution.

Unprecedented financial incentives were granted to foreign companies by the Mexican government: factories could be 100 percent foreign-owned and managed; low taxes on profits and sales were offered, with some Mexican states giving full tax exemption; and land could be purchased or leased on favorable terms. Unofficially, corporations were given carte blanche to conduct business and labor affairs without government interference.

The Mexican government had considered BIP a temporary response to a crisis situation. But in 1972, BIP was expanded from the original 12.5-mile stretch of the border to include all of Mexico, opening up the entire country to a new form of colonization in which labor, not raw materials, was the main prize (Fernandez Kelly 1981: 5).

Maquila *women*

From the start, BIP was a lopsided arrangement offering Mexico little in return for its concessions. Rather than alleviate massive unemployment among male workers in the border area, the program targeted a new source of cheap factory labor. Corporations aimed to draw unprecedented numbers of women into the industrial labor force just as they had done in East Asia. Arthur D. Little, a United States consulting firm that had designed several industrial parks under BIP, did a study in 1966 that outlined strategy for United States business on the border: "The present industrial pool of about 25,000 can increase severalfold through greater use of female labor (only one-fifth of the labor pool is female at present), through the conversion to industrial work of low-income agricultural and commercial labor, and through the attraction of further immigration from central Mexico" (NACLA 1975: 11).

By 1974, there were about 500 *maquiladoras* operating on the border, employing some 80,000 people, 85 percent of whom were women. The majority were between 16 and 25 years old and came to the border zone from small towns and cities. Entire families moved north in the hope that their daughters could find work. Mexican women were targeted for assembly jobs for the same reasons as their Asian sisters: they could be paid less than men because of their disadvantaged position in society and because their wages were considered only supplementary to male sources of family income. *Maquiladora* workers average 48 hours a week on the job for the minimum wage of 455 pesos a day – about 77 US cents an hour. (With the recent devaluations of the Mexican peso, the real wages of Mexican workers have dropped sharply.)

As in East Asia, low wages are not the only reason multinationals prefer women. Social and cultural stereotypes of docile and uncomplaining "girls" apply here as well. A primer for businesses setting up *maquiladoras* states that "from their earliest conditioning women show respect and obedience to authority, especially men. The women follow orders willingly, accept change and adjustments easily and are considerably less demanding . . ." According to an electronics plant manager in Ciudad Juarez men are much more difficult: "The man in Mexico is still the man. This kind of job is not doing much for his macho image. It's just a little quirk of a different culture. They'd rather run a factory" (*Cleveland Plain Dealer* 1981).

There are presently over 600 *maquiladoras* on the border, accounting for half of all the assembled products which enter the United States under lenient tariff codes designed to nurture offshore manufacturing. With companies streaming down to the border to exploit Mexico's growing economic difficulties – aggravated by the drop in oil export earnings – the future of the *maquiladora* looks rosy.

The picture is not so rosy, however, for the 135,000 women working the *maquiladoras*, nor the hundred of thousands who will be drawn into the labor market in the coming years. The National Bank of Mexico predicts that the *maquiladora* work force will reach half a million by 1990. Companies routinely violate federal labor laws on minimum wages and social security and frequently require women to sign temporary work contracts to prevent them from accruing seniority and the increased salaries that go with it. As in the Philippines, a medical certificate proving that a job applicant is not pregnant is often required, eliminating any expenses for maternity benefits.

Workers in electronics plants, which account for 60 percent of the *maquiladoras*, are regularly exposed to toxic chemicals. Because women's work is assumed to be a temporary hiatus from their usual domestic tasks, health and safety concerns are brushed aside. "We don't worry too much about these matters; these girls don't stay on the job long enough to get sick," claims a plant manager in Ciudad Juarez (Fernandez Kelly n.d.: 15). But in garment factories, which comprise 30 percent of all border industry, chronic back problems, asthma, conjunctivitis, bronchitis, and brown-lung are common occupational diseases. With the intense pressure of assembly work, *maquila* women experience high levels of gastrointestinal disorders, insomnia, and menstrual irregularities. Bladder problems are common because women cannot use the toilets or drink water freely.

Almost two decades after the first *maquiladora* started operating, BIP is generally recognized as a failure in terms of the Mexican government's initial expectations. Male unemployment along the border has reached 67 percent; transfer of skills to the work force and technology to Mexican industry has been minimal (learning to stitch 1,000 shirt cuffs per day may lead to a shirt sleeve, but not much else); and capital-intensive technology remains in the United States. Adding insult to injury up to 70 percent of *maquiladora* workers' wages are spent across the border in the United States and do not contribute to the Mexican economy (Woog 1980: 103). What began as a short-term remedy for Mexico's economic malaise has only deepened dependency on the United States and generated new problems for the Mexican people.

The answer is global

Women all over the world are becoming a giant reserve army of labor at the disposal of globe-trotting multinationals. No woman can feel job security on the assembly line as long as the profit motive guides multinational activities. Runaways are now occurring *within* the Third World. Sri Lanka, which recently opened an export processing zone, has become a haven for companies fleeing the labor militancy in South Korea and the Philippines.

Charito Planas, former director of the Philippine Chamber of Commerce and a Marcos opponent living in exile when we wrote this chapter, says many women do not realize they are being exploited. "Because we've been dominated by foreigners, women employed in foreign corporations feel superior to those in local factories owned by Filipino businessmen . . . But there are some women who are aware of their situation and are organizing and involved in the struggle for better working conditions. Their numbers are growing despite government arrests. It's just a matter of time," she believes. "There's no stopping the pendulum of change."

Some corporate strategists are now suggesting that offshore factories are no longer viable. An editor of *Semiconductor International* argues that "if political turmoil begins to haunt the world, especially in those areas where U.S. companies have their assembly operations, it would be a disaster for the U.S. semiconductor industry. . . . With the new, more vigorous U.S. defense posture, political polarization and turmoil are bound to occur. We can expect that some countries which now openly welcome the semiconductor industry will make greater demands on companies . . ." (Levinthal 1981: 6). The solution? Automated facilities in the United States to assure cheap labor *and* stability.

Automation without worker control and full employment is a threat to working people. In the electronics industry, women are assembling the very components which may be used to make their jobs and those of other workers obsolete. Faced with sexual and racial discrimination, women will be further hurt as remaining technical and managerial jobs go mainly to white men.

With continued economic crisis, when even low-paid jobs are hard to come by, it is especially easy for companies to play off their employees against each other. As sociologist Cynthia Enloe says, "We're all being fed the line that we are each other's competitors." Women in a Tennessee garment factory are threatened with competition from Mexican workers, and women in the Philippines are threatened with competition from Sri Lanka. It is a competition in which all workers are losers; wages are driven down everywhere and health and safety conditions deteriorate, but job security is never achieved. As garment worker Min Chong Suk asserts, "The people who are called economic scholars use 'international competition' when they talk. But we know they mean a way to squeeze workers."

"Bound together with one string"

Rachel Grossman (1979) argues, "Protectionism and nationalist attitudes that view Third World imports and workers as competition are lagging behind the times. The international nature of production has been an economic reality for some time now. Multinationals don't deal in terms of individual countries, but on a global scale." Any strategy to further women's control over their worklives must take into account that new economic reality. Saralee Hamilton, coordinator of the AFSC Nationwide Women's Program, says: "The multinational corporations have deliberately targeted women for exploitation. If feminism is going to mean anything to women all over the world, it's going to have to find new ways to resist corporate power internationally."

One way to resist that power is to use organized pressure in specific cases of corporate abuse. The boycott of Nestlé products to protest their infant formula promotion in Third World countries is a good example of a successful consumer action. But a general boycott of consumer goods from Third World countries is unrealistic, and may hurt working people more than anything else.

Another important strategy is to foster an information exchange between Third World activists and their counterparts in the industrialized countries. Information on hazardous substances at the workplace or on corporate structures and strategies is often easier to obtain in the "home" countries of the multinationals where there are more resources at hand. Sharing the knowledge that will empower women workers in their struggle is a priority of solidarity work.

The most difficult, yet most important, task in confronting multinational domination is to create direct links between women workers around the world. International travel is expensive and few women have the money for long-distance phone calls or even postage. But some links are being made, such as UE's developing relationship with KMU of the Philippines. The Nationwide Women's Program organized a conference in 1978 on women and global corporations which brought together women from the Third World and the United States to share information and ideas. Out of that conference came the Women and Global Corporations project which encourages networking of working women in the Third World with women in the Western countries to provide support for their common struggles.

It may take years before international links are extensive and powerful enough to challenge successfully multinational corporations and the governments which support them, but women's lives grow closer all the time. "We all have the same hard life," wrote Min Chong Suk. "We are bound together with one string."

Note

1   From a slide show on women in the Philippines by the Philippine Solidarity Network, San Francisco, California.

References

Arrigo, L. G. 1980. The industrial workforce of young women in Taiwan. *Bulletin of Concerned Asian Scholars* April–June.

Ball, G. 1967. Cosmocorp: the importance of being stateless. *Columbia Journal of World Business* November and December, 26.

Cantwell, B., D. Luce and L. Weinglass 1978. *Made in Taiwan*. New York: Asia Center.

Chhachi, A. 1981. *The experiences of retrenchment: women textile workers in India*. Paper presented at textile workers conference of the Transnational Institute, Amsterdam, October.

Cleveland Plain Dealer 1981. June 2, 1975.

Fernandez Kelly, M. P. 1981. *Women's industrial employment, migration and health status along the U.S.–Mexican Border*. Working paper for Program in US Mexican Studies. San Diego: University of California.

Fernandez Kelly, M. P. *Maquiladoras and women in Ciudad Juarez: the paradoxes of industrialization under global capitalism*, Unpublished paper, Center for Latin American Studies. Palo Alto, Calif.: Stanford University.

Flannery, M. 1978. America's sweatshop in the sun. *AFL–CIO American Federationist* May, 16.

Global Electronics Information Newsletter (Pacific Studies Center, Mountain View, California), February 1982.

Grossman, R. 1979. Changing role of Southeast Asian women: the global assembly line and the social manipulation of women on the job. *Southeast Asia Chronicle* January–February.

Isis International Bulletin 1978–9. 10, Women workers in Asia. Rome and Geneva, Winter.

Levinthal, D. J. 1981. Automate, but bring it back onshore. *Semiconductor International*, April.

Lim, L. Y. C. 1980. *Women in the redeployment of manufacturing industry to developing countries*, UNIDO Working Papers on Structural Changes, 18.

Meier, R. L. 1977. Multinationals as agents of social development. *Bulletin of the Atomic Scientists* November.

NACLA (North American Congress on Latin America) 1975. Hit and Run: U.S. runaway shops on the Mexican border. *Latin American and Empire Report*, July–August.

New Straits Times (Singapore), 1978. Our fussy factory workers. June 18.

Saffioto, H. I. B. 1981. *The impact of industrialization on the structure of female employment*. Paper presented at textile workers conference of the Transnational Institute, Amsterdam, October.

UNIDO (United Nations Industrial Development Organization) 1980. *Export processing zones in developing countries*. UNIDO Working Papers on Structural Changes, 19 (Global and Conceptual Studies Section). International Center for Industrial Studies, August 18. New York: UNIDO.

Woog, M. A. 1980. *El Programa Mexicana de maquiladoras: una respuesta a las necesidades de la industia norteamericana*. Guadalajara: Universidad de Guadalajara.

13 Export-led industrialization in the Third World: Manufacturing imperialism*

MARTIN LANDSBERG

With 1979 marking the end of the Second United Nations Development Decade, the problems of poverty and underdevelopment in the Third World remain at least as great as they were at the beginning of the First United Nations Development Decade. Many Third World governments, increasingly worried that capitalism's failure to induce Third World development will eventually undermine their power, are desperately searching for an economic strategy that will lead to self-expanding capitalist industrialization. According to many bourgeois economists, the solution is industrialization based on the export of manufactures.

These economists point to countries like South Korea, Taiwan, Singapore, and Hong Kong, all of which follow this strategy, as examples of Third World nations on the road to capitalist industrialization and development. The undeniable growth in production and export of manufactures by these countries, in conjunction with support from international economic institutions and developed capitalist country governments, has led to a growing number of Third World nations adopting a similar development program. Export-led industrialization is now the dominant Third World strategy for achieving capitalist development.

My investigation begins with an analysis of the failure of import-substitution industrialization as a model for the Third World development, and the historical conditions and pressures created by imperialism which led a number of Third World nations to adopt a new

* Reprinted from Landsberg, M. 1979, Export-led industrialization in the Third World: manufacturing imperialism, *Review of Radical Political Economics* **11** (4, winter), 50–63, by permission of the author and the Union for Radical Political Economics. (© 1979 *Review of Radical Political Economics.*)

strategy: industrialization based on the production and export of manufactures. Next, I identify the Third World countries which lead in the export of manufactures and the types of goods they export, showing how transnational corporations have played a major rôle in shaping export-led industrialization and control most Third World exports in the process of transnational corporate profit maximization. By studying the impact of export-led industrialization on the political economy of Third World nations, I conclude that this strategy will lead not to the creation of indigenous, self-expanding capitalist development in the Third World but to dependent industrialization as part of a new form of imperialist domination.

The failure of import-substitution industrialization

At the close of World War II, foreign domination of the Third World had not been broken.[1] Domestic planning and development were squeezed and limited by two interconnected pressures. First, with little industrial base, countries were forced to spend large sums of foreign exchange to import almost all manufactured goods. Second, necessary foreign exchange could be earned only through primary commodity exports to the developed capitalist countries (DCCs), but these exports were continually subject to violent swings in demand and reduced purchasing power. The lack of foreign exchange sufficient to maintain even minimal levels of growth and consumption necessitated substantial foreign debt with continued foreign domination the result.

Fearful of growing internal pressures for change, and desiring to insure and expand their power, the national bourgeoise in a number of Third World countries sought to break out of this position of dependence. Generalizing, their goal was to initiate self-expanding capitalist development, and their strategy was to pursue import-substitution industrialization (ISI). This choice of ISI as a development strategy flowed out of the constraints described above. Since primary commodity trade had proven unreliable, it was to have reduced emphasis. Since dependence appeared to rest on a continual lack of foreign exchange and the need to import all manufactured goods, ISI would pursue the replacement of these imports by boosting domestic production.

The logic of imperialism, however, kept this from succeeding. In choosing which goods to produce, the market, as always, responded to the existing class structure. The mass of the population remained poor, tied to the land for survival, and unable to provide a market for goods. Thus the decision to produce domestic manufactured goods could not mean the production of mass-consumption goods.

Only the bourgeoisie was capable of supporting a domestic market and thus industrialization had to focus on luxuries and consumer durables and be concentrated in existing urban areas (further aggravating regional imbalances). The fact that tariffs would reduce finished imports from advanced capitalist countries, however, did not mean that the local bourgeoisie had the capital or technology to begin their own domestic industrialization. The result was foreign debt and participation by foreign (primarily United States) transnational corporations. Although projects were often joint ventures with contribution by local capital, "independent" development was soon transformed into dependent industrialization under the leadership of foreign capital. Moreover, although local production did at first lead to a reduction in imports, after a brief period the foreign exchange saved was far surpassed by the foreign exchange spent for the importation of basic inputs and capital goods, and by the massive outflow of profits back to the transnational corporations' home countries, primarily the United States. Thus, although the composition of Third World countries' imports did change, their balance of payments deficits continued to grow.

For Third World countries, the results of ISI were anything but positive: (1) greater starvation for the majority of the people, (2) limited industrialization, (3) growing regional inequalities, and (4) larger deficits and debt.

The new strategy: export-led industrialization

By the 1960s, the bourgeoisie in most Third-World nations were forced to admit that ISI had been a failure. Their goals of diversified and self-generating industrialization and economic independence had both been frustrated. With internal class pressures building and national liberation struggles successfully organizing people around an anticapitalist ideology, the national bourgeoisie realized a change in strategy was necessary. And so, in the early 1960s, a new approach to development (once again flowing out of the logic of imperialism) was advanced.

Given the precarious debt position facing most Third World nations, it was not surprising that the linchpin of this new strategy was increased exports. Unless foreign exchange pressures could be alleviated, no real planning was possible. In a sense this strategy completed a full circle: once again Third World development was to be tied to the external market. However, with industrialization still a major goal, there was to be a change in the composition of exports. In the past, export-led development concentrated upon primary commodity sales to the developed capitalist countries. Now, it was to be based upon the production and export of manufactures. By this strategy, the bourgeoisie hoped to industrialize, reduce domestic tensions through increased employment, earn foreign exchange, and stimulate the process of domestic capitalist development.

The Third World's shift to production of manufactures for export is documented in Table 13.1. Between 1960 and 1969, total world exports grew at an average annual rate of 8.8 percent. Breaking down that total reveals a 10.8 percent increase for manufactured goods compared to a 5.7 percent increase for primary commodities. This trend toward greater trade in manufactures (by 1969 they accounted for 60.5 percent of total exports) was, as shown in Table 13.1, most pronounced among Third World nations.

Third World countries continued to trade mostly in primary commodities. But, as a result of this new development strategy, manufactured exports (narrowly defined) as a percentage of total Third World exports increased from 9.2 percent in 1960 to almost 17 percent in 1969. Manufactured goods narrowly defined refers to chemicals, basic manufactures, machinery and transport equipment, and miscellaneous light manufactures. Manufactured goods broadly defined includes additional items such as a number of processed products, e.g., processed foods and wood and paper products.[2] Using the broader definition of manufactures, the share of manufactures in total Third World exports increased from 21 percent in 1967 to 27 percent in 1971 to 40 percent in 1976 (UNCTAD Secretariat 1978a: 5). In fact, between

Table 13.1 Trends and characteristics of world trade in manufactures 1960–69[a]

World trade in manufactures	World[b] total	Developed countries	Developing countries
Percentage share in world exports			
1960	100.0	83.9	3.8
1969	100.0	84.6	5.1
Cumulative annual growth rates 1960–9			
manufactures	10.8	10.9	14.3
primary commodities	5.7	5.9	5.8
Percentage share of exports of manufactures in total exports of goods			
1960	51.3	64.4	9.2
1969	60.5	72.3	16.8

Source: *Economic Bulletin for Latin America* 17:1 (1972) p. 42.

Notes
[a] SITC sections 5, 6, 7 and 8, excluding division 68.
[b] Includes socialist world.

1970 and 1976, Third World exports of manufactured goods (broadly defined) to DCCs increased in volume terms at an annual rate of 14 percent – or more than twice as fast as imports of manufactures into DCCs from the world, twice as fast as manufacturing output growth in the Third World, and four times as fast as manufacturing output growth in the DCCs (UNCTAD Secretariat 1978b).

Third World production and export of manufactures is characteristic of a new international division of labor. The classical international division of labor was based upon a small core of heavily industrialized developed capitalist countries trading with a larger number of raw-material supplying Third World nations. The production and export of manufactures has now spread to new locations in the Third World.

Countries and products: who is exporting what to whom?

In order to evaluate manufactured export-led industrialization (MEI) as a development strategy, it is necessary to examine specific Third World nations and their export performance. This task is facilitated by the fact that relatively few Third World countries produce the great majority of manufactured exports.

Table 13.2 The top eight Third World[a] exporters of manufactures[b] to 21 developed capitalist countries in 1973 (in million US$)

Country	Value	Percentage of total Third World exports to 21 developed capitalist countries
Hong Kong	3,260	23.0
Republic of Korea	2,234	15.7
Mexico	1,260	8.9
Brazil	1,139	8.0
India	872	6.1
Singapore	840	5.9
Malaysia	560	3.9
Argentina	443	3.1
total	10,608	74.7

Source: UNCTAD Secretariat (1976: 26).

Notes

[a] Yugoslavia and Israel are not considered Third World countries, Taiwan is not included in UN computations.

[b] Excluding petroleum products and unwrought nonferrous metals.

In 1973, for example, Hong Kong, South Korea, Singapore, Malaysia, Mexico, Argentina, Brazil, and India accounted for approximately 75 percent of all Third World manufactured exports (broadly defined) to DCCs (see Table 13.2).[3] More specifically, Table 13.3 shows that our eight countries accounted for an overwhelming percentage of all Third World exports to DCCs in three product lines: engineering and metal products, clothing, and miscellaneous light manufacturing. They were also well represented in leather and footwear, wood products and furniture, and textiles. Using the most restrictive definition of manufactures, and 1972 data, these eight countries accounted for almost 60 percent of *total* Third World exports of manufactures and over 65 percent of *total* Third World industrial production.

There are, however, some important differences among these eight leading exporters. Mexico, Brazil, Argentina, and India (Group A) accounted for over 55 percent of all Third World industrial production but only about 25 percent of all Third World manufactured exports (narrowly defined). Hong Kong, Malaysia, Singapore, and South Korea (Group B) were responsible for less than 10 percent of Third World production *but* 35 percent of all Third World manufactured exports (narrowly defined) (Nayyar 1978: 61).

It is not surprising that Mexico, Brazil, Argentina and India are leading Third World exporters of manufactures because each has a relatively large domestic industrial base and established infrastructure. Hong Kong, Malaysia, Singapore, and South Korea represent almost a completely opposite situation. They have few natural resources, small domestic markets, and little infrastructure. Yet, as the data presented above show, by rooting their industrial base in the needs and logic of the international capitalist economy, they have become very successful exporters (see Table 13.4), especially to DCCs.[4]

The differences between Groups A and B are significant to our understanding of export-led industrialization. In order to appreciate these differences more fully, we shall look at the structure of each of the eight nations' manufactured exports to the developed capitalist world. The focus will be on exports to DCCs because these make up the great majority of Third World exports.

We now examine the data in Table 13.3 by country, starting with those in Group A. Argentina's exports are primarily food products and leather and footwear. India is the leading exporter of textiles and leather and footwear. Brazil is the leading exporter of food products and has significant sales in wood products and furniture, textiles, and leather and footwear. It is important to note that all three of these countries are primarily exporters of traditional manufactured goods, and that many of these processed raw-material exports occur because of natural-resource conditions in the country.

Mexico stands as an exception to the other countries in Group A. It is

Table 13.3 Exports of manufactures[a] to 21 developed capitalist countries, 1973 (in million US$).

	Hong Kong	Republic of Korea	Mexico	Brazil	India	Singapore	Malaysia	Argentina	21 DCC[b]	Percentage by[c]
clothing	1,393	644	106	44	80	116	20	18	2,650	91.4
other engineering and metal products	649	337	559	115	48	472	81	35	2,453	93.6
textiles	336	308	100	143	432	32	16	10	2,275	60.5
wood products and furniture	35	330	52	163	8	141	385	1	1,587	70.3
miscellaneous light manufactures	719	230	93	22	25	38	5	16	1,292	88.9
food products	23	67	73	308	17	19	36	159	1,217	57.7
leather and footwear	59	109	26	140	195	3	4	102	823	77.5
chemicals	15	35	89	75	24	17	6	47	614	50.2
iron and steel	3	115	26	69	31	1	—	43	552	52.2
drink and tobacco products	—	1	73	5	—	—	—	3	220	37.3
others	28	58	63	55	12	2	6	9	506	46.0
total above	3,260	2,234	1,260	1,139	872	842	560	443	14,189	74.8

Source: UNCTAD Secretariat (1976: 48–50).

Notes

[a] Excluding petroleum products and unworked nonferrous metals.
[b] Total imports by DCCs from the Third World by product line. Yugoslavia and Israel are not considered Third World countries. Taiwan is not included in UN computations.
[c] The percentage of total imports by DCCs from the Third World accounted for by the eight Third World countries listed.

Table 13.4 Per capita exports of manufactures[a] by selected Third World countries to the developed capitalist countries, 1973.

Country	Population mid-1973 (millions)	Manufactured[a] exports per capita in dollars
Hong Kong	4.2	784
Singapore	2.2	384
Korea	32.9	68
Malaysia	11.3	49
Mexico	54.3	23
Argentina	24.3	18
Brazil	101.4	11
India	574.2	1.5

Source: UNCTAD Secretariat (1976: 28).

Note
[a] Excluding petroleum products and unworked nonferrous metals.

a major exporter of engineering and metal products and has significant sales in clothing, textiles, and light manufacturing. These export categories, except textiles, represent components of a less traditional, more modern industrial base. Mexico's success in these areas, however, is tied to its Border Industrialization Program. Production in the border area accounts for over 25 percent of total exports and almost all the exports of nontraditional manufactures (Nayyar 1978: 81). If the border area were considered part of Group B, Mexico would no longer be considered an exception.

If we look at countries in Group B we see a contrasting situation. Hong Kong, for example, is the leading exporter in clothing, light manufactures, and engineering and metal products. South Korea exports a significant amount of clothing, and engineering and metal products. Singapore specializes in engineering and metal products. Malaysia, the exception in Group B, concentrates on export of traditional manufactures – wood products and furniture. It is, however, currently increasing its exports of engineering products.

With reference to those product categories in which the eight countries account for a majority of Third World exports to DCCs, it appears that Group A (with the Mexican border area as an exception) specializes in traditional resource-based exports and that Group B specializes in more modern industrial product exports. This difference in emphasis is part of an important trend. In the early 1960s, about 67 percent of all manufactured goods which Third World countries exported to DCCs were products made from foodstuffs, tobacco, wood, textiles, and leather. The nontraditional manufactured exports (clothing, engineering goods, and light manufacturing) accounted for only 18 percent. By 1973 the situation was reversed with traditional exports accounting for only 40 percent of total export value and the nontraditional products 45 percent (Nayyar 1978: 74).

This point is made even sharper if we concentrate on exports to the United States. Group B countries – Hong Kong, South Korea, and Singapore – emphasize exports in clothing, engineering and metal products, and light manufactures. Group A countries – Argentina, India, and Brazil – emphasize more traditional exports in product lines like leather and footwear, food products and textiles. Looking at the overall composition of imports into the United States from the Third World, we see that almost 60 percent of the total imports are clothing, engineering and metal products, and light manufactures.

We can now generalize the differences between Group A and Group B. The countries in Group A are large, have significant natural resources and appear to have a base for successfully exporting a broad range of manufactures. Yet their exports to the DCCs are concentrated on those goods that are connected to their natural resource of endowment and that represent a declining percentage of total imports into the United States and other DCCs. Group B countries have small internal markets and relatively undeveloped industrial infrastructures. Yet they specialize in nontraditional manufactures and successfully compete against larger and more developed Third World countries in DCC markets.

Export-led industrialization: what is behind its growth?

Central to the growth of Third World exports of manufactures to DCCs is "international subcontracting."[5] The term refers to a relationship whereby, in order to cover markets in an advanced capitalist country, transnational corporations arrange to use Third World firms to produce entire products, components, or services. The arrangement can be initiated by a producer firm, i.e., a firm that produces similar products, or by a retailing firm, i.e., a firm primarily involved in product distribution. Regardless, the transnational corporation will always control final marketing of the product and, more often than not, provide technical assistance, management, loan capital, and physical equipment for the subcontractor. Although there are a variety of possible legal relationships between the transnational corporation and the subcontractor, ranging from wholly owned subsidiary to independent producer, the key point is that Third World exports to DCCs are part of a complete organizational structure dominated by firms from advanced capitalist countries. For example, while Sears may contract with an independent firm in Hong Kong to produce standard white polyester shirts, Sears retains complete control over research, advertising, and marketing.

No one knows the exact size or rate of growth of Third World international subcontracting. A rough estimate of growth for the United States can be calculated by using figures for United States imports under Tariff Items 806.30 and 807.00. These tariff items levy import duties on value added abroad if the inputs originated in the United States. These figures are not identical with international subcontracting as defined above since they do not include products produced completely abroad. These figures also differ from the real figures for international sub-contracting because technicalities in the tariff items exclude many imports produced as a result of subcontracting. For example, United States cloth cut in the United States and sewn abroad is included in the data, but United States cloth cut and sewn abroad is not.

In spite of the above limitations, Table 13.5 does give information on the rapid growth of international subcontracting with the Third World in the late 1960's and early 1970's. We see that the share of imports allowed under these two items, accounted for by the Third World, increased from 6.4 percent in 1966 to 21.4 percent in 1969 to 35.9 percent in 1973. Although Third World imports under these two items remain small relative to total United States imports, the rate of growth is significant. From the viewpoint of many Third World countries, that increase represents substantial economic activity.

There are perhaps three main reasons for the major growth of international subcontracting. The first, primarily "economic," is the growth of new labor-intensive manufacturing industries like electronics and light manufacturing, joining older labor-intensive-industries like clothing and shoes. This has taken place because many advanced consumer products in the DCCs have become standardized and sold in mass markets. The development of international subcontracting in these product lines has also been advanced by new technological innovations in transportation and communication. With improved air freight, containerization, and tele-communication, transnational corporations could dispatch products and components more quickly, more cheaply and more safely.

The second reason for subcontracting is capitalist rivalry. Immediately after World War II, the United States was the dominant capitalist power. When Third World nations embarked upon their import-substitution industrialization plan by shutting off their markets to imported finished products, only United States transnational corporations could undertake large-scale direct investment in Third World manufacturing. United States expansion during this period was directed at securing markets in the Third World, not at establishing export bases in order to supply home markets. (The majority of direct investment was in Latin American countries with sizeable domestic markets – Mexico, Brazil, and Argentina.)

Table 13.5 United States imports under Tariff Items 806.30 and 807.00 (in millions of dollars).

	1966	1967	1968	1969	1970	1971	1972	1973
total imports into United States under Tariff Items 806.30 and 807.00	953.0	1,035.1	1,554.4	1,841.8	2,212.7	2,768.2	3,408.7	4,242.1
total imports under Tariff Items 806.30 and 807.00 from the Third World	60.7	99	221.7	394.8	541.5	652.5	1,031.7	1,522.9
Third World imports into the United States as a percentage of total imports under Tariff Items 806.30 and 807.00	6.4%	9.6%	14.3%	21.4%	24.5%	23.6%	30.3%	35.9%

Source: Sharpston (1975: 96–7).

In the mid-1960s, however, the international situation began to change as Germany and Japan competed heavily against the United States. These two countries had developed as export-led economies and increasingly challenged United States business for markets because they had relatively cheap labor, more government assistance, and more modern plants and equipment. United States transnational capital met this challenge partly by means of international subcontracting. By employing Third World labor, United States markets were protected. (United States action, as one would expect, has forced Japan and Germany into a similar strategy.[6])

The third reason for business to engage in international subcontracting was growing internal class pressures and struggles. In the United States, for instance, by the mid-1960s, capitalists were no longer able to maintain high profit margins and yield to working-class demands for material and political gains. Given international economic pressures (large balance of payments deficits) and domestic economic pressures (inflation, full-employment profit squeeze), United States capitalists could not successfully restore profit margins through continued price increases. One way of reducing costs and combatting full-employment pressures at home was to involve Third World workers, through international subcontracting, more directly in production for the United States market. Thus the logic of global capitalism led to the expansion of a new international division of labor under the control and direction of transnational corporations.

It is essential to indicate the profitability of subcontracting because this is an obvious motivating concern of transnational corporations. Since subcontracted jobs tend to be labor intensive, we look at figures for productivity and wage differentials. Beginning with productivity, a Tariff Commission report in 1970 found that the greatest difference between labor productivity in the United States and other countries was in garment making in Mexico – just over 60 percent of the United States level (United States Tariff Commission 1970). For electronics assembly, foreign productivity was, on average, almost 90 percent of the United States levels, and for many other products it was found to be even higher than in the United States (NACLA 1975, 1977). Productivity tended to be high under subcontracting because management, design, and even technology might be identical to that used in the DCC. In addition, labor problems – unions, strikes, absenteeism – are kept down by the fear of starvation, repressive labor legislation, or armed force.

Although foreign productivity certainly compares favorably with United States levels, it is only one side of unit labor costs. Turning to wages we see more clearly the gains to capitalists from subcontracting. Differences in wages are so great that, according to Sharpston (1975: 98), "Even if U.S. wages go up by 5% and Korean by 20% – the absolute differential between the rates becomes larger." According to

data from the United States Tariff Commission, and net Far East labor
cost for electronic assembly works out to be only 8 percent of that in the
United States. International subcontracting for certain manufactures
appears to be very, very profitable.

Given the growth of international subcontracting, Group B countries were the ideal candidates. Since labor is the key variable, the
poorer countries – those with less industry to compete for workers –
appear most desirable. Since the final market to be served is the
developed capitalist market, the internal market size of the Third World
country is not a key factor. Economies of scale, and modern capital-
intensive technology are all possible, even in a small, underdeveloped
Third World country, because production is geared for export.
Another factor determining the countries in which corporations choose
to subcontract is the countries' dependence on foreign trade. The more
dependent on foreign trade, the more likely they are to offer business
attractive terms, e.g., tax holidays, free trade zones, and repressive
labor conditions, and the less likely they are to disrupt the international
movement of goods for domestic purposes. Above all, however, is the
concern transnational corporations have for the political safety of their
investments. By subcontracting, corporations are relying upon Third
World production to assist in supplying the important home market; it
is therefore not surprising that subcontracting has been concentrated in
only a few politically safe countries. United States transnational corporations, for example, have over 85 percent of all subcontracting work
done in five countries, most of whose governments are directly dependent upon the United States for survival – Mexico, Taiwan, Hong
Kong, Singapore, and South Korea.[7]

Although advantages from subcontracting are obvious for transnational
corporations, the bourgeoisie in countries like South Korea, Taiwan,
Malaysia, Hong Kong, and Singapore also saw possible gain. They were
willing to give up control over design, research, advertising, and
marketing in order to follow a strategy they hoped would lead to self-
expanding capitalist industrialization and thus increased power and wealth
for themselves. Since Group B countries are presently the most committed
to the strategy of export–led industrialization, the remainder of this chapter
will focus on the impact of MEI relative to them. This simplification is
made because Group A countries appear to occupy a very different place in
the international capitalist system and require separate study.

Export-led industrialization: a false promise

I have shown that MEI is an important phenomenon, that its growth can
be understood as part of the development of a new international division of labor under the direction of transnational capital. In this section I

show that, for the Third World, MEI represents only a new form of international capitalist domination, not a program for establishing indigenous capitalist development or for meeting the needs of Third World workers and peasants.

Export-led industrialization strategy blocks the development of an internally articulated self-expanding economy. An economy which responds to the needs of the majority of the population is characterized by *convergence* between needs, domestic demand, investment, and resource use. In other words, the needs of the people must create effective demand calling forth investment and development of appropriate technology, domestic resource use, and production. Domestic consumption both completes the production–consumption cycle and provides the basis for a new cycle by creating new needs and demands. By responding to the needs of workers and peasants, such an economy generates employment, technology, and growth as part of a self-expanding process.

The above sketch of an ideal-type, the self-expanding economy, contrasts sharply with the *dynamic divergence* of Third World export-led industrialization. Due to inadequate income, workers and peasants are usually unable to translate their needs into effective demand. Market demand comes largely from the small middle and upper classes and is heavily oriented toward products not produced domestically. As a result, a rise in Third World demand leads to an increase in imports rather than domestic production. And since the workers and peasants lack income, domestic production is largely for export. Thus investment, technology, and resource use develop in response to demand in DCCs and tend to be unrelated to the needs of workers and peasants in countries following this road to economic "growth."

The dynamic divergence economy has no internal linkage between production and consumption. Goods produced are not consumed domestically; goods consumed are not produced domestically. It is, of course, possible for both the consumption of the middle and upper classes (largely imports) and domestic production (largely exports) to increase at the same time. This usually occurs, however, without creating the basis for self-generating economic expansion and blocks fulfillment of the needs of most Third World people. With both production and consumption tied to the developed capitalist economies, economic "development" of a Third World nation following a strategy of export-led industrialization only reinforces its dependence on DCCs.[8]

Subcontracting operations normally specialize in the use of low-skilled labor. The jobs tend to be those which are not easily mechanized, such as sewing. Since 80 percent of the labor costs in clothing manufacturing are sewing costs, clothing manufacturing is often subcontracted. Another example is assembly work, such as in the production of semiconductors. Corporations bring chips and other components together in Taiwan, hire workers to assemble them under magnification, and then export the assembled semiconductors back to the United States. Although the overall production of semiconductors is both skilled and capital intensive, it is the assembly process that is labor intensive in DCCs and therefore suitable for the Third World. Since related operations are either capital intensive or require skilled labor, transnational corporations do not usually subcontract them. The logic of subcontracting, therefore, makes it very unlikely that a Third World country will be able to establish forward or backward linkages to produce the entire product, or upgrade the skill level of its work force.

There are limits built into a development process based on subcontracting such tasks. In the DCCs, corporations tend to use technology to mechanize manufacturing operations as much as possible, and to reduce the importance of parts and processes that cannot be mechanized (e.g., fewer parts to be assembled). This tendency, which obviously can be influenced by the relative costs of mechanization in the DCCs and labor in the Third World, would seem to place limits on the expansion of employment and on the number of processes to be subcontracted.

Transnational corporations also subcontract production which is standardized, technologically simple, and requires little capital overhead. Examples of products are sporting goods, toys, wigs, and plastics. These goods can be produced anywhere and transnational corporations subcontract their production in order to minimize possible future competition from other corporations which might take advantage of cheap foreign labor.

All of the operations described above can be characterized by their use of unskilled labor and elementary production processes. In general, there appears to be no basis for assuming that such economic activity will result in the transfer of useful technology or the upgrading of skill levels in the Third World. Moreover, little of this production will generate internal linkages, support a domestic mass-consumer market, or meet vital social needs.

The increase in Third World manufacturing production has resulted, however, in a significant growth in the size of the industrial working class. One United Nations publication describes this fact:

> In developed market-economy countries employment in manufacturing increased at an annual rate of 1.4 percent between 1955 and 1974, but in the most recent period, 1970–1974, the annual increase was merely 0.3 percent. In developing countries, employment in manufacturing increased by 4.3 percent per annum between 1955 and 1974 and by as much as 6.5 percent per annum between 1970 and 1974. (UNCTAD Secretariat 1978b: 26)

A changing class structure in the Third World should have profound political significance. The substantial growth in the industrial work force may, for example, provide a new and significant base for anti-imperialist, anticapitalist activities. Export-led industrialization may reinforce *existing* Third World dependence, but it also produces important changes in the political economy of the Third World.

Subcontracting production can take place under a number of different relationships: transnational foreign-affiliate production, joint venture, or independent Third World production. Transnational foreign-affiliate production accounts for most Third World production of semiconductors, electronic memory circuits, engineering products, and capital intensive goods. Most manufactured exports, however, are not produced under this legal structure. Estimates of the percentage of Third World manufacturing exports which were produced by majority-owned foreign affiliates in 1972 are: Hong Kong, 10 percent; Taiwan, 20 percent; South Korea, 15 percent; and Singapore, 70 percent (Singapore's percentage is high because of a concentration in engineering exports, (Nayyar 1978: 62).

Independent Third World firms and firms from DCCs working in joint ventures with Third World firms produce finished consumer electrical products, small machines, machine tools, cameras, clothing, sporting goods, toys, and wigs. Superficially, this situation looks like diversified independent production and industrialization.[9] In the great majority of cases, however, transnational corporations retain complete control over the entire process (research, design, transport, processing, storage, and marketing). Even when an independent Third World firm controls production, advertising, technology and management are almost always under the complete control of either a purely retailing corporation (such as J. C. Penney, Sears & Roebuck, Macy's, Bloomingdale's) or a trading or distributing company established by a producing transnational corporation.[10]

The result is that independent Third World firms can be prevented, by transnational corporations, from producing for the local market or direct exporting. Third World firms are dependent upon DCC firms for inputs and access to markets, and since Third World firms undertake a little research or development on their own, they lack skilled personnel and experience in home production and direct exporting. Local firms use technology chosen by transnational corporations and depend upon them for service and technical assistance. Subcontracting under these conditions only advances a process of dependent industrialization, not self-generating capitalist reproduction. It does highlight, however, the importance to transnational corporations of technology and marketing as weapons of dominance.

It is true that at present some upgrading and expansion is taking place in certain Third World countries. In Hong Kong and Singapore some foreign affiliates now completely produce transistors and integrated circuits locally. In South Korea networks of small manufacturers subcontract some work domestically and a South Korean program to encourage export diversification includes shipbuilding and steel production. Singapore no longer gives as many advantages to firms considering setting up plants for very low-skilled subcontracting. For example, "Hewlett Packard was denied tax incentives in connection with packaging integrated circuits, but did secure tax concessions for the production of electronic calculators" (Sharpston 1975: 126).

In some cases such development is nothing but an enlargement of an already existing manufacturing enclave.[11] In other cases, as in South Korea, it may represent attempts by the domestic bourgeoisie to gain a measure of independence from transnational corporations. Within the context of a strong commitment to export-led industrialization, it is not surprising that the bourgeoisie in Group B countries are trying to upgrade and diversify their exports in order to build a more dynamic economic base and increase their own independence and power. There are, however, a number of checks on their ability to succeed. One of the most important is the creation, with the support of transnational corporations, of new rival export centers.

Countries in Asia (Indonesia, Philippines, Thailand), the Caribbean and Central America (Haiti, El Salvador),[12] and the West Indies (Netherlands Antilles) are now competing for new and existing subcontracting work. Competition between Third World countries for export business takes place in a number of different ways, and all of them increase the profits and power of transnational corporations at the expense of Third World workers and peasants. Some countries compete in terms of financial policies. They offer generous tax holidays, although there is no proof that these have any effect, other than to reduce government revenues. Many countries are forced to offer corporations subsidized credit even though it is illogical for a capital-scarce nation to offer funds to capital-rich transnational corporations.[13]

Many countries compete for subcontracts by offering bonus exchange rates and other export subsidies; if the bonuses become too large, however, the Third World country can lose foreign exchange by exporting. This can happen, since under subcontracting most components or capital inputs must be imported and thus paid for with foreign exchange. When a final product is exported, only part of what is earned can be considered as net foreign exchange. So, if the imports are expensive and the price of exports artificially lowered, the entire transaction can result in a loss for the Third World nation.

Third World governments also try to encourage subcontracting in their countries by allocating foreign exchange and duty-free importation of supplies and equipment to corporations if they produce goods for export. Both foreign-exchange and tariff advantages, however, work to ensure that production will be biased toward producing goods for DCC markets, local supplies or suppliers will not be used, and internal linkages will not take place.

Finally, competition is also carried out through the establishment of free trade zones.[14] These are industrial parks, constructed and paid for by Third World nations who turn over their governance and administration to foreign capital engaged in exporting. Countries anxious to encourage exports are literally willing to give up sovereignty to foreign capital in order to foster industrialization.[15]

The competition for subcontracting has already begun to hurt Group B countries. For example, in Hong Kong and Singapore, labor costs are rising; in the former, industrial land is become scarce. As a result, transnational corporations are slowing employment and production of semiconductors and memory arrays in those countries, and new production (sometimes even transfer of existing work) is being shifted to Malaysia, El Salvador, Thailand, and Indonesia (UNCTAD Secretariat 1978a: 17). Jobs and production are lost and export diversification and capital accumulation is retarded. The development of new export centers and the resulting competition increases the flexibility and profits of transnational corporations. In the Third World it limits wage increases, thus maintaining poverty and underdevelopment, and it reinforces reliance on the external market, thus strengthening internal disarticulation and dependence.

Export-led industrialization and the crisis of capitalism

Some countries have increased output and employment through subcontracting. Continued gains, however, depend upon the stability and growth of markets in DCCs and such dependence is fraught with danger. That danger is the instability of the global capitalist economy on which the MEI development strategy depends. There was a sharp drop in Third World manufactured exports resulting from the downturn experienced by the capitalist system in 1974–5.

The cyclical downturn of 1974–5 hurt Third World manufacturing output and export.[16] The growth rate of manufacturing output in the Third World fell from 9.5 percent in 1973 to 6.5 percent in 1974 to 3 percent in 1975. The 1975 reduction was especially severe in Hong Kong, South Korea, and Singapore, since these countries rely heavily on exports to the DCCs. The overall volume of world trade in manufactures decreased by 5 percent between 1974 and 1975, but Third World exports to DCCs decreased by even more, producing an overall decrease in the Third World's share of imports into the DCCs. In 1975 the Third World's share fell in 11 of the 21 DCCs. Even during the downturn, however, the Third World did not stop exporting

manufactures. Thus, in 1975, the market share of Third World manufactured exports was higher for every DCC than it had been in 1970; in
nine countries it was higher than it had been in 1974.

The international capitalist world is currently facing serious
economic problems and they are not ones of short-term business–cycle
management, but of cyclical instability in the context of global stagnation. With all nations moving along the same path and thus subject to
the same forces, trends are exaggerated rather than stabilized.

In 1974–5, the unified business cycle turned down producing the
most serious economic crisis since World War II. In 1979, with the
bottom of that cycle in the past, most bourgeois analysts (especially in
the United States) are congratulating themselves for having guided
their countries into the fourth year of recovery. Even a casual look at
international data, however, suggests that after four years of recovery,
world capitalism, far from enjoying prosperity, has entered into a
period of growing stagnation. Well into the "recovery" period, unemployment in almost all capitalist countries is at record levels, inflation is
rising from an already historically high plateau, industrial production is
lagging and investment is weak.[17] With the business press forecasting a
normal cyclical downturn in the near future, one can only conclude that
capitalists, and those who depend upon them, have hard times ahead.

With markets tightening in DCCs as a result of economic stagnation,
Third World countries pursuing an export-led industrialization
strategy will find it increasingly difficult to maintain overall production
and export levels. It is quite likely that these countries will experience a
sharp decline in earnings and growth with workers and peasants experiencing a simultaneous increase in unemployment and poverty. I am
not arguing that transnational corporations will cease to use international subcontracting. On the contrary, I have shown that subcontracting is integral to transnational operations; it may become even
more important, in a period of economic crisis. It is reasonable to
expect, however, that diversified and independent Third World
exports of manufactures to the DCCs will be greatly reduced during
the upcoming period of economic stagnation. In other words, although
Third World exports that are tied to the needs of transnational corporations through subcontracting will probably grow, overall Third
World exports of manufactures will suffer.

Trends suggesting this development are already visible. First, data
shows that Third World exports of manufactures have recovered since
1975, but that the gains are concentrated among those countries most
committed to subcontracting – Group B. In one example of Group B
growth, export values increased by 50 percent for Hong Kong and
South Korea and 30 percent for Singapore between 1975 and 1976.
Most other Third World nations, however, continue to experience
weak export demand.

The second trend suggesting that Third World countries' overall exports of manufactures will decrease and exports resulting from sub-contracting will increase is the growing pressure for protectionism in the international capitalist system. Protectionism, currently taking the form of quotas, special levies, unofficial cartels, and orderly marketing agreements, constrains world trade, especially that of Third World nations. The impact of protectionism on the Third World, however, tends to be limited to nonsubcontracted goods.

This limitation occurs because when a majority–owned foreign affiliate of a transnational corporation undertakes production the parent firm uses its political power to prevent any domestic protectionist movement from threatening the trade. Similarly, when an independent Third World firm undertakes production under a subcontract with powerful retailing cor-porations or trading divisions of producing firms, these international companies will resist any legislation unfavorable to their trade. When Third World companies independently produce and directly export goods, however, there is little reason for transnational corporations to oppose protectionism. In fact, there are times when they will promote it so as to create divisions between Third World and DCC workers.

As Sharpston (1975: 131) puts it, "This no doubt goes to explain why (despite political resistance) it has been possible for imports to take over nearly all the U.S. market for many consumer electronic products, whereas much more limited penetration of the U.S. textile market (less than 15 percent of consumption of cotton textiles) led to official or 'voluntary' quotas on cotton textiles and increasingly on all textiles." This also helps to explain the recent passage of orderly marketing arrangements which limit exports from South Korea's steel, ship-building, shoe, and auto industries.

Concluding remarks

A number of Third World governments have adopted an export–led development strategy in hopes of achieving rapid capitalist industriali-zation. I have attempted to analyze the historical context in which certain governments adopted this strategy, the rapid expansion of Third World production and export of manufactures, and the impact of this strategy on Third World development. I have concluded that although export–led industrialization leads to growth in industrial production and the industrial work force, it will not lead to the creation of an indigenous, self–expanding capitalist economy. Moreover, in the context of the deepening economic stagnation in the core capitalist economies, such an externally based development strategy is likely to produce increased poverty and suffering for workers and peasants in the Third World.

Two final comments are in order, First, conclusions reached in this study should not be generalized to Group A countries. Due to their size and abundant natural resources, Group A countries will probably play a very different rôle in the world economy than will Group B countries and thus require separate study.

Second, the growth of Third World manufacturing means the development of a new international division of labor in that it creates an industrial working class in the Third World. This change in the class structure of certain Third World countries and in international capitalism requires serious study. The new international division of labor may be expanding in response to the needs of transnational capital, but the resulting Third World industrial working class could become the base for important anticapitalist struggles in the future. With continued economic instability forecast for Third World countries, this will indeed become more likely.

Moreover, this new international division of labor produces changes in the political economy of the DCCs. Effects of the international restructuring of production have already been felt by the United States working class in declining manufacturing employment, intensification of regional and urban crises, and growing domestic economic instability. Transnational capital has attempted to exploit this situation by encouraging competition and antagonism between Third World and DCC workers. After winning numerous concessions in the Third World, e.g., free trade zones, antiunion legislation, and lack of health standards, capitalists are trying to win similar concessions here in the United States. The result is a relentless attack on the quality of life and standard of living of workers in this country. Pressure for such concessions to capitalists, in the midst of growing economic stagnation, could result in the development of a strong anticapitalist labor movement.

While capitalists try to exploit the current situation at the expense of workers everywhere, the expansion of the new international division of labor embodies its own contradictions. In fact, as stated above, it appears to be intensifying them in both DCCs and the Third World. In the exploited Third World, global capitalism is enlarging the working class. In the DCCs, the working class is becoming increasingly exploited. Since workers in DCCs and the Third World increasingly share interests in opposing the new international division of labor, the circumstances which now exploit them also strengthen the basis for greater international working-class solidarity.

Notes

1   Amin (1977) provides a good historical analysis of the impact of imperialism on Third World development. Weisskopf (1972) and the articles in *Review of Radical Political Economics* (Spring 1971) are also valuable.

2   Manufactures are defined according to the UNCTAD Standard International Trade Classification (SITC). The *broad* definition used in this chapter includes chemicals (SITC 5), basic manufactures (SITC 6), machinery and transport equipment (SITC 7), miscellaneous light manufactures (SITC 8) plus a number of processed food products contained in SITC sections 0–4. The most important are certain processed foods, alcoholic beverages, tobacco manufactures, and wood and paper products. Petroleum products (SITC 3) and unworked non-ferrous metals (SITC division 68) are excluded. The *narrow* definition includes only SITC sections 5 to 8 minus SITC division 68.

3   The United Nations officially includes Yugoslavia and Israel as part of the Third World. It does not, however, include Taiwan in its data collection or calculations. I do not consider Yugoslavia or Israel as Third World countries in this chapter, and therefore have removed them from my calculations. Since the United Nations does not collect data on Taiwan, that country is not included in most calculations.

4   Because of its Border Industrialization Program. Mexico actually contains aspects of both groups. The program, started in 1965, was designed to speed Mexican development in the areas bordering the United States. It established the border area as a free trade zone with separate administration and regulation. Although I have not made the separation, in terms of my two groups the Mexican border area could be considered a separate geographic area and part of Group B with the rest of Mexico remaining in Group A.

For an analysis of the border area see Baerresen (1971), NACLA (1975, 1977) and Fernandez (1973).

5   For an in-depth discussion of international subcontracting see Sharpston (1975).

6   By 1971, one-half of Japanese direct foreign investment was in the Third World and over two-thirds was in manufacturing. According to Nayyar (1978: 70), "A large proportion of these investments were directed toward the small Asian economies such as Hong Kong, Taiwan, South Korea, and Singapore in order to reap the benefits of abundant unskilled labour and low wage rates. . . . Consequently, exports to Japan became a primary function of some Japanese manufacturing investments in Asia. In fact, by 1973, exports back to Japan accounted for nearly 25 percent of the total sales by Japanese-affiliated manufacturing firms located in Asia: for some industries – clothing (60 percent) and electrical machinery (30 percent) – this share was even higher. . . ."

7   The next three countries are Jamaica, Philippines, and Haiti.

8   For a more detailed theoretical analysis of export-led industrialization and its impact on Third World economic disarticulation and underdevelopment. See Thomas (1974) and de Janvry & Garramon (1977).

9   This arrangement also tends to minimize direct conflict between transnational corporations and Third World labor. With no foreign "owners" of the plant, labor discipline is left to nationals. This helps to explain why nations that are successful subcontractors have such reactionary antilabor policies.

10   Quoting a report from the UNCTAD Secretariat (1978a: 11): "An example

is that of the marketing of leather footwear for export in Argentina and Brazil. The main feature of this marketing system is the presence in the country of a large number of buying agents, representatives of large United States importing firms, established in the big centers of the shoe industry, who are in control of the marketing operation. 'They buy directly from the numerous firms established in the country for the account of United States principals with specific orders for very large volumes: they indicate the design and styles required, fix prices and delivery dates, control the production process and quality of the product and organize the shipment and the marketing of the footwear exports.'"

11   Quite often, expansion by transnational corporations represents acquisitions or takeovers of existing local firms. This is especially true in Latin America. According to a report issued by the UNCTAD Secretariat (1978a: 15), "A survey of 396 United States and other TNCs operating in developing countries showed that close to 60 percent of the 2,904 subsidiaries existing in the late 1960s had been set up by acquisitions rather than by new investment. . . . The electrical industry in Brazil and Mexico provides an outstanding example of the 'denationalization process' (transfer of ownership to foreign companies) of well-established national industries in developing countries through acquisitions of local firms by TNCs." This type of expansion, all too common, certainly does not contribute to Third World development.

12   Given United States transnational concerns with political "safety," repressive Haiti is more attractive than progressive Jamaica. The result is a growing concentration of subcontracting in the former at the expense of the latter.

13   An additional point that needs further research concerns the growing rôle of transnational banks. In order to export products, competition among Third World countries has led to the creation of different financing schemes designed to provide easily available and competitive low-cost financing and insurance against foreign trade risks. These schemes require access to funds that most Third World banks are unable to secure. The result is that transnational banks become increasingly important and powerful in the Third World.

14   For a discussion of free trade zones see Tsuchiya (1978).

15   "Workers employed in the zone are often subject to special regulations (prohibition of labor disputes, for instance), have to show special passes to enter, and must often undergo body checks when they finish a day's toil. This latter is to prevent 'smuggling' of the zone's products into the workers' own country" (Tsuchiya 1978: 30).

16   Information on the recession comes from the UNCTAD Secretariat (1977).

17   For a more complete description of long-term trends in industrial production see Sweezy (1978). See recent issues of the OECD *Economic Outlook*, published by the OECD.

References

Amin, S. 1977. Self Reliance and the New International Economic Order. *Monthly Review* **29**, 3 (July–August).

Baerresen, D. W. 1971. *The border industrialization program of Mexico*. Lexington, Mass.: Heath.

Fernandez, R. A. 1973. The border industrialization program on the United States–Mexican border. *Review of Radical Political Economics* **5** (1, Spring).

Janvry, A. de and C. Garramon 1977. Laws of motion of capital in the center-periphery structure. *Review of Radical Political Economics* **9** (2, Summer).

North American Congress on Latin America (NACLA) 1975. *Hit and run: runaway shops on the Mexican border*. Latin America and Empire Report, 5. New York: NACLA.

NACLA 1977. *Electronics: the global industry*. Latin America and Empire Report, 11. New York: NACLA.

Nayyar, D. 1978. Transitional corporations and manufactured exports from poor-countries. *The Economic Journal* **88**, 349 (March).

Sharpston, M. 1975. International subcontracting. *Oxford Economic Papers* **27** (1, March).

Sweezy, P. M. 1978. The present global crisis of capitalism. *Montly Review* April.

Thomas, C. Y. 1974. *Dependence and transformation*. New York. Monthly Review Press.

Tsuchiya, T. 1978. Free trade zones in Southeast Asia. *Monthly Review* **29** (9, February).

Union for Radical Political Economics 1971. Case studies in imperialism and underdevelopment. *Review of Radical Political Economics* **3**, 1 (Spring).

UNCTAD Secretariat 1976. *Trade in manufactures of developing countries and territories, 1974 Review*. New York: UNCTAD.

UNCTAD Secretariat 1977. *Recent trends and developments in trade of manufactures and semi-manufactures*. TD/B/C.2/1975.11, May. New York: UNCTAD.

UNCTAD Secretariat 1978a. *The role of transnational corporations in the marketing and distribution of exports and imports of developing countries*. TD/B/C.2/197, 16, March. New York: UNCTAD.

UNCTAD Secretariat 1978b. *Review of recent trends and developments in trade in manufactures and semi-manufactures*. TD/B/C.2/190, 21, March. New York: UNCTAD.

UNCTAD Secretariat 1978c. *International subcontracting arrangements in electronics between developed market-economy countries and developing countries*. TD/B/C.2/144/supp.1. New York: UNCTAD.

United States Tariff Commission 1970. *Economic factors affecting the use of the Items 807.00 and 806.30 of the Tariff Schedules of the United States*. Washington, D.C.: USGPO.

Weisskopf, T. E. 1972. Capitalism, underdevelopment and the future of the poor countries. *Review of Radical Political Economics* **6** (1, Winter).

Part V
Industrial policy reexamined

14 Introduction

RICHARD PEET

The phenomenon of export-led industrialization in parts of the Third World was examined in Part IV. It was argued that a precarious form of dependent industrialization, involving deleterious consequences for exploited workers, particularly women, cannot and should not be emulated by Third World countries in general. In this part of the book we turn to the question of capitalist society's control over its manufacturing development. Industrial production is a social activity. Broad sections of the population are involved in it. Even more people depend on it. However, under capitalism, the control of industrial production, both what is produced and who is employed, is vested in individuals pursuing private profit. Profit determines what is produced where using whom.

Certain deficiencies in this method of allocating work have prompted action by the capitalist state representing, in some degree, the people as a whole. In some cases this goes as far as the state actually controlling parts of production, for example the nationalized industries in Britain. These industries are run by public corporations under the prevailing business practices, often using managers borrowed from private corporations. Workers frequently strike against public corporations: the 1984 miners' strike in Britain against the National Coal Board was longer, more violent, and involved more people than any recent strike against a private corporation. Truly social decision making, in which industrial decisions are made for the common good, is virtually unknown in the West. Because basic economic decisions are privately made, state industrial policy can only entail ephemeral modifications made in the public interest.

Even such ephemeral public policy has been opposed by the conservative theories recently in vogue, and, more importantly, guiding those in power in the United States, Britain, and elsewhere. These conservative theories have a base in the dominant school of bourgeois economics which stresses the efficiency of the market as allocator of productive resources. For example, arguing that deindustrialization is a myth in the United States, Branson (1983) redefines the loss of jobs in traditional sectors as merely a movement of resources from low-productivity industries (autos, textiles, steel) towards high-productivity areas of expansion in which the country retains a comparative advantage (agriculture and human-resource intensive industries). Jobs may be lost to firms but workers simply move on to more productive, and perhaps higher paying, kinds of employment (cf. the evidence presented in Chapter 5). He finds it appropriate that the government use tax revenues to minimize the costs of adjustment and speed the process of transition. By and large, however, "capital markets move resources in the right direction, so there is no need for an industrial policy that directs the allocation of resources. What we do need, however, is a program that provides retraining and relocation assistance for workers who have to adjust and some sort of interim support for the affected communities" (Branson 1983: 54). Or, as an advisor to the Carter administration in the United States puts it, "I don't believe you can deal with economic change by trying to stop it or slow it down. You can only try to maximize the positive side" (Schultze *et al.* 1985: 38).

Even liberal theoreticians accept the basic premise of the market as an efficient allocator of resources. Liberal proponents of industrial policy, such as Reich, Rohatyn, and Thurow in the United States disagree on details but essentially agree that the government should facilitate industrial change in the direction indicated by competition in the market – from sunset to sunrise industries, from low to high technology, and from uncompetitive to competitive activities. Most advocate setting up a planning board or cooperation council, with members from industry, labor, banking, government, and public interest groups, backed by an investment bank or reconstruction finance corporation. Funds would be directed into research, retraining, and the mitigation of the harmful effects stemming from rapid economic change. Japan's Ministry of International Trade and Industry, which has intervened to help industries in which it has a competitive advantage, is held up as the model to emulate (*New York Times* 1983: 1, 30). In the words of Robert Reich (*New York Times* 1983: 1), "Improving competitiveness is a goal almost everyone can endorse."

However, a fringe of social democratic theories takes the argument in a somewhat different direction by advocating that serious thought be given to national economic planning. The "radical reindustrialization" policy outlined by Bluestone & Harrison (1982: Ch. 8) uses principles of economic democracy (equality, production for need, better working conditions, popular participation) as its political–economic theoretical base. At any time there will be new products which entrepreneurs want to make yet have difficulty in doing so because of competition from government-subsidized producers elsewhere. The government should subsidize these sunrise industries under a system of "public–private partnership" (i.e., partial public ownership of subsidized private companies). Sunset industries, which the private sector is abandoning or rationalizing because they are no longer profitable, need public monitoring to determine the real reason for abandonment, and to see if plant and equipment can be used for alternative purposes. Here the example given is Lucas Aerospace in Britain, where workers outlined 150 new product lines for the company to pursue (although the plan failed because of lack of government support). Plant-closing legislation can also be used to slow down disinvestment and geographic abandonment. When the government intervenes to bail out industries, or when unions are asked to give concessions, management should be restructured in a more democratic direction. Bluestone & Harrison (1982: 257–62) advocate worker or community ownership of certain industries with the aid of the government.

Worker control of selected industries is the left frontier of the industrial policy debate. But even this "radical" proposal does not really broach the topic of social control over economic activity, for worker-controlled industries would be expected to make a profit and operate within the existing market framework. According to the analysis presented in this book this would hardly differentiate them from private corporations.

The lack of real social power over the economy is most evident where the state has long intervened in the public interest: the area of the location of economic activity. To what extent, and in what ways, do capitalist governments influence the location of industrial production? In Chapter 15 Ross examines the relatively long history of regional and local policy influencing the geography of production in the United States and Britain. State intervention in the United States, he concludes, is more effective in altering capital–labor relations in the corporate interest than directing companies to socially desirable places through financial incentives. In Britain, where the idea of state direction of business was more acceptable (until recently), state subsidies have a slight locational effect during economic expansion, but little during recession. This influence has certainly not been sufficient substantially to alleviate economic decline in old industrial areas of the country. Unemployment rates in regions like the North, Northwest, West Midlands, Wales, and Northern Ireland have continued to be substantially higher than the national average in the recession years of the 1970s and 1980s (Central Statistical Office (UK) 1984: 91, see also Ch. 6).

One reaction to the state's failure to direct employment to the places most in need is to selectively *decrease* government intervention in areas designated as "enterprise zones," an idea first proposed by the British geographer Peter Hall. The article by Goldsmith, reproduced as Chapter 16, examines the United States version of enterprise zones. This proposal by the Reagan administration envisions a mixture of policies designed to reduce controls on freedom of enterprise and give tax incentives to businesses in designated zones of high unemployment. Minimum wage laws for teenagers would be waived in an effort to reduce wage costs to levels competitive with the platform economies of the Third World. However, as Goldsmith points out, industrial wages of $14 a week are not compatible with the United States cost of living. He calls enterprise zones planned areas of depression and fears that the measures first proposed for small areas would spread to the entire country. They would enshrine not just a dual labor market but a dual citizenry.

Enterprise zones in the First World are modeled after free trade zones (FTZs) in the Third. One of the earliest assessments of this method of attracting economic activity to certain parts of Third World countries, written by Tsuchiya, is reproduced here as Chapter 17. In the FTZ government intervention takes a positive form for business, in the sense of providing some capital and all necessary services, and a negative form for labor, in the sense that labor unions and industrial disputes are prohibited or strictly controlled. This makes the FTZ a paradise for international capital. From the critical point of view of Tsuchiya's article, by contrast, the FTZs are concentrated spatial indicators of the whole process of Third World domination by outside powers.

In capitalist countries the state *must* take the side of its most powerful economic institutions – the corporations. It would be foolish, indeed, to limit the competitiveness of nationally based corporations when others are not so limited. Intervention in the "public interest" can only occur within this disciplining framework: that is, the public interest is served best by leaving the corporations free to compete, succeed, and generate jobs and the state should encourage them positively, by channeling public funds in the direction of new, growing companies. Attempts to restrain entrepreneurial activity by imposing social accountability or restricting locational freedom have had limited effects because they violate the most basic premise of capitalist production, freedom of entrepreneurship. Hence proposals for industrial policy have increasingly moved in the direction of the encouragement of competitiveness. There is, however, a basic question of whether the existing proposals for industrial policy would only accelerate a long-term trend towards economic depression caused *by* international competition. In the polarized ideological climate which must eventually result from the failure of liberal policy, increased attention must be given to what has hitherto been dismissed as pragmatically irrelevant – social control over economic activity and directing the economy through democratic planning. This is further discussed in Chapter 18, which provides a brief summary and conclusion to the book.

References

Bluestone, B. & B. Harrison 1982. *The deindustrialization of America*. New York: Basic Books.

Branson, W. H. 1983. The myth of de-industrialization. *Regulation: AEI Journal on Government and Society*. September–October, 24–29, 53–54.

Central Statistical Office (UK) 1984. *Regional trends*. London: HMSO.

New York Times 1983. Debate grows over adoption of national industrial policy. June 19, 1, 30.

New York Times 1983. How to help America compete. September 30, 31.

Schultze, C. L. *et al*. 1985. Do we need an industrial policy? *Harpers* **270** (1617, February), 35–48.

15 Facing Leviathan: Public policy and global capitalism*

ROBERT J. S. ROSS

The capitalist system is to be understood as global rather than national. Rapid mobility has diffused manufacturing around the globe, increasingly to nations formerly considered peripheral sources of primary extraction. The large global enterprise (the multinational corporation or MNC) is the main, though not the only, institutional form and channel of this mobility. At the local level of metropolis and region the engine driving development and prosperity is the investment localized there. Economic decline results from capital outflow which is the aggregate result of numerous location decisions by firms and investors. Chief among the considerations to stay, leave, or enter a locality are considerations of wages, the discipline of the labor force, and public policy perceived to be favorable to capital. In the course of the past decade we have learned that the consequences of a net outward flow of capital include many personal and community manifestations which have come to be called social problems.

Much of the analysis of the above familiar trends is cast in tones of concern and indignation. It remains for social scientists to bring to bear on such questions conceptual tools based on a theoretical perspective. The proximate goal of such an enterprise is the portrayal of fundamental processes in a consistent and objective manner. That goal can be advanced by enlisting concepts of the balance of class forces and the strategic situation in which classes and their segments are embedded. Such work lies in the intermediate ground between an abstract discussion of the crisis tendencies inherent in capitalism and the empirical details of particular social events. This intermediate level is an appropriate ground upon which to interpret particular kinds of state or public policy. The task of such analysis is to apply a larger theoretical framework to particular phenomena. At the intermediate level policies constitute both products of larger processes, i.e., they register changes in the relative power of classes as evidenced in state activity, and also constitute *de facto* propositions about the dynamics of the political economy.

* Reprinted from Ross, R. J. S. 1983, Facing Leviathan: public policy and global capitalism, *Economic Geography* **59** (2, April), 144–60, by permission of the editor.

The theoretical framework referred to in this interpretation of public policies responding to capital mobility is that of *global capitalism*. By global capitalism one refers to a form of capitalism now becoming dominant, characterized by the operations of the multinational corporation – or the global firm (Gibson *et al*. 1983, Ross 1982 a & b, Ross *et al*. 1980, Williams 1982, Ross *et al*. 1983, Ross & Trachte 1983). This form of capitalist organization separates the production process over space and national boundaries, as the number of viable production sites expands. The global choice which results permits investors a wider field of discretion. In turn, this discretion allows MNCs and other institutions which direct capital flows to use capital mobility as one of their chief instruments in the class struggle with labor. In this process state structures and state policies both reflect and enhance capital's new powers.

For the working class and many public officials the era of global capitalism pits them against a Leviathan. Each local advance or reform may be subverted by the investors' ability to evade it by moving away. Moreover, the recent stagnation of the advanced capitalist economies has added to the leverage which capital can bring to bear on labor. This chapter focuses on the nature of some major public policies which reflect and contribute to the renewed power which the global expansion of capitalism gives to employers; it depicts the new Leviathan.

Viewed from the office towers of the global cities at the centers of the world communications and control system, the space economy of capitalism is a mosaic of regional opportunities for investment. The forces determining the opportunity structure of space are relatively complex. Each part of the mosaic represents a conjunctural outcome of world systemic tendencies and local historical and geographic particularities. That is, at any given moment each area's particular rôle in the structure of world capitalism is the outcome of numerous contingencies, including political factors (Ross 1982a, Ross *et al*. 1983). As the internationalization of production proceeds, broader parts of the world's regional mosaic are brought into candidacy as viable sites for manufacturing (NACLA 1977 a & b, Evans 1979, Hymer 1979). Social differences among viable sites also grow. Capitalism becomes a spatially dispersed system of production, and firms are vertically integrated across national boundaries (Barnett & Mueller 1974, Szymanski 1981). Places of resource extraction and commodity distribution previously at the periphery of the world system now become internal to the manufacturing system itself (Evans 1979, Froebel 1980). In such an unevenly developed extensive system, rife with extremes in local conditions, industrial location becomes a buyers' market. Among the matters subject to explicit or implicit bargaining between location buyers and local sellers are aspects of local public policy.

Throughout the current world system, states attempt to encourage or attract localization of investment within their areas of jurisdiction.

Such public policies are intended to alter or influence the regional deployment of capital and labor. Some of these policies are explicitly intended to alter regional structures of capital and labor. Others that are only implicit may nevertheless produce regional differences which are as important and as powerful in their influence on investment. Every local variation in public policy is susceptible to influence by capital by virtue of its claimed status as an attractor or repellant to investment.

The mobility of capital represents bargaining potential (Fayerweather 1981). Capital's demands on public policy receive ever more positive consideration from local states. Putting this another way: the global submode of capitalism entails an increase in the strategic power of capital as against labor which is revealed in public policy.

Class forces and the strategic situation

A relative balance between local class forces exists at each location in the world mosaic. The contention between capital and labor leads to changing results as the structure of these relations changes over time (Ross 1982). Within a given variant of capitalism, and a given location in space and time, the resources available to class actors have a particular structure. Across space there is a mosaic of variation in those structures. The major dimensions which form the matrix of structural constraint are: (1) the form taken by the dominant fractions of capital (competitive, monopoly, or global); (2) the structure of state authority (its democratic or authoritarian nature and the fraction of capital dominant within it) and the structure of constitutional authority (the federalist or centralist nature of the state); (3) the rôle of the social formation in the worldwide division of labor. In direct confrontation over production relations, or through the mediated relations of political or cultural life, one class achieves its aims with increasing frequency. When the working class increases its relative ability to achieve material, cultural, or political goals, capitalist class actors take counter steps to reassert dominance. Alternatively, capitalist firms and class fractions may leave a problematic region. Class struggle of this regionally varying type results in institutional changes, for example, the emergence of the conglomerate widely dispersed over different national territories, industrial sectors, and with a variety of investment areas. Should such institutional innovations fail to restore a balance in which capital can continue to expand, crises and further changes may be expected.

The matrix of class forces and resources may be seen as a strategic situation which differentially constrains the probability of success of its various actors. As they struggle to also advance their material and ideological interests, they attempt to use the power of the state for more propitious policies. Although in general the state may be dominated by the interests of capital, or at least constrained by the structure of capitalist relations as a whole, nevertheless, variations exist in the success workers achieve in obtaining policies in their interests. Without engaging in the specific dispute over the nature of the capitalist state, we can at least say that each local strategic situation includes a relative probability of workers or capitalists successfully obtaining state policies in their interests.

The following discussion interprets certain public policies from the framework of global capitalism. It distinguishes three levels and contexts of public policy as these affect capital mobility:

a   the interstate mobility of capital in the United States, as an example of federalism and regional competition;
b   the impact of United Kingdom regional development policy, as an example of the influence of the central state on the restructuring of capital and labor;
c   the international migration of manufacturing capital to previously nonindustrial areas, as an example of the expanded range of investor choice and the competition among national states for capital.

Regional and local public policy in the United States

Three broad areas of public policy are distinguished here, with an examination of prominent cases of each: (a) policies which affect the reproduction of labor, through wages and the social wage,[1] especially as these are effected by unionization; (b) policies intended to attract capital by the provision of it (subsidies); (c) tax policies and incentives.

UNION LEGISLATION, THE SOCIAL WAGE, AND LOCATION
The shift of capital from older to newer areas of industrial development has been motivated to a considerable degree by the minimization of wages and the avoidance of unions. This shift has also expressed capital's preference for environments in which local and state policy makes the least contribution to the social wage.

Federal labor law gives each of the 50 states the option of outlawing the "union shop," i.e., a collective bargaining agreement which makes union membership compulsory at the end of a new employee's probationary period. The union movement contends that this substantially hinders their ability to organize. Lower rates of unionization, in turn, are associated with lower wages. Higher rates of unionization are associated with public policies which contribute to the social wage. Examples of such policies include workmen's compensation awards and consequently employer-borne insurance costs, welfare benefits, and regulations concerning eligibility for unemployment compensation. Unionization rates vary considerably among the 50 states, as do policies which reflect labor's political strength. This political strength has material consequences for employers. Such policies contribute directly to the relative costs of employing labor among the states. Higher levels of social benefits contribute indirectly to labor's ability to bargain, for the resultant "social safety net" emboldens workers in their relations with employers (Piven & Cloward 1982). These policies are sometimes reported as part of a bundle of perceptual or indirect considerations loosely termed the "business climate." States whose social policies reflect a higher social wage are considered to have poor business climates. With some exceptions, such as California, manufacturing capital has tended to flow towards states with low wages, low rates of unionization, lower legally mandated employer contributions to extra-wage benefits, and which discourage unionization through the enactment of the local option "right-to-work" (RTW) laws (Rones 1980). Right-to-work laws are associated with low unionization, lower wages, and somewhat lighter tax burdens (Table 15.1).

Table 15.2 shows that capital has flowed towards RTW states. An increasing proportion of jobs were created in those states between 1969 and 1976. In the states without the RTW constraint on union organizing and union wage and political demands, 85 jobs were destroyed for every 100 created. In RTW states, only 70 jobs were destroyed by closings, failures, or removals for every 100 created. This difference is substantially as powerful as when the more popular Frostbelt–Sunbelt distinction is employed. In Frostbelt states 89 jobs were lost to every 100 created; the ratio in Sunbelt states was 72.

Table 15.1 Unionization, wages and taxes in 20 right-to-work states and the United States.

	20 RTW states 1980	US 50-state average	$\dfrac{\text{RTW}}{\text{US}} \times 100$
Percentage of labor force[a] unionized, 1980	14.0	24.0	58.3
Index of hourly wage[b] and fringe benefits, 1980	89.5	100	89.5
Taxes per capita[b]	$537	$665	80.8
State and local effective business taxes as percentage[a] of total sales, 1975	1.60	1.69	94.7

Sources
[a] Bluestone & Harrison (1982: 186).
[b] Kuldarsham (1981: 96–7).

The differential rate of economic growth between more and less unionized states has contributed to a long-run decline in union membership. Also contributing to this are differential growth rates among industries, with those having traditions of unionization and associations with class-based communities declining. The proportion of workers unionized in the United States peaked in 1954 at 35 percent and has now declined to approximately 24 percent (Bluestone & Harrison 1982: 138).

These data support the proposition that capital is attracted to areas in which the public policy mix constrains unions and their wage and political demands. In this context note the recent experience of New England. Having suffered sharp declines in manufacturing employment in the postwar period, New England workers suffered higher than average unemployment rates throughout much of the post-World War II period. The 1975 recession was notably more severe in the region than in the nation. By the late 1970s this had changed, and by 1982 the New England states had some of the lowest unemployment rates of the industrial states. Of potential significance is that New England wages in manufacturing, as of the summer of 1982, were but 87 percent of the national average. Apparently the discipline of high unemployment has had a tonic effect on investment. In an interregional comparison of the severity of the 1981–2 recession, low wages (by state) were associated with smaller job loss (Browne 1982). By contrast, the higher wage, and social wage, and more unionized states of the Mid-Atlantic and Midwestern regions are still losing manufacturing jobs and have high unemployment rates. In such areas pressure mounts on those labor-related costs associated with public policy. A consultant thus urged the State of Michigan to improve its business climate in order to attract the robotics industry by recommending reform of the state's workmen's compensation laws (Battelle Columbus Laboratories 1982).

Table 15.2 Ratio of jobs destroyed to jobs created, 1969–76, by right-to-work (RTW) status, 1980.

States	Jobs destroyed	Jobs created	Ratio of jobs destroyed to jobs created	Percentage of United States total	
				Destroyed	Created
RTW states	10,383,527	14,898,214	0.70	29.3	33.6
Non-RTW states	25,101,917	29,439,329	0.85	70.7	66.4
All United States states	35,485,444	44,337,453	0.80		

Source: Calculated from Bluestone & Harrison (1982: 265–7).

LOCAL CAPITAL SUBSIDY: INDUSTRIAL REVENUE BONDS

States are able to proffer capital at lower than market rates through the offering of bonds whose income is not taxable by the federal government – industrial revenue bonds (IRBs). These are paid back by the recipient firms. Most state and local authorities define taxable income like the federal government. The preference for such instruments results in a loss of public revenue at the local level, but does not entail direct outlay by the local authority.[2]

In the 1950s local officials in the northern states apparently believed that IRBs were giving southern states an advantage in attracting investment. In 1960, $100 million in such loans was made available; by 1963 it had become apparent to some officials that "self-defense will drive local governments everywhere into participation" (Congressional Budget Office 1981: 8); and by the mid-1960s the IRB mechanism was available in 17 states. Even then, they accounted for only 1.4 percent of new plant and equipment nationwide (Congressional Budget Office 1978: 28). By 1981, however, 47 states offered this subsidy, and the volume grew from $1.3 billion in 1975 to $8.4 billion in 1980 (Congressional Budget Office 1981: 14). The high-job-loss states of the Northeast used 38.5 percent, the North Central region used 28.1, and the South used 29.8 percent. Pennsylvania, Minnesota, New Jersey, and Ohio, the four largest users, accounted for 45 percent of total issues (Congressional Budget Office 1981: 27–8).

The tax-free nature of income received by holders of IRBs (and similar instruments such as municipal bonds) allows their interest rates to be lower than the market rate for similar bonds of private firms. As of 1979, municipal bonds (and thus, in general, IRBs) offered only 61 percent of the interest rates that similar quality private paper offered. Firms receiving their financing through IRBs would therefore pay interest charges roughly 40 percent lower than they could obtain on the private market (Congressional Budget Office 1981: 17). In the aggregate, one projection estimates that by 1986 such offerings might have the effect of increasing GNP quite modestly – by $1.78 billion. Their effects on regional location decisions are more difficult to gauge, however, in part because they are so widely available. In general, few firms consider such public sector incentives among their most important domestic location criteria (Congressional Budget Office 1981: 96). If two areas are physically proximate and otherwise comparable, the offer of an IRB or other subsidy may then enter into the location decisions of large firms. Small firms, on the other hand, tend to be locationally constrained by the proprietor's place of residence. There is, therefore, little likelihood that considerable location-specific effects are traceable to IRBs. They do tend to erode the progressive nature of the tax structure (as does all municipal debt which is tax free, and thus worth more to high income earners than to others). Critics of the IRB system suggest various limits on their use; of possible relevance to this discussion is the proposal that they be limited in geographic or sectoral utilization, restricting their use to distressed areas (Congressional Budget Office, 1981). The diffusion of this mechanism is an example of the competitive process referred to by Goodman as public sector entrepreneurship in offering attractions to capital (Goodman 1979). Although IRBs are but one of many subsidies, they exemplify the general process by which the spatial expansion of investor discretion amounts to leverage over local (and federal) public policy.

LOCAL TAXES AND LOCATION IN THE UNITED STATES

Political discussion of state and local taxes in the United States is almost wholly dominated by capital's hostility to both taxes and growth of the public sector. With local political agendas heavily concerned with retaining or attracting jobs, the view of the capitalist class of the rôle of local taxes has dominated the political process. Lowering taxes in one form or another is now the chief "development" tool of state and local governments. This political outcome is a measure of the leverage investors have in their relations with local governments. It is also the occasion of a major discrepancy between the claims made by our local business and political actors and the results of research on industrial location.

Opinion surveys among business executives would appear to indicate that state and local tax burdens may influence location decisions. When the "business climate" of alternative states (or other areas) is rated by managers, local tax burdens are prominent as negative considerations (Padda 1981). However, survey studies of *actual* location decisions show that business climate considerations[3] are of but moderate direct influence. Right-to-work laws and low unionization are by far the most powerful (Schmenner 1980), whereas state and local taxes have a moderate to low ranking in most location surveys (Congressional Budget Office 1978: 28, Townroe 1979: 77–9, 130–1). There is little evidence that, directly or indirectly, state and local taxes have a potent impact on interregional or interstate capital mobility.[4] Bluestone & Harrison (1982: 186) show that the reason for this is that by 1975 interstate variations in tax burdens had become relatively small. Short-distance moves or proximate alternatives may be influenced by tax differerences – as with intrametropolitan moves from city to suburb. Recalling Table 15.1, we note that RTW laws are associated more closely with unionization and wage rates than with tax rates. Right-to-work laws rate more highly than local tax burdens in surveys of location decisions. Public officials, however, appear to be persuaded that tax incentives must be offered. Virtually all the voluminous office construction in Manhattan since the fiscal crisis of 1975 has benefitted from major property tax relief, yet it is extremely questionable whether

Lower Manhattan requires such incentives for major real estate investment (Bahl 1980: 19). In New York, as elsewhere, public officials and
their constituencies are subject to an ideology which associates tax
burdens with capital flight and low taxes with an attractive business
climate.

Business climate may be understood as the result of joint interests and
mutual reinforcement between local business-class political actors and
national or international firms. Locally based business interests have
discrete interests in local growth (Molotch 1982). Newspaper, bank
and media holdings, and real estate, for example, prosper more or less
directly with market size and local demand. As with all taxpayers they
wish others to bear as much of the tax burden as possible. In particular,
local business interests wish to restrain those public sector expenditures
which boost the social wage and thereby labor's overall bargaining
position. Without the threat of capital's flight and its consequent stagnation and decline, this preference has limited efficacy where labor and
working-class organizations are vocal. In the face of such threatening
realities, however, the argument of local business leaders is more
credible and effective.

Local and outside investors claim that low or lower taxes will be
effective in producing jobs. Surveys may be used to document this
claim. Sometimes this may be accomplished by the mechanism of an
outside consultant giving local leaders the message they wish to publi-
cize. The result is a problem definition which constrains policy choice
to use tax relief as a development tool.

Within the United States, variations in most locally controlled explicit incentives are probably weak in influencing capital flow. They have
less influence than the broader elements of capital–labor relations, i.e.,
wages, the social wage, and labor relations laws. The latter are policies
of implicit but powerful relevance for the regional deployment of
capital.

There is a paradox here. The electoral structure impels public officials
to claim that their actions can provide employment: they are forced to
promise what they cannot deliver. This is one factor in the rotation of
politicians. Since local business persons are most vocal about local
taxation, much of the local politics of economic development involves
crafting incentives and tax policies to attract investors. The overall
effect exerts a downward force on the effective tax burden borne by
businesses. Yet the degree to which local authorities influence the larger
operating cost and investment paybacks is constrained. Consequently,
the more powerful variables governing capital's success in relation to
labor are a kind of subagenda in those states with an historically well
organized and relatively well paid labor force. It is difficult for capitalist
class political actors to directly confront working-class interests over
social benefits and community services where unions and neigh-

borhood organizations are vocal. Candidates in Detroit, for example, will not be elected by condemning unions, by advocating even more austere welfare benefits, and the like. But once elected, even liberal officals find that the large firm has immense bargaining power in the face of scarce work. The razing of the Poletown community in Detroit to make way for a General Motors facility is a symbol of the decline of working-class political power in a region where this power was once higher than anywhere else in the country (Bluestone & Harrison 1982: 184).

FEDERAL POLICY AND LOCATION

The United States has never had an overall regional policy, although in the 1960s the Appalachian region was the recipient of large grants used mainly for roads. However, many policy analysts claim that certain features of the national tax code influence regional growth. Investment tax credits which encourage the purchase of new machinery and accelerated depreciation allowances appear to encourage new plant construction (Kopcke & Syron 1978). In the context of regional variation in the age of infrastructure, wages, and unionization levels, this set of incentives may produce decisions to build new plants in the new industrial regions of the country. Quantitative estimates of such effects do not exist; but the belief that they contribute to industrial shift is widespread (Peterson 1980: 4–20), if still a matter of contention.[5]

It should be noted, however, that the magnitude of such national tax incentives is very much larger than any of those available to local governments. This relative difference will become even larger as a result of the combined effects of increased investment credits and faster depreciation allowances advanced by the Reagan administration.

Another area with an implicit impact on interregional capital mobility is the flow of federal funds for defense procurement and grants-in-aid to local government. As industry declined in the Northeast–Midwest in the 1970s, congressional representatives were alerted to federal expenditure patterns which apparently favored the so-called Sunbelt. In the 1970s various programs which responded to cyclical downturns or other federal contribution to local government began to take into account the needs of distressed older areas in the distribution of federal money to urban areas or the poor. In general, however, federal funds have tended to flow disproportionately towards areas of recent industrialization: because they were poorer than others (Mississippi), specialized in defense production (Texas), or were arid and received large federal expenditures on dams and irrigation (Anton *et al.* 1981, Markusen *et al.* 1981).

The Carter administration attemped to formulate, for the first time, an urban and regional policy aimed at retaining the economic viability of the older cities of the Northeast–Midwest. The programs proposed modest tax incentives which were not accepted by Congress. Administratively, the policy aimed at changing procurement policies, for example in the Department of Defense, to include quotas set aside for small businesses and central city producers. There was an announced intention of favoring central city rather than suburban locations for new federal facilities. The Urban Development Action Grant (UDAG) program, making use of federal grants to attract private investment, was made available to distressed cities. The Reagan administration changed this development policy. Since the end of Carter's administration a Schumpeterian view of regional shift has predominated: the redistribution of employment and investment is seen as efficient, the rise of new regions is preferred to the uneconomic subsidy of older ones, and as a result federal policy should be to encourage people to move.

Regional policy in the United Kingdom

The United Kingdom does have explicit regional development policies. Peripheral areas of the country, designated "Development Areas" or "Special Development Areas," may offer incoming firms capital grants (up to 22 percent of a firm's investment), other financial assistance, and employment bounties (Rhodes & Moore 1976, Townroe 1979, Keeble 1981: 123–33). Such expenditures are derived from national budgetary outlays. Local taxes are minor, although sometimes local authorities include tax relief in industrial recruitment. The program has at least two objectives: an active attempt to mold the spatial structure of industry, and a defensive intent to limit massive unemployment. In some places as much as 43 percent of the value of new capital investment has been extended to firms by combinations of these programs (Keeble 1981: 207).

A number of reviews have been made of this policy. There is some evidence that during the economic expansion of the 1960s, the investment incentive programs produced jobs which otherwise would not have appeared in the Development Areas (Congressional Budget Office 1978: 198, Townroe 1979: 123–8): estimates range from 90,000 to 168,000 jobs attributed to the regional subsidy effects in the 1960–71 period (Rhodes & Moore 1976: 27, Ashcroft & Taylor 1977). During the early and mid-1970s, under conditions of national losses of manufacturing employment, however, regional incentives did not appear to produce development. Keeble (1981: 212) speculates that Assisted Areas might have lost even more jobs in this period without the regional subsidies. United Kingdom regional subsidies are substantially larger than those which result from United States tax and financing subsidies at the local level. It is, therefore, not surprising that

Townroe reports on a British government survey which suggests that British employers seemed more influenced by regional investment incentives than United States employers are by state and local incentives (Townroe 1979: 129, cf. 68, 106, 130). At the level of the firm, the magnitude of a full panopoly of investment, financing, employment premiums, and local authority provision of industrial estate space can produce substantial differences in costs and investment payback times (De Meirleir 1982, Plant Location International 1981).

United Kingdom regional incentives appear large enough to attract expanding firms when the British national economy is expanding too. The evidence about the structural dimensions of capital flows to the Assisted Areas, however, indicates that British regional policy also supports a qualitative restructuring of economic space. Massey's (1978) study of the electronics industry found that routine production functions grew in the Assisted Areas, leading to more electronics job growth in such areas than elsewhere. In Massey's study, the ability of firms to separate aspects of the production process over space led them to place these routine assembly tasks in the high-subsidy areas, but to maintain headquarters and research and development functions in the south-east of England. Similarly, Watts found that large United States- and foreign-based corporations were more likely to use the regional incentives than were British-based firms. These same firms, Watts also found, located more of their white-collar work force in the Southeast (Watts 1979). Apparently, British regional policy supports the emergence of some areas concentrating in routine production and others specializing in headquarters functions. This spatial structure is consistent with a labor-control strategy of location by multinational capital. In the lower-wage, high-subsidy, and generally more rural areas (Keeble 1981), industrial militance may be contained by the disciplining effect of past unemployment and by insulating other employee groups from the traditionally more militant ranks of production workers. In regions more prosperous by conventional criteria, regions where white-collar jobs are predominant, wage and other labor conflicts are dampened by the cultural emphasis on the worker's identification with the employer. Class conflict in the Assisted Area may be reduced by the possibility of firms moving to areas where labor is more manageable, such as Ireland or the Asian export platforms.

To summarize, in contrast to state and local governments in the United States, United Kingdom regional policy offers sizeable incentives. This has not, however, turned the Development Areas into prosperous regions. In fact, unemployment has been higher than in the nation, despite the subsidies. Leakage of regional benefits and lower wage employment are among the probable reasons (Ross et al. 1983). The following examination of the global context of investment choice contributes further to an understanding of that relative failure.

The global market in industrial sites

Although the local and regional incentives available to national governments may become quite large, they are but one factor in the formation
of the worldwide mosaic of opportunities for investment in production
facilities. Increasingly, that mosaic includes regions of the world with
starkly different levels of living and working-class material and political
success.

The Organization for Economic Cooperation and Development
(OECD) has recently published data on MNCs and the structure of
direct foreign investment. These data show that direct foreign investment controlled by firms located in OECD countries has grown
significantly more rapidly than the GDPs of any of the OECD countries. From 1960 to 1973, the growth of outward direct investment
grew at 150 percent of the average rate of growth of GDP in these
countries (OECD 1981: 29). Although this process slowed from 1973
to 1979, foreign investment has remained more buoyant than net
domestic investment.

The same report also shows that manufacturing investment controlled
by OECD firms is growing more rapidly in certain newly industrializing
regions than in older ones. The OECD report cites the favorable (i.e.,
lower) wage situation and the labor discipline in such places as South
Korea, Taiwan, Singapore, and Brazil as attracting investment (OECD
1981: 18). Although United States MNCs are dominant in international
investment, German and Japanese firms command increasing shares of
the flows. And among the more recent changes, the OECD notes that
inward foreign investment to the United States accounts for increasing
portions of the total (OECD 1981: 24). The decreasing differential
between formerly higher United States labor costs and some OECD
countries, in particular those in northern Europe, are cited by the report
as important factors in this change.

The internationalization of productive investment is not restricted to
the giant MNCs. The OECD reports that medium and even smaller
firms have begun to invest across national boundaries (OECD
1981: 29). The sectoral diversity of internationalization is demonstrated
by its vigorous appearance in otherwise contrasting industries such as
apparel (NACLA 1977b), electronics (NACLA 1977a), and automobile production (Fieleke 1981).

Global choice by investors brings older and newer industrial regions
of the advanced capitalist countries into competition with each other
and with previously peripheral or less industrial nations. Public policies
are relevant to this structure of competition.

Many Third World countries offer tax relief and capital subsidies for
new industries. For example, Singapore offers ten years of tax freedom
(Singapore Chamber of Commerce 1981). Nigeria offers "pioneer

status" in some sectors, leading to five or more years of tax holiday (Johnston 1982). For firms whose core-country operating environments include corporate and other taxes, these may amount to substantial inducements. For firms with globally integrated production and distribution subsidiaries, such tax havens offer the additional virtue of providing opportunities for transfer pricing, i.e., showing higher profits in a subsidiary located in a low-tax environment and lower profits elsewhere. Similarly, generous capital grants and subsidized financing reduce cost, risk, and payback times.

These incentive policies have been subject to much discussion, especially in the case of the United Kingdom and the United States where "enterprise zones" of tax forgiveness and permissive regulation have been proposed as ways of emulating Third World incentives (Ross et al. 1980, Bluestone & Harrison 1982). Nationally leveraged incentives appear to present more powerful inducements to mobility than local and regional ones. What is not clear is whether these incentives are as significant in the internationalization of production as current discussion might imply.

Table 15.3 shows wage rates in apparel production in a number of countries. Discrepancies of the order shown cannot be compensated for by "tax relief" in older areas, and may not require subsidies in low-wage areas. Similar wage differences are exhibited in other industries, e.g., automobile production. To the extent that capital mobility is wage driven, even national-level incentives are not apt to deter it; and when low wages are combined with very large subsidies, the drift of routine production outwards from the core countries appears certain (Barnet & Mueller 1974, Froebel et al. 1980, Gibson et al. 1983).

Table 15.3 Hourly wages and fringe benefits in the apparel industry (in US$).

Sweden	7.22
Netherlands	5.68
Belgium	5.49
New York (legal)[a]	4.58
United States	4.35
Puerto Rico	2.57
New York (sweatshops)[a]	1.75
Singapore[a]	1.10
Hong Kong	0.96
Brazil	0.86
Taiwan	0.56
Korea (South)	0.41

Note
[a] Does not include fringe benefits.
Source: Ross & Trachte (1983: 417).

What is frequently overlooked in public policy discussions are policies intended to maintain wage and labor control, the main attractions in low-wage and weakly unionized regions. Authoritarian repression, especially directed against labor, is a prominent feature of the policies of the countries singled out by the OECD as developing due to "attractive" wage conditions. Singapore's Chamber of Commerce (1981), for example, points out that in 1981 *no* working days were lost to strikes. State policies which prohibit or control unions and/or workers' ability to act in their industrial or political interests are, from this perspective, the basic policies attracting investment from global firms.

Investors and their consultants discuss these matters in their own language. For example, in discussing the attractiveness of high-wage West Germany as an investment site, in comparison to other European nations, one consulting firm mentions the "responsible" attitude of German trade unions, i.e., the lowest work stoppage rates in the EEC (DeMeirleir 1982). The advent of a socialist government in France was seen by this firm as cause for concern in the investment community. And in an interview with a small New England computer firm, this author was told that for routine production United Kingdom regional development assistance was not as important as its (negative) labor relations, or the Far East's wage rates.

The ability to suppress labor's demands at an offshore site of production has direct implications for workers in the older industrial areas. In apparel, the pressure of competition on the domestic United States industry has caused a search for low-wage sites of assembly in the Caribbean Basin and the Pacific Rim. Apparel imports to the domestic American market have risen dramatically, reaching 25 percent of sales by 1977 and maintaining that level (NACLA 1977b, United States Bureau of the Census 1981: 812, 853). Labor control elsewhere has changed the strategic relation between apparel labor and capital in the United States. The competitive pressure on United States producers has produced sweatshop conditions in New York, Los Angeles, and elsewhere. Here is the way the system of internationalization appears to a New York contractor (Ross & Trachte 1983: 415).

A manufacturer will tell me he has 2,000 twelve-piece blouses he needs sewn. I tell him I need at least $10 per blouse to do a decent job on a garment that complicated. So then he tells me to get lost – he offers me $2. If I don't take that, he tells me he can have it sent to Taiwan or South America somewhere, and have it done for 50 cents. So we haggle – sometimes I might bring him up to $4 per blouse.

Now, you tell me, how can I pay someone "union scale" ($3.80) or even the minimum wage ($2.90), when I'm only getting $4 per blouse? With overhead and everything else, I may be able to pay the ladies $1.20 per blouse, but that's tops. There's nothing on paper. I get it in cash.

Significant fractions of all New York garment labor toils in turn-of-the-century sweatshops. The illegal wages of New York's sweatshops are induced by control of labor in newer industrial areas.

Policy and authority structure

Two themes in the foregoing can now be summarized. First, public policies which intend to affect the localization of jobs through financial inducements are probably not as powerful as public policy which mediates capital-labor relations. On both the world and national scales, capital flows towards places in which its control of labor is more secure and its rate of exploitation higher (Carney 1980). Although cost and control are not always the same (e.g., West Germany) they tend to be similar. The result is to heighten the ability of capital to secure benefits everywhere.

The second theme concerns the levels of state authority engaged in producing incentives. The explicit local competition between states and cities in the United States, although furious, actually engages relatively marginal location factors. But the general result is broader latitude and more control over local politics by business interests. Federalism allows the investor to benefit from a buyers' market in production sites: many wish to be called, few are chosen.

More substantial leverage is obtained when the tax and capital resources of a national government are engaged, as in United Kingdom regional policy. These are of little solace in times of absolute economic shrinkage. In the long run, their magnitude is rarely sufficient to outweigh wage savings available in poor countries. When international mobility is examined, the differences in national incentives may be substantial. But it remains probable that the more powerful policies are those which cheapen labor and inhibit its organized representation.

These processes result in three kinds of political initiatives. At the national level, unions and parties (or tendencies within parties, e.g, the Left of the British Labour party) are attracted to protectionist policies which promise to sustain employment in wage-sensitive industries. An example is domestic content legislation proposed by United States auto workers and legislators from areas affected by the auto industry's collapse. Simultaneously with protectionist pressure, labor and capital in declining and import-impacted industries have called for subsidies of various types. A wide variety of such specific proposals come under the rubric "reindustrialization." The task of crafting such policies faces two difficulties. One difficulty is the interest group process of politics: once begun, it is hard to deny tax and other benefits to a broadcasting set of industrial sectors and firms. When the benefits are granted universally (as by the 1981 United States tax revisions), it is probable that no particular flow of capital to distressed industries or regions will result. Instead, the general conditions for capital accumulation may be supported, but the renewed cashflows may not necessarily benefit older regions or the domestic economy. The second problem of reindustrialization policies of either centrist or leftist origin resides in their global context. The advanced capitalist countries possess costly infrastructures, including the levels of reproduction of their working classes. These are products of decades of material development and democratic and other class conflict. It is doubtful that any given package of subsidies can obviate the global firms' search for cheap labor, especially in distressed industries.

A third political initiative now appearing in the core capitalist countries is a recognition by the labor movement of the *de facto* creation of a worldwide pool of labor: global capitalism creates a global working class. The internationalization of workers' employers now makes cooperation among national fractions of workers a material necessity. Whether concrete cooperation can be implemented is at least as difficult to anticipate as any other complex diplomatic problem. The reconciliation of protectionist job defense and international solidarity is the daunting task of the contemporary labor movement. It appears, for the moment, that protectionism is dominant. To the extent to which protectionist working-class politics hinders labor cooperation, the medium-term prospect is not promising.

State structures and ideology

The formulation of a concept of global capitalism brings into focus particular issues which have been submerged in political economy. Although theoretical discussions of the "relative autonomy of the state" are many, particular applications to the changing matrix of the world system are scarce.

The geographic structure of state authority is one dimension of this. The extreme decentralization of local authority in the United States has material and ideological ramifications. Federalism deflects the policies of economic change onto a local competitive matrix. It focuses conflict onto marginal issues and produces an ideological environment extremely favorable to local business-class interests. For, instead of class contention over the origins and destination of capital investment, one observes local and regional competition over taxes and subsidies. From this perspective, under contemporary conditions, federalism itself is an important political resource for capital. This implies that the form of the spatial structure of state authority has differential relevance at different moments of capitalist development. This is not adequately comprehended by terming it a "reflection" of economic process: it is a major resource *within* that process. One would welcome comparative research on the class implications of federalist versus centralist authority structures (Williams 1981, Ross 1982).

Finally, we can consider the relation between the shifting world structure of capitalism and contradictions within various ideological contenders for hegemony. The richer capitalist states are juridically democratic. For their political stability and social cohesion they depend on ideological legitimacy. The political accompaniment to the restructuring of regions has at least the following ideological tendencies.

The first tendency is conservative and it produces support for the policies pursued by the administrations of Ronald Reagan and Margaret Thatcher. It responds to the threat of capital flight by acceding to the redistribution of market and social wages towards capital. When this conservatism is broadly accepted, workers adopt an attitude of resignation toward the "natural" necessities of capitalist reorganization. They expect and accept more modest rewards from their labors. They support conservative policies for fear that they will be hurt more than helped by policies emphasizing equality, public goods and service delivery, or power over economic life. At its extreme, such an attitude adopts a fearful intolerance of anticapitalist dissidence: authoritarianism may result.

Although this result could be understood as the unalloyed hegemony of capitalist ideology, such dominance cannot be total. Lodged in this result are the contradictions between nationalist and regional sentiment mobilized to attract capital and the thoroughgoing internationalism of the global firms' operations. An internationalized fascism is hard to conjure.

The second tendency produced by global restructuring is the delegitimation of capitalist "success." The welfare state was to have abolished the massive deprivation and cyclical intensity of an earlier era. Its failure under current conditions may thus weaken the attractiveness of the "social contract" of the postwar era. A more ambitious socialist politics emerges, as in the British Labour Left, or the French Socialist party Left. The contradiction embedded in contemporary socialist politics is that, short of simultaneous socialist political victories among major trading partners, short-run success is unlikely. Capital outflow would immediately subvert socialist reconstruction. The result would be extended austerity. In turn, this austerity would stand as a negative example for other socialist movements.

This interpretation of public policy and the politics which surround contemporary capital mobility, although not optimistic, does suggest approaches to the problem which contrast to many currently in vogue. Rather than suggesting that workers can defend themselves and their communities through an exclusively regional or local consciousness, or with the political demand for "participation" for example, the more

How??

urgent need is for national means of controlling and generating capital
and for international perspectives on labor cooperation. Rather than a
political claim that the right tax incentive will save an older city or
region, this approach emphasizes the need to control the global firm
itself. Public policy which serves the interests of workers and older
regions must go beyond the current fashion of subsidizing capital in the
hope that it will stay in a given place. In the era of global capitalism, the
problem for workers is that their employers have a world of choices.

Notes

1 The social wage: "that amalgam of benefits, worker protections, and legal
  rights that acts to generally increase the social security of the working class"
  (Bluestone & Harrison 1982: 133). We note that these protections also
  support labor's bargaining power.
2 Estimates of the magnitude of these local revenue effects are not available.
3 Business climate is reviewed as that amalgam of locally variable policies
  which indicate the degree of dominance of capitalist class interests over the
  local state (Goodman 1979, Rones 1980, Anonymous 1981, Padda 1981,
  Bluestone & Harrison 1982, De Meirleir 1982, Ross 1982).
4 Responses to surveys are subject to variation depending on how questions are
  asked. When openended questions probe location criteria, state and local
  taxes rarely appear as high among the influencing factors. However, when
  prompted, business persons abhor high taxes. There is an implicitly
  "correct" position which inheres in the respondent's world view. Most
  surveys of location have not been explicitly crafted to discern the sequence of
  steps and the spatial terms of reference of each location criterion. This may
  account for some of the indeterminancy between different studies (McMillan
  1965, Nishioka & Krumme 1973).
5 Bluestone & Harrison (1982: 300) review this debate in some detail. Their
  view is that though such features of the tax code help capital to shift tax
  burdens onto workers' incomes it is not clear that they contribute to regional
  change in the United States. Marcuse (1981), by comparison, writing about
  central cities rather than broad regions, and about a series of implicit policies,
  asserts that investment tax credits do produce capital flow out of cities.

References

Anonymous 1981. The art of site selection. Interview with Maurice Fulton.
  Electronic Business, May 15.
Anton, T. J., J. P. Cawley and K. L. Kramer 1981. Federal spending in regions:
  Patterns of stability and change. In *Cities under stress*, R. Burchell and D.
  Listokin (eds). Piscataway, N.J.: Center for Urban Policy Research.
Ashcroft, B. and J. Taylor 1977. The movement of manufacturing firms and
  the effect of regional policy, *Oxford Economic Papers* **29**(1).

Bahl, R. 1980. *The impact of local tax policy on urban economic development.* Urban Consortium Bulletin, United States Department of Commerce, Economic Development Administration, September.

Barnet, R. and R. Mueller 1974. *Global reach.* New York: Simon & Shuster 1982.

Battelle Columbus Laboratories 1982. *Identification of location criteria related to the development of robotics and biotechnology in the state of Michigan.* Report to the High Technology Task Force and Michigan Department of Commerce, September 24.

Bluestone, B. and B. Harrison 1982. *The deindustrialization of America.* New York: Basic Books.

Browne, L. E. 1982. Two years of stagnation: a regional perspective. *New England Economic Review.* September–October, 35–44.

Carney, J. 1980. Regions in crisis: accumulation regional problems and crisis formation. In *Regions in crisis,* J. Carney, R. Judson, and J. Lewis (eds). London: Croom Helm.

Congressional Budget Office 1978. *Barriers to urban economic development.* Washington, D.C.: United States Government Printing Office.

Congressional Budget Office 1981. *Small issue industrial revenue bonds.* Washington, D.C.: United States Government Printing Office, April.

De Meirleir, M. J. 1982. The realities of development policy implementation and incentives for the electronics industry in the EEC countries. *Investing in the European Economic Community* May, 20.

Evans, P. 1979. *Dependent development: the alliance of multinational, state, and local capital in Brazil.* Princeton, N.J.: Princeton University Press.

Fayerweather, J. 1981. Four winning strategies for the international corporation, *Journal of Business Strategy* 2, 25–36.

Fieleke, N. 1981. Challenge and response in the automobile industry. *New England Economic Review* July–August, 37–48.

Frobel, F., et al. 1980. *The new international division of labor.* Cambridge: Cambridge University Press.

Gibson, J., J. Graham, D. Shakow and R. Ross 1983. Theoretical approaches to capital and labor restructuring. In *Restructuring regions: Marxist interpretations of regional change in advanced capitalism,* J. Carney and P. O'Keefe (eds). London: Croom Helm.

Goodman, R. 1979. *The last entrepreneurs.* New York: Simon & Schuster.

Hymer, S. 1979. The multinational corporation and the law of uneven development. In *Transnational corporations and world order,* G. Modelski (ed.). New York: W. H. Freeman.

Johnston, I. 1982. *The development of a Third World city: Lagos and Nigeria.* Clark University, Department of Geography, Fall.

Keeble, D. 1981. Manufacturing dispersion and government policy in a declining industrial system: the United Kingdom case, 1971–76. In *Industrial location and regional systems,* J. Reese, G. J. D. Hewings, and H. A. Stafford (eds). New York: J. F. Bergin.

Kopcke, R. W. and R. F. Syron 1978. Tax incentives: their impact on invest-ment decisions and their cost to the treasury. *New England Economic Review* January–February, 19–32.

McMillan, T. E., Jr. 1965. Why manufacturers choose plant locations vs. determinants of plant location. *Land Economics* August, 239–46.

Marcuse, P. 1981. The targeted crisis: on the ideology of the urban fiscal crisis and its uses. *International Journal of Urban and Regional Research*, 330–55.

Markusen, A. R., A. Saxenian and M. Weis 1981. Who benefits from inter-government formulas. In *Cities under stress*, R. Burchell and D. Lisokin (eds). Piscataway, N.J.: Center for Urban Policy Research.

Massey, D. 1978. Capital and locational change: the UK electrical engineering and electronics industries. *Review of Radical Political Economics* Fall, 39–54.

Molotch, H. 1982. The city as a growth machine. *American Journals of Sociology* **2**, 309–32.

Nishioka, H. and G. Krumme 1973. Location conditions, factors and decisions: an evaluation of selected location survey. *Land Economics* **49**, 195–205.

NACLA (North American Congress on Latin America) 1977a. *Electronics: the global industry*. Special issue of *Latin America and Empire Report* 4 (April).

NACLA 1977b. *Capital's flight: The apparel industry moves south*. Special Issue of *Latin America and Empire Report*, **XI** (3, March).

OECD (Organization for Economic Cooperation and Development) 1981. *International investments and multinational enterprises: recent international direct investment trends*. Paris: OECD.

Padda, K. 1981. Report card on the States, *Inc.* October, 90–8.

Peterson, G. E. 1980. *The impact of federal fiscal policies on urban economic development*. Urban Consortium Information Bulletin. United States Department of Commerce, Economic Development Administration, September.

Piven, F. F. and R. Cloward 1982. *The new class war*. New York: St. Martins Press.

Plant Location International 1981. *Derwentside study*. Brussels: Plant Location International.

Rhodes, J. and B. Moore 1976. Regional economic policy and the movement of manufacturing firms to development areas. *Economics* **43**.

Rones, P. 1980. Moving to the sun: regional job growth, 1968–78. *Monthly Labor Review*, March.

Ross, R. 1982a. *Capital mobility, branch plant location and class power*. Paper delivered at Society for the Study of Social Problems Annual Meeting, San Francisco.

Ross, R. 1982b. Regional illusion, capitalist reality. *Democracy* April, 93–8.

Ross, R. and K. Trachte 1983. Global cities, global classes: the peripheralization of labor in New York City. *Review* **VI**(3) (Winter), 393–431.

Ross, R., D. Shakow and P. Susman 1980. Local planners – Global constraints. *Policy Sciences* **12**, 1–25.

Ross, R., K. Gibson, J. Graham, P. O'Keefe, D. Shakow and P. Susman 1983. Global capitalism and regional decline: the strategies of classes in the older regions. In *Restructuring regions*, J. Carney and P. O'Keefe (eds). London: Croom Helm.

Schmenner, R. 1980. *The location decisions of large, multiplant companies*. Cambridge, Mass.: MIT–Harvard Joint Center for Urban Studies.

Singapore Chamber of Commerce 1981. *Facts for business*. Singapore: Singapore Chamber of Commerce.

Szymanski, A. 1981. *The logic of imperialism*. New York: Praeger.

Townroe, P. M. 1979. *Industrial movement: experience in the US and the UK*. Farnborough, England: Saxon House.

United States Bureau of the Census 1981. *Statistical abstract of the United States: 1981*, 102nd edn. Washington, D.C.: United States Bureau of the Census.

Watts, H. D. 1979. Large firms, multinationals, and regional development: some new evidence from the United Kingdom. *Environment and Planning A* **II**, 71–81.

Williams, W. A. 1981. Radicals and regionalism. *Democracy*, **1**, 87–98.

Williams, W. A. 1982. Procedure becomes substance. *Democracy* April, 100–2.

16   *Bringing the Third World home*[*]

WILLIAM W. GOLDSMITH

The centerpiece of the Reagan urban program is a development scheme called "enterprise zones." The plan would offer extra tax and regulatory concessions to induce business to invest in depressed areas. The problem is that Reagan has already given away so much of business' tax base that he has little left to offer. The enterprise zone idea leads logically to concessions by the only group left with much to concede – workers. Trade unionists are already facing widespread demands for givebacks. In their pure form, enterprise zones attract industry by insisting on wage concessions, as well as waivers of health, safety, and environmental regulation. Reagan's version begins by waiving the minimum wage for youths.

It is a mark of the exhaustion of liberal postwar policies in urban renewal, housing, and job development that this approach is being taken very seriously, and not just by conservatives. A key congressional enthusiast is the Democrat from the South Bronx, Representative Robert Garcia. Across America, mayors, city councils, and state administrations hungry for jobs are debating the shape of enterprise zones.

What makes this idea thinkable is the radical change in the structure of the world economy. During the past 20 years, corporate capital has become increasingly diffused. Modern communications have permitted central financial and accounting controls over far-flung manufacturing networks. Today, complex industrial goods can be fabricated in relatively primitive settings, by a work force paid far below levels prevailing in industrial societies.

In this new global economy, private capital enjoys vastly increased leverage to extract wage concessions as its price for staying put. The result is nothing less than a serious erosion of economic and political rights. Enterprise zones do far more than retain and attract jobs: they

[*] Reprinted from Goldsmith, W. W. 1982, Bringing the Third World home, *Working Papers Magazine,* with permission of *Working Papers Magazine.* (© 1982 Trusteeship Institute Inc.)

become a wedge to cut deeply into the social safety net of the modern welfare state and reduce the political power of workers in advanced industrial countries.

This idea did not spring full-blown from the brow of some conservative policy intellectual. The Third World already has a good deal of experience with the special production enclaves, often known as "platform economies" or "free production zones." Conditions in these tax-free, duty-free, subminimum wage areas suggest the sort of economic development that enterprise zones portend for the United States. And even the relatively successful cases, like Singapore and Puerto Rico, are nothing we should wish to emulate, economically or politically.

As Berkeley planner Manuel Castells has suggested, national governments in the Third World increasingly serve as political intermediaries, caught between the demands of their displaced, urbanized populations and requirements set by global corporations. The enterprise zone idea reflects the growing pressure on governments of advanced countries to play essentially the same rôle.

In effect, enterprise zones would keep American jobs from being exported – by bringing the Third World home to the United States.

Before turning to enterprise zones in greater detail, one should stop to recall just how radically the new global economy has changed the relations between industrial capital and the Third World. Historically, early industrial expansion sought trade in commodities. Raw materials were imported from underdeveloped countries; manufactured goods were produced in the mother country for sale at home and overseas. This process built industry in Europe, and later in America and Japan, at the expense of local Third World industry. For example, English cities exploded with textile production, whereas the traditional Indian textile manufacturing industry collapsed.

Later, manufacturing operations were established in overseas territories, but mainly to serve local markets. As European and North American industry established outposts in the Third World, however, they remained something essentially grafted onto local social systems. This external sector was seldom fully integrated into the local economy.

In this long process of the expansion of industrial capital, the great bulk of benefits went to the already industrialized countries. Development elsewhere was stunted, skewed, even reversed. André Gunder Frank has termed this process "the development of underdevelopment."

But, traditionally, the poor countries were not really part of a worldwide production system, except as suppliers of raw materials. In the past two decades that has all changed. Today, worldwide corporations can supervise minutely specialized manufacturing operations from distant headquarters, so that in the industrial sector of the global economy relations between workers and owners increasingly ignore national boundaries.

In the new international economy, global corporations manufacture at multiple sites for export to world markets. They also import Third World labor to the metropolitan countries. Hence, we purchase underwear and transistor radios made in Kuala Lumpur, Volkswagens made in Germany by Turks, and beans harvested by Mexicans in the United States. In this context, it becomes harder and harder for the domestic work forces of the industrialized countries to defend their privileged position as islands of high wages, relatively decent work conditions, and social benefits.

This internationalization of industrial production is all remarkably recent. As late as 1960, there was virtually no Third World production of manufactured goods for export. By the late 1970s, however, there were many hundreds of thousands of workers in multinational corporate plants producing for export from scores of sites in more than 60 countries of Asia, Africa, and Latin America. Today there are probably millions of such workers. Aside from the availability of raw materials or energy sources, such production is based on three main considerations: an available labor force that will do good work for low wages, an international transport and communication system, and a system for dividing tasks, allowing subdivision into easily organized, supervised, and controlled units of production.

Although foreign plants may be located all over some Third World countries, many "world market factories" are located in some free production zones. These zones are legal islands, "where foreign corporations and their officers are usually treated to the special considerations that are recommended by the United Nations Industrial Development Organization: exemption from duty on machinery and raw materials, from income tax, and from other normally applicable taxes; freedom from restrictions on foreign exchange; preferential rates on financing, local transportation, and facility rental; provision of utilities, roads, office buildings, and factories; and provision of multiple business and personal services. Usually health and safety regulations are minimal, labor has few rights, and there is little environmental protection.

American domestic corporations are also assisted by special provisions of the United States Tariff Code, which allows duty-free reimportation to the United States of products assembled abroad. Under articles 806 and 807, components may be shipped abroad for processing, then reimported with a sizeable duty exemption as long as there will be further processing in the United States. Duty is not assessed on the original components but only on fabrication costs overseas. In 1978, after six years of growth at 20 percent per year, imports under this preference amounted to $7.2 billion. Of this, one-third was from underdeveloped countries, where such exports grew at a rate of 26 percent per year.

These tariff provisions accelerate the movement towards runaway shops. Among the world's poor countries, Mexico is a striking example of the ability of low-wage areas to attract runaway industry. Mostly along the border with the United States, more than 100,000 workers, almost exclusively young women, work in scores of factories that reexport goods to the United States.

In Ciudad Juarez, many work in the large Bermudez Industrial Park, where they process or assemble components for such corporations as GE, Westinghouse, Bendix, American Hospital Supply, RCA, and Sylvania. At the other extreme, in Tijuana, young women sew clothing in fly-by-night sweatshops. In 1978 firms shipped over $700 million in taxable value under 806–807 from Mexico alone. The actual value of the goods was approximately twice as much. From Taiwan came $400 million, and from Singapore, Malaysia, and Hong Kong about $200 million each.

The idea of enterprise zones in advanced industrial countries was first promoted in Great Britain by Professor Peter Hall of Reading University as a means to cut wages so that British workers could somehow compete with their brethren in the colonies. The so-called "free ports . . . to be based on fairly shameless free enterprise," as Professor Hall expressed it, would abate taxes on profits, capital gains, sales and personal income, allow imports and sales free of duty, eliminate all but the most basic regulations, and cut social services and labor protection to the bone. Strong trade unions would be officially discouraged. As Professor Hall put it, "Wages would find their own level. . . . Small, selected areas of inner cities would be simply thrown open to all kinds of initiative, with minimum control. In other words, we would aim to recreate the Hong Kong of the 1950s and 1960s inside inner Liverpool or inner Glasgow." Such legislation, watered down to meet political realities, has become the cornerstone of the urban program in Mrs. Thatcher's Conservative government.

British enterprise zones are now defined as depressed areas in big cities in which local taxes on industrial and commercial property are to be abolished (municipalities to be reimbursed by the national government), capital gains and corporate income taxes are to be reduced, local zoning waived and government paperwork simplified to aid business and encourage international trade. These provisions are to apply for a decade and are to be renewable. To date, three such zones have been formally recognized by British government, but no new enterprises are operating yet.

In the United States the idea was promoted first by the ultraconservative Heritage Foundation, in Washington, which put out an American version of the British proposal in 1980. Now embodied in at least five federal bills, in proposed legislation in more than 20 states, and under active discussion in city halls everywhere, enterprise zones promise to become the main element in United States urban policy. An Illinois bill, for example, although successfully vetoed by Governor Thompson in September 1981, was nearly repassed over his veto. Organized labor and civic groups played a large rôle in the defeat. The bill provides useful illustrations of the possibilities for local legislation. The original Illinois proposal called for suspending all zoning and building codes, eliminating minimum wages, initially abolishing property taxes, prohibiting any state aid not provided in the enterprise act itself, weakening unions (through right-to-work laws), and weakening or eliminating all environmental regulations and health and safety laws.

Besides Reagan's new plan, one key federal bill is the proposal by Congressmen Jack Kemp and Robert Garcia, the 1981 Urban Jobs and Enterprise Zone Act. The Kemp–Garcia Bill would eliminate taxes on capital gains, halve taxes on corporate income, liberalise treatment of business losses, and give the firm a tax credit equal to 5 percent of the wages paid each employee in the zone, with another 5 percent when employees are low-income people.

An earlier draft also eliminated social security taxes and drastically cut regulations. Because of opposition from Garcia, the minimum wage reductions and drastic regulation waivers were dropped from the bill. Ironically, technical analysis shows that the remaining provisions are unlikely to attract investment or provide jobs. The current White House version of an enterprise zone emphasizes tax cuts mainly, but President Reagan has also been an enthusiastic advocate of subminimum youth wages and freer entry for foreign guest workers.

Except for the special cases of Taiwan, South Korea, and Singapore, not a single poor, capitalist country since World War II has developed in a way that both increased incomes and improved income distribution. As it turns out, even the successful cases, which were continuously stimulated by our Asian military preparations and by wars in Korea and Vietnam, are problematic.

Before moving to evidence about the majority – the places that *did not* develop – let us consider two of these peculiar "successes," Singapore and Puerto Rico. They are particularly interesting, even though exceptional, because they survive almost entirely as "factories" producing for the global marketplace. They really are precursors of today's enterprise zones.

The international development community considers the city–state of Singapore a model of successful development. It is an almost laboratory-controlled case illustrating the effect of investment by global corporations in branch plants that manufacture products for re-export to world markets. It also suggests how this process influences domestic political life.

As in much of the Third World, political life in Singapore is controlled by a corporatist state, whose eagerness to help depress wages and control labor strife in order to attract multinational investment has undermined the domestic business class and stunted political opposition. The economic relationship between domestic workers and their foreign employers virtually dominates the political context in Singapore. The constant threat that these employers will move their operations elsewhere determines to a great extent how, when, and why local business and the government act.

In the 1960s, the ruling People's Action Party embarked upon a program to attract foreign industrial investment. They began by cutting corporate taxes for investors from 40 to 4 percent. This did attract new investment, but because it was highly capital intensive, unemployment continued to grow, worsened by the loss of domestic markets when Singapore became independent from Malaysia in 1965 and British military bases were closed after 1966.

Then, in 1968, tough new labor legislation effectively eliminated collective bargaining by reducing benefits to laid-off workers, cutting bonuses and pay for overtime work, reducing maternity leaves, holiday leaves, and fringe benefits, and authorizing full management control over promotion, transfer, and dismissal. This left for negotiation only wages, on which disputes go to the Ministry of Labor and a special labor court. Since the government also acted drastically to weaken unions, decisions have consistently favored management. Strikes and lockouts have been virtually eliminated. In 1955 strikes cost industry nearly a million lost person-days, and in 1963 nearly 400,000 lost person-days; since 1970 the losses have dropped to no more than a few thousand per year, an average of only five or ten workers out on strike each day in a country of 2 million.

In this "favorable investment climate," as it is called in the business press, manufacturing investment in labor-intensive industries shot up. From 1963 to 1974 industrial employment increased 560 percent, by 170,000 workers, the biggest increases being in textiles and electronics, the bulk of the new employees being young, unskilled women. Immigrant workers (one-eighth of the labor force by 1973) and children, whose legal work age was reduced to 12, were needed to fill labor shortages.

Although Singapore is something of a success story compared to the even worse conditions of much of the Third World, wages remain shockingly depressed. The prevailing wage for all production work in 1974, for example, was $16.72 for a 44-hour week – under $900 a year. Worker dissatisfaction is now expressed in high absenteeism, high quit rates, and of course pressure to raise wages, all of which makes Singapore somewhat less desirable for foreign investors.

Puerto Rico's foreign investment history, although it began 15 or 20 years earlier, is remarkably similar. After some experimentation with planning and nationalization, the Puerto Rican leadership decided in the late 1940s to open the island to foreign corporations for branch plant manufacturing.

Under "Operation Bootstrap," special provisions of United States law abolished corporate income taxes in Puerto Rico, provided subsidized feasibility studies and infrastructure investment, and guaranteed to investors the protections of domestic United States law and American courts. Initially, this program did succeed in attracting outside investment to produce growth rates that were extraordinarily high, averaging about 35 percent per year in textiles, metal, and machinery, and well over 8 percent in every other sector but agriculture and food. Per capita GNP grew 354 percent in real terms from 1947 to 1973. This was a heyday for government-assisted free enterprise, with subsidies for feasibility studies, roads, utilities and factory buildings, free labor training, and active recruitment, all close to home and under the full protection of United States laws.

The Singapore development may still progress in a fashion, but the Puerto Rican experiment is in real trouble. Even with 40 percent of its population having left for the United States mainland, conditions on the island are difficult. First, export growth has virtually ceased. From 1968 to 1974, while Asian producers increased their apparel exports to the United States market by 370 percent, Puerto Rican exports stagnated, leading to net factory layoffs for 23,000 workers. Second, unemployment, always a problem in Puerto Rico, has hovered between 30 and 40 percent since 1974. Third, family poverty is severe, and without food stamps, which go to seven of every ten families, there would be widespread hunger and disruption.

Why did Puerto Rico decline? In a sense, the entire development strategy was contradictory. To the extent that it succeeded, thereby raising wages, it reduced the attraction for investors, and therefore failed. There was no mechanism for internal generation of development, no central planning, no government investment, no real development policy aside from *laissez-faire*. Inherent in a mode of development that emphasizes low-skill, high-tech production and depends on corporations' ability to operate anywhere in the world, is the danger that corporations can simply relocate whenever wages threaten to rise. In this sort of global economy, in which selling prices are rigid and only low-labor-cost operations can survive, it is all too easy for new plants to open and for orders to be shifted from one source of supply to another. Such a dependent development program causes local employment to be whipsawed between local wage increases and foreign low-wage competition.

For years, the government in San Juan has been troubled by this dilemma. To attract branch plants, it has kept wages down, but as its own statistics show, this is a losing game. Although the average hourly wage in Puerto Rican textile factories was just $2 in 1974, in its competitors – the Philippines, Sri Lanka, Haiti, Malaysia, India, Pakistan, Singapore, and the Dominican Republic – hourly wages in textiles were grouped between 14 and 33 cents. At the same time, pressured by the workforce, which is itself heavily influenced by mainland United States wages and prices, the government has allowed wages to rise (although they have not risen above 50 percent of United States mainland wages). Once again we see a government stuck between the unyielding demands of global industry and the unfulfilled aspirations of its people.

When Third World countries gear themselves to become low-wage outposts of global industry, stagnation seems to be the logical outcome. Hospitality to branch plants of multinational corporations fails to generate a balanced local economy. Wages stay low, because other Third World countries always are available to pay even lower wages.

Puerto Rico and Singapore, as even partial successes, are very much the exception. Singapore is small. It can expel its foreign labor. It has no impoverished rural hinterland. It may survive on receipts of international banking, commerce, and commodity trade because it is at an extraordinary international crossroads. And it may capitalize on its educated labor force through centralized planning to introduce more technically advanced manufacturing, with higher wages.

In the rest of the world, things are worse. Just as global competition has snatched textile employment away from Puerto Rico, first to Asia and then back to Haiti, the Dominican Republic, and Central America, so it will displace employment elsewhere too. In general the vast majority of the sixty-odd countries that hope to develop with platform economies cannot succeed because there are not enough jobs to go around. For to the degree any country threatens or manages to raise its wages, the global corporations will threaten to or actually move elsewhere, where wages are still lower.

Consequently, aside from the exceptional cases, things are dismal indeed. In most countries with free production zones, labor is astonishingly cheap. Hourly wages for unskilled manufacturing workers in branch plants in 1975 were about 15 cents or less in India, the Philippines, Thailand, Mauritius, and Haiti; they were 25 cents or less in Indonesia, Malaysia, Taiwan, Lesotho, Liberia, Swaziland, Colombia, and Honduras. Add it up: 25 cents an hour is $10 a week, hardly more than $500 a year for the best of these cases.

Given levels of productivity that are comparable to plants in the United States, it is difficult for any industrialist to resist foreign location, and fewer and fewer with the capability have resisted each year. Even in nearby Mexico unskilled labor is paid as low as $1 an hour. Giant corporations are closing United States plants more rapidly than small firms because the former are more easily able to modify their operations in industrial countries and then organize and finance operations abroad.

This brings us back to the United States, where the problems of plant closing and capital flight lie behind the urban unemployment that stimulates calls for enterprise zones. Let us try now to make sense of the situation.

The prospects for American workers in the new global economy bring to mind a rather disreputable Marxian phrase that was all but laughed out of the vocabulary of mainstream economics during the postwar era – the reserve army of the unemployed. During a brief 30 year moment of the "American Century," United States workers could enjoy the benefits of America's remarkable dominance of the world economy. Granted even America has always had its secondary labor market where racial minorities, women, and foreign migrants worked at low-paying, unskilled jobs. But there remained a substantial primary labor market as well, where many American workers (the vast majority of them white and male) were protected, whether by trade barriers, technological limits to a truly global factory system, American dominance of manufacturing for export or, most important of all, the hard-won gains of the American labor movement. Just as all these factors helped to expand the boundaries of the primary labor market, the new international economy and its offspring, urban enterprise zones, are potent weapons for shrinking them. The underemployed people of the Third World constitute an authentic reserve army that can undermine the wages and benefits of workers all over the world.

It is of course very unlikely that wages of American workers can be cut so low, even in enterprise zones, that they could compete effectively with the platform economies of the Third World. If nothing else, the high cost of living in the United States precludes industrial wages of $14 a week.

But even the attempt to impose this competition on American workers will radically reduce their standard of living and their political power, and will transform the rôle of the state. During the period of American domination of world trade, American workers were able to seize a measure of political power and the state was more or less neutral in labor relations. Measures like the Wagner Act helped labor to organize, and unemployment insurance, minimum wage, and occupational health and safety laws improved labor's economic capacity to bargain.

But the new global economy radically changes the bargaining power of domestic labor, and the enterprise zone proposal is a device to shift explicitly government's rôle from neutral party to overt ally of corporate industry. Even without government playing this rôle, workers have already felt the growing pressure for wage concessions. In November 1981, the Ford Motor Company threatened to close a plant employing 1,300 workers in Sheffield, Alabama, unless the workers agreed to a 50 percent cut in wages and fringe benefits, to bring costs at the plant in line with global competition. In December, the United Auto Workers released its locals to negotiate separately, to reduce wages where they felt it necessary to provide assistance to otherwise unprofitable plants. Perhaps the most astonishing evidence of such a long-run plan is Ford's for duplicating production plants in Western Europe. Their plants are designed normally to operate at half capacity precisely so that managers can confront labor with a stronger hand.

In this climate, financiers and corporate planners are increasingly candid about what they expect from governments. Does a country have the temerity to raise minimum wages or impose regulations? Walter Wriston, Chairman of Citicorp, has a ready reply. "As a last resort, all the multinational company can do in its relation with a sovereign state is to make an appeal to reason. If this fails, capital, both human and material, will leave for countries where it is more welcome." Wriston, it turns out, was not lecturing some obscure Third World country. His words were directed to the British (in 1976).

In pure form, enterprise zones call upon government to create planned depressions, rather than letting the market generate chaotic spontaneous ones. They are quite consistent with other proposals of the Reagan administration, such as more liberal entry for "guest workers," tolerance of high unemployment rates, and reduction of a broad range of social supports, all of which depress wages. In effect, enterprise zones would officially bless the *de facto* dual labor market, since workers in such zones would have fewer protections and rights than other workers.

The danger, however, is that enterprise zones would not stay contained. Once industry became accustomed to lower wages, lower taxes, and limits on workers' rights in enterprise zones, these provisions would tend to spill over elsewhere. Why should GM tolerate a high wage, unionized work force in Detroit when a government-approved domestic Third World is available, say, in St. Louis?

As medicine to rejuvenate American cities, the enterprise zone proposal is entirely self-defeating. Rather than creating new opportunities for depressed areas, it would mainly depress standards elsewhere in America. It would accelerate the erosion of America's status as a relative island of affluence. The worst affront, however, is to political democracy. For enterprise zones enshrine not just a dual labor market but a dual citizenry. And in time, the result would be a single pool of low-wage workers with diminished rights as citizens.

17   Free trade zones in Southeast Asia*

TAKEO TSUCHIYA

What is the free trade zone?

The "free trade zone" (FTZ) is like a country within a country. Cut off by barbed wire or concrete walls from the rest of the country and guarded in some cases by "zone police," the zone is "an enclave in terms of the customs-territorial aspect and possibly other aspects such as total or partial exemption from laws and decrees of the country concerned," as a survey on FTZs for the Asian Productivity Organization (APO) puts it (APO 1975:86). The zone has its own authority to which government functions are largely relegated to providing all necessary services related to export–import transactions and facilitating intrazone production by its occupant foreign investors, 100 percent (or nearly 100 percent) of whose products are exported abroad. Workers employed in the zone are often subject to special regulations (prohibition of labor disputes, for instance), have to show special passes to enter, and must often undergo body checks when they finish a day's toil. This latter is to prevent "smuggling" of the zone's products into the workers' own country.

The free trade zone is a relatively new phenomenon, though free ports or free trade areas have existed for a long time as ex-custom, bonded territory where imported goods are stored, partially processed, and exported without interference by the customs authority as long as they do not cross the national border line which separates the zone from the customs territory. But in the last ten years or so, a new concept of free zones has emerged. In contrast to the conventional free ports, this new type of zone is a manufacturing zone where foreign investors are invited to operate their manufacturing plants to produce export goods. "Whereas the commercial free zones chiefly function as warehousing, distributing, and re-exporting depots, the main thrust of activities of the industrial free zones is directed toward industrial manufacturing

* Reprinted from Tsuchiya, T. 1978, Free trade zones in Southeast Asia, *Monthly Review* **29**(9), 29–39, by permission of Monthly Review Foundation. (© 1979 Monthly Review Inc.)

activities" (UNIDO 1971:6). The customs-free privileges of the traditional free zone are not only retained here but new incentives are also added to entice foreign investors.

Entrepreneurs are invited to carry out manufacturing activities within the fenced-in area of the free zone. Here, customs freedom is offered on imported production means and equipment, raw materials, and components. Also, preferential treatment is given on capital and income taxes, repatriation of profits, cost of utilities, etc. In many cases, various other kinds of fiscal and physical incentives are additionally provided to attract entrepreneurs to establish themselves in the industrial free zone. (UNIDO 1971:6).

The South Korean government describes its "zone" thus:

(a)   The export processing zone (or free export zone) is a specifically designated industrial area where foreign companies (as well as joint venture firms with Korean nationals as partners) can import raw materials or semi-finished goods free of duty, and manufacture, process, or assemble export products.

(b)   The zone has characteristics of a bonded area where the application of pertinent laws and regulations is waived or relaxed, in whole or in part.

(c)   It is a specifically designated industrial estate where the government constructs various facilities for sale or lease, including plant sites or factory (standard type) buildings for occupant firms.

(d)   It is an industrial area where various privileges in legal aspects and tax incentives are provided to foreign-invested (including joint venture) firms. (Industrial Administration, the Government of Korea 1974:8.)

These zones are referred to by different names, such as Industrial Free Zone, Free Export Zone, Export Processing Zone, etc. But we shall call them "free trade zones" (FTZ) for the sake of convenience.

The first such zone, the Shannon International Free Port, was established in 1958 in Shannon, Ireland, with the local airport as its core. In the latter half of the 1960s, a number of countries in East Asia began to establish FTZs in their territories, the first being Taiwan's Kaohsiung Export Processing Zone, set up in 1965. In 1970 Taiwan established two other zones, Taichung Export Processing Zone and Nantze Export Processing Zone. The Park Chung Hee régime in South Korea set up the Masan Free Export Zone the same year. The Philippines under Ferdinand Marcos set up the Bataan Export Processing Zone in Bataan in 1972, and in the same year Malaysia established the Bayan Lepas Free Trade Zone.

The FTZ has two main characteristics. On the one hand, it is an industrial estate where land, factory buildings, electric power, industrial water, and other infrastructure elements are furnished by the host governments for the convenience of the manufacturing firms operating there. On the other hand, it is a free trade zone in the traditional sense of the word. Although there is nothing novel about either of these features, their combination in the FTZ creates something entirely new – an alien territory within a national territory – having an authority which acts as the zone government and is responsible for supplying cheap local labor and for controlling the zone workers. The combination of these three factors makes the FTZ system highly attractive to foreign investors, a veritable paradise for international capital.

Economy in a capsule

The free trade zone is not an isolated system. On the one hand it is part and parcel of the "export-oriented industrialization" that has been promoted by most Third World countries since the late 1960s. On the other hand it is a product of the industrialized capitalist countries' efforts to organize the Third World into production bases, both for their home markets and for the world market, and to integrate the Third World into regional markets for their produce. The tremendous growth in investments by these imperial metropolitan countries in the Third World's manufacturing industries since the late 1960s goes hand in hand with the proliferation of free trade zones.

The significance of the FTZ to the host governments is said to consist in the following: (1) promotion of export for the acquisition of more foreign exchange; (2) creation of new job opportunities for the local labor force; and (3) hastening the transfer of technology to their own countries. Apart from whether the FTZ actually serves these purposes, the goals reflect an attempt to remedy ills that preceded the establishment of FTZs: (1) growing deficits in international payments accounts; (2) growing unemployment, particularly through the influx of poor populations into urban centers; and (3) widening technological gaps. Since these negative phenomena resulted from the host countries' relationships with the imperial metropolises (the United States, Europe, and Japan), these preceding relationships must first be examined.

Though varying country by country, the period preceding "export-oriented industrialization," or the period of FTZs, is characterized by the efforts of Third World countries (in this case Asian countries) to promote "import substitution" industries. Simply put, this pattern of economic efforts began as an endeavor to substantiate the political independence they had won by boosting local production of goods that had been imported from industrialized capitalist countries. They wanted to create industries which would produce goods for the domestic market and reduce imports of goods for domestic consumption, thus saving foreign exchange.

But this policy was doomed to fail. The absence of thorough going land reform and the resultant poverty of the peasantry limited the size of the domestic market, undercutting the prospects for the newly encouraged industries. The domestic industries, furthermore, did not have the competitive capacity to export industrial products in sizeable amounts to foreign markets. Governments set up customs barriers to prevent foreign finished goods from flowing in, but foreign investors, eager to secure shares of the home markets of these countries, got around these barriers and set up subsidiary assembly factories which they supplied with semifinished products. These foreign firms in some cases grabbed even the key import-substitution sectors such as textiles (for production for the local market) and in others began manufacturing useless products such as Coca Cola locally. The entire import-substitution period for Asian countries was, from the point of view of Japanese corporations, the age of "export-substitution" investments, meaning that they invested in Asia to start local production of goods that would otherwise be exported from Japan.

The import-substitution policy succeeded to a certain extent in boosting the "substitution rates" for some commodities in some countries. But this type of industrialization, by bringing commodity relationships into the rural areas, accelerated class differentiation among the peasantry and caused an inflow of rural poor into urban centers. On the other hand, the expansion of the import-substitution industries to new areas served to increase imports of industrial materials and semifinished products to be fed to local industries, and eventually imports began to exceed the value saved by domestic production. This again caused a serious imbalance in the international balance of payments.

In the case of Asia, the balance-of-payments deficits used to be offset significantly by the United States government's military and economic aid. Though this factor continued to play a major rôle during the Vietnam War for some countries, the United States had begun to cut grant-aid drastically in the early 1960s, on account of the dollar crisis that had by then set in. Under the circumstances, this practically dealt a fatal blow to import-substitution industrialization.

This development led to a shift in the late 1960s to "export-oriented industrialization." This formula combines two things – export promotion and industrialization – as though they were a natural pair. Instead of protective barriers, the countries concerned are to promote free trade and concentrate on the industrial production of goods for the world market. This is supposed to bring in more foreign exchange, rescue them from their perpetual debtor's status, and at the same time accomplish the process of industrializing their countries.

It must be remembered, however, that this policy did not flow naturally from the preceding policy. It was not introduced *after* an industrial base had been built strong enough to support the export of commodities able to compete with imperialist metropolises. On the contrary, it is the negative consequences of the preceeding period that forced this new policy upon these countries. But having decided to sell their products on the world market, they must do so within the framework of free trade. There is a tremendous gap between the goal and the reality, and if this gap is to be filled, there is only one way to do it – massive injections of foreign capital to produce export goods.

Export-oriented industrialization is thus intrinsically linked with the domination of the economy by foreign capital. And to attract foreign capital the host countries had to offer all they had: cheap labor, tax incentives, low-priced factory sites, and "political stability" maintained through extremely repressive measures.

The FTZ contains all these relationships in one package, and as such is a sort of concentrated expression of the "export-oriented industrialization" being promoted so actively by dictatorial régimes and encouraged so enthusiastically by the businessmen, bureaucrats, and economists of the imperialist capitalist countries.

Proliferation of free trade zones

Free trade zones are now proliferating and their establishment is energetically promoted on an international level. The experience of the first FTZ, Shannon International Free Port, was spread abroad by the staff of the Shannon Free Airport Development Co., mainly through the United Nations Industrial Development Organization (UNIDO).

In Asia, the Kaohsiung Export Processing Zone in Taiwan served as a model. In 1958 Professor Paul F. Keim of California State University advised that the Kaohsiung port development project be combined with the establishment of an FTZ there. In 1963 the establishment of an Export Processing Zone at Kaohsiung was officially decided and it was formally set up in 1965.

The Kaohsiung FTZ not only served as a moral spur but also rendered material help to other countries interested in the establishment of FTZs. South Korea, for instance, sent a survey mission to Kaohsiung in 1969. The Nguyen Van Thieu régime in South Vietnam actually set up an FTZ in Saigon (Long Binh) and planned to establish another on Cam Ranh Bay, a huge military installation evacuated by United States troops following the Paris agreement. In 1972 Thieu's government, with the help of the Agency for International Development (AID) of the United States, invited leaders of the Nantze EPZ in Taiwan to ask for cooperation in the management of the Long Binh EPZ. Thieu also sent a survey team to South Korea to investigate the Masan Free Export Zone.

The central body energetically spreading the idea of FTZs is UNIDO, which states: "Through its Free Zone Unit, within the Industrial Policies and Programming Division, UNIDO is constantly in touch with developments in the field of export processing zones internationally. There cannot be many zones being planned of which UNIDO is not aware. UNIDO has been asked for and has been offering assistance on different aspects of free zone development since 1970" (UNIDO 1975). UNIDO states further that "more and more countries, especially the developing countries, are interested in creating an industrial free zone. The existence of such plans has been announced by more than 30 developing countries, many of them also expressing their desire to obtain the technical assistance services of UNIDO" (UNIDO 1971:6).

UNIDO was founded in 1967, on the basis of a UN General Assembly resolution, to promote industrialization of developing countries. It was from the outset an organization which aimed to create receptivity to greater amounts of foreign capital on the part of developing countries and to promote the latter's export-oriented industrialization. In 1975, UNIDO became a specialized organization of the United Nations.

UNIDO provides assistance in the establishment of FTZs in the form of preliminary surveys, feasibility studies, and various other services short of actually operating the zones. UNIDO is assisted by the Shannon Free Airport Development Co., Ltd. (SFADCO) staff and the World Bank. In the case of Masan, in 1971 UNIDO entrusted Bechtel International to do an appraisal of the Masan works.

UNIDO has also been working to internationalize FTZs into a global system. In October 1974 it sponsored the Regional Expert Working Group Meeting on Industrial Free Zones at Barranquilla, Colombia. At this meeting it was decided that a federation of free trade zones operating in various countries should be organized. In line with this decision a broader international conference was convened in December 1975 in Vienna, the Expert Working Group on the Establishment of an Association of Export Processing Zone Authorities (AEPZA). Out of this grew the decision to found the World Industrial Free Zone Association (WIFZA) in June 1976. This WIFZA operates internationally to facilitate conditions in the host countries for the acceptance of foreign capital in their FTZs in correspondence with the global activities of transnational corporations.

Besides UNIDO, the Asian Productivity Organization (APO) is another important international body anxious to promote FTZs. With the support of UNIDO, it sponsored an international symposium on export-processing zones in ESCAP areas in Seoul, South Korea, in

October 1975. APO, based in Tokyo, is the internationalized version of the Japan Productivity Center, the organization that in the 1950s and 1960s energetically and successfully guided Japanese big-business industrial rationalization campaigns centering on the introduction of "scientific labor management."

Free trade zones: the tip of the iceberg

Since free trade zones, as we have seen, are but the visible tip of a whole iceberg, we have to deal with the iceberg itself, that is the current stage of integration of Third World (Asian) countries by international capital based on the imperialist metropolises, the stage at which large-scale and transnational investments in manufacturing industries in the Third World by metropolitan capital are complemented by plans on the part of the Third World countries to build up export-oriented economies. This stage of imperialism as understood in this light could be tentatively called modern-day integrative imperialism.

Free trade zones as systems are concentrated, though initial, expressions of this reality. By taking them as an indicator of the whole process of dominance of international capital export-oriented industrialization, we can obtain a glimpse into the Asian reality, a reality which, though it assumes ominous forms, also generates rightful resistance by the masses to the system being imposed upon them.

For metropolitan capital, FTZs are like beachheads, ensuring operations which will integrate the entire economies of the host countries. More and more countries, with the help of UNIDO, are inclined to build such beachheads themselves for foreign investors: already in 1974, Egypt, Gambia, Ivory Coast, Kenya, Senegal, Sri Lanka, Jamaica, Liberia, Syria, Trinidad and Tobago, and Sudan were asking UNIDO to draw up plans for FTZs (UNIDO 1974:140).

The nature of FTZs and their meaning become more visible when we deal with para-FTZ-type projects which stem from like motivations, such as the Kawasaki Steel Corporation's sintering plant project in a new industrial estate in Mindanao, the Philippines, and the aluminium-producing project promoted by giant Japanese corporations at Asahan, Indonesia. The former has recently been classified as a free trade zone, and the latter, though it is a mixture of extraction and manufacturing industries, has nearly the same traits as FTZs in the general framework of 'export promotion.'

Our criticism of FTZs and the structure which generates them relates simultaneously to the mode of economy, the structure, and the ideology of the countries which export capital to Third World countries. The Japanese, for instance, wear shirts made in Masan by underpaid young Korean girls and eat bananas produced in plantations in the

Philippines owned by Japanese trading firms where workers are paid less than a dollar a day. Sintered ore made in Mindano at the expense of the livelihood and health of the local fishermen–peasants is brought to Chiba City in Japan where it is used in steelmaking at the sacrifice of the health of local citizens. To change things on the one side would require corresponding changes on the other, though developments may often be uneven. This chapter is intended as a modest first step toward giving more clarity to this consciousness at a time when the internationalization of capital is still far more advanced than the solidarity among the working people of the world.

References

APO (Asian Productivity Organization) 1975. *Survey on duty-free export zones in APO member countries*. Asian Productivity Center, Syp/11/75, July. APO.

Industrial Administration, the Government of Korea, 1974. *A case study of the Masan Free Export Zone*. Seoul: The Government of Korea, March.

UNIDO (United Nations Industrial Development Organization) 1971. *Industrial Free Zones as incentives to promote export-oriented industries*. ID/WG, 112/3, October. New York: UNIDO.

UNIDO 1974. *Annual report*. New York: UNIDO.

UNIDO 1975. *Export Processing Zones in non-APO regions*. APO Symposium, Seoul, October.

18 Conclusion: Restructuring control over industrial development

RICHARD PEET

This book began by arguing that manufacturing industry was *the* significant economic activity of advanced societies. It provides essential material
inputs into human existence. It is the source of its own means of improvement and can be rapidly expanded. Workers in manufacturing are more
highly organized than workers in general and have been able to gain a share
of the income produced by the high productivity of manufacturing.
Industrial workers provide a rapidly expanding mass market for the
products and services of other economic activities. This produces growth
in the whole economy. What happens to manufacturing is of fundamental
importance to the future of all developed economies and gaining a manufacturing base is the key to development in the Third World.

Any society desiring to control its economic destiny has to achieve
social control over its most basic activity. Issues like where manufacturing is located, how much and what it produces, whom it employs,
and how it changes must be subject to popular, democratic debate by a
people who have power over their economy because they own it.
Instead there are many signs that changes in manufacturing occur 'by
themselves' as the result of an autonomous process driven by competition, certainly as far as the workers are concerned and arguably also
as far as corporate management and ownership are concerned. Manufacturing employment is being rapidly decreased by an automation
driven by competitive necessity. Manufacturing employment is moving geographically, also under the impetus of competitive necessity.
Both remove whole sections of the productive process at the center of
the world capitalist system and undercut the mass markets provided by
unionized workers in manufacturing. They are essential components of
a long-term tendency towards world economic recession.

The various parts of the book exemplify different aspects of this
general process. Part I connects industrial devolution at the center with
recession, and this with debt crises in the periphery. Export-oriented
industrialization in the Third World has been bought for a high price,

the newly industrialized countries are vulnerable to external fluctuations, and the capitalist world of the 1980s is economically unstable. In Part II it was argued that the loss of manufacturing in the old regions of the center is caused by the abandonment of unionized labor by corporations and that this results in the destruction of many of the institutions of industrial society like powerful unions and organized oppositional politics. It was argued in Part III that the solutions proposed for rectifying problems in the First World, the Japanese model and high-technology industries, are unlikely to work. Additionally, the few central regions characterized by industrial development are also characterized by social and environmental crises: the existing model of growth is highly contradictory. In Part IV export-oriented manufacturing as a Third World growth model was examined and it was shown that it is not generalizable to all the periphery. In any case it produces disorganic development which injures people, cultures, and societies. In Part V we reexamined industrial policy to demonstrate that capitalist societies lack the power effectively to intervene in a competition-driven economic history and to plan their futures according to socially desirable ends. The overall conclusion is that capitalism has entered a long period of crisis which already has drastic consequences for millions of unemployed workers and threatens further more extensive damage in the future. These issues are further examined in a concluding contribution by Frank, reproduced here as Part VI.

Humans are conscious beings, capable of directing their own history. But consciousness cannot be finely tuned to reality, nor history accurately directed, if fundamental issues are disguised or alternative ways of organizing the world kept hidden from effective scrutiny. Accurate comprehension is not provided by the existing, dominant social theory, nor workable solutions proposed by the hegemonic politics. New kinds of explanation are needed as the theoretical basis of a democratic-socialist politics.

What would we propose instead? (Here we can only point in the general direction of a solution, for this is a book of criticism rather than constructive proposals). The need for societies to control the basis of their economies becomes acute at time of crisis. This is revealed in measures whereby the "national" economy is protected from "unfair" foreign competition. But consumers in capitalist countries have little allegiance to producers located within the same national boundaries, especially as these same corporations also produce internationally. Purely nationalist protectionism does not and cannot work when the consuming individual mirrors the corporation striving only for his or her own benefit. Yet it is indeed necessary that an economy be protected from changes which destroy its effectiveness as provider of basic necessities, like essential manufactured goods and jobs for the coming generations of workers. How can these be achieved?

All society suffers from the loss, or lack, of essential economic activities like manufacturing. Society must therefore control its own process of economic development. But the existing models of state ownership, or state direction, of economic activity have not worked well. Workers can be as alienated from a centralized state as they can from a distant private corporation. State direction also yields as much consumer apathy as does the market. We would therefore suggest direct worker ownership of economic activity – grass-root control of workers' self-managed institutions, with coordination provided by a democratically determined state. Social planning should be substituted for the market as arbiter of changes which affect millions of lives. Social and intersocietal cooperation must replace competition as the mainspring of economic action. The satisfaction of need should replace the making of profit as the objective of work. And "efficiency" should be redefined to include an appraisal of all costs and benefits over the long term, rather than purely and (narrowly) "economic" costs in the short term. The economic crisis of the late 20th century can be solved only by creating a new social order. Industrial restructuring creates the need for social restructuring. This book is a modest attempt at shifting the focus of debate in new, more revealing directions.

Part VI

*Conclusion: the transformation of
international capitalism*

19 Global crisis and transformation[*]

ANDRÉ GUNDER FRANK

The world economic system is undergoing another of its historically recurrent crises which, like previous ones, is generating far-reaching and deep-going economic, social and political transformation through technological change, and modifications in the division of labor and power. I shall briefly review some of the manifestations of the contemporary crisis and then examine two of the attempted alternative transformation responses: further integration in the world economy by adapting to the changing division of labor through export promotion in the Third World and the socialist economies, or resistance and rebellion against this integration by attempts to delink from the world economy through national liberation and the promotion of self-reliance and socialism. I shall examine some of the economic possibilities and limitations, social consequences, and political implications of these apparently alternative responses to crisis and approaches to transformation in the recent past and foreseeable future.

The world system has experienced periodic crises throughout its history. A crisis is a period in which the previous expansion cannot continue on the same basis. In order to survive at all, it is necessary for the system to undergo vast economic, social, political, and cultural transformations, including technological change. During these periods of crisis there is a need for costs of production to be reduced: lowering wages, moving production to places where it is cheaper and, very importantly in the long run, technological change that lowers costs of production. In the periods of crisis, there are new inventions which require vast investments in order to transform them into a new basis for production during the subsequent expansion. The world system is in such a crisis today. The question is whether the world capitalist system will be able to make the necessary readjustment. If it cannot, then of course the system will destroy itself. But if it can make these readjustments, then there is reason to believe that it might subsequently

[*] Reprinted from Frank, A. G. 1983. Global crisis and transformation, *Development and Change* 14 (3), 323–46, by permission of Sage Publications, London, © Sage Publications Ltd.

have another period of expansion similar to that of the postwar years, perhaps in 10 or 15 years from now or perhaps longer. During this period of readjustment, there will again be vast economic, social, political, and cultural convulsions in the world. These readjustments appear as significant transformations of economy and society in the various parts of the world, North and South, East and West. From a worldwide and longer historical perspective, however, the question remains open whether these apparently frequent revolutionary changes really represent a fundamental transformation of the unequal regional, sectoral and class structure and the uneven temporal or even cyclical development of this world economic system. Perhaps these local, sectoral and national transformations represent changes of position in a global game of musical chairs to the tune of economic crisis, in which the fundamental structure of polarity, exploitation and oppression, and the long rhythm of uneven world development remain fundamentally unaltered.

The present world economic crisis is another general crisis of capital accumulation in the world capitalist system analogous to those of a half-century (1914 to 1940–5) and a century (1873–96) ago. Such crises in capitalist development have occurred for several hundred years, and they are a natural part of the historical process of world capitalist development. After the last major crisis during the interwar years, there was a renewed expansion during the postwar period. This apparently lasted until 1973, but really had already begun to slow down in 1967 and to turn into a renewed period of relative stagnation and crisis. Initially, this crisis took the form of reduced rates of profit and a renewed increase in recessions. There was one in 1967, which excluded the United States and Japan, the former (and in part the latter) because of American expenditures to finance its war in Vietnam. In this recession, official unemployment in the industrial capitalist countries (of North America, Western Europe, Japan, Australia, and New Zealand) rose to 5 million. It then declined again in the 1968–9 recovery. Then came the 1969–70 recession, in which the United States and Japan also participated. Unemployment in the industrialized countries then grew to ten million.

This recession had very serious consequences. Before it, the world had been flooded with dollars issued by the United States in order to finance the Vietnam war. There had been important changes in relative productivity among industrial producers during the 1960s. Productivity in Europe had grown twice as fast as in the United States and in Japan twice as fast again as in Western Europe or nearly four times as fast as in the United States. This change in the relative competitive abilities on the world market and the flood of dollars were exacerbated when growth rates declined during the 1969–70 recession. On August 15, 1971, they led to what President Nixon called a New Economic Policy and what the Japanese called Nixon Shokku: Nixon imposed wage and price controls in the United States, took the dollar off its fixed relation to gold, permitting it to be devalued, and imposed a special discriminatory surtax of 10 percent on imports from Japan. Thereby he effectively destroyed the basis of the international monetary system that had been established at Bretton Woods after World War II with fixed exchange rates, and opened the way to widespread currency fluctuations and further devaluations of the dollar. This decision was an attempt to increase American competitiveness in world markets again and led to the rapid increase of American exports, especially armaments, and agricultural products. Then followed the shortlived recovery from 1971 to 1973. This led to the major 1973–5 recession, which was worldwide, and in which official unemployment grew to 15 million, nearly 9 million of whom were in the United States.

The world recession of 1973–5 also led to an end of the high Japanese growth rates and to a decline in output in 1974 in Japan as well as in other industrial countries. Then there was another recovery – from 1975 to 1979 – in which unemployment again decreased in the United States but continued to increase in Canada, Western Europe, Japan, Australia, and New Zealand. Total unemployment in the industrialized world during the so-called recovery rose from 15 to 17 million. In 1979–80 the renewed recession began and, of course, unemployment again increased very substantially, to about 23 million in 1980, with the OECD experiencing a total of 30 million in 1982, equivalent to almost the entire labor force of a major industrial country. These unemployment figures, moreover, are the officially recorded ones. Real unemployment is much higher, particularly in Japan where, in 1974, registered unemployment was 730,000. According to an Employment Status Survey, however, real unemployment was 3,276,000; male unemployment was twice as high and female unemployment *ten times* as high as officially registered unemployment. These figures for Japan still do not include the 4 million other people who either work part-time but wanted to work more, or those who were discouraged from looking for work. This problem is now exacerbated by the enforced earlier retirement age. Real unemployment in the industrialized world is very much higher than is admitted by governments.

Investments have also declined. The rate of profit began to drop in 1967. The major consequence for economic policy everywhere has been that the expansionist, demand-maintaining Keynesian policy has been abandoned on the argument that it would be inflationary. Everywhere it has been replaced by deflationary policies, the decline of the welfare state, and the attempt to reduce real wages, the latter being more successful in some countries than others. Real wages have certainly declined in the United States and Great Britain, and during part of the 1970s they also declined in Japan as inflation grew more than money wages. The drive to reduce costs of production has also led to changes in the nature of investment in order to reduce labor and its costs in the industrial process.

In an attempt to justify and legitimize these measures, it has become common to appeal to the return to traditional values, to national unity, and to economic and political nationalism. In a word, there has been a very marked political shift to the Right in the industrialized world. This shift is visible in the election and policies of Ronald Reagan in the United States and of Margaret Thatcher in Britain, but also extended to the former Frazer and the Muldoon governments in Australia and New Zealand and to the pronounced rightward shift in the municipal and parliamentary elections and the government of Japan. Even the labor and social democratic parties have experienced very significant shifts to the Right and are pursuing more conservative economic policies in Germany, Scandinavia, and elsewhere. Indeed, it was the Labour government of James Callaghan in Britain and the Democratic President Jimmy Carter in the United States first abandoned Keynesian economic measures and imposed new austerity policies. That is why they lost their electoral support to the Conservative and Republican parties which, however, only continued and further extended these same monetarist austerity policies. Among the industrial countries only France has moved somewhat to the Left, but with severe limitations to the economic policy of the Mitterrand government.

Another very significant way to reduce costs of production has been to move parts of the productive process from areas where labor costs are high to areas where they are lower. The policy is to move particularly those industrial processes that use much labor, e.g., the textile, clothing, shoe, toy, and electronic components industries. More recently, capital-intensive crisis-ridden industries (and those that are polluting or incur high antipollution costs), such as automobiles, shipbuilding, steel, and petrochemicals, are also being moved increasingly to Third World and socialist countries. In the 1960s, the northern border of Mexico south of the Rio Grande began to see the establishment of factories for production for export to the American market. South Korea, Hong Kong, Taiwan, and Singapore began their so-called export-led growth in the late 1960s, based on the production of labor-intensive commodities for export to the world market. In South Korea and Southeast Asia (excluding Hong Kong), much of this investment was by foreign capital, especially Japanese.

Under the impact of the growing economic crisis of the 1970s, this process of industrial relocation spread to Malaysia and the Philippines (it is no accident that Mr. Marcos imposed martial law in 1972 when this policy began), Thailand, Sri Lanka, and to India, Pakistan, Egypt, Tunisia, Morocco, various countries in sub-Saharan Africa, the Caribbean (except Cuba), and through most of Latin America. In this rapid change in the international division of labor under the impact of this world economic crisis, the Third World is also becoming a place for increased production of agricultural commodities for export by agribusiness. New mining methods on land and on the sea bottom are also being introduced. What the Third World countries have to offer is first and foremost cheap labor. Additionally, their governments offer all kinds of concessions to international capital, including tax-free holidays to the corporation for several years. Third World states provide the infrastructure of ports, airports, railways, cheap electricity, cheap water, free land, etc.; often they even build the factories and lend international capital the money, or at least guarantee private loans in order that production may be set up in their countries to export to the world market, in competition with other countries that bid to do the same.

The worldwide political economic mechanism to promote a new international division of labor by relocating manufacturing, agricultural and mining, and even some financial processes in the Third World and the socialist countries is fuelled and oiled by the international financial system. Firstly the recessions and inflation (so-called "stagflation") in the industrial capitalist countries and secondly the increases in the price of oil (part of the cost of which to the First World has also been shifted to the Third World) have sharply aggravated the balance of payments deficits of those countries in the Third World that do not export oil (and some socialist countries such as Poland). To cover these growing deficits, such countries have turned increasingly to the private international capital markets. These have recycled OPEC surplus funds towards them and have additionally lent them other funds at high rates of interest, funds that found no borrowers in industrial countries where investment has been low. The extension of these loans, and particularly their rollover rescheduling in order to finance the growing debt service when borrowers are unable to pay, has become the basis of stringent economic and political conditions that the private banks, and/or the International Monetary Fund acting as their intermediary, have imposed on Third World (and some socialist and developed) countries. The standard "conditionality" to the IMF package which governments are obliged to accept in their "letter of intent" before being certified to receive further loans always includes devaluation of the currency, reduction in government expenditure, especially on consumer subsidies and welfare, the reduction of the wage rate through various devices, and more favorable treatment for private and especially foreign capital. These conditions have sometimes led to "IMF riots" as the people have sought to resist the enforced curtailment of their standards of living. It has been said that the IMF has overthrown more governments than Marx and Lenin put together. An important political economic consequence, if not rationale, of these IMF-promoted government policies in the Third World is to promote "export-led growth" by cheapening Third World labor and its products for international capital and foreign importers (by lowering the price of Third World wages and currencies) and to lend support to domestic forces that have an economic interest in export promotion. Thus, the international financial system and the financing of the Third World debt serves to fuel and oil the mechanism of the emerging international division of labor based on Third World export promotion. A political consequence of all these economic policies is that it is necessary to repress the labor force in order to keep wages low or to reduce wages. In Brazil which, after Mexico, has been the principal example of this process in Latin America since the military coup in 1964, wages were reduced by over 40 percent. In Argentina, since the military coup in 1976, wages have been reduced by over 50 percent. But even before the coup, real wages were going down as a result of the economic policies of the right wing of the Peronist government in 1974–5. In Chile, real wages since the coup were reduced by two-thirds, that is to say, from an index of 100 almost to an index of 30, and unemployment increased from 4 to 20 percent before levelling off at 12–15 percent. To be able to do this it was necessary first to destroy or to control the unions, to eliminate – often physically – the leadership, to repress all political opposition and to throw people in jail, torture, murder, exile them, etc. Secondly, it was necessary to reorganize the economy from producing for the internal market, through so-called import substitution, to producing for export.

During the last major crisis of the 1930s and early 1940s, when the Third World had a balance of payments crisis and was unable to earn foreign exchange to buy imports, countries such as Mexico, Brazil, Argentina, India, South Africa, started to produce manufactures internally for the internal market, substituting these for imports. To be able to do so, however, they had to import capital goods. They had to import machinery and later technology with which to produce these, and they had to pay for such capital imports through exports. In order to earn these exports, they had to invite the multinational corporation which they thought would bring capital equipment and capital into the country, and they had to borrow and increase their debt. Then, in the 1950s and 1960s, this movement spread through other parts of the Third World and most particularly through many countries of Latin America. The process of import substitution for the internal market required people with incomes with which to purchase the commodities. Therefore, there were political alliances between the labor movement and the sector of the bourgeoisie which worked for the internal market, to support populist, more or less democratic nationalist governments. When these economies switch from this import substitution model of economic growth to that of "export-led growth" by promoting exports for the world market, they no longer require this effective demand on the internal market to purchase the industrial or agricultural commodities which they produce. Manufactured and agricultural commodities are exported, and they now require a world market. They also require the lowest possible costs of production. Therefore, their main objective now is to reduce the wage cost of production. They do not care if that reduces internal demand because they do not want to sell internally: they want to sell externally.

This requires a significant reorganization of the economic and political structure of Brazil, Argentina, Chile, and elsewhere in the Third World, i.e., from producing for the internal market to producing for the external market. This means that the sector of industry as well as the labor that had been producing for the internal market, or that wants to produce for the internal market, now has to be repressed politically. This leads to political measures being taken by these authoritarian and military régimes, and to the imposition of martial law and of emergency rule that was seen almost everywhere in the Third World in the 1970s. The repression is used first and foremost against labor, and secondly against a sector of the bourgeoisie itself in order to restructure the economy and to reorient it towards export production. This political economic process behind the political repression of Kim in South Korea and Aquino in the Philippines, both of whom were bourgeois leaders who did not propose a revolutionary alternative but simply a more democratic alternative. They are the political representatives of bourgeois capitalist interests in countries dependent on the development of the internal market. These economic interests and their political representatives have at least to be eliminated politically. The whole political régime is based on an alliance between the sector of the bourgeoisie that is allied to international capital and particularly to the multinationals of the United States, West Germany, and Japan. Internally, the alliance rests politically on the military as the force that cements such relationships. This is the political–economic basis of the events that have been observed in South Korea, the Philippines, Chile, Argentina, and so forth. This crisis-generated political–economic exigency is what really explains the wave of political repression throughout the Third World.

Two major kinds of alternative responses and transformations may be distinguished in the Third World and the socialist countries with regard to these crisis developments: acceptance and rejection. Recent experience offers examples of both approaches, each of which is proposed as a "model" of development policy for others to follow, until supposedly the whole world is transformed in their image. The acceptance policy of integration in the emerging division of labor is associated particularly with the so-called Newly Industrializing Countries

(NICs) of the Asian Gang of Four (South Korea, Taiwan, Hong Kong, and Singapore), plus Brazil and Mexico in Latin America, whose development "miracles" supposedly offer a "model" of "export-led growth" and socioeconomic transformation or development strategy to be pursued by the remainder of the Third World, and even parts of the socialist (Second) and industrial (First) world. The alternative rejection policy of delinking from the world economy and promoting self-reliance as much as possible is associated with the struggle for national liberation from colonialism and neocolonialism or imperialism and the transition to or promotion of socialism from the Soviet Union and Eastern Europe to China, North Korea, Vietnam, and Cuba, as well as more recently Nicaragua and Grenada, Angola and Mozambique, Zimbabwe and Ethiopia, etc. Both approaches may be and often are regarded as major sociopolitical transformations in response to economic crisis, the former, so to say, accepting and promoting the transformations generated from the center or demanded from above and the latter rejecting the same and initiating and participating in a transformation at the periphery and from below. We may examine some of the economic limitations, social consequences, and political implications of these transformation responses in the recent past and foreseeable future.

The thesis and policy that the miraculuous success of the Asian Gang of Four and Latin American NICs offer a model of development and transformation for the Third World and elsewhere is internally inconsistent and contradictory. If the experience of South Korea, Taiwan, Hong Kong, Singapore (and sometimes of Mexico's border region with the United States and São Paulo in Brazil) are really miraculous, i.e., extraordinary and almost inexplicable in normal terms, then they can hardly serve as a model for the remainder of the Third World, which would be hard put to duplicate the same circumstances and experiences. This limitation is at least twofold: general and particular.

The general limitation is that export-led growth by a few small countries and the absorption of their exports as imports by the rest of the world is one thing; the generalization of the same export-led growth to that same rest of the world (To whom would it export? What would be imported by whom?) is another matter. Consider the prospects and problems of Hong Kong and Taiwan-style exports on an all Chinese or Indian, let alone Third World scale. The sheer impossibility of such a "model" is intuitively clear. World systems analysis can offer the "scientific" reasons: particularly growth experiences, such as those of the NICs, that of postwar Europe and Japan, or indeed of the industrial revolution itself, can and could not be generalized to the rest of the world, precisely because they took place where and when they did and thereby exclude(d) and prevent(ed) the rest of the world from doing the same. Eric Hobsbawm has already pointed out, without the benefit of "world systems analysis," that in 1800 there was room in the world for no more than the industrial revolution in Britain. He had in mind, apparently, demand-side limitations to British, let alone other, export-led growth. Similar demand-side limitations obtain with regard to the NICs; and today we can see that there are resource supply-side limitations as well (one-fourth of the world's population uses three-fourths of the world resources). But as the analysis of imperialism, dependence, and the world system has emphasized, the very growth pattern of the "leaders" has been based on, indeed has generated, the *inability* of much of the world to follow. The underlying reason, as world systems analysis would have it, is that this development or ascent has been misperceived as taking place in particular countries when it has really been one of the processes of the world system itself. The recent export-led growth of the NICs is also part and parcel of the process of capital accumulation on a world scale (to cite the appropriate title of Samir Amin). To reduce costs of production and to make room for more technologically advanced development elsewhere, a part of the labor-intensive production (and some capital-intensive production) is relocated to the NICs and the "socialist" countries. However, this process is far from trouble free, as it generates protectionist pressures in the "traditional" producing countries, exacerbates trade and financial imbalances, and is threatened by the possible breakdown of the world trade and financial system, to whose instability this process itself contributes. More NICs would only do more of the same.

But there are many limitations to the generalization of NIC export-led growth on the "gang of four" NICs model which are particular to these countries and to others that may seek to follow in their footsteps. All four of the Asian NICs are fundamentally characterized by very particular *political* reasons for their establishment and survival; two of them are, additionally, city–states for the same reason. South Korea and Taiwan clearly were created as "independent" entities as a result of the Cold War against China and the Soviet Union, and have been politically supported and economically subsidized as strategic pawns against them. Hong Kong emerged from history to a similarly peculiar position, and Singapore became a state because of the preponderance of overseas Chinese populations on the Malay Peninsula (and behind them also the perceived threat of China). These world political circumstances, let alone the advantages of city–states that draw on their respective hinterlands without economic and political responsibility for them, may be politically miraculous, and go some way toward accounting for their economic miracles; but they hardly offer a model to be duplicated *ad infinitum* elsewhere in the Third World (except with modifications in Israel). It would be tedious and should be unnecessary to review particularities elsewhere in the Third World to establish that they do not and cannot match those of the Asian NICs. Suffice it to point out the obvious: that India, or even Pakistan or Bangladesh, is in no position to duplicate the *relatively* socially incorporative or nonmarginalizing growth patterns of "gang of four" export-led growth; and that the larger Brazil and Mexico have completely failed to do so – witness the 50 percent unemployment rate in Mexico *after* exporting several million workers to the United States. Indeed, even tiny Hong Kong excludes a large proportion of its population from the benefits, if not from the costs, of export-led growth, if its world's most unequal distribution of income is any measure.

Beyond the impossibility of following the gang of four NICs as a model, the desirability of their "miracles" as models of development is also questionable, to say the least. The supposed merits of export-led growth are that it generates foreign exchange to improve the balance of payments, that it provides employment to eliminate or reduce unemployment, that it imports technology and improves skills to advance technological development, and that it furthers integral national development generally. But export-led growth scores very badly in the test of experience on each of these four counts of its supposed merits, and for very good reasons.

Far from improving the balance of payments, export-led growth deteriorates it to the point of generating serious balance of payments crises, as the three largest NIC exporters, South Korea, Brazil, and Mexico, have found to their, and the banking community's, alarm. To export, the NICs have to import raw materials, components, technology, and high-priced businessmen. These are frequently overpriced through transfer pricing within the multinationals who in turn underprice the resulting exports, thus reducing or eliminating the foreign exchange earning and tax-paying value added in the NIC. But since the principal attraction of the NICs is low wages, and secondarily the state subsidies that often involve imported components for local infrastructure as well, the national value added and export-minus-import foreign exchange earning was low to begin with, and only becomes lower through transfer pricing and other tricks. The result is that the NICs have to borrow increasingly to pay for their import requirements, which grow additionally as export production interferes with domestic production; therefore import requirements increase, especially for agricultural products. The NICs then have to finance and roll over their debts at increasingly onerous interest costs and other conditions.

Export-led growth undoubtedly generates employment, but apart from being unsteady due to ups and downs in the world market and/or the market penetration of the particular NIC industry, this employment itself generates unemployment as it interferes with domestically oriented industry and agriculture and draws more labor into the cities than the jobs that it creates. In Hong Kong and Singapore this process is invisible within the "country," but in Mexico and Brazil, as well as

Malaysia, the Philippines and elsewhere, and now in China itself, this structurally generated unemployment is increasingly evident. Technological development is also uncertain. To the extent that NIC export production is of a component or process which is produced through labor-intensive routine operations, on an assembly line that is no more than part of a worldwide industrial process in which other places specialize in the more advanced technological processes and in advancing the technological development itself, the NIC experiences only questionable technological development and skilling of its labor force. Even where the NICs produce entire end products such as shirts, radios, or even automobiles, they are simply increasing their dependent integration into a worldwide division of labor and technological development in which they are allocated the least remunerative and technologically obsolete contributions and the correspondingly meagre benefits. Far from contributing to, or even laying the basis for, relatively autonomous and self-propelling technological development based on national resources and capacities as North Korea has pioneered, dependent export-led growth on the South Korean model renders integrated national development increasingly impossible. At the same time, it still keeps the economy low on the totem pole of world technological development.

It should not be forgotten that "export-led growth" is nothing new in the history of world development. Beyond British growth on its own terms, and American, Canadian, and Australian export-led growth in exceptionally favorable times and circumstances within the process of world capital accumulation, much of the Third World went in for, or was pushed or pulled into, raw-materials export-led growth on unfavorable terms dictated by the requirements of accumulation on a world scale, but elsewhere in the world, without themselves becoming developed beneficiaries of this process. The new dependent export-led growth of manufacturing and agribusiness production for the world market are in no way significantly different from the old raw-materials export-led growth which underdeveloped the Third World in the first place. However, if it does turn out to be different, the recent experiences of South Korea, Brazil, and Mexico, with their resultant export-led growth-generated economic, social, and political crises of recent years certainly does not augur well for this difference.

Finally, we should consider the political costs of export-led growth, which have found echos even in the halls of the United States Congress. Testimony there established how:

> at the heart of South Korea's human rights problems is the economic growth strategy of the country, a strategy which requires the repression and manipulation of labor . . . and the tight control of free political expression. . . . The absence of full human rights is neither

arbitrary nor coincidental; it is the product of the choice to have an export-oriented economy which leaves internal needs unmet.

(United States Congress 1978)

The United States Senate itself prepared a document in which:

> as we have shown, in many countries there seems to be a direct correlation between economic difficulties and political repression. . . . The problem with these measures [to create a favorable climate for foreign investment and for the private sector in general] is that . . . they can also lead to greater unemployment, to the reductions of social welfare, and to a lower standard of living for the people. . . . Creditor demands to implant drastic economic austerity programs . . . could only be imposed at the expense of civil liberties in the countries that adopt them.

(United States Senate Foreign Relations Committee 1977)

These unpalatable truths, which have been recognized even by the unimpeachable authorities quoted above, have in turn led to Right and Left political responses which, however different, seem to have in common that they both appear as "lesser evil" policies. The right-wing response is to justify and support these authoritarian tendencies and régimes as lesser evils than, and as necessary and useful allied bulwarks against, "totalitarian" world communism and socialism led by the Soviet Union. (This response is typified by the United States representative to the United Nations, Mrs. Jeane Kirkpatrick, and the Reagan Administration generally.) Short of the rejectionist answer, the Left responses are to limit some of the economic excesses of export-led growth through some measures of return to import substitution and economic nationalism and to curb the political excesses through the return to some form of democracy under the title of "viable democracy," "popular government," or some other variation on that theme, which would be a lesser evil than military or other authoritarian rule. Thus, since 1977–8, there has been an apparent redemocratization and the installation of what United States President Carter called Viable Democracy. Elections have been held, as in India, in Sri Lanka, even in Bangladesh. There has been the replacement of military régimes by civilian ones in Ghana and Nigeria. There have been elections or the proposals for elections in a number of countries in Latin America: Bolivia, Peru, Ecuador, etc. Is this a new wave of democratization that represents a return to the period of import substitution and the kinds of political alliances between labor and peasantry and the bourgeoisie of the period of import substitution?

A number of people believe or at least hope that. I also hope so, but I do not believe it. On the contrary, my impression is that this move to what President Carter called Viable Democracy is rather the institutionalization of the same model of export-led economic growth that had already been imposed during the 1970s through the use of force. Once this model is operating, it is possible to use a bit less force in some places to keep it going and therefore it is possible to have some democratization. In other places not even this relative democratization is possible and it is necessary to use force, particularly if and when there is a renewed recession, such as there has been since 1978, and the economic problems increase again. As President Marcos said, he could not afford to abandon martial law or to democratize. (The subsequent replacement of martial by another law has everywhere been condemned as a farce and the "elections" as largely meaningless.) Thus, this apparent democratization is really making the model of export-led growth viable for the 1980s.

This viability takes the following political expression among others. In Chile former Christian Democratic President Eduardo Frei was leading (until his recent death) the opposition to General Pinochet. In Peru in the recent election Belaunde, the same man who was president until 1968 prior to the military coup, became president again. In this election Belaunde was supported by many sectors of the Left. In Bolivia, Siles Suazo and Paz Estensoro, both previous presidents before the military government, were candidates for president. Siles Suazo was elected but prevented from taking office by the military. Since then a compromise candidate was deposed by another coup. In Brazil Magalhaes Pinto and Brizola, both important political figures from the 1960s, have been active again politically. In Nigeria Azkwe and Awolowo, politicians from the 1960s, were candidates again in the recent elections. In Ghana, of course, N'Krumah is dead; but the people from his movement were candidates. In India, Mrs. Gandhi was reelected. In the Philippines Mr. Aquino was again the main opposition leader, etc. Two things are remarkable about these old political leaders from the 1960s who reappear in the 1980s after this period of military rule. The first is that today they all have political and economic programs that are much further to the right than those they had in the 1960s. And the second thing is that the progressive and revolutionary forces of the Left, who in the 1960s opposed these political leaders as too conservative, today support these same political leaders although now they have a much more conservative right-wing program than in the 1960s, when the Left opposed them. This is a political measure of how much there has been an effective shift to the Right even among the progressive and in many cases revolutionary forces in the Third World who, in pursuit of a lesser-evil policy, find themselves obliged to support old politicians who have programs that are much more to the Right than those they had years ago. In a sense this means that General Pinochet is in part realistic when he says that there is no real alternative to him in Chile. Maybe there is another political formula that might replace

Pinochet. The supposed alternative was Frei, who also proposed a much more right-wing program than he did when he was president until 1970.

The economic program that all these politicians are proposing and which the new civilian governments in Peru, Ghana, and Nigeria are promoting, is the very same export-led growth model that the previous military régime put into place. In Peru before the election there was reason to believe, and events now bear out, that the civilian government of Belaunde would be even more to the Right than the military government that he replaced. Moreover, the deeper the world economic crisis manifests itself in any new cyclical economic recession or depression in such countries as Peru, Brazil, Nigeria, South Korea, etc. in the early and mid-1980s, the greater the realpolitic regression to the already latent authoritarianism is likely to be.

Thus, it appears that the economic crisis transformation of the world economic system, as it is implemented through the positive acceptance, response, and transformation of the Third World and some other (including socialist) export promotion, is beset by a number of very serious economic, social, and political limitations and costs.

The apparently opposite and supposedly alternative response to crisis and approach to transformation is to reject the imperialist world economy and to seek self-reliance through delinking, national liberation, and socialism.

The widely felt negative consequences of imperialism, colonialism, neocolonialism, and dependent capitalism generally, and now the pressures and economic, political, and social costs of export promotion, have led to numerous movements in the Third World for national liberation, socialist revolution, African socialism, delinking, collective and national self-reliance, etc. But, as many revolutionaries have observed, if taking political power is difficult, its subsequent use in the pursuit of popular liberation is even more problematic. A review of some recent experiences can provide a guide to the limitations and, perhaps through their better understanding, to the means to overcome them.

Take the case, for instance, of President Mugabe of Zimbabwe. He came to power after a long guerilla struggle, followed by negotiations with the British and the Rhodesian Right leading to an election, and after having long had the support of Samora Machel in neighboring Mozambique and of other Front Line states and leaders in Africa. But Samora Machel told Mugabe even before the election that he should become very moderate in order to be elected at all and that, if he did not, Mozambique would not be able to continue to support him, because it was costing Mozambique too much economically and politically to do so. Since Mugabe became president of Zimbabwe, he has completely failed to pursue the policies that he had promised. First, he has not instituted the land reform that he had promised as his first priority. President Mugabe recently gave an interview in which he said, "I am not only a practising Marxist but also a practical Marxist." Therefore, he said, he now recognizes a need for foreign capital, for the multi-nationals, for good relations with South Africa, etc. Thus, the "terrorist" Mugabe has now become a super moderate.

The newly independent ex-Portuguese territories in Guinea-Bissau, Angola, and Mozambique also reached independence through prolonged revolutionary guerilla struggle (as well as the thereby induced 1974 revolution in Portugal). Yet none of them has sought to delink significantly from the world capitalist economy. Angola was enjoined by the Soviet Union not to become another Cuba, and the Cubans in Angola are guarding the Gulf Oil installations which provide Angola's principal source of foreign exchange, the remainder coming from coffee and minerals which are also sold primarily to the West. Mozambique still depends on South Africa (and its supply of labor to the mines there is due less to Mozambican policy than to changes in the price and production of gold), and the FRELIMO régime has recently backtracked on its earlier policies and is again renewing Mozambican reliance on Western aid and trade and private enterprise at home.

In Nicaragua the Sandinistas have had a very spectacular and important success. Nonetheless, they have assumed the foreign debt of about US$1.2 billion (a big sum for small Nicaragua), which Somoza had accumulated under his dictatorial régime. To pay this debt, the Sandinistas have had to borrow more money from international banks, the IMF and even $70 million from the United States in order to roll over the previous debt and to finance current imports, which they also have to curtail. Thus, they have to accept the imposition of important economic and political conditions which make it extremely difficult for the Sandinistas to pursue a progressive, let alone revolutionary, economic policy at home and a supportive foreign policy toward the revolutionary movements in El Salvador and elsewhere in Central America. That is, of course, the express objective, at least of the United States. Thus, the Sandinistas are caught in a dilemma. Either they say no to international capital by renouncing the Somoza debt, in which case they receive no further loans or export credits and are subjected to an economic blockade that would be even more severe than that which Chile suffered under President Allende and which contributed to his downfall. Or the Sandinistas accept paying the Somoza debt and play along with international capital; but thereby they also accept the conditions that international capital imposes on them and which considerably restrict their ability to act. In the conditions of the current world economic crisis and the already very serious domestic economic crisis in Nicaragua itself, these conditions imposed on the Sandinista government will cost the Nicaraguan people dearly in terms of their well-being. Therefore, these conditions may reduce popular political support for the Sandinistas, and thus help the bourgeois forces in Nicaragua to undermine and challenge Sandinista political power. That is, of course, precisely what the United States government is trying to achieve through its own policy. This poses a very serious danger.

In Jamaica, the intervention of the IMF, and the conditions that it imposed on the progressive government of Prime Minister Michael Manley, served to undermine his economic and political base and finally defeated him in the elections. He was replaced by the avowedly right-wing pro-American government of Edward Seaga, who immediately received ample American and international economic, financial, and political support. Recently, there has also been a significant shift to the conservative Right in progressive Tanzania, which is also doing valiant battles with the IMF. President Nyerere still commands substantial respect although he is trying to hold out against the conditions the IMF seeks to impose, but at the same time a significant shift to the Right has occurred in the last elections and in administrative policy. As the economic crisis deepens, President Nyerere is under increasing pressure to abandon the policy of self-reliance for which Tanzania had become a model in the Third World.

The political exigencies of deepening economic crisis are having similar effects elsewhere in the Third World. Angola, Mozambique, and Guinea-Bissau have renounced any substantial delinking of their economies from the world capitalist system and are moving back to greater reliance on market incentives and private enterprise in their domestic economies. Vietnam and China, not to mention Poland, have been facing serious economic crisis by attempts increasingly to relink their economies to the still capitalist world economy, and to place renewed reliance on market organization and private initiative and reward in their domestic economies, especially in agricultural production and distribution. The recognition of these realities in no way belittles the major progressive popular achievements in these countries and offers a realistic basis to safeguard and advance their progress.

The real economic limitations, social costs, and political shortcomings of both the integrationist and rejectionist options – and the failure of Marxist theory and socialist models in the Soviet Union, China, and elsewhere to offer sufficiently persuasive alternatives – are also bringing novel populist movements and policy options to the fore in which a combination of nationalist and religious values mobilizes millions of people against the status quo, apparently more massively and effectively so than the more secular alternatives. The Ayatolla Khomeini's revolution in Iran – perhaps the vanguard of a Muslim revival around half the globe – and Lech Walesa's Solidarity movement in Poland are the most notable recent expressions of this new (or renewed) motive force. We cannot exclude the possibility that the near future will witness the development of analogous movements and the spread of their force, possibly also incorporating appeals to race or racism, in such regions as Southeast Asia (with special reference to China and overseas Chinese), South Asia (through the spread of communalist forces), the Middle East (as a response to the complex economic–political–military–social– cultural–religious conflicts), Southern Africa (as a legacy of colonialism and apartheid), Latin America (as a repercussion in part of the realignments generated by the Falklands (Malvinas) war), and last but not least, within and between the capitalist West and the socialist East. It is too early to foretell the prospects and possible consequences of such social movements and their politico-economic consequences.

The observation and comparison of past experiences with other recent projects at delinking and transition to socialism, however, suggest the following theoretical or at least classificatory reflections on transformation and development policy in the foreseeable future of the present world crisis. A break with capitalism and the transition to socialism requires a revolutionary process, an internal transfer of power and popular participation, and the achievement of a greater degree of external independence. Attempts at transitions in the Third World have attempted neither, one or the other, or both. In some cases there has been no real attempt at either delinking or at a redistribution of power and popular participation. I am thinking, for instance, of Indonesia under Sukarno, India, much of the so-called African socialism, Brazil in the time of Goulart from 1961 to 1964. All these attempts failed miserably. In some places, there has been an attempt at external *delinking*, so to say external isolation from the world capitalist system but without concomitant, simultaneous, far-reaching internal social and political changes. I am thinking particularly of Nasser's Egypt and of Burma until recently. These régimes have lasted a bit longer but in the medium run have been very substantial failures. The policies of subservient relinking undertaken by Sadat were in part attributable to the important failures of the Nasser régime. Burma is now also relinking at a very rapid rate. Other countries have attempted some kind of internal reorganization without the external delinking; for instance, the Ghana of N'Krumah and, in a certain sense, Allende's Chile. These have also been disastrous failures.

One of the lessons of this experience is that to try neither delinking nor popular participation gets you nowhere. To try only external delinking without internal participation also gets you nowhere and leads back to rapid relinking. To try only internal participation without external delinking is extremely dangerous, very difficult to do, and is likely to lead to disaster. External delinking and internal participation, social and political mobilization, reinforce each other and are necessary in order to be able to pursue rapid structural change to a threshold from which one would not immediately slide backward. The only countries where this has been possible are those that we today call socialist. That is to say that external delinking and internal political change have been carried so far as to call them socialist. None of the other ways, the noncapitalist path, the popular democracy path of African socialism, etc. have produced results.

One paradox of these experiences and attempts at delinking, with or without internal political change, is that delinking is in essence voluntary; but it is immediately complemented, supplemented by involuntary delinking or "destabilization", the term Kissinger applied to this policy towards the Allende régime in Chile. That is to say, there are attempts, both internationally and through the normal operation of the market system, to undermine this process of delinking and internal political change from the outside and, through the Quisling fifth column inside the country, to delink the country even faster or farther than it would like to go, or at least to delink it under control of the opposition to this process (externally and internally) rather than to delink it voluntarily under control of the political forces which are carrying the process forward. This in itself gives cause to ponder the real possibilities of delinking. The very fact that delinking is not only a policy that is attempted by progressive governments but is also an arm that is used against the progressive governments gives cause for reflection about the rational utility of delinking in the world today.

The socialist East is also caught up in this world capitalist crisis and provides another cause for concern. There is a process of increasingly rapid reintegration or "relinking" into the capitalist international division of labor, not only through trade but also through production. There is also an increasing productivity crisis throughout the COMECON countries in general; separately and together they have achieved only half or less of their growth targets for the 1976–80 five-year plan.

In Poland production declined and "growth" was negative by 2 percent in 1979, by 4 percent in 1980 and 14 percent in 1981. Poland is perhaps the most extreme crisis case in this regard, being caught between the increased oil prices that the Soviet Union charges to its partners in Eastern Europe on the one hand, and on the other hand, the export difficulties due to recession in the West. These Eastern European countries are thus caught in a "scissors crisis" on an international level, reminiscent of that during and after NEP in the Soviet Union on an internal plane. Inflation is increasing: as the papers say, inflation goes East. They have been unable to isolate themselves from the effects of this crisis. This is not unrelated to the workers' revolt and the deepening economic crisis of 1980 and 1981 and the subsequent repression.

In the major crisis of the depression and war, socialists and socialism welcomed the capitalist crisis; they were in favor of the crisis and against capitalism. In the present crisis, it seems very evident that the socialist world does not welcome the capitalist crisis at all; in fact, it is anticrisis and procapitalist. That is to say, it is doing all it can to contribute to the recovery of capitalism and even to eliminate the effects of the crisis. The prime minister of Bulgaria, Theodore Zivkoff, put this very clearly, in saying that "the crisis in the West affects us immediately and very deeply, because of our trade and other ties with the West. We hope that this crisis will pass as soon as possible." Socialism could then get back to business as usual. Deng Ziaoping in China speaks very eloquently for himself and, at least for the time being, for many millions of Chinese in his alliance with American imperialism and in the attempt to reintegrate China into the world capitalist economy as quickly as possible, with the proclaimed end of making China a world industrial power by the year 2000.

The economic and then political crisis in Poland and the growing economic crisis in Czechoslovakia and Rumania, as well as the general economic difficulties in Eastern Europe and the Soviet Union, show that fundamental economic reorganization and concomitant political adjustment is becoming (in Poland has already become) imperative. A major source of this impasse has been the attempt to graft extensive integration into the world capitalist economy (itself in crisis) onto inflexibility in economic and political organization in Comecon and at home, except in Hungary. One possible way out of the impasse might be through retreat and involution to delink again. But even if that is possible, which is doubtful, it might require unacceptable economic and political readjustments at home. The other option is a forward flight to remedy the capitalist integration–socialist inflexibility impasse by, para-doxically, even further relinking with the capitalist world economy and greater, but politically perhaps ultimately less costly, complementary flexibility at home. That has been the option so far followed in China and Vietnam (not to mention Kampuchea whose ousted Khmer Rouge now renounce communism and socialism for the rest of the century), and it is the policy of those in North Korea who seek to avoid the son of Kim II Sung as his successor and maintainer of past policies.

All this is not to say that the attempts at socialism were mistaken or useless. The socialist countries have all made significant advances of considerable benefit to their populations; they have very much increased social services. What the World Bank now calls "basic needs" are met in the socialist countries; they have increased production; but they have not been very successful in increasing productivity. They have managed to produce an important expansion in production by mobilizing all inputs and therefore increasing outputs. Compare China with India, for instance, or Rumania, Bulgaria, etc. with Turkey or Greece, or take the most obvious case of the Soviet Union: by having made a socialist revolution, they are now able to rejoin the world capitalist division of labor, but with an entirely different productive basis internally (in one word, industrialization) and an entirely different bargaining power externally.

This expansive growth approaches limits, however, which seem to have been reached in many socialist economies around 1970, unless and until they reorganize production to increase it intensively by raising productivity. Here the socialist economies have been much less able to show successes. The need for increased productivity is the major reason why they are now turning to technology from the West and are trying to reorganize their economies internally. But, very significantly, productivity comes at the cost of the relative equality that has been achieved during the earlier period, as experience in Eastern Europe and now China suggests.

Thus, these socialist experiences have been very important and useful, but they have not produced precisely what was expected of them, either internally or externally. As the French Revolution did not bring the peasants to power, so the Soviet Revolution certainly did not bring the Russian proletariat to power, and internationally they have not brought what we previously understood by socialism. Originally, socialism was understood to be a process of transition to communism. It seems extremely difficult if not impossible today to sustain the thesis that the "really existing socialist societies" in Eastern Europe are in any sense in a transition to communism. On the contrary, if they are in transition to anything today, they are more likely to be in a transition to capitalism. But capitalism itself is undergoing another crisis-generated transition or transformation, of which the relinking of the socialist economies and the analogous reorganization of the Third World to participate in a new international division of labour through so-called export-led growth, are integral elements. Both contribute to the necessary lowering of production costs, and to capital's ability to reorganize the world economy during this period of crisis and to lay the basis for a possible period of renewed capitalist expansion. Whether these and other developments will fundamentally alter the structure and operation of the world capitalist system remains to be seen, but it seems unlikely for the foreseeable future.

References

United States Congress 1978. *Congressional Record, April 5: H 2517*. Washington, D.C.: United States Government Printing Office.

United States Senate, Foreign Relations Committee 1977. *Foreign debts, the banks and US foreign policy*. Washington, D.C.: United States Government Printing Office.

Index

Betts Letts
good

sa'
decision
makes
NO P243
explores
for age

Corbyn
Hope it
impossible
what is this
Each when
give answers
seen old.

P212
How?

Swanda

Lambery

No amount
of follow

Any and ranges good
to get together

Rest good if
rather simple

Important v. good
Zephir & evidence...

Stationers ... ...
Clear

So much eloquence

Already read more

Evidence

Polemic imp — Cerer

Very rubbish

some chaps just what to offer
but explain why restore & needed
what a offer